Ohio's Natural Heritage

Ohio's Natural Heritage

Michael B. Lafferty
Editor-in-Chief

Published by
The Ohio Academy of Science
Columbus, Ohio

This publication was produced jointly by The Ohio Academy of Science and the Ohio Department of Natural Resources.

Grateful acknowledgment is made to the following publishers for permission to reproduce illustrations that originally appeared in their publications:

The Ohio State University Press, for pen and ink botanical illustrations by Elizabeth Dalve on pages 60, 64, 119, 122, 124, 134, 146, 157, 160, 226, 236, 240, 250, 252, 254, 292, and 328 in *The Woody Plants of Ohio* by E. Lucy Braun. Copyright© 1961 by The Ohio State University Press.

The Ohio State University Press, for pen and ink botanical illustrations by Elizabeth Dalve on pages 54, 136, 168, 172, 212, and 315 in *The Monocotyledoneae - Cat-tails to Orchids* by E. Lucy Braun with Gramineae by Clara G. Weishaupt. Copyright© 1967 by The Ohio State University Press.

The Ohio State University Press, for pen and ink illustrations of fish on pages 153, 197, 200, 218, 486, 493, 525, and 531 in *The Fishes of Ohio* by Milton B. Trautman. Copyright© 1957 by The Ohio State University Press.

The Ohio Historical Society, for pen and ink illustrations of Indian artifacts on pages 11, 13, 22, 26, 30, 36, 52, 45, and 50 in *Ohio's Prehistoric Peoples* by Martha A Potter. Copyright© 1968 by the Ohio Historical Society.

Copyright © 1979 by The Ohio Academy of Science

All rights reserved. Except for purposes of review, no part of this book may be reproduced or utilized in any form or by any means, electronic or mechanical, including photocopying, recording, or by any information storage and retreival system, without written permission from the Publisher. Address all inquiries to:

The Ohio Academy of Science
445 King Avenue
Columbus, Ohio 43201

Printed and bound by
Kingsport Press
Kingsport, Tennessee

Color separation negatives by
Printing Preparations, Inc.
Dayton, Ohio

Designed by Gene Hite
Design Communications, Inc.
Columbus, Ohio

Library of Congress Cataloging in
Publication Data

Ohio's Natural Heritage

Bibliography: p. 314
Includes index

1. Ohio — Description and travel.
2. Natural history — Ohio.
I. Lafferty, Michael B., 1947 -
II. The Ohio Academy of Science.

F491.0398   500.9'771   78-60505
ISBN 0-933128-01-0

Second Printing, May 1980
7.5 M

This book is dedicated to

Trent D. Sickles

whose tireless devotion to human welfare in so many phases of life motivated others into joining his lifetime efforts to help make Ohio bountiful and beautiful for the benefit of all. His work and the benefits from it continue despite his absence.

Acknowledgments

by Lynn Edward Elfner

Many people made this book possible. All were necessary. Some contributed money and other kinds of support; others offered ideas; still others provided creative talent. We especially want to thank several persons who played key roles in making *Ohio's Natural Heritage* a reality: **Arvin J. Alexander, Richard J. Anderson, J. Richard Bull, DeVere E. Burt, James H. Edwards, John E. Fisher, Mr. and Mrs. John B. Greene, Charles Harper, Dean W. Jeffers, Mr. and Mrs. Charles Y. Lazarus, Mr. and Mrs. Robert Lazarus, Jr., Richard H. Oman, W. Mills Parker, Everett D. Reese, Mr. and Mrs. John Sawyer, and Robert W. Teater.** Their assistance was invaluable.

Four very special contributions enabled the Academy to take a giant step forward in the publishing field:

Nationwide Insurance, The Ohio Department of Natural Resources, Battelle Memorial Institute Foundation, and **The Everett D. Reese Fund of the Columbus Foundation.**

This book was built upon a literary framework hammered out by the Editorial Committee, the Editor-in-Chief and the authors. Serving on the Editorial Committee were: Carl W. Albrecht, DeVere E. Burt, C. Wayne Ellett, Ernest E. Good, Edward F. Hutchins, Charles C. King, E.J. Koestner, Harold D. Mahan, Richard E. Moseley, Jr. and Ralph E. Ramey. Charles C. King chaired the Editorial Committee. This book began with Charlie when he brought the success story of the Alberta book to Ohio. And, in the end, it was Charlie who put the final polish on the manuscript. Ohioans should be grateful for his painstaking efforts on behalf of the Academy and *Ohio's Natural Heritage*.

We gratefully acknowledge the generous financial contributions of the following individuals, corporations, foundations, and organizations:

Akron Garden Club	Mr. and Mrs. Robert Lazarus, Jr.
Arvin J. Alexander	Eleanor Longbrake
Jack C. Antrim	Stephen F. Maurer
Dr. and Mrs. Thomas J. Atchison	R. Jon McQuillin
Battelle Memorial Institute Foundation	The Montgomery Foundation
	R.H. Mosteller
M.B. Belden	Nationwide Foundation
George Bidinger	Nationwide Insurance
Russell A. Brant	Wayne S. Nichols
Bryce C. Browning	The Ohio Chapter of The Nature Conservancy
Canton Garden Center	
Lloyd A. Chacey	The Ohio Department of Natural Resources
Garden Club of Cincinnati	
Warren J. Cremean	The Clifford Ozias Fund of The Columbus Foundation
Pauline F. Cucerzan	
Jacob E. Davis II	F.L. Paillet
N. William Easterly	Kenneth L. Powell
Barbara Ely	W.D. Pratner
C. Wayne Ellett	Joseph A. Ralston
Bob Evans Farms, Inc.	W.W. Randolph, Jr.
H.E. Figgie, Jr.	The Everett D. Reese Fund of The Columbus Foundation
Harold Fox	
Robert Fulton	James R. Riley
C.E. Fultz	Virginia Sand
Donald E. Geist	Mr. and Mrs. John Sawyer
Mr. and Mrs. John B. Greene	Seward D. Schooler
Hamilton Community Fund	Alexander M. Smith
James R. Hanson	Marion L. Smith
Jane C. Harris	Marian K. Thomas
Howard S. Hintz	Richard L. Tully
Huntington National Bank	Waite-Brand Foundation
Indian Hill Garden Club	Floyd R. West
Paul S. Kennedy	The Wheaton Club
Mr. and Mrs. Charles Y. Lazarus	George W. White
The F & R Lazarus Co.	Wolf Associates, Inc.

In addition to the review provided by the Editorial Committee and by various authors, many people read parts of this book in manuscript and galley form and offered valuable advice and criticism: Dennis M. Anderson, John Burke, Charles H. Carter, Denis S. Case, Richard L. Christman, Tom S. Cooperrider, Rhea K. Copening, William F. Cowen, Jr., Ann W. Crowner, Ralph Ewers, James G. Griffin, Robert B. Gordon, John D. Harder, Janet V. Jenks, Howard S. Kenny, Mrs. M.C. Markham, Muriel N. King, John H. Olive, Kenneth L. Powell, Alexander Ritchie, Jr., Emanuel D. Rudolph, William T. Schultz, G. Chris Stotler, Myron T. Sturgeon, and George W. White.

It is a special pleasure to acknowledge the imagination and tireless professional assistance of Gene Ilite of Design Communication, Inc. Assisting in the production of this book were several people from the Ohio Department of Natural Resources. We especially want to thank W. David F.J. Crosson, Jack Pennell, Thomas James, Virginia S. Mindigo, and Kay Hall. Patricia B. Walker of the Ohio Biological Survey and Jane S. Burns and Ardath M. Meier of The Ohio Academy of Science have lived with both the frustrations and the joys of this project and deserve special mention for their support, patience and understanding.

And last, I want to acknowledge the thousands of researchers whose work has gone before us. This book is but a brief summary of their many hours of dedication to the advancement of science. Without their efforts we could never have written the story of Ohio's natural heritage.

Preface

For the past 11 years, *Ohio's Natural Heritage* has been the passion of Charles C. King, Executive Director of the Ohio Biological Survey. Charlie acquired the idea for the book in 1968 while studying in Alberta, Canada, where he was introduced to a publication called *Alberta — A Natural History*. Upon returning to Ohio, he set out to develop support for a similar book for our state. *Ohio's Natural Heritage* exists largely because he never gave up his dream.

The book is written by authorities, but for the lay citizen who may, or may not, know much about the plants, animals, wind and water, soil, and geology of the state. Each of the 28 authors approaches his or her subject from a slightly different perspective, thus reflecting a broad range of thought in the environmental field. *Ohio's Natural Heritage* was designed not only to be read cover-to-cover as a unit, but also to have each chapter sufficiently complete to stand on its own. Some overlap of information was unavoidable to achieve these objectives, but this should in no way detract from the reader's enjoyment of the book. The language is simple and direct — suitable not only for casual enjoyment in the home, but also for use as a text or supplement to a high school or college course. Common names rather than scientific names are used in most instances to simplify reading.

Ohio's Natural Heritage was written to fill a void, very apparent when one walks through almost any bookstore or library. There are books on the high Sierras, the Rocky Mountains, the Great Plains...but not one book concerning the natural wonders in our own back yard. This book will help explain the natural history of Ohio for years to come.

Michael B. Lafferty, Editor-in-Chief
Granville, Ohio
May 1979

Contents

Preface ix
Contents xi
Introduction 1

Part I THE LAND 2

1. The Ohio Country 4
   Edward F. Hutchins

2. Written in the Rocks 16
   Robert L. Bates

3. Ice Over Ohio 32
   Richard P. Goldthwait

4. Today's Landscape 48
   Lucile M. and Richard H. Durrell

5. Climate and Weather 58
   Richard D. Goddard

6. Cradle of Life 70
   Nicholas Holowaychuk

7. Ohio Forests 80
   Ernest E. Good

8. Ohio Waters 110
   David H. Stansbery
   Michael B. Lafferty

9. Relicts of the Past 132
   Prairies/*K. Roger Troutman*
   Bogs/*Guy Denny*
   Caves/*Roger W. Brucker*

Part II NATURAL REGIONS 158

10. Hill Country 160
    Charles C. King

11. Glaciated Plateau 182
    James K. Bissell
    Glenn W. Frank

12. Till Plains 198
    Jane L. Forsyth

13. Lake Erie and the Islands 214
    Charles E. Herdendorf
    Ronald L. Stuckey

14. Lake Plain 236
    Louis W. Campbell

15. The Bluegrass 252
    Lynn Edward Elfner

Part III THE IMPACT OF MAN 260

16. The First Ohioans 262
    Martha Potter Otto

17. Changing Land Use 272
    Forests, Farm Lands, and Wildlife/*Kenneth W. Laub*
    Water/*Sherman L. Frost*
    Hidden Wealth/*Ruth W. Melvin*

18. The Naturalists 294
    Ralph W. Dexter

19. Preserving the Heritage 304
    Richard E. Moseley, Jr.
    Ralph E. Ramey

Additional Readings 314
About the Authors 316
Illustration Credits 318
Index 319

Introduction

by Robert W. Teater

For millions of years, nature had its own way in forming what is now Ohio. Then mankind arrived and began changing the environment. Our first centuries were spent surviving the perils of nature. But more recently, we have assaulted nature with relentless force — discovering, building, modifying, and sometimes pillaging.

Today, Ohio is rich and prosperous. Crops grow in the fertile soil. Valuable minerals provide building materials and energy to power our machines, fuel our factories, and heat our homes. Abundant water graces our boundaries, laces the state with beautiful rivers, and flows quietly in underground aquifers. Forests cover a quarter of the state, and wildlife abounds in field and stream. And amidst all of our works, there are still some remnants of Ohio's past as sobering reminders of our great natural heritage.

Nature has been good to us. But as nature can be our ally, so can it be our adversary. If we move forward in ignorance and indifference, then future generations will pay a terrible price in scarcity, ugliness, and social conflict. If we move forward with knowledge and concern, then continued prosperity can be assured.

This book is about Ohio's rich natural heritage. Knowing more about our state's environment and natural resources will encourage all of us to appreciate them better and to take a more active role in conservation and resource management, so that future generations will be able to enjoy Ohio as we have.

Part I
The Land

Chapter 1
The Ohio Country

IN the 1700s a green blanket of forest, interrupted here and there by open prairies, bogs, and marshes covered what is now Ohio. Although the rich woodland was probably among the greatest forests ever to grace the earth, the settlers were more interested in other riches. Pioneers were impressed by the deep soils of the west, the lake to the north and river to the south, the magnificent wildlife, and the clear and cool streams. But they feared the forest.

Today, as Ohioans walk through second-growth woodlands and the few small tracts of preserved virgin timber, they can only try to imagine the dark and forbidding grandeur of this forest—the harborer of darkness, strange beasts, and hostile Indians, which Ohio settlers fought and, at least for a time, conquered.

by Edward F. Hutchins

Settlement

The Ohio Country, one of the first regions settled west of the Alleghenies, was the object of fierce competition between the British and the French. In 1748, the British formed the Ohio Company to secure the Indian trade and to check the progress of the French who were pushing south from Canada. The first Ohio Company trading post, Pickawillany (near present-day Piqua), built on the Great Miami River in 1749, was

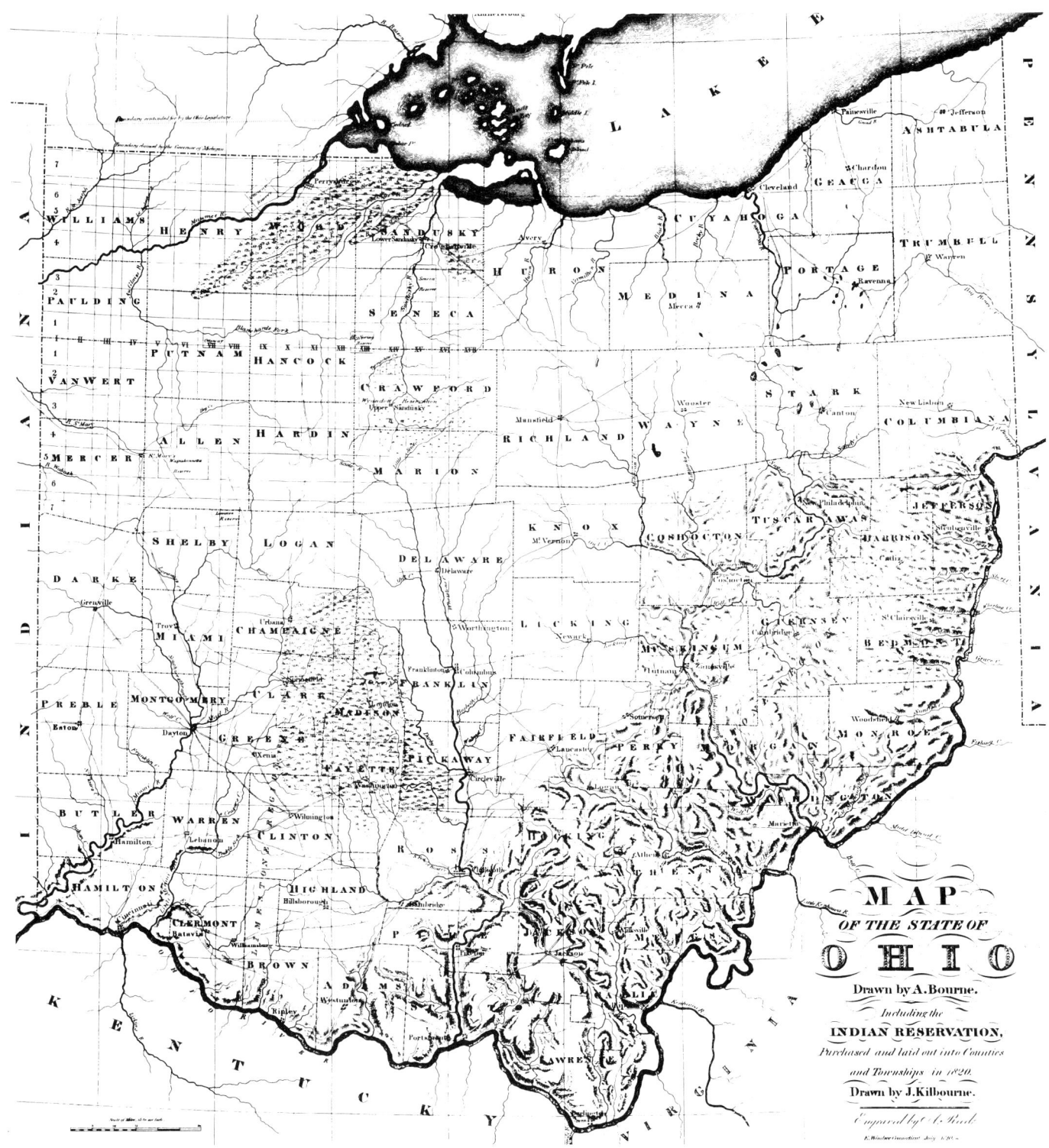

This 1820 map by Alexander Bourne is one of the earliest records of the location of natural features in Ohio.

destroyed by a force of about 200 Ottawa Indians led by Charles Langlade, a half-breed trader from Canada. Notwithstanding the battles of the French and Indian War and the Revolutionary War later, the eighteenth century was essentially a time of relentless elimination of the native Americans, the Indians. During the early settlement of Ohio, many atrocities were committed by the settlers and their militia as well as by the Indians — outrages perhaps highlighted by the systematic slaughter in 1782 of 94 unarmed, Christianized, agrarian Indians at the Moravian mission town of Gnadenhutten (in what is now Tuscarawas County) by militia troops.

In addition to the military considerations, settlers were very strongly motivated by such factors as population pressures in New England,

Virginia, and Germany, relief from traditional civil and religious authority, and the possibility of quick rewards from a bountiful wilderness.

Like Marietta, which had its beginnings with the erection of Fort Harmar in 1785, the earliest settlements in the Ohio Country were situated along the major rivers. During high water, flatboats ascended many miles up the larger streams to deposit pioneers and their livestock and farm implements. Lake Erie was also quite important to early transportation. Early travel by land mostly followed the ancient Indian and game trails, and was fraught with great hardship and risk.

Among the first new trails were the so-called traces hacked through the forest by such men as Ebenezer Zane. Zane's Trace, authorized by Congress in 1796, extended from Wheeling, in what was then Virginia, to Zanesville, then through Lancaster and Chillicothe, ending at Limestone (now Maysville), Kentucky. The cutting out of a trace was probably a fairly quick process since it involved nothing more than making the trail passable for horseback riders.

The vast forest was awe inspiring to these early travelers, especially to those who could view it objectively. Morris Schaff, in his account of the building of the "National Road and the United States Road" through Licking County, recalled that in his boyhood, about 1840-58:

> ...Three fourths of Etna Township was covered by a noble primeval forest. And now, as I recall the stately grandeur of the red oaks and white

Goll Woods State Nature Preserve in Fulton County

Dysart Woods in Belmont County remains today as a living link with the past.

oaks, many of them six feet and more in diameter, towering up royally fifty and sixty feet without a limb; the shellbark hickories and the glowing maples, both with tops far aloft; the mold- and moss-covered ash trees, some of them over four feet through; the elms and beeches, the great black walnuts and the ghostly-robed sycamores, huge in limb and body, along the creek bottoms, I consider it fortunate that I was reared among them and walked beneath them.

Despite its grandeur, the forest of giant trees that dominated the Ohio Country was a formidable enemy to farmers. Eager to establish a corn patch and vegetable garden, the backwoods settler attacked and conquered the forest armed with little more than great fortitude, a sharp axe, and a fagot. The "deadenings" created by girdling the giant trees, followed by log-heap fires, became a common sight.

This assault on nature originated out of need, but in less than half a century had established a record of destruction of flora and fauna that perhaps stands unequalled. Under frontier conditions, ecological and aesthetic consideration for the Ohio forest was out of the question. The commercial lumbering operation that followed a generation or so later merely completed the job at a faster pace. The tragedy of the reckless removal of the primeval forest was further compounded by the nearly complete waste of what was perhaps the finest lumber in North America. More than likely, the timber market arrived soon enough that many of the former backwoods settlers recalled with regret the prime timber which they had reduced to ash piles in their younger days.

Prairies in the glaciated western and north-central sections of the future state were permanent openings in the forest–some were several miles in length. And there were short-term natural openings created by tornadoes, deadfalls, and fires set by lightning (and possibly some set by Indians). Numerous frontiersmen, soldiers, and pioneers prayed in relief when, at last, they emerged from the dense canopied forest into the sunlit openings.

The prairies were too wet in spring and too dry in summer and autumn to support trees, except in their more elevated portions called "islands,"

An early 20th century logging operation in Geauga County

The Ohio Country 9

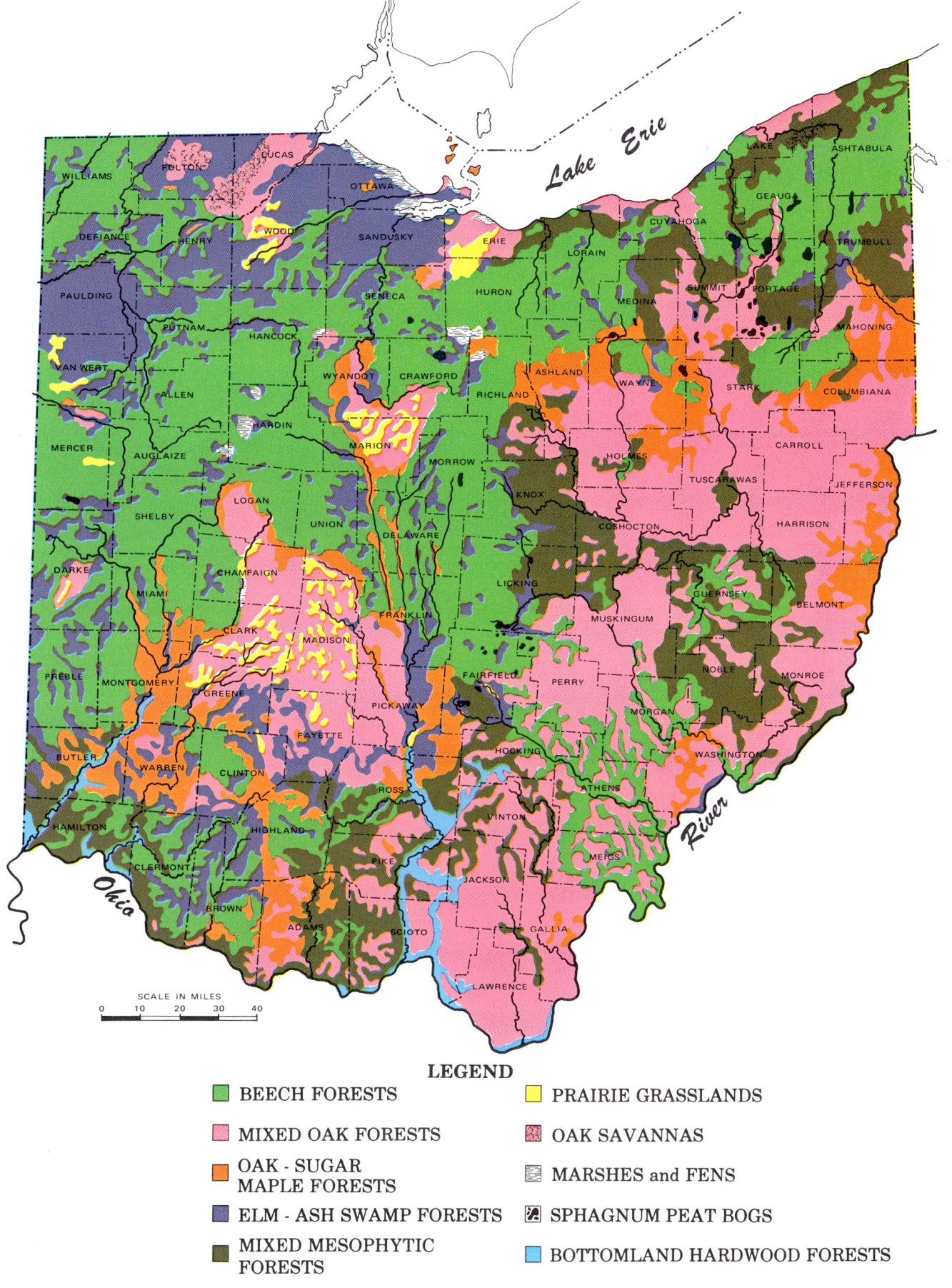

Original Vegetation of Ohio
At the Time of the Earliest Land Surveys

Elk

Buffalo

where oak-hickory forests grew. James Kilbourne, in his *Report to the Scioto Company,* described a "clear meadow" of a thousand acres that existed in central Ohio in 1802, in which the grasses grew "higher than a horse's back" and was "without a tree or bush in the whole extent." Samuel R. Brown, writing in 1815, described "open and extensive prairies" surrounded by "fine oak and chestnut land in the vicinity of Sandusky Bay"; also "a natural meadow...90 miles long and from two to ten wide, extending from the mouth of the Portage" River, Ottawa County, westward around the western end of Lake Erie "to Brownstown" south of Detroit, Michigan.

The Great Black Swamp of northwestern Ohio ranked as one of the region's greatest natural features and is estimated to have been 40 miles wide and 120 miles long, covering part or all of 18 present-day counties.

The Ohio Country was as rich in wildlife as it was in vegetation. Prior to the arrival of the settlers the abundant wildlife populations were evidently in balance with one another and with the habitat. The Indians apparently had little impact on fish and game populations. Identification of skeletal remains from midden or refuse piles indicate Indian diets included all species of native mammals present in Ohio today, plus black bear, puma, and wolf. Elk and buffalo were present in at least limited numbers. The white-tailed deer was most important, but the Indians also ate passenger pigeon, wild turkey, grouse, quail, Canada goose, and many kinds of ducks. From all indications the rivers provided an abundance of fishes, mollusks, turtles, and amphibians. It is believed that the elk and the buffalo were gone before many whites arrived, but during settlement times the balance of the wildlife community was intact.

Pumas, Bears, and the Big Hunts

Of the many wild creatures inhabiting the Ohio wilderness, probably the most feared and hated was the puma. It was also known as mountain lion, mountain tiger, cougar, panther, or catamount. How common pumas were is not known, but it is certain they were well known to the Indians. Puma bones have been recovered at many village sites, caves, and mounds of prehistoric Ohio Indians. A combination of heavy hunting and trapping pressure by whites and Indians alike, with drastic changes in land use, was probably responsible for the rapid demise of the puma in Ohio. In *The History of Athens County,* in 1869, C.M. Walker reported: "The first board of county commissioners offered a bounty of three dollars for wolf and panther scalps under six months old, and four dollars on those over six months old. This bounty was discontinued in 1818." Dr. Jared P. Kirtland of the Ohio Geological Survey reported in 1838 that the mountain tiger had by then disappeared from the state.

Timber wolves also were common. Wolf skeletal parts, clearly showing evidence of having been worked by humans, have been discovered in a number of prehistoric Indian burial sites. In fact, timber wolves were so abundant and well distributed when Ohio was being settled that at least 28 streams have been named for them. Ohio has one "Wolf Ditch," 15 "Wolf Creeks," and 12 "Wolf Runs." Norton S. Townshend, first professor of agriculture, botany, and veterinary science at The Ohio State University, wrote about "mischievous animals" encountered May 1, 1830, while he, with two companions,

Puma or mountain lion

"...walked from Cleveland some 18 miles on the state road westward. The place of destination was not reached until late in the evening, when conversation became difficult from the incessant howling of wolves." There are many records of the timber wolf in southern Ohio. In *The Pioneer History of the Ohio Valley,* in 1848, Hildreth reported, "The wolf for thirty years was a great hindrance to the raising of sheep, and for a long period the state paid a bounty for the scalps. Neighboring farmers often associated and paid an additional bounty of ten or fifteen dollars, so as to make it an object of profit for certain old hunters to employ their whole time and skill in entrapping them." Hildreth further reported, "The race is now nearly extinct in the Ohio Company's lands."

Wolf

Black bears were very common in early Ohio and possibly ranked next to the deer in importance as a source of food and hides for the Indians. Bear bones are almost always found in prehistoric Indian sites. One of the earliest accounts of bears in Ohio is in the journal of Major John Rogers. He reported in January, 1761: "We traveled eleven miles and encamped, having killed in our march, this day, three bears and two elks." Hildreth, in 1848, wrote, "...one day during the year 1805, two children of John Spencer were playing in the yard of the cabin at the 'Big Spring' when a huge bear came along, seized a pig near them and made off with it. Had Bruin selected the youngest of those children instead of the pig, the career of the late Colonel William Spencer would have been cut short."

Gray squirrels also were abundant in early Ohio. In fact they destroyed so much corn and other crops in some places that in 1807 the Ohio General Assembly required that each person subject to payment of a county tax "...shall in addition thereto, produce to the clerk of the township in which he may reside such number of squirrel scalps, as the trustees shall, at their annual meeting, apportion, in proportion to their county levies, provided that it does not exceed 100 or be less than ten." The law authorized a penalty of three cents a scalp for the number not turned in. Great migrations of squirrels reportedly occurred in five-year cycles with many drowning in their attempt to cross streams. The cause

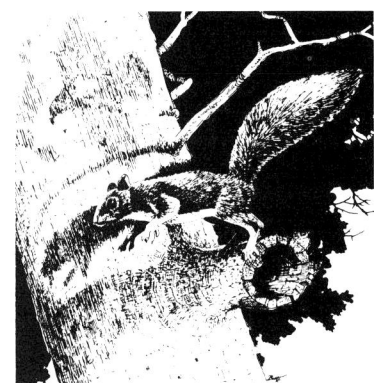
Gray squirrel

Artist's conception of the Great Hinckley Hunt

of these migrations is uncertain, but reliable observers indicated the squirrels were fat so it could not have been from a shortage of food. In fact, they left areas abounding with food. Like most bounty schemes intended to reduce the abundance of wildlife, Ohio's "Squirrel Scalp Law" had little, if any, effect on squirrel populations, and the squirrel problem lasted several decades more. Massive, countywide squirrel hunts were organized. One of the largest hunts took place in Franklin County in 1822. The county was divided into two districts, and a barrel of whiskey was awarded to the district producing the most squirrel scalps. After the three-day hunt, the Columbus *Gazette* reported 19,666 scalps turned in. Many more were probably killed, since the paper reported many hunters did not bother to report their kills. Ohio's last mass squirrel hunts occurred in the 1850s.

The Great Hinckley Hunt of December 24, 1818, was undoubtedly the best organized and most successful, large-scale hunt in Ohio history. A fantastic amount of game was killed: 300 deer, 21 bears, 17 wolves, and fair numbers of turkeys, foxes, and raccoons. In the autumn of 1818, according to Captain Milton B. Pierce, writing in *The American Field,* Chicago, January 4, 1890, a number of meetings were held in the townships surrounding Hinckley to make arrangements for "a war of extermination" upon bears and wolves. Committees were appointed and arrangements were made for "...a grand hunt which would embrace the entire township of Hinckley and the forest lands adjacent thereto."

In justifying the hunt, Pierce reported that the settlers were "seriously embarrassed" by the many wolves that ravaged their sheep. Once wolves killed more than 100 sheep in one night on a few farms near Hinckley. They also said bears frequently raided pig pens.

The War of 1812 had ended only three years before, so there were plenty of officers who could handle a large body of men. Plans for the hunt were advertised as far away as 20 miles. At sunrise, December 24, 1818, 600 men and boys formed on a battle line around the perimeter of the township. Most families had at least one musket, but there were not enough to go around. Bayonets and butcher knives were mounted on poles; some men used axes. Many carried hatchets and butcher knives in waist belts. Soon after daybreak, the commander gave the words, "All ready!" and the skirmish lines began moving into the Hinckley woods, with most of the game animals moving ahead of the hunters. By previous arrangement, a general halt was made at a line of blazed trees half a mile from the center of the township. Dogs were then released into the circle and this served to drive most of the animals out into the musket fire of the hunters.

Inside the circle of hunters, a frozen stream with high banks served as a final hiding place for bears, wolves, deer, and turkeys; and it was an

Now extinct, both the Passenger Pigeon (left) and Carolina Parakeet were once common in Ohio.

easy matter for the hunters to fire down on the trapped animals. Soon the hunt was over. The game was divided equally among the participants, and by evening a large bear had been dressed and was barbecued. An ample supply of "honest" whiskey is said to have contributed to the all-night festivities that followed.

The Passenger Pigeon

Ohio figured prominently in the history of the now extinct passenger pigeon. In 1882 Dr. J.M. Wheaton, in his *Report on the Birds of Ohio,* described flights of passenger pigeons from the great roost at Bloody Run Swamp at Buckeye Lake (formerly the Great Buffalo Swamp): "On several occasions we have been favored with a general migration of these birds, when they have appeared in congregated millions. This was the case in 1854, when the light of the sun was perceptibly obscured by the immense, unbroken, and apparently limitless flock which for several hours passed over the City [Columbus]." The passenger pigeon bore a family resemblance to the mourning dove, but it was about four inches longer and perhaps three or four ounces heavier. Like the still-existent mourning dove the passenger pigeon was migratory. Unfortunately, most of the history of the passenger pigeon is recorded in terms of how it was hunted and marketed. Alexander Wilson, the great American pioneer ornithologist, wrote of a passenger pigeon flock in 1806 that was estimated to have been one mile wide and 240 miles long, moving one mile a minute. The pigeons passed by for several hours, and Wilson estimated the flock contained more than two billion birds.

The passenger pigeon, probably the most abundant bird the world has known, went from great abundance to extinction in one human generation. A low biotic potential (one egg per clutch) and the removal of the forests are often cited as the reasons they became extinct, but the principal blame is more logically laid to uncontrolled market hunting. The extent of the hunting pressure is well documented. Most of the shooting took place at the great nesting concentrations, and nowhere could it have been more deadly. When a passenger pigeon nesting concentration was destroyed, it would have made little difference whether the birds had one egg per nest or four. Although the clearing of the forests deprived the pigeons of a great percentage of their nesting habitat and food sources, the supply of beechnuts and acorns remained far in excess of the needs of the pigeons throughout the last half century of their existence. Furthermore, the pigeons ate a great variety of foods, including farm crops.

Nearly 12 million brooding pigeons were killed from 1866 to 1876. The loss of six million eggs or squabs left to die in the nest must be added to this figure. The expenditure of ammunition gives an indication of the extent of the pigeon slaughter. The Sparta [Wisconsin] *Herald,* May 23, 1882, reported that an ammunition dealer handled three tons of powder and 16 tons of shot during a single nesting near Sparta.

The last record of a passenger pigeon killed in Ohio was March 24, 1900, near the town of Sargent in Pike County. The small boy who killed the bird was unable to identify it and took it to an amateur taxidermist. Despite sizable collections of passenger pigeons in zoos, breeders were usually unsuccessful at propagating the birds. The last captive passenger pigeon, "Martha," died at the Cincinnati Zoological Gardens

A Currier and Ives interpretation of how hunters "decoyed" passenger pigeons into area for slaughter

September 1, 1914. Her age has been variously reported from 12 years to 29 years. But regardless of the accuracy of that detail, Martha's death was just not the death of an individual, but the death of a species.

Another bird species now extinct, the Carolina parakeet, was well known in the Ohio Country. Likenesses of the bird exist in the art of prehistoric Ohio Indians, and it was well known to early Ohio ornithologists. In 1862, William S. Sullivant, a prominent Columbus citizen and a highly respected naturalist, watched a flock of 25 to 30 parakeets in elm trees across from the new state capital square. Sullivant's observation of Carolina parakeets in Columbus is no doubt one of the last records of this bird in Ohio. The parakeet was about 13 inches long and had lustrous green body feathers. The head was bright yellow, and a mask around the bill was flaming scarlet. Great numbers of the birds were killed for their plumage which was used on ladies' hats. Many others were trapped live and sold as pets. The parakeet was also good to eat, so it was hunted as a game bird. But hunting for sport was not an important factor in its decline and extinction. Instead, many thousands of parakeets were destroyed as agricultural pests. Not only did they eat corn, they had the interesting but obnoxious habit of twisting green fruit off fruit trees. Old-time hunters reported the parakeets would not desert fallen comrades, and this habit made it easy to kill every member of a flock once the first bird was downed.

The prairie chicken, another once common bird, was extirpated from Ohio by about 1900. Prairie chickens were once hunted commercially for food, but their decline is blamed primarily on the elimination of prairie habitat for agriculture. Some wildlife species actually increased in numbers with the removal of the large forests and the concurrent increase in abundance of fields and forest edge. The ruffed grouse was among these species and at one time occurred in every county of the state. The bobwhite quail, which prior to 1800 was found primarily in the prairie areas of the Ohio Country, increased in numbers as the forest was cut. By 1880 it was widely hunted for sport and market. But by 1913 quail populations had declined so much that the legislature closed the quail-hunting season. Four years later the quail was placed on the so-called "songbird list" and protected from hunting for another 38 years. The white-tailed deer and the wild turkey were extirpated from the state by about 1900. Fortunately, both species were reestablished a half

Prairie chicken

century later through efforts of the Ohio Division of Wildlife. Non-game wildlife prospered or declined in response to land-use changes much the same as did game species, although these events are not as well documented.

Clear Waters

Just as the forests teemed with wildlife, Lake Erie and the streams of the Ohio Country teemed with many kinds of fish. Early Ohio streams were probably a paradise for people who fished since most of the species were the better-flavored and larger varieties such as muskellunge, walleye, perch, and catfish. Since these fishes generally need streams with clean waters and bottoms, many Ohio streams were perfect, with narrow, deep channels, heavily forested banks holding the soil and a canopy of trees shading the water.

Muskellunge

Fish were important food for the Indians, especially when hunting was bad or when crops failed. And fish continued to be of great importance to the settlers after they began moving into the Ohio Country. Early explorers reported streams teeming with fish. The settlers caught the fish by hook and line, gigging or spearing them or with trotlines. Sometimes settlers could catch half a barrel of fish in one night using a trotline. Kinds of fish as named by the settlers which were especially important as food included pike (or muskellunge), white perch (drum), salmon (walleye), sturgeon, buffalofish, black bass, and several species of catfish. Early naturalist Samuel Hildreth reported that settlers caught a 96-pound black (either the blue or the flathead) catfish in 1792, while a year later, soldiers caught 5,000 pounds of fish in two nights using a home-made fish trap stretched across the Great Miami River.

Sturgeon

Huge numbers of fish also lived in Lake Erie, and by the late 1800s the lake supported a large commercial fishing industry. Commercial fishermen caught more than one million pounds of whitefish annually between 1885 and 1900. Unfortunately, these good times did not last. Overfishing combined with dam construction, pollution, siltation and ditching of tributary streams, and the introduction of non-native species as settlement progressed, worked against the fish. Populations as well as the number of desirable species in many streams declined drastically.

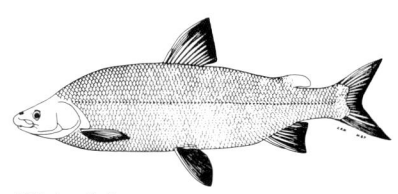
Whitefish

The conquest and development of the Ohio Country unfortunately cannot be viewed impartially. History has shown that the relative success of a civilization is never considered with objectivity until after it collapses. Exploitation of natural resources was clearly part of the price of development and the accommodation of the vast human population that now inhabits Ohio. In less than 200 years the Ohio Country was transformed from a land of magnificent forests and clean waters, occupied by no more than a few thousand Indians clearly in balance with the available wildlife resources, to a land occupied by 11 million people whose living requirements not only exceed the natural carrying capacity of Ohio, but drain heavily on national and world resources. In light of pollution in its many forms, the social deterioration besetting cities, and the growing scarcities of essential resources, our civilization would clearly have benefitted by an attempt to keep population growth and development in some logical relationship with natural systems. The history of the vanquishing of the Ohio Country cannot be reversed, and relatively few would want it changed. It has long been recognized that in the mind of the individual a loss which is unknown is no loss at all.

Chapter 2
Written in the Rocks

by Robert L. Bates

BEDROCK is the foundation of the state and the raw material which makes life possible. Eroded by wind and water, pulverized by ice sheets, the rock has been slowly ground to dust and incorporated into the soil.

Soil is the basis of the natural history of Ohio. Influenced by the bedrock below and the climate above, a myriad of soils have developed that support different kinds of vegetation. Plant life, in turn, attracts and supports many different animals. The bedrock directly determines where a waterfall will be, or how high it will be, or the length and depth of a river rapids. It supports skyscrapers in Ohio cities, and, dug out of the ground, is used to construct buildings, fertilize crops, make steel, and melt ice on roads.

With all of these different uses, Ohio's bedrock varies considerably, and in fact is composed of many different kinds of rocks. However, it is not necessary to bore deep into the earth to learn of Devonian shale or Silurian limestone. Across Ohio, the bedrock is exposed in roadcuts, cliffs, ledges, and innumerable ravines and deep valleys. Gypsum is quarried near Port Clinton, limestone is quarried at Columbus, and coal is mined in southeastern Ohio. Shale is present in cliffs overlooking Lake Erie, and sandstone and conglomerate are exposed in the Hocking Hills.

Altogether, 11 kinds of rock comprise the bedrock of Ohio. They include:

conglomerate – pebbles and coarse sand, plus the natural cement that binds them into solid rock

sandstone – sand grains, plus the natural cement that solidifies the mass

shale – compacted and consolidated mud

siltstone – rock grains finer than sand but coarser than those of shale, cemented or compacted into rock

limestone – fossil seashells, shell fragments, and limy mud, compacted and cemented into rock, main mineral calcite (calcium carbonate)

dolomite – resembling limestone, but containing few recognizable fossils, main mineral dolomite (calcium magnesium carbonate)

chert – mineral silica

clay – extremely small grains of mica, quartz, and various clay minerals

gypsum – the mineral gypsum (hydrous calcium sulfate)

coal – compacted plant remains, largely carbon

salt – crystalline halite (sodium chloride)

These rocks are similar in one respect. They are stratified, which means they occur in layers or strata. Each layer was formed from sediment deposited in ancient seas, marshes, or swamps which covered all or portions of the state at times over the past 500 million years.

In a quarry or road cut, these layers of rock usually appear horizontal. In reality, most of the strata are gently inclined, or tilted. In eastern Ohio, the bedrock slopes gently toward the southeast. In extreme northwest Ohio, the layers dip to the northwest. The only place where the layers are really nearly level is in a belt extending from Cincinnati through Dayton, Bellefontaine, and Findlay to Toledo. This belt marks the crest of a broad, low, dome-like feature of Ohio's bedrock called the Cincinnati Arch. The arch is a feature of the bedrock strata, not the land surface. So, although the bedrock is tilted, the land surface, which is nearly level, cuts across the arch, exposing the edges of the rock layers that were once continuous across it.

Time, Fossils, and the Geologic Calendar

By studying cores and other records from oil and gas wells, geologists know there are several thousand feet of sedimentary rock beneath Ohio. Over millions of years, sediments were deposited in ancient seas, solidified into rock, and eventually uplifted forming dry land. Animals and plants became embedded in the sediments, and today, these fossils reveal the ages of various rocks. For example, Devonian rocks contain fossils which lived about 375 million years ago. These fossils show that corals, clams, and other shelly marine creatures of Devonian times were more advanced than those found in Silurian rocks (below the Devonian). But they are not so advanced as forms found in Mississippian rocks (next above). Fossils from the oldest rocks at the bottom of the strata are very different from plants and animals living today, while fossils from progressively younger rocks are more and more like living forms.

But fossils tell us only the relative age of rocks. Scientists need more precision, which they achieve by studying radioactive chemical

Written in the Rocks 19

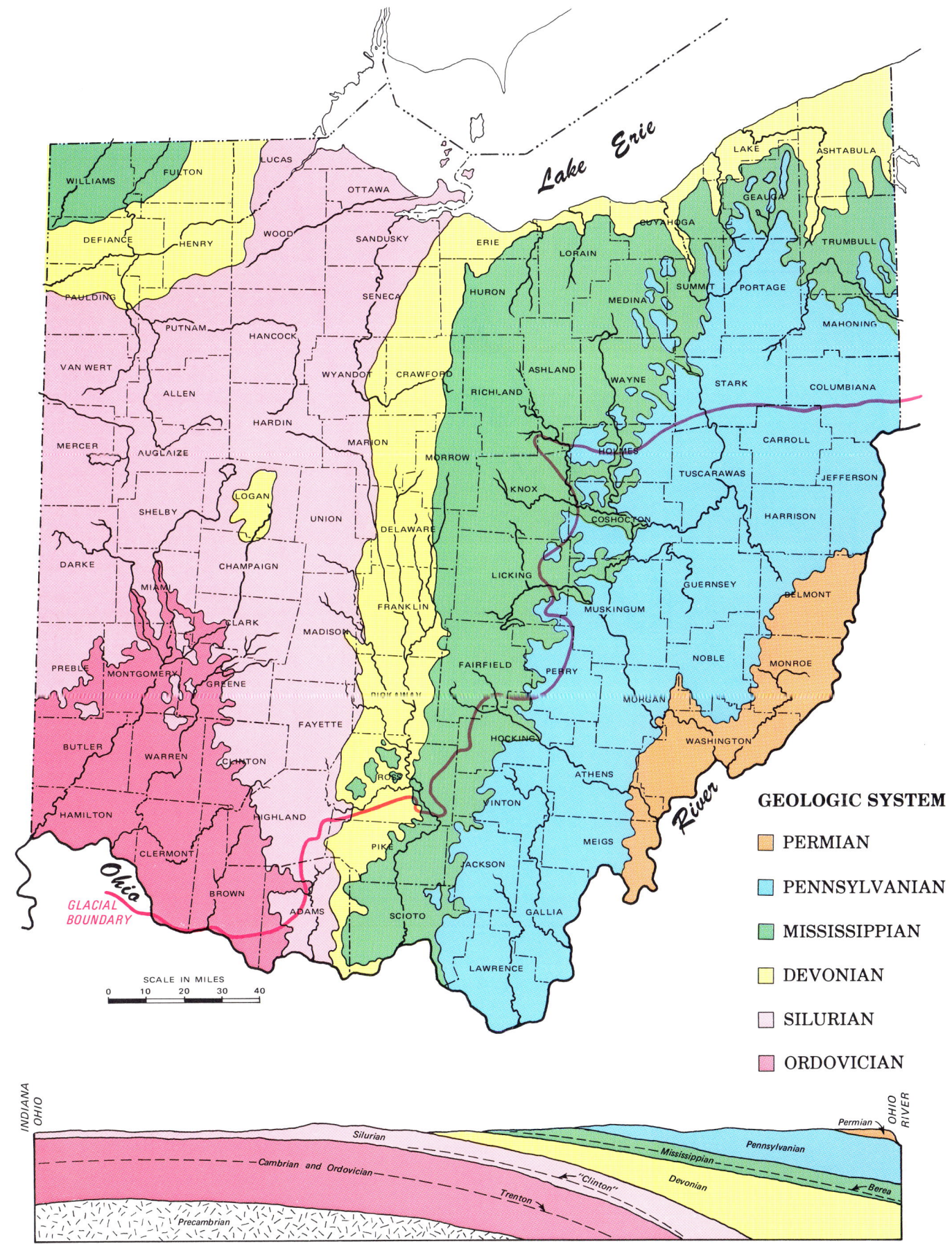

Geologic Map and Cross Section of Ohio

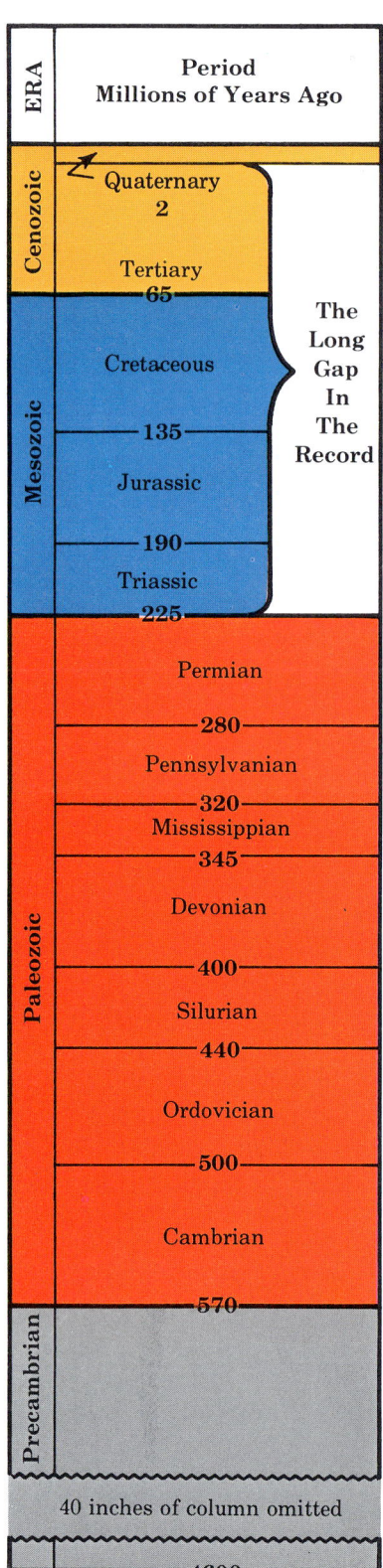

Ohio's Geologic Timetable

elements in the rocks which change to other elements, or "daughter" elements at a constant rate. The age of a rock is determined by measuring the amount of a daughter element present and then comparing it with the rate at which it formed. This is how we know the Paleozoic Era began about 580 million years ago and lasted about 330 million years. The Mesozoic Era began about 255 million years ago, and the Cenozoic Era about 65 million years ago. Not only do these numbers serve as reminders of the enormous length of geologic time, they also show how very short human history is in comparison.

Ohio's Share of Geologic History

All of Ohio's upper bedrock layers are sedimentary, and they fit easily into the standard geologic time scale because all of them contain abundant fossils. The fossils show that the rocks are of Paleozoic age. The Paleozoic is further divided into time periods, all of which, from Cambrian to Permian, are represented in Ohio. The oldest rocks are buried and can be seen only in the records of deep wells. But the younger rocks — from Ordovician to Permian — are close to or at the surface and some of them have been eroded away.

In many regions of the world, Paleozoic rocks are overlain by Mesozoic rocks, but not in Ohio. There are no Mesozoic rocks in the state. There are no Cenozoic rocks either. The only covering of Ohio's bedrock is the deposit of clay, gravel, and boulders associated with the ice sheets of late Cenozoic (Pleistocene) time. For more than 225 million years, since before the end of the Permian Period, we have no record in Ohio. Perhaps thick beds of rock were deposited, only to be worn away, or perhaps the state was above sea level and was undergoing erosion instead of deposition. Whatever happened, the Paleozoic rocks remain, providing a rich and fascinating record of that portion of geologic history.

The Precambrian Floor

Ohio's bedrock is stacked in layers. The stack of Paleozoic strata, with Cambrian at the bottom, lies on much older rocks called Precambrian. Ohio's Precambrian rocks are a southward extension of the Canadian Shield and a part of the primordial crust of North America. These rocks are not sedimentary. They consist of granitic rocks (formed by the cooling of molten earth material) and metamorphic rocks (formed by heat and intense pressure deep within the earth's crust). They contain no fossils, and are of no economic value in Ohio because they are so deeply buried.

The Precambrian rocks which lie in the upper portion of the lithosphere are probably the roots of mountain systems that were ultimately worn down in the incredibly long stretches of Precambrian time. In turn, this surface is covered by sediments of Cambrian age which constitute the foundation of Ohio's sedimentary rocks.

Our Oldest Sedimentary Rocks

Sandstone is the oldest and lowest of the Cambrian strata. Above the sandstone are several hundred feet of gray, sandy limestone and dolomite. Fossils in these rocks show that the lower part is of Cambrian age and the upper part is early Ordovician (about 550 to 480 million years ago). During this time Ohio was just off the coast of the North American land mass, covered by an extremely clear sea teeming with marine life. Trilobites, one of the first animals with a complex exoskeleton, appeared at this time, and the sea also was full of primitive sponges, jellyfish, and brachiopods. The trilobite probably is related to the common ancestor of almost all arthropods — crabs, insects, spiders, and the like — which together make up about 90 percent of the animal species on earth.

The skeletons and shells of these dead animals fell to the sea floor and solidified with other materials, forming thick layers of limestone and dolomite. Both of these rocks are very important economically because they contain oil about 4,000 feet beneath the surface. The oil is formed from the decomposed remains of other microscopic animals, and occurs in porous zones in the rock produced by the partial dissolving of the dolomite after it was formed.

Cincinnati's Ordovician Rocks

In Ohio, Cambrian rocks are covered by younger bedrock. Near Cincinnati some extremely old rocks of Middle Ordovician age are exposed at the surface. These rocks lie directly above the Lower Ordovician strata, and they are the oldest rocks uncovered in Ohio. These beds of limestone and shale were exposed as streams eroded their valleys deeper into the Cincinnati Arch, and they are best seen at a few places along the Ohio River upstream from Cincinnati.

Even though these rocks are the oldest uncovered, much more interesting are the slightly younger rocks of Upper Ordovician age. These rocks, also exposed near Cincinnati, are more than 500 feet thick. They consist of shale beds a few inches thick alternating with very thin beds of limestone.

The shales are gray and quite ordinary, but the limestones are packed with fossil shells and shell fragments. Mud for the shale and shells for the limestone were deposited when Ohio was once again covered by an arm of the ocean. This ancient sea stretched from the Gulf of St. Lawrence far south and west and was part of one of the greatest inundations in the history of North America. Actually, the water covering Ohio was fairly shallow — less than 100 feet in most places — about the depth of the Atlantic over much of the continental shelf.

At times the water receded and the western third of the state emerged as a series of low, flat islands. When the water was muddy, life was not abundant. However, most often the water was warm and clear and the sea floor was covered with small twig-like creatures called bryozoans, creatures still alive and similar to corals. In addition to the bryozoans, this sea contained many kinds of clams, lobster-like animals, snails, and chambered nautiloids. The largest nautiloid found in Ohio is about three feet long — a large animal compared to present-day nautiloids, but puny when compared to the giant 15-foot-long nautiloid found in Quebec near Montreal.

Later in the Ordovician, life was even more abundant. Today, scientists and collectors from around the world search for the remains of this life in the rich fossil beds in the Upper Ordovician rocks near Cincinnati. These fossils also can be seen at many places along the valleys of the Great Miami and Little Miami rivers and their tributaries;

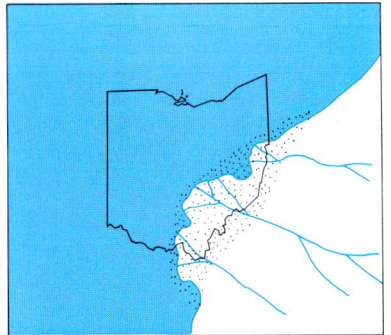
Early Silurian sea

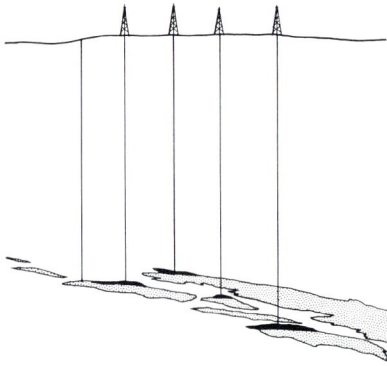
Clinton Sand

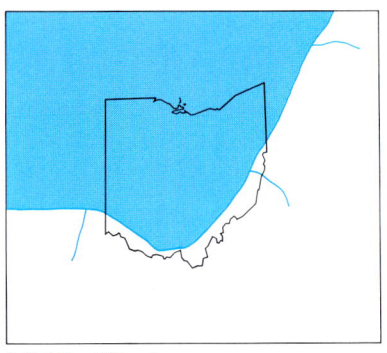
Middle Silurian sea

Megalomus or "beef heart" fossil

in highway cuts along U.S. routes 62 and 68 north of Ripley, Ohio, and south of Maysville, Kentucky (just across the river from Aberdeen); near Fort Ancient; and at Hueston Woods State Park near Oxford.

Silurian Rocks and Their History

During the early part of the Silurian Period, most of Ohio was dry land. But toward the middle of Silurian times, seas spread from both the north and south and again covered most of the state. At times, mud washing into the sea clouded the water. Most of the time, however, the water was clear and this is why most Silurian rocks in Ohio are limestone and dolomite.

As in Ordovician times, when the sea was clear, it teemed with life, especially corals. These tiny animals first appeared during the Ordovician, but they reached peak abundance in Silurian oceans and seas. In those days, they formed hundreds of small, mound-like reefs, many of which are exposed today in quarries and are penetrated by wells. In addition to corals, many kinds of animals and lime-secreting algae added to the reefs, and soft-bodied animals living in the sea probably decomposed forming the oil found in these Silurian reefs today.

The Clinton Sand. Before Silurian times, during the Middle Ordovician, there was a high range of mountains bordering the Atlantic coast. These were not the Appalachian Mountains because the area now containing the Appalachians was covered by a narrow, shallow arm of the sea. Over millions of years, the mountains eroded and mountain streams spread sand, silt, and mud into this sea. At times, these sedimentary deposits even spread as far west as Ohio. One such flood of sandy sediment occurred early in the Silurian, about 430 million years ago, and produced a deposit that oil drillers refer to as the Clinton Sand.

The Clinton Sand is really a sandstone. In Ohio, it is never seen at the surface, but it enters the state from the southeast and extends only about one third of the way across the state. In central Ohio, it becomes thinner and finally disappears, or pinches out as geologists say, before reaching the surface. Even so, the Clinton is far better known than the older buried rocks because it contains much of Ohio's oil and gas.

Middle Silurian Dolomite. When the shelly marine creatures in Silurian seas died, they accumulated on the sea floor and eventually were hardened into limestone and then changed into dolomite, the most common rock found today from the Silurian Period. A light-colored and porous rock formed about 420 million years ago, dolomite is almost pure calcium-magnesium carbonate. Its porosity is due to fossil shells which dissolved in the rock when the original limestone was converted to dolomite. At some places in the rock, there are mound-like masses which are the remains of ancient reefs, while a common fossil type often found is the internal filling or mold of a large clam called *Megalomus,* — known among quarrymen and collectors as a "beef heart."

Two good places to see natural exposures of Middle Silurian dolomite are at the dam at Rocky Fork in Highland County, and at John Bryan State Park in Greene County. Dolomite is used in making firebrick and other heat-resistant materials, smelting iron ore, manufacturing magnesium compounds, and as lime for farm fields.

Upper Silurian gypsum and salt. Late in Silurian times, Ohio's climate turned hot and arid and the sea started to dry. As the water

Silurian dolomite at Plum Run quarry, Adams County

evaporated, two minerals — gypsum and halite — were precipitated in extensive beds on the sea floor. These beds, among the largest in the world, are found in northern Ohio, New York, Pennsylvania, and Ontario.

Both minerals, known as evaporites, are quarried in Ohio. Gypsum is mined near the town of Gypsum, east of Port Clinton in Ottawa County. Chemically, gypsum consists of hydrous calcium sulfate; it is the raw material for plaster and wallboard manufactured at a plant near the quarry. The gypsum, which contains no fossils, occurs as beds and irregular masses mixed with beds of dense, compact dolomite and gray shale.

Halite, or rock salt, is mined at two spots in northern Ohio. Both mines are underground and extend beneath Lake Erie. One mine is on Whiskey Island at Cleveland and the other is at Fairport Harbor in Lake County. The salt is used mainly to melt ice and snow on roads. At Painesville in Lake County, at Barberton in Summit County, and at Rittman in Wayne County wells have been drilled into the salt beds. Water is pumped down these wells to dissolve the salt and the resulting brine is pumped to the surface for use in manufacturing soda ash, caustic soda, chlorine, and many other products. No salt is exposed at the surface in Ohio, and like gypsum, the salt does not contain fossils.

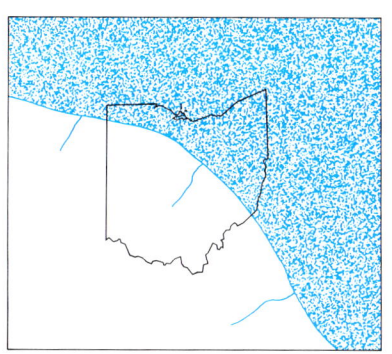

Late Silurian sea

The Devonian Period — Rise of the Fishes

There are no rocks of Early Devonian age in Ohio. By the Middle Devonian, seas again surged over the state, except for a series of low islands in western Ohio. As in previous periods, the climate was warm and the sea was mostly shallow and clear and supported extensive coral reefs.

Shell life and mud were deposited in this warm sea, later to harden into limestone and shale. Today, these Devonian rocks are exposed in a belt extending from the Ohio River west of Portsmouth, north to Lake Erie, then swinging east into northeast Ohio. A small area of Devonian rocks also is exposed in a curved band in northwestern Ohio and in a very small area near Bellefontaine in Logan County.

Columbus Limestone in a quarry west of Delaware, Ohio. Glacially smoothed surface with till removed.

The Columbus Limestone. Most Middle Devonian rocks are limestone. One of the most important of these rocks is the Columbus Limestone, a light gray, compact rock about 100 feet thick. The Columbus Limestone is loaded with fossils, the remains of shellfish which littered the sea floor in the Middle Devonian times. The limestone contains fossils of a number of clams, brachiopods, marine snails, and corals. The corals include solitary forms called "cup" corals, as well as colonial forms that are often more than one foot in diameter and contain thousands of tiny openings where individual coral polyps lived.

The Devonian also is remarkable because, for the first time, fishes swam in the oceans of the world. Some of the fish were up to 25 feet long, and their fossils are now very abundant in the Columbus Limestone. The fossils are in the forms of small dark grains or chips, mostly of scales and teeth because these early fish lacked bony skeletons. These fish were the largest forms of life in seas of Devonian time, a period often known as the Age of Fishes.

The lower part of the Columbus Limestone contains layers and small masses of chert (silica), and some dolomite. But the upper 45 to 50 feet is composed of exceptionally pure calcite — the mineral which composes the shells and shelly fragments. This makes it a valuable rock, and the Columbus Limestone is quarried at many places, from Columbus north to Marblehead in Ottawa County. Early in this century, so much of the upper Columbus Limestone was removed from Kelleys Island that in effect much of the island was one big quarry. About the only limestone remaining on the island is a small area famous today for the deep grooves cut by glaciers. At Barberton, where the limestone is buried by younger rocks, Columbus Limestone is removed from a mine nearly 2,000 feet deep.

Pure limestone is one of the most useful rocks. The Columbus Limestone is, or has been, used to manufacture cement, burned to make lime, quarried for building stone, crushed for use in concrete, and — especially important — used as fluxstone, to remove impurities from iron ore in the smelting process.

The Ohio Shale. Right on top of the Devonian limestones and contrasting with them is a bed of shale some 500 feet thick. This is the Upper Devonian rock called the Ohio Shale, which is also known as the Cleveland and Huron shales in northern Ohio. The most striking characteristic of the rock is that it breaks into thin, flat plates and chips. The shale contains few recognizable fossils, although fossil fishes have been found in the Cleveland Shale of northern Ohio. It consists of extremely small grains of quartz, mica, and clay minerals, plus a large amount of equally fine-grained coaly matter. This dark organic matter is the remains of plants which lived on the land, were washed into the Late Devonian sea, and were carbonized about 350 million years ago.

Unlike many sedimentary rocks, the shale contains rounded masses of rock the size of cannonballs or larger, that are different from the shale. These rocks are concretions formed when minerals collected around a sand grain, a fragment of a plant, or some other foreign object. The larger the object grew, the more minerals were collected; so it enlarged faster and faster and became very hard. Later, mud and other sediments were deposited around the concretions, solidifying through the ages into shale. That is why the bedding of the shale conforms to the concretions by bending around them. Most of the concretions are made of dolomite and a related mineral called siderite (iron carbonate), although some have an outer shell of pyrite (iron sulfide). Others have shrunk and cracked, the cracks filling with other minerals.

Reconstructed fossil fish (*Dunkleosteus*) from near Cleveland, Ohio

Chagrin Shale along Mill Creek in Lake County

Concretion in shale

The Ohio Shale is exposed in the walls of many valleys and ravines. Two of the best places to observe it are Highbanks Metropolitan Park along the Olentangy River north of Columbus, and along the Rocky River in the Cleveland Metropolitan Park system.

Although the shale currently has no economic value, it does contain natural gas and very small amounts of uranium. The natural gas is held tightly between the fine grains of shale and is very difficult to remove, although research eventually may allow the use of this storehouse of energy.

Great Deltas of the Mississippian Period

Black shale was still accumulating in Ohio seas at the beginning of the Mississippian Period. Gradually, these muds gave way to silts, fine sands, and gravel which formed shale, siltstone, sandstone and conglomerate. The rocks range in age from 345 to 320 million years and are derived from sediments that washed into Ohio from the Canadian Shield and from high mountains to the east.

Mississippian rocks do not contain as many fossils as Devonian rocks, even though the animal population then was just as great as earlier. Corals lived in the sea, but they were less common because the water was muddier. Instead, corals were replaced by mud-loving brachiopods, pelecypods, gastropods, and bryozoans. Fish also were common.

Ancient ripple marks in sandstone walk at Adena State Memorial

On land, amphibians continued to develop. The land was covered with lush vegetation. Trees grew large and, when they died, toppled over, their logs to be preserved in sediments. A large number of ferns and other plants also grew on land.

The Bedford Shale and the Berea Sandstone. Black shale similar to that of Devonian times continued to accumulate early in the Mississippian Period. The sediments came from uplands south and east of Ohio. In time, mud gave way to silt, sand, and fine gravel, all of which accumulated in large, fan-shaped deltas. Waves, in turn, picked up the sediment and distributed it across the sea floor.

A good place to see two very interesting Mississippian formations is Tinkers Creek Gorge in Cuyahoga County. The gorge, part of the Cleveland Metropolitan Park District, has about 75 feet of gray shale exposed in its lower half. Directly above is a massive sandstone which forms a vertical or overhanging cliff about 40 feet high. The lower rock is the Bedford Shale and the upper, more resistant rock is the Berea Sandstone.

The Bedford Shale at Tinkers Creek is softer and not so splintery as the Devonian black shale that underlies it. Interestingly, a few miles west in the Rocky River section of the metropolitan park at Berea, the Bedford Shale is not gray. Instead it is a deep, chocolate red, a color maintained farther south. Like most shales, this formation is not very resistant to erosion, so the best exposures are usually found where the rock has been protected from weathering by the overhanging Berea Sandstone.

In eastern Franklin County, the Bedford Shale has been quarried for brickmaking. Here it is a dark red, soft, crumbly rock which geologists classify as a "mudstone" rather than typical shale.

The Berea Sandstone is a gray compact rock composed of quartz grains firmly cemented by a small amount of clay. At Tinkers Creek Gorge and elsewhere, it commonly contains ripple marks. These are just like the ripples seen in present-day sands that are accumulating in water, so the Berea probably was deposited in shallow water near shore.

Berea Sandstone quarry at South Amherst in Lorain County.

The sandstone is also strongly crossbedded, showing that much of the sand was washed into position by currents from several different directions. In most places, the Berea Sandstone is only 10 to 40 feet thick, as at Tinkers Creek, in the ravine of Rocky Fork northeast of Gahanna in Franklin County, and along U.S. Route 23 near Waverly in Pike County. However, it is considerably thicker at Berea in Cuyahoga County, and at Deep Lock Quarry near Peninsula in Summit County. At these places the rock was quarried for more than a century to make millstones and grindstones. The old quarries at Berea are now filled and built over, and Deep Lock is a part of the Akron Metropolitan Park District. The Berea Sandstone is still mined at South Amherst in Lorain County, where it reaches its maximum thickness — more than 200 feet.

The Black Hand Sandstone. The Hocking Hills is one of the most scenic regions in the state. From Cantwell Cliffs to Ash Cave, this rough, wooded area of high cliffs, rock recesses, bluffs, deep hemlock-fringed gorges and rock shelters is particularly popular because of the Middle Mississippian formation called the Black Hand Sandstone.

The sandstone was formed when coarse sand and pebbles were washed northward by a large stream flowing out of mountains to the southeast about 330 million years ago. The sands accumulated in deltas, and each of the present areas of sandstone represents a finger, or lobe, of this delta. The sands and pebbles were washed onto a muddy bottom and covered by muds which eventually solidified to siltstone and shale.

The rock is buff colored and massive — 80 to 250 feet thick. Coarse-grained, it contains some layers that are so pebbly they are actually conglomerate. The rock is much more resistant to erosion than the shales and siltstones that lie below and above it, so it stands in spectacular cliffs as much as 100 feet high. Water erosion and weathering have carved the less resistant middle part of the Black Hand into recesses and rockshelters. This erosion is especially severe along vertical fractures cutting through the sandstone.

The Black Hand receives its rather unusual name from a black figure of a large human hand which Indians inscribed in soot on a cliff in Black Hand Gorge east of Newark. Unfortunately, the hand was destroyed when the Ohio Canal was constructed in the late 1820s, but the site is now part of Black Hand Gorge State Nature Preserve.

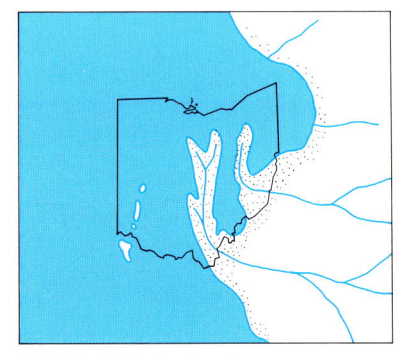

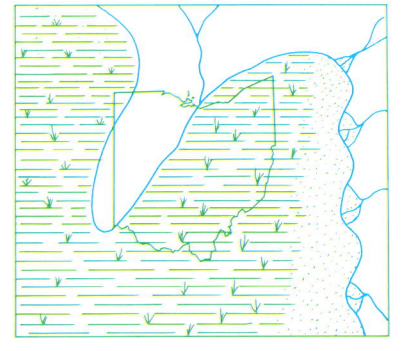

Pennsylvanian and Permian Rocks

About 320 million years ago, at the beginning of the Pennsylvanian Period, Ohio was again covered by a shallow sea. The climate was warm and extensive forests grew in great coastal swamps. The trees and shrubs in these swamps grew almost to the edge of the water, and, for millions of years land battled sea, with the salt water advancing and retreating many times. As a result, Pennsylvanian rocks are both marine and nonmarine in origin. Fossils from these ancient seas include mollusks (clams, cephalopods, and snails), brachiopods, crinoids, and many kinds of fishes.

However, the Pennsylvanian Period is best known for what happened on land. The coastal swamp forests were extremely luxuriant and dead leaves, stems, and other plant parts accumulated to great thicknesses, leaving scientists a rich record of what Pennsylvanian land-life was like. In time, the sea rose, flooding the swamps, killing the trees and burying everything under a blanket of sand and clay. The clay sealed off

Middle Mississippian sea

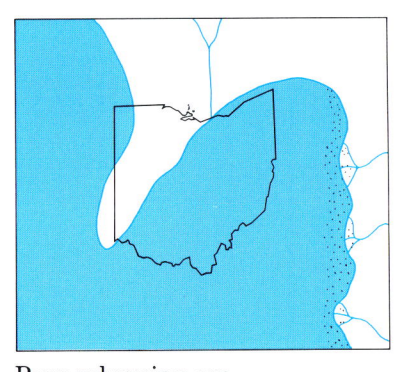

Pennsylvanian sea

Pennsylvanian swamp

oxygen, and the weight of the sediment compressed the vegetation through millions of years, eventually forming coal.

Pennsylvanian swamps swarmed with amphibians. For the first time, reptiles walked. These reptiles were only one or two feet long — small compared to the amphibians which attained lengths of up to 10 feet. Fresh water snails and clams also lived in the swamps. Fossil tree stumps are found occasionally. Three hundred million years ago, small animals lived, hid, and died in the stumps. When these stumps are discovered and broken apart, the skeletons of lizards, amphibians, spiders, snails, and millipedes are often found.

The Sharon Conglomerate. The Sharon Conglomerate is the oldest Pennsylvanian rock in Ohio. The Sharon was formed after fast-moving mountain streams, in uplands to the north and east, washed gravel into ancient seas covering the state. The sediment accumulated in a broad delta, much larger than the present-day Mississippi delta, and through time compacted, forming conglomerate rock. The rock is formed from small quartz pebbles, worn almost perfectly round from the continual tumbling in the fast-moving, primeval streams.

The rock is named for the city of Sharon, just across the Ohio state line in Pennsylvania. However, the most spectacular formations are seen at Gorge Metropolitan Park in Cuyahoga Falls. Here, the Cuyahoga River has cut deeply into the rock, and the conglomerate forms high, massive cliffs. Other good exposures are at Virginia Kendall Park in the Cuyahoga Valley National Recreation Area north of Cuyahoga Falls, Nelson-Kennedy Ledges State Park in Portage County, and many locations in Jackson County 150 miles to the south.

The Vanport Flint. Shells of marine animals also accumulated, forming sediments which eventualy solidified into limestone in these Pennsylvanian seas. Some of these limestone beds, including the Vanport Limestone, were transformed in part to silica by the action of the water. The result is flint. One of the most extensive deposits of this unusual rock is in Ohio at Flint Ridge in Licking County. Prehistoric Indians traveled hundreds of miles to Flint Ridge to pry chunks of flint from shallow pits. The flint probably also was traded among Indian tribes. The flint, Ohio's state mineral, makes excellent arrowheads, spear points, knives, and scrapers, and flint from Flint Ridge has been found as far away as the Atlantic coast, Louisiana, and Missouri.

Dense and hard, the flint breaks forming curved, sharp edges. A trace of organic matter colors most flint black or gray, but small amounts of iron oxide also colors some flints red, orange, or brown.

The Coal Measures. South and east of Flint Ridge lie millions of tons of coal — Ohio's most important mineral. Beneath the hills of eastern Ohio, the coal is interspersed with layers of shale, siltstone, sandstone, clay, and limestone in beds collectively up to 2,000 feet thick. These rocks deposited in the Pennsylvanian and Permian periods, are known informally as the Coal Measures. Because of the heavy forest cover, natural exposures are rare, so the Coal Measures are best seen in interstate highway cuts and the walls of strip mines.

In contrast to other sedimentary rocks, the parent material of the coal beds was not transported by streams or currents. It accumulated right where it grew—"in place", as the geologist says. Rather puzzling is the fact that thin limestones overlying some coal beds in the Coal Measures, together with the shales that accompany them, contain marine fossils. Putting these factors together, it is likely that during Pennsylvanian

Sharon Conglomerate at Thompson's Ledges, Geauga County.

and Permian times the middle of the continent was a vast lowland very near sea level. At times, fresh-water swamps flourished and a thick layer of peat, or semi-decayed plant material, accumulated. Then the land sank a few feet and the sea flooded over. This killed the plants and covered the peat with layers of marine mud and silt. Later, sediments from highlands to the east were spread in delta-like sheets of sand and clay, burying the marine muds. This action forced the shoreline westward and set the stage for the growth of another coal swamp.

Plant remains usually decompose quickly. Why was coal formed in these formations? The answer is that the plant debris accumulated in swamp water which shut off the air, thus slowing decomposition. This process still occurs in swamps today. Instead of breaking down, the plant material is attacked by anaerobic bacteria (non-users of free oxygen) which partly decompose it, splitting off oxygen and hydrogen. These two gases escape and what remains is carbon, which becomes more and more concentrated. In turn, the bacteria are killed by poisons released in the decomposition. At this point, the plant debris is peat.

As the peat is buried beneath more and more plant debris and more and more clay, sand, and silt, water is squeezed out along with such gases as methane. This usually concentrates the carbon, first forming lignite, then sub-bituminous coal, and finally bituminous coal.

Ohio's coals are all bituminous, consisting of compacted, carbonized plant remains. Some of the thicker coal beds extend over thousands of square miles, into Pennsylvania, West Virginia, and Kentucky. Only six or seven of Ohio's coals are thick enough to be extensively mined. In places, the underclays are thick enough to be mined too, and they are the principal materials for the state's brick and tile industries.

In the largest surface coal mines, giant machines known as draglines are used to strip off the rocks above the coal bed. Smaller power shovels are then used to remove the coal for use in electric generating plants. So great is the demand for Ohio's coal that miners may strip away more than 100 feet of rock and soil in order to uncover only four feet of coal.

The Long Gap in the Record

On top of hills in extreme southeastern Ohio are rocks of Permian age, the youngest rocks in the state. In many regions — the Rocky Mountains, for example — Permian rocks are overlain by Triassic rocks, and these in turn by Jurassic, Cretaceous, and Cenozoic strata. Altogether, these rocks, which are not found in Ohio, represent some 225 million years of time. Ohio rocks contain many fossils of earlier Paleozoic sea life and of late Paleozoic land plants. However, these rocks do not contain any dinosaur skeletons or bones of early mammals. These creatures developed during Mesozoic and Cenozoic times and no deposits from these times are found in Ohio.

What was going on in Ohio during this immense time interval? The answer is almost certainly erosion. Many of Ohio's bedrock formations must have once been far more extensive than they are today. For example, consider the "island" of Devonian rocks lying on Silurian strata near Bellefontaine. This is a remnant of a sheet of Devonian shales and limestones originally extending across the state, blanketing the Cincinnati Arch and continuing into the Michigan Basin. Erosion has removed all but this little patch. Or, consider the Pennsylvanian Coal Measures. They once extended without interruption from West Virginia through Ohio and Kentucky into Indiana and Illinois. Parts were eroded during the long interval of time not recorded in the rock record. It was undoubtedly this Mesozoic and Cenozoic erosion that produced the pattern of rock formations over which the glaciers later slid.

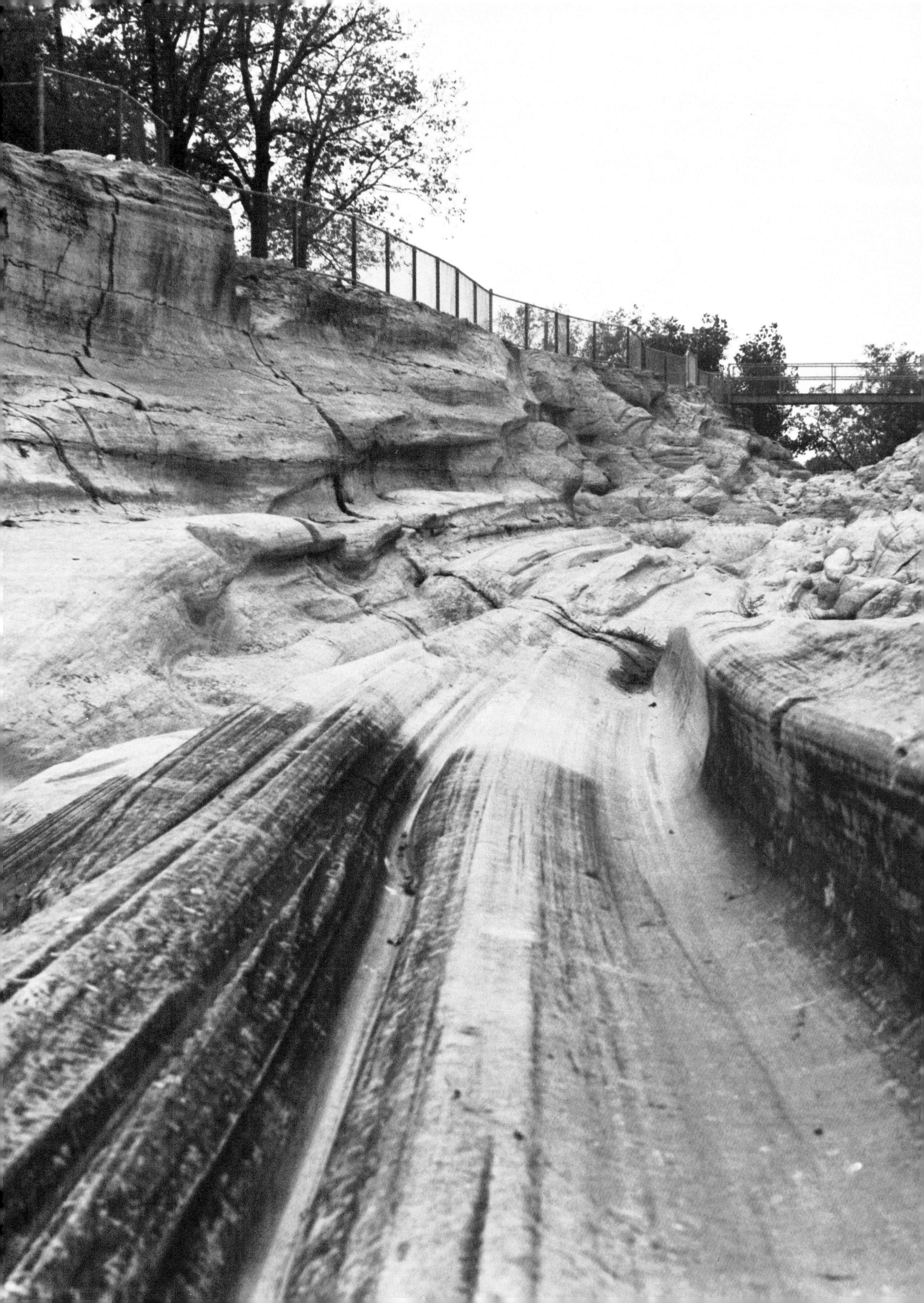

Chapter 3
Ice Over Ohio

THE long break in the geologic record in Ohio after Permian time ended in a series of spectacular events only about two million years ago. In the northern hemisphere the weather turned colder, spawning enormous ice caps which grew repeatedly in the Arctic. They spread southward, covering Canada, practically all of the northern United States, and 56 of Ohio's 88 counties, in a frozen mass 1,000 to 8,000 feet thick. Fourteen more counties were partially covered. The glaciers moved as giant bulldozers, pulverizing earth and rock beneath them, smoothing broad plains, rounding sharp hilltops, shredding and smashing trees as if they were toothpicks, and only stopping when slowed by high hills and warmer weather. Despite several retreats the glaciers left an indelible impression on the earth.

by Richard P. Goldthwait

Invasion by Ice

Ohio has experienced more than four separate ice ages during the last two million years. How fast did each invasion come on? Very slowly — at least in human terms. By studying trees which were pushed over and dragged a short distance by the ice and preserved in glacial material, geologists know ice from the last glacial stage (the Wisconsinan) entered Ohio about 25,400 years ago, advancing at the average of nearly 160 feet a year.

The Last Ice

The ice spread southward over Ohio in four great lobes. Two lobes extended down the broad valleys of the Scioto and Miami rivers. Two shorter lobes in northeast Ohio came down the Grand River and Killbuck Creek. After reaching central Ohio the ice speeded up, pushed forward by continually thickening ice farther north. By the time the glacier reached central Ohio 22,000 years ago, it was overrunning 200 feet of ground each year. South of what is now Columbus in the Scioto Valley, it moved even faster at 360 feet a year. In western Ohio, the same ice sheet moved a little more slowly. The expansion from Sandusky to Sidney was made at nearly 220 feet a year, while the leg south from Sidney to Hamilton was about 170 feet a year.

Actually, the speed of the glacier at any given time was probably double or triple the average. But every now and then, when the weather warmed slightly, the glacier halted. In every ice sheet known today, the ice really moves double to 10 times the yearly advance of the ice edge (from one to six feet daily) because of summer melting. So, we see an annually pulsating advance of a steep ice edge moving 100 yards farther south than the previous year.

As the ice took over 6,000 years to spread across what is now Lake Erie and Ohio, how long did it encase the state? Well, this last time it remained within 50 miles of its farthest limit for 3,000 to 4,000 years. Fringing forests were repeatedly annihilated each time the ice readvanced a few miles. Actually the ice first reached its southern limit down the Scioto Valley 21,300 years ago, and down the Miami Valley about 19,700 years ago. After a brief 2,000- to 3,000-year retreat, it last pushed all the way down the Scioto Valley and bulged westward to Xenia in Greene County 18,000 years ago. Then it melted back, only to readvance to Jamestown, east of Xenia, 1,000 years later.

Thick ice under its own pressure squeezes out slowly like plastic. But the advancing face of the last glacier was only 50 to 200 feet high (as in Greenland today). To squeeze from Cleveland to Chillicothe or Hamilton would require 5,000- to 8,000-foot-thick ice over Cleveland. Certainly it had to be over 1,000 feet thick where it entered even the outer counties (like Stark, Knox, Fairfield, or Butler). Present-day ice sheets in Greenland, Iceland, or Antarctica are more than a mile deep only 200 miles back from the ice edge. In northern Canada the ice was probably two to three miles deep. One striking evidence of such deep ice burial is the great elevation of the first seashores in the St. Lawrence Valley and around Hudson Bay when the ice melted. These beaches are as much as 1,000 feet above sea level, which shows that ice was thick and heavy enough to depress the land, allowing the seawater to flood the terrain. The surface was never depressed so far that the postglacial seas reached Ohio, but they did reach as near as Niagara Falls.

Earlier Glaciations

Invasion by creeping, thick ice was not an isolated event. Ice has formed between eight and 12 separate times in the north during the last two million years. Not much evidence remains of earlier glaciations because many signs have been scraped away by later ice sheets. But each one of four long classical glaciations (Nebraskan, Kansan, Illinoian, and Wisconsinan) left sheets of glacial debris called till, and

Ice Over Ohio 39

Mammoth tooth

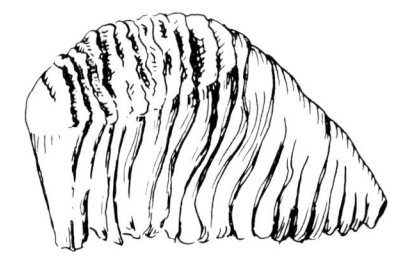

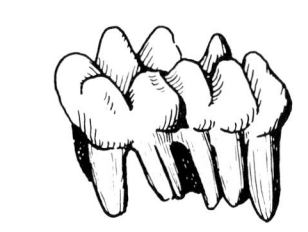

Mastodon tooth

was typical of many Ohio bogs and must have been a favorite watering and hunting spot through the ages. A large collection of the bones of other animals was discovered with the mastodon skeleton. The Orleton mastodon was immature when it died, but it was big for its age. One of its molar teeth was 6½ inches long.

Unfortunately, the mastodon and most of the other megafauna are extinct. Only the muskoxen still lives in the frozen wastes of Siberia, Alaska, Canada, and Greenland. Although simple climatic change was certainly responsible for the changes in the forests, it does not explain the disappearance of so many animals in so short a time. The climate today is different, but not that much different from 8,000 years ago. Besides, the climate of central Ontario probably closely matches the climate of Ohio in the ice ages. But no megafauna live in Ontario. When the megafauna died suddenly, they were not succeeded by anything remotely resembling the species of that day. In Ohio, the mass death began about 11,000 years ago and must have been nearly completed when the Orleton mastodon died. One much-argued but logical explanation would be overhunting by the first Indian ancestors of Pleistocene times.

Glacial Erosion

Before the last ice age, most of Ohio must have been rolling, steep, and hilly country, much like the southeastern part of the state today. Those hills were the product of 60 million years of erosion. Running water, wind, expansion by summer heat, and the freezing and thawing of winter cold have etched the face of the earth ever since the formation of the planet. They eroded the land surface left by the retreat of ancient seas, transforming it into a region of deep valleys, high cliffs and bluffs, and rock outcrops. Giant blocks of rock split from hilltop outcrops covered the hillsides. But, all of this changed as the dozen or so continental ice sheets made successive advances every 20,000 or 90,000 years. The ice deposited till in the valleys, resulting in a flat plain. Thus, the 18 southeastern Ohio counties left untouched by the ice stand as monuments to the weathering of the previous millions of years.

Polished Rock Surfaces

Glacial ice builds up more than one mile thick, and from a distance, a glacier looks like a stationary, quiet, deep-freeze blanket. In reality, all ice caps from Greenland to Antarctica, are torn at their brittle surfaces by crevasses. These giant ice cracks are more or less parallel to the edge of the glacier and are within 100 miles of the ice margin. No matter if a glacier is advancing or retreating, the ice behind the ice margin is always moving forward. The crevasses form as a result of this forward movement, which can be as little as one foot or as much as 60 feet a day whether or not there is a new advance or retreat.

An advancing glacier is so cold at its margins that soil is frozen solid ahead of it. This is why glacial soil layers in counties fringing the glacial ice are preserved so well. However, wherever the ice becomes deep and lasts many centuries, the internal heat of the earth accumulates and gradually the ice base melts. When this happens, the ice slides along its rocky base, - only an inch or two daily, - but fast enough to pick up old pre-glacial soil and rock. Most of this debris is either gathered up in wet ice or is frozen to the bottom of the ice and carried along. Thus the ice sheet acts like a gigantic sandpaper which, under great pressure, slowly grinds the bedrock down to fresh, solid rock.

As more and more rock and debris are dragged over the land surface, the top layers of the bedrock are slowly worn away, exposing the glossy sheen of fresh rock. When exposed, the sheen weathers away, but scratches called striae, produced in the bedrock, remain for decades, and sometimes for thousands of years. These scratches mark the glacier's course over the solid rock, and usually only scratches etched by the most recent ice remain. However some earlier markings are not completely worn away. Bedrock in Greene County, which shows the direction of the early Scioto lobe 21,000 years ago, is cross-marked at right angles by the push of the Miami lobe 1,500 years later.

Glacial scratches on piece of bedrock

Limestone and dolomite are easily eroded by glaciers and, since they comprise much of the state's bedrock, quite a bit of Ohio's upper bedrock layers have been removed. In fact, geologists calculate that between 10 and 60 inches of the limestone were eroded by the last glacier, while the total amount of soil and rock eroded by all the glaciers varies from 20 to 40 feet.

The results of this immense power are best seen at Kelleys Island in Lake Erie. Here, mile-thick ice gouged deep grooves in the limestone. The groups of grooves are three to fifteen feet deep, and at one time were 400 to 600 feet long. The ice must have been channeled up little stream valleys scoured in the limestone, thus concentrating its force along very narrow lines. The ice might have been moving very fast because "turbulent," sweeping gouges are found in the sides of some grooves. Several parallel grooves are separated by smooth, rounded rock ridges. These may be due to clumps of fossil coral in the rock which more successfully resisted the glacier's cutting action. Unfortunately, most of these grooves were quarried away when the limestone was extensively mined in the late nineteenth and early twentieth centuries. Today, one 400-foot-long section is preserved by the Ohio Historical Society. There are smaller and less impressive grooves close by on Marblehead Peninsula, South Bass Island, and Pelee Island.

Deep Old Valleys and New Lakes

The glacial deposits are thickest–200 to 500 feet–along the sites of old preglacial valleys. Instead of eroding more deeply under the flowing ice, these ancient, deep valleys simply filled with dirt dragged at the bottom of each glacier. For example, under the Cuyahoga River is a northward sloping narrow river valley in bedrock buried by 500 feet of till, sand, and silt. Before the several ice advances, it flowed at a level below present sea level. Similarly, Dayton is built over a buried valley 400 feet deep, filled with seven or more layers of glacial till and several layers of sandy gravel. Chillicothe, Akron, Hamilton, and many other Ohio cities also are built over deep glacial deposits. The ice pushed rock and soil into these valleys filling some and completely burying others. Today, the deep sands and gravels provide huge underground reservoirs of water.

Best known of these ancient buried river valleys is the Teays, which runs northwest through Ohio from Chillicothe to Celina and is buried under 200 to 600 feet of till and sand. More than one million years ago, when the Teays was a surface stream, water flowed downhill into Indiana. Today, the river can be traced westward through Indiana–all buried–then southwest across Illinois as the buried Mahomet Valley, before finally emptying into the pre-glacial Mississippi system. The Ice Age glacier blocked all of this northward and westward flow in Ohio, changing the scene drastically. Deep valleys were filled and river waters backed up. Eventually, these lakes overflowed, forming new streams or new connections of old streams.

Where the last four glaciers did not reach, the ancient valleys are still exposed. Parts of the unburied Teays Valley are filled with silts and clays deposited in old, glacier-formed lakes. In Jackson and Pike counties, the Teays is filled with 50 to 100 feet of silt and clay called Minford Silt.

In west-central Ohio, the Kansan glacier dammed a stream 690,000 years ago, leaving as evidence fresh glacial rock flour in the lake-deposited clay. The clay is magnetically reversed — that is north and south poles are reversed in the magnetic clay particles. The last time that happened long enough to record was nearly 700,000 years ago, and thus the minimum age of the glacier which blocked the stream is known.

Still more ice-dammed lakes are left from the Illinoian age glaciations. The blockage of former Teays tributaries produced a lake over Cincinnati, as well as 125,000- to 200,000-year-old ghost lakes at Cynthiana flats in Pike County, lower Massie Creek and Salt Creek in Ross County, Rush Creek in Fairfield County, and lower Wakatomika Creek in Muskingum County.

The locations of these ancient lakes are known because fine clay sediment accumulated on the lake bottoms. The Wisconsinan Stage also created small lakes, none hardly more than three miles long, which stretched up small valleys occupied previously by the Illinoian ice. At least 20 such ice-marginal clay deposits have been found. The end moraines trapped another 20 lakes in the early deglaciation phases 18,000 to 15,000 years ago. Still later, about 14,000 years ago, when the melting ice lay north of the watershed between Lake Erie and the Ohio River, 15 broad, big, shallow lakes, like Celeryville Bog in Huron County, were trapped between broad moraine ridges. In most of these, the water outlet cut down as the lake filled up with silt and peat. Only a few shallow, swampy lakes such as Indian Lake, Buckeye Lake, and Grand Lake remained when white men settled Ohio.

The granddaddy of Ohio glacial lakes is Lake Erie itself. As the ice melted back, it blocked the Erie basin drainage at Buffalo. This ice was the last to melt, and it forced the water to rise high enough to overflow to the west near Fort Wayne, Indiana. Indeed, when geologists traced the fossil lake beaches leading to this outlet it became evident that when the lake existed, ice still occupied most of the lower eastern basin even as far west as Toledo. This early lake, called Lake Maumee, flooded the broad, flat areas of northwest Ohio and northeast Indiana, 200 feet above present Lake Erie. After a while, the lake levels dropped. This is indicated by a series of lower beaches which lead off into outlets across Grand River, Michigan into Lake Michigan. The glaciers had depressed the Lake Huron basin so much that water flowed across the lower peninsula of Michigan. As the glacier melted north, it created a series of lakes at successively lower levels named Whittlesey, Arkona, Warren, Wayne, and Lundy. This last one existed 8,500 years ago and was 43 feet above present Lake Erie. This series of low beach ridges — each lower than the last — was utilized for early roadways and even today many main highways follow them.

Minford Silt deposited at the bottom of ancient glacial Lake Tight in southern Ohio.

Till, We Meet Again

Till is the dirt of glaciers — a mixture of old soils, fresh ground rock, and boulders all from up-glacier. Till made a one-way trip from the north where the ice was thick, to margins where ice became patchy and thin. Ohio is in the outer quarter of the area overspread repeatedly by thick ice; so, as one might expect, Ohio accumulated more of this unsorted mixture of glacial debris than areas much farther north. In northern Ontario much bedrock is exposed and the irregular till blanket averages only five to 15 feet deep. In contrast, Ohio has only knobs of exposed bedrock. In most counties the average depth to rock in thousands of water wells exceeds 50 feet. High, hilly areas near the ice margin do not have nearly that much — perhaps 20 or 25 feet of dirt cover — so solid rock hills and cliffs show through in many places.

This is the soil we live on, build on, and dig in, so it is important. If modern glaciers are a clue, the till was deposited late in each ice invasion at a rate up to a half inch a year. Unlike the sandy soils of northern Ontario, Wisconsin, or New England, the glacier brought vast quantities of clay to Ohio and this makes soils heavy, sticky, or very hard when dry. The common shale rock, both weathered and fresh, with the abraded limestone-dolomite yielded most of this fine material. Most till particles have been moved by ice no more than 50 miles. Where the glacier eroded sandstone bedrock in eastern Ohio, sand may comprise as much as 50 percent of the till.

Stones — pebbles and boulders — are liberally mixed in till. In western Ohio these may be only one percent to five percent of the till. The bigger

Rocky Fork stream cut east of Columbus. The latest Wisconsinan age till (brown) occupies the top of the cliff. Older (about 18,000 years ago) tills (gray) lie below it and the lower third is sand and gravel outwash with buried wood dated about 45,000 years ago

the boulder, the farther away is its source. For example only two to fifteen percent of the pebbles in central-southwest Ohio came from exclusively Canadian rock types (granite, quartzites), whereas 90 percent of the boulders over one-foot in diameter are Canadian crystalline-type rocks. The biggest boulder in each county is often more than 10 feet long and is invariably a granite, granite gneiss, or some rock type from north of the Great Lakes. Such huge chunks weighing many tons are seen riding along the outer surface of modern ice sheets where solid ice is exposed in summer. This is especially true in the boulder belts, which are in reality end moraines where the ice edge stood for decades dumping its boulder load across the surface.

Ice-contact Kames and Eskers

A few selected areas in Logan and Greene counties and in Portage, Summit, and Stark counties which were between the great lobes of the last ice sheet received hilly, thick, sand and gravel deposits, called kames. Some river valleys such as the lower Paint Creek and middle Licking and Black rivers are speckled with these deposits.

What was it like in these areas of Ohio? Invariably, the ice was thin and irregular and had just about stopped advancing. All the water melting from dirty ice surface washed and sorted out the dirt. The fine silts and clays were carried off as "glacier milk" to a lake or the sea, whereas the sand and gravel often lodged in silt-free layers on top of ice or against it.

A glacial kame in Salt Creek Valley east of Laurelville in Hocking County

Buried ice lasted longest where it was covered by dirt, although it always melted within a few centuries to a millennium. Where thin, decaying ice melted from under the washed sand it left small kettle ponds and bogs among the kame hummocks mostly 14,000 to 16,500 years ago.

More widespread but relatively rare in Ohio are the elongated, crooked ridges of sandy gravel called eskers. They accumulated under the ice in an ice tube or cave as meltwaters opened passages in honeycombed ice. Good examples of eskers in Ohio are only one to 10 miles long, and between five and 50 feet high. Together with channels cut in earlier till, they mark the passage of subglacial waters which sorted basal till and carried away the silt and clay. The eskers almost always end in nearby dry water courses cut through end moraines. The ice usually did not pause long and most ridges were formed in fewer than 10 years.

A kettle lake west of Mechanicsburg in Champaign County

Flooded Valleys

The rivers which flowed from the retreating Wisconsinan ice were very different from rivers today, even through they flowed in the same valleys. Today, streams are fullest in spring, but glacial streams flowed only during June, July, and August when the warm summer days melted the ice. Every fair summer day a huge and rapidly swelling flood issued from the ice face. The waters were so vast that some main valleys were oversized cuts under the ice even before meltwater deposits were made. Consider the Mad River Valley. It is four miles wide, but contains a relatively small river. Almost 18,000 years ago, western Ohio's Mad River originated under the melting ice. It was fed by several "tunnel valleys" like Nettle Creek and was much bigger than it is today. It was even larger than the Miami River 17,000 years ago, although the reverse is now true. The lower Scioto, Hocking, Licking, Kokosing, Mohican, and Tuscarawas rivers, and Sandy, Nimishillen, and Killbuck creeks all were glacial streams for a thousand years with flows 100 times greater than in summer today.

As each glacier melted back, flooded valleys filled slowly with sandy gravel deposits reworked from the stream valley cuttings under the ice and from dirt in lower ice layers. Such layered, gently sloping "valley trains" are characteristic of every glaciated area today. Instead of a single meandering stream in each valley there were many braided channels shifting from side to side. In a few hundred or a thousand years, each of these main valleys was filled partially with sandy gravel layers 50 to 100 feet thick, accumulating at five to 10 feet a century.

Today, many valley trains have been eroded away by docile postglacial rivers. These have removed the central parts of these old valley trains, leaving terraces of outwash on the valley sides up to 50 feet above present flood plains. Together with the ice-contact eskers and kames, these outwashes are our principal source of clean washed sand and gravel — a very important resource for concrete, road making, and fill.

Outwash was deposited, not once but many times, as ice sheets melted. For example, 18,000 years ago the Mad River Valley was still full of ice. But thinning between the Scioto and Miami ice lobes allowed the outwash to pour into that first opening and build the high Kennard

Crossbedded glacial outwash sand and gravel

outwash from Castle Piatt Mac-A-Cheek and Ohio Caverns in Logan County south through Champaign County and Clark County east of Springfield to Clifton Gorge. There the gravel deposits ended and meltwaters vastly swelled the Little Miami River, cutting Clifton Gorge and the stream's huge potholes west of Clifton. The still earlier Wisconsinan, Illinoian, and Kansan glaciations all left terraces stacked one above another like stairs up the walls of many Ohio stream valleys.

In Ohio, the unglaciated hills just east of glaciated counties and Illinoian age till all have the thickest blanket of loess. In some places the loessial soil may be as much as 15 feet deep. This means that some loess storms occurred as early as Illinoian time. The largest dust storms rose off the outwash of the White, Little Miami, Scioto, and Muskingum rivers because the loess cover is thickest in the lee of each of these trains.

Suddenly, just about 17,000 years ago, the loess supply was cut off. Dust cover is not found (more than a few inches) on till of the 17,000- to 16,000-year-old retreats, or on till and outwash of the 15,000-year readvance. Even the glacial lake shores 12,000 to 14,000 years ago supplied little dust. Big dust storms were over until the next glaciation.

Time Table for the Next Ice Age

The Wisconsinan Stage ice withdrew from Ohio about 12,000 years ago, but it is probably not the last time the glaciers will advance from the north. On the average, 50,000 to 100,000 years have elapsed between the most extended pushes of the last four glaciations. So the next ice sheet may not reach its climax for another 40,000 to 90,000 years. Then again, the climate does change in shorter cycles, and the ice may begin advancing within the next decade. What is known for certain is that 120 to 230 years ago the Arctic glaciers were advancing and now they are mostly retreating. All this minor fluctuation is during an interglacial (between glaciers) stage when glaciers cover less than one third their maximum area. None come near enough to affect Ohio profoundly — the entire hemisphere is simply a very few degrees colder and wetter.

Now the scientists who explore ocean floor sediments and its life find that cool glacial-stage waters lasted much longer during the two million years just ending than did warm interglacial-stage waters. In other words, the warmest interglacial times are short, and most of the 50,000 to 100,000 years between maximal ice sheets is a cycling climate distinctly cooler than today. Ice may not cover Ohio in less than 50,000 to 100,000 years, but it will certainly regenerate on the highlands of Canada and Europe long before that, conceivably in our lifetime. Which single advance will continue long enough to bring thick ice to Ohio is now nearly impossible to predict. Its lumbering expansion has always been slow enough that weather modification countermeasures may be possible next time.

Less flat and better drained than the Lake Plain, the Till Plains are the result of the deposition and smoothing action of the glaciers.

The terrain in the northern Till Plains is much more youthful than that in the south. Streams such as the St. Marys River in Auglaize, Mercer, and Van Wert counties have a much lower gradient than streams farther south such as the Great and Little Miami rivers. The latter two streams are former glacial outwash streams and today are cutting down more rapidly to the lower baselevel of the Ohio River.

The plains receives its name from the glacial debris, or till, which covers preglacial hills and valleys, except where it thins along the southern glacial boundary. Most hills in the Till Plains are mounds of boulders and soil left by the retreating Wisconsinan glacier. Sometimes the ice front remained stationary for 100 to 200 years — just long enough for a few million tons of rock and soil to pile up in a series of broad moraines up to 100 feet high and six miles wide. Eight of these moraines loop across the Till Plains. In Logan County they drape around the Bellefontaine Outlier, a hilly belt of bedrock that rises to 1,549 feet, the highest point in the state.

Till Plains

Farther south, fast-flowing meltwater washed huge amounts of sand and gravel into valleys south of the ice front. In some places, the outwash partially filled the valleys. Later, water eroded parts of these deposits, leaving the uneroded remains as terraces along the valley sides. Their elevation above flood level gives protection, and the terraces are now the sites of Cincinnati, Terrace Park, Springfield, and other cities.

The succession of glaciers also changed drainage patterns. Advancing ice fronts often dammed streams, backing them up forming lakes. Eventually, the water overflowed and the streams cut new courses. This is the way the Ohio River was created after the Kansan glacier dammed the Teays River, former master stream east of the Mississippi River. Made up of a patchwork of the courses of former streams, the Ohio River gradually evolved along the margin of the continental glacier. The Teays, which had formerly drained much of the eastern and southeastern United States, ceased to exist. North of Chillicothe its channel lies buried under up to 400 feet of glacial till. Only in southern Ohio, where the glaciers never reached, is the Teays Valley clearly visible.

Crawfish chimney

Water flowing from glaciers into Ohio River tributaries also quickly cut new stream channels. The process was speeded because there was little vegetation to slow the meltwater. The Little Miami River, which lost its old channel by blockage, cut a spectacular, narrow gorge 70 feet deep through bedrock near Clifton. Wherever particularly hard bedrock is encountered, streams form waterfalls.

A warmer climate stopped the southern advance of the Wisconsinan glacier about 19,000 years ago; so this ice did not completely cover the older till plains. Today the ice advance is marked by two terminal moraines (Hartwell on the west and Cuba on the east). South of this belt, Illinoian till (400,000 years old) underlies the Till Plains section. The Illinoian till is much flatter and is less well-drained. It also has been weathered for a much longer time, and the weathering has leached many plant nutrients downward forming a hardpan about nine feet below the surface. This hardpan is almost watertight, and it slows drainage from the surface so much that the upper soil levels are frequently wet, especially in woodland depressions. The local term for this is "crawfish land," a name derived from the large numbers of crawfish which burrow in the slow-draining soil. The clay soil of the area holds together exceptionally well, and the crawfish mound the soil up to several inches high around their burrow entrances. Some fields have hundreds of these "chimneys" before farmers plow in the spring.

The Bluegrass

The Bluegrass

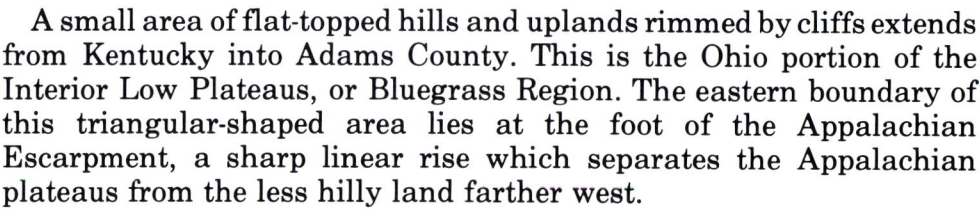

A small area of flat-topped hills and uplands rimmed by cliffs extends from Kentucky into Adams County. This is the Ohio portion of the Interior Low Plateaus, or Bluegrass Region. The eastern boundary of this triangular-shaped area lies at the foot of the Appalachian Escarpment, a sharp linear rise which separates the Appalachian plateaus from the less hilly land farther west.

Limestone, dolomite, and shale bedrock formed in Ordovician and Silurian times dip gently eastward. These rocks vary greatly in resistance to erosion, and they control the land forms. The easily eroded shales form gentle slopes, which are often interrupted by level areas called benches underlain by more resistant limestone and dolomite. The dolomites and limestones rim the valleys forming cliffs or very steep slopes, or they cap the flat-topped ridges with resistant rock. The edges of some of the uplands are dotted with sink holes or depressions made by solution of the calcareous rocks.

Although the Wisconsinan glacier did not reach as far as the Bluegrass, it still left its imprint. From Manchester to Portsmouth, tributaries enter the Ohio River at abnormal angles. These "barbed" tributaries are inherited from the preglacial Portsmouth River which flowed eastward from a preglacial divide at Manchester into the Teays system. Blocked by ice, the resulting Lake Tight overflowed westward and breached a divide, and thus this part of the Ohio came into being. Today the Ohio Valley narrows where the river cuts across the old north-south divide.

One of the unique land forms in the United States is near the Adams-Highland County line. It is called the Serpent Mound Cryptoexplosion Structure and was created when a cataclysmic explosion occurred sometime after the Mississippian Period 325 million years ago. Scientists believe a meteor struck the area. The force of the explosion must have been immense. Immediately after impact, the center rebounded, lifting Ordovician rocks 950 feet above their normal positions. In contrast, an outer ring of younger Mississippian sandstone and shale was depressed nearly 400 feet. As these sandstones are harder than the surrounding rocks, erosion has resulted in a circle of hills clearly visible from the air. Since land use depends on the different types of exposed rocks, the terrain here has a great impact on area agriculture. The high center of limestone and shale is mostly given over to pasture, while a surrounding inner ring on Silurian dolomite supports crops. The hilly outer rim of sandstone and shale is forested. The famous Indian effigy mound, Serpent Mound, is located on a depressed block of Silurian dolomite on the southwest side of this structure.

Unglaciated Appalachian Plateau

The remote hill country of the unglaciated plateau lies in southeastern Ohio. This is a region of deep valleys, high hills, and winding streams. The plateau has the greatest relief in the state, and some of the hill tops are 1,200 to 1,400 feet above sea level. Roads follow either the narrow ridge tops or valley floors, and forests cloak most of the steep slopes.

In Adams County, the western boundary of the unglaciated plateau forms a great step in the landscape running north and south. Here there is a difference of 765 feet from the valley of Ohio Brush Creek, with an elevation of about 500 feet, to the top of Greenbrier Ridge, with an elevation of 1,265 feet. From the west, this escarpment appears as a wall of wooded mountains in front of which rise isolated hills. These hills, or knobs, once were joined to the plateau, but through the eons the connecting land eroded away.

Sandstone, one of the principal bedrock outcroppings in the region, is very resistant to erosion and supports the uplands and steep sides of the valleys. This results in a variety of cliffs, gorges, rockbridges, and waterfalls. Hocking County has a rich treasury of such sandstone features. In contrast, a more subdued topography and lower elevations develop where shale dominates the rock section.

A long belt of higher hills in the east-central part of the plateau extends from Monroe County northeast to Columbiana County. Referred to as the Flushing Escarpment, this higher, rough hill country is the divide area between steeper eastward-flowing streams that enter the Ohio and longer, more gently west-flowing streams tributary to the Muskingum.

Viewed from a fire tower, the plateau in Carroll and adjoining counties in southeastern Ohio, has two levels of hills within 200 to 300 feet of one another in elevation. The higher-level hills have an average elevation of about 1,270 feet above sea level and are thought by some scientists to be remnants of a very old land surface known as the Harrisburg peneplain. The lower-level hills, commonly 930 to 990 feet high, are the remnants of a younger erosion surface — the Lexington peneplain. A third, and still more recent partial erosion cycle was cut by the Teays drainage system before the first of the great continental ice sheets invaded Ohio over one million years ago.

Because of the roughness of the plateau and its infertile soils, this area is less prosperous and less populated than all adjoining regions. Agriculture must be confined to floodplains, flat-topped remnants, or shale areas. One of the best farming areas in the plateau is a remarkable agricultural valley which curves through the plateau north of the Ohio River near Wheelersburg. No stream flows there today. This is an abandoned segment of the preglacial Teays River. Cut off by an early glacier, this segment remains an undisturbed relict of geologic history. It is partially filled with lake clays called the Minford Silts which settled out of Lake Tight, the vast, winding, marginal lake dammed by ice.

The Teays began in North Carolina, flowed across Virginia, West Virginia, and northwest across Ohio, Indiana, and Illinois. Numerous tributaries of the Teays have been incorporated into the modern drainage patterns. For example, in southcentral Ohio, creeks heading very close to Ohio Brush Creek flow eastward joining the Scioto River.

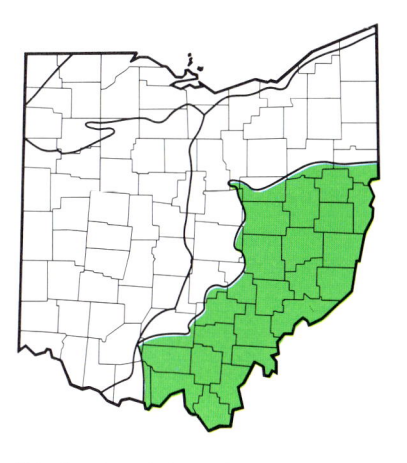

Unglaciated Appalachian Plateau of the hill country

The preglacial Teays River and various tributaries in relation to modern Ohio boundaries

Teays River in relation to nearby states

Abandoned Teays River valley east of Vigo in Ross County

When the water reaches the Ohio it turns and flows west. This route takes the runoff more than 40 extra miles. Elsewhere, modern streams crisscross the old Teays drainage and then follow the former valley for short distances.

Glaciated Appalachian Plateau

The ice sheets pushed up and over the western and northern fronts of the Appalachian Plateau, and glacial deposits cover the former stream-carved topography. The glaciated plateau, less hilly except on the south, is more suitable for agriculture and lacks the wilderness quality of the unglaciated section.

A frayed escarpment with outliers displays a ragged skyline southwest of Chillicothe. Just northeast, Mt. Logan rises 600 feet above that city. It is a well-known landmark and appears on the Great Seal of Ohio. Where Paint Creek is cutting at the side of its valley the creek has cut Copperas Cliffs, a spectacular cliff 220 feet high in the Ohio Black Shale.

In addition to obliterating streams, the glaciers, combined with water erosion, changed the course of many streams along the margin of the ice. A number of Ohio streams have had their courses changed by the Kansan, Illinoian, and Wisconsinan glaciers. For example, the Cuyahoga and Grand rivers follow odd courses to Lake Erie, partly inherited and partly new. A classic example of stream reversal is that of Salt Creek in Hocking County. Here, the Illinoian glacier advanced as far as present-day Haynes in the Salt Creek Valley. The ice dammed the northwest-flowing creek and its tributaries. The water backed up until it overflowed to the southeast at the head of a tributary. As the water spilled over the divide, it deepened the escape channel, cutting a narrow, steep-sided gorge. Salt Creek follows this reversed drainage route today to the Scioto River far south of Chillicothe.

Tributary streams normally flow in the same general direction as the main stream in a pattern that resembles the branching of a tree. However, the "barbed" tributaries of Salt Creek upstream from the gorge enter the creek at an acute angle and still flow in the same direction they did before the reversal occurred.

In Highland County, Rocky Fork at Seven Caves and Baker Fork near Fort Hill have both lost their preglacial channels. Misplaced over massive Silurian dolomites, they have produced spectacular gorges which we can enjoy today. Other "reversed" streams include the Mohican, Kokosing, Licking, Hocking, and Tuscarawas rivers, and Killbuck Creek.

East of Columbus elevations of 1,000 feet are more common, and glacial deposition controls the landscape, almost obscuring the Allegheny Escarpment. In northeast Ohio south of Lake Erie, the terminal moraines loop into pre-existing lowlands. Kames, terraces, and kettles abound. Bogs are numerous in Portage County, and they also are common in Fairfield, Licking, Stark, and Summit counties. Brown's Lake Bog, a nature preserve in Wayne County, lies in a kettle hole.

Glaciated Appalachian Plateau

Our Inheritance of Water

Of the 38 inches of rain that fall on Ohio each year, 12 inches or about one-third, run off into streams and lakes. Part of the flow goes into Lake Erie, which stores 100 billion gallons of water from Ohio and the northern Great Lakes; and part drains into the Ohio River, which carries 23 billion gallons past Cincinnati every year.

Over 6,000 streams in 18 major watersheds drain the state. Each stream has its own flow characteristics, chemical quality, and unfortunately, its own sources of pollution. Those streams in the Till Plains, such as the Mad and Great Miami rivers, tend to have more uniform flow and maintain a high summer volume. Water seeping from outwash and underlying limestone strata recharges both of these rivers. Unglaciated plateau streams, because of small recharge from bedrock, often show a very low summer flow.

Perhaps as much as one third of rainfall is lost into the air by direct evaporation or transpiration through plants. Slightly more than one third runs off in streams and rivers. Thus less than one third of the precipitation sinks into the ground filling the voids in the soil, glacial deposits, and bedrock. The top of this underground zone of saturation is called the water table, and these reserves are frequently tapped by households, towns, and cities. Although ground water comprises only about five percent of the state's total water supply, about 900 million gallons of water are pumped for use every day. More than 75 percent of the ground water pumped comes from beds of sand and gravel, while much of the remainder (about 160 million gallons a day) is pumped from limestone and sandstone formations.

Western Ohio furnishes much more ground water then the eastern part of the state because of the large areas of limestone bedrock close to the surface and the extensive deposits of permeable glacial outwash. Buried valleys, such as the preglacial Teays River, are substantial reservoirs of underground water. Wells drilled in buried valleys can yield more than 500 gallons per minute (gpm) of "blue gold." Two wells in western Hamilton County, in the buried ancestral Ohio, produce 17

56 Ohio's Natural Heritage

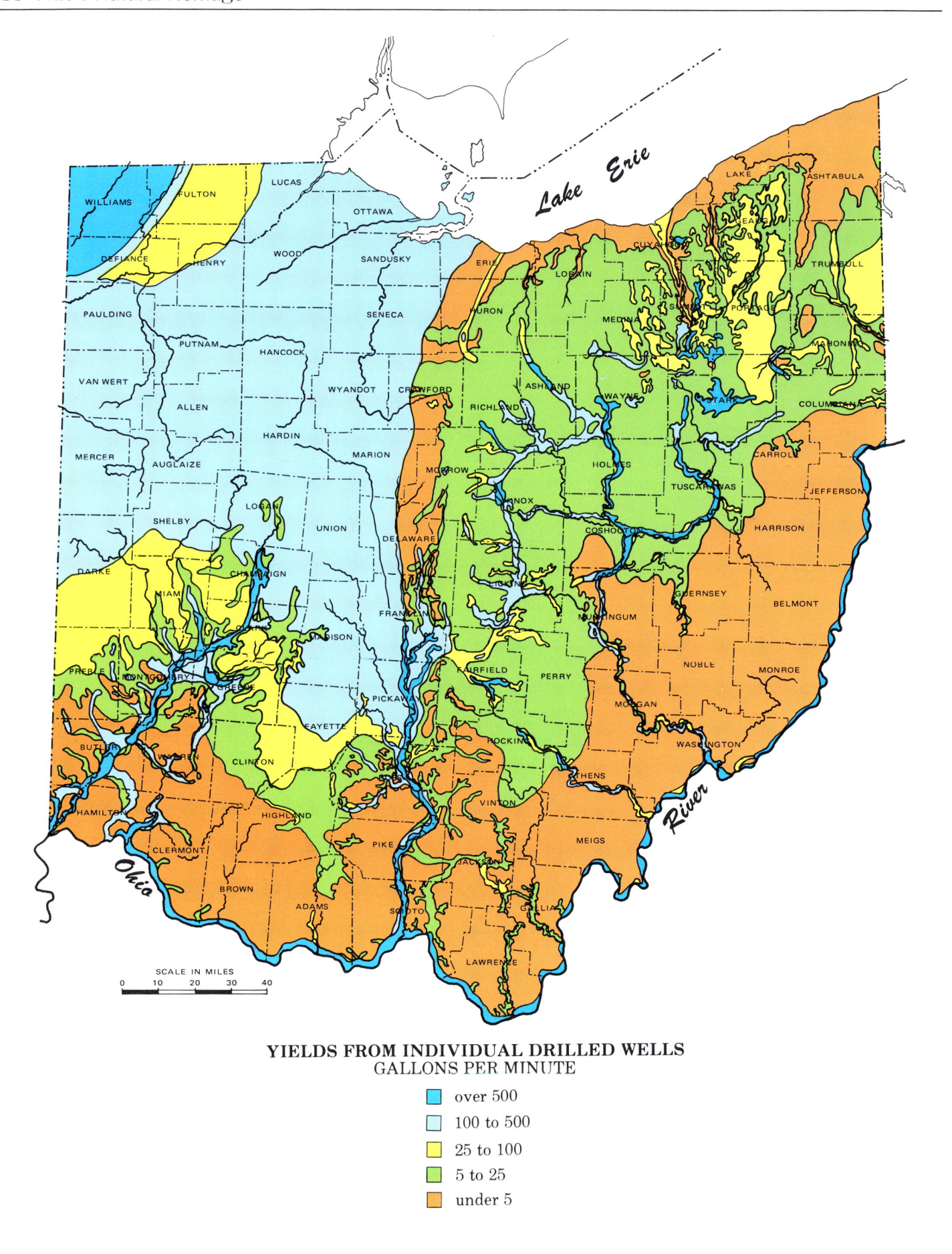

YIELDS FROM INDIVIDUAL DRILLED WELLS
GALLONS PER MINUTE

- over 500
- 100 to 500
- 25 to 100
- 5 to 25
- under 5

Groundwater Resources Of Ohio

The "yellow spring" at Yellow Springs in Greene County

million gallons per day for industrial use. This well water is a constant 55°F, the mean annual temperature of the region, and is prized for industrial use because of its even temperature and consistent chemical quality.

Water is also stored in the tiny pores, minute cracks, and fissures of consolidated rock. The amount of flow from wells or springs varies with the kind of rock. For example, a well from limestone and dolomite can produce 100 to 400 gpm. A good sandstone well yields 25 to 70 gpm, while water-tight shales supply less than 2 gpm. During droughts, ground water maintains stream flow, and it furnishes all the water for springs. A spring emerges at the surface when a water-bearing layer, or the water table, intersects a valley slope. The Yellow Springs at Glen Helen in Greene County issues from a fissure in the Cedarville dolomite just below a few feet of glacial till. Its flow varies from 60 to 100 gpm. Iron in the water imparts a yellow color to the calcareous spring deposits which preserve twigs and leaves that fall in the water. Water percolating downward through glacial deposits sometimes stops at the top of the bedrock. Then it flows along the top of the bedrock until emerging as a small spring or seep, very common in glaciated areas.

Water in the Blue Hole near Castalia bubbles up out of a sink hole in the Columbus Limestone aquifer, a rock formation which holds much water. Its large flow, averaging 5,000 gpm, increases after heavy rains. The overflow is used in a trout hatchery, but the water, having traveled many miles from its entry point, must be aerated to increase the oxygen for the fish to live.

Surface drainage often contaminates shallow wells and springs; thus much water consumed in rural areas is unfit for human consumption. Deeper wells provide purer water.

Ohio is fortunate with its wealth of water. In 1970 it ranked fifth in the nation in use. Use averaged about 12,500 million gallons per day (mgd) that year by electrical generating companies, 2,400 mgd by manufacturers, 1,300 mgd by municipalities, and 350 mgd by farmers and other rural residents.

Ohio's abundant water supply stems from its ample rain and its geologic history. Seas of the ancient past have given us our limestones and dolomite. From the ice ages we have inherited a bounteous storage capacity from the unconsolidated deposits and buried valleys plus a great lake on the north. Water is precious, and in the future we will probably be demanding ever increasing amounts.

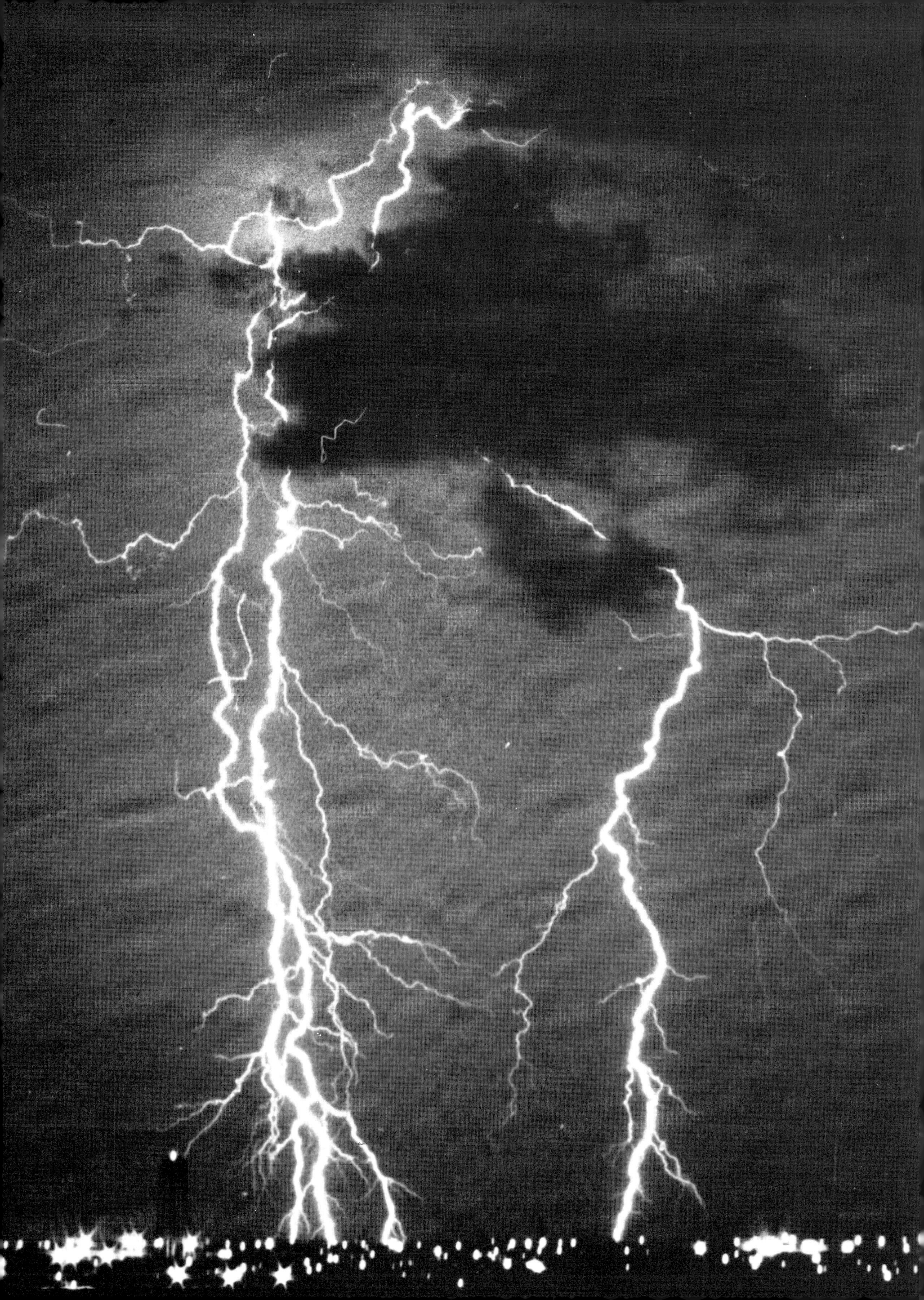

Chapter 5
Climate and Weather

IF weather were a product like coffee, iron, or steel, Ohio would be on the short end of the trade balance. While relatively little weather is produced in the state, we consume a great deal of it. Ohio lies in the midst of a busy weather traffic pattern. The wind at this latitude (prevailing westerlies) sends an unending parade of weather fronts, high and low pressure systems, from west to east across the state. Weather is the current temperature, precipitation, humidity, wind, barometric pressure, and cloudiness. Climate is the long-term tendency of the weather. Ohio's climate is classified as "continental" but with moderate extremes of wetness and dryness, heat and cold. Indeed, the state is blessed with fairly even precipitation, and spring, summer, and autumn days are often sunny. In northeast Ohio near Lake Erie, this continental climate is modified even further by the lake waters.

Ohio weather can come from any direction. But generally, shifting jet streams, which blow around the world at 100 to 200 miles an hour and at heights of 30,000 to 40,000 feet, control the direction of three major continental storm tracks in the United States. A shift of just a few degrees in the movement of one of these tracks can mean the difference between a major blizzard or just a few light flurries.

One track originates in the Gulf of Alaska, enters North America in western Canada, then makes a huge loop south to the Gulf of Mexico before turning north into the northeastern states. Another track begins farther south off the coast of Washington, crosses the Rocky Mountains,

by Richard D. Goddard

Continental storm tracks

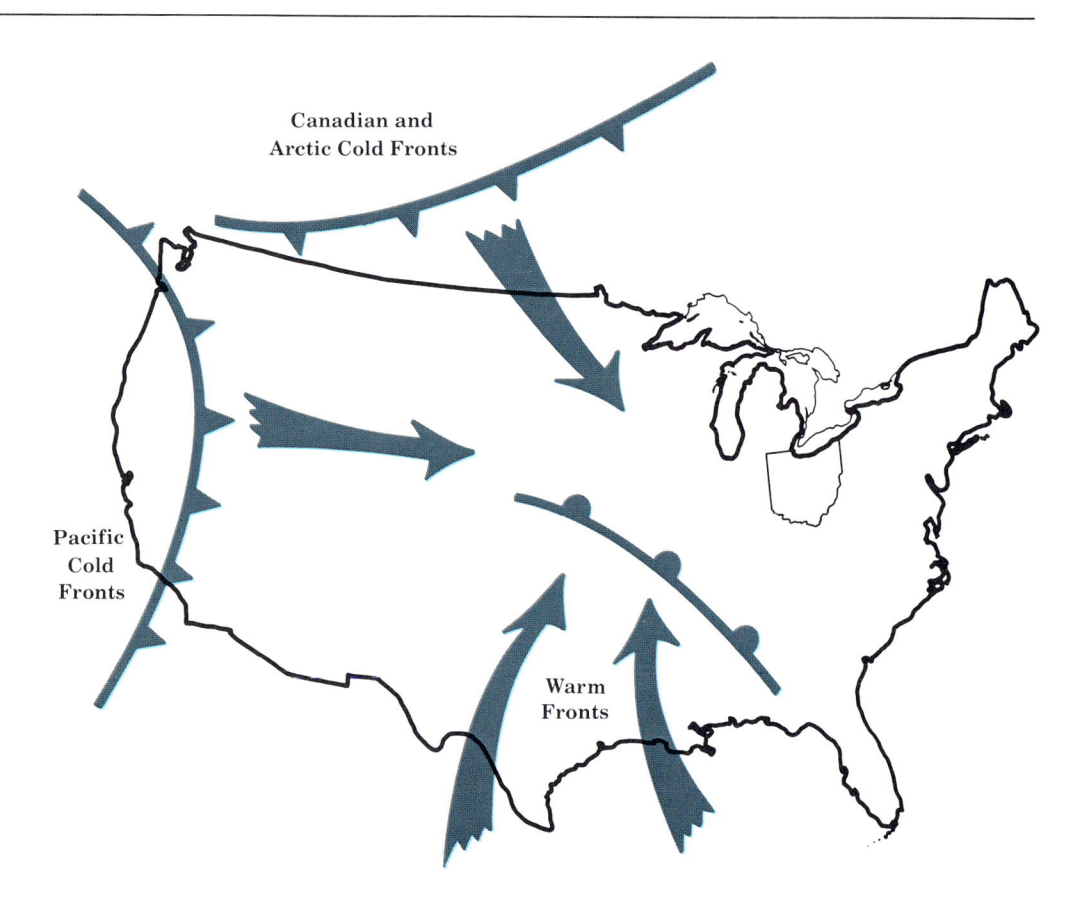

then loops far south into the gulf before it heads northeast. The third track begins off the coast of southern California, loops northeast through the Great Plains and then southeast through Indiana, Ohio, and Kentucky into the southeastern U.S. The first two tracks bring wet weather — snow or rain — which is picked up in the Gulf of Mexico, while the third track usually carries less moisture.

In Ohio, Lake Erie is the major weather producer. The lake's influence is felt most strongly in late autumn and early winter when west by northwest winds blow across the water, picking up moisture and depositing it as heavy snow inland over high land elevations. Snow bursts of one to two feet are not uncommon in snowbelt communities south and east of Cleveland.

Spring

Early spring produces Ohio's most fitful and chaotic weather. Weather fronts from the northwest and southwest arrive with great regularity. Onrushing warm and humid air from the Gulf of Mexico often collides with cool Pacific Ocean air directly over the state, resulting in frequent severe thunderstorm and tornado watches and warnings.

Tornadoes

Nearly 70 percent of all Ohio tornadoes occur during spring. The state averages about one dozen tornadoes annually, but this number is low compared with states farther west. Still, Ohio's death rate from tornadoes is high. Just as many people die from tornadoes in Ohio as in Kansas, which has about eight times as many of the storms. The reason is that Ohio is a much more populous state. Buckeye tornadoes also have a reputation for severity.

Ohio shared in the greatest tornado outbreak in American history April 3, 1974, when 37 people were killed in the state and damage totaled more than $100 million. One hundred forty-eight tornadoes were reported in the U.S. that day — 12 of them striking Ohio. Xenia, in Greene County, bore the brunt of the onslaught. A giant twister roared out of the late afternoon sky and wound through the city for 35 minutes. This storm was extremely wide and its winds were estimated at 316 miles an hour.

Nine years earlier, a series of killer tornadoes ripped through northern and central Ohio on Palm Sunday, April 11, 1965. The 12 tornadoes that touched ground resulted in 57 deaths, more than 300 injuries, and nearly $41 million in property damage.

Scientists do not completely understand how a tornado forms. However, they do know there must be layers of air contrasting in temperature, moisture, density, and wind flow. Tornadoes usually form within well developed thunderstorms, and tornado weather is characteristically warm, humid, and unsettled. A tornado develops several thousand feet above ground and is normally accompanied by great displays of lightning. This electrification is often continuous and many scientists believe that this is an important link between a thunderstorm and tornado formation. As water vapor condenses and becomes visible, a funnel dangles from the base of the thunderstorm cloud. This funnel may remain suspended in the air or reach earth, picking up dirt and debris which darkens the funnel. Tornadoes may skip, alternately lifting and touching down again, as the thunderstorm moves along. Winds may reach 300 miles an hour or more, as they rip and twist. Buildings with normal air pressure inside may explode as the partial vacuum within the tornado funnel passes over. Unfortunately, these deadly storms cannot be forecast. When conditions seem ripe for development, a "tornado watch" is issued. But, only half the time a tornado watch is issued will such a storm occur.

Approximately 90 percent of all Ohio tornadoes come from the southwest, west-southwest, or west. Most Ohio tornadoes are 300 to 400 yards wide and remain on the ground for about 13 miles. Their average forward speed is 25 to 40 miles an hour. It is important to remember that three of every four tornadoes last 15 minutes, or less. The storms form fast and strike so suddenly that warning time may be only minutes, if at all. Three of every four tornadoes touch down between 2 p.m. and 10 p.m. The first recorded tornado in Ohio was in Geauga County in August 1804, and only one Ohio county, Vinton, has never recorded a twister.

Xenia tornado destruction

Tornado at Sayler Park near Cincinnati on April 3, 1974.

Floods

Early spring and late winter flooding also is common in Ohio. Flooding usually results when frozen ground cannot absorb heavy spring rains — precisely the conditions that led to the 1913 flood, worst in Ohio history.

Heavy January rains that year soaked into the ground which then froze in a succeeding cold snap. The ground remained frozen until March. In late March, temperatures rose into the seventies and nearly

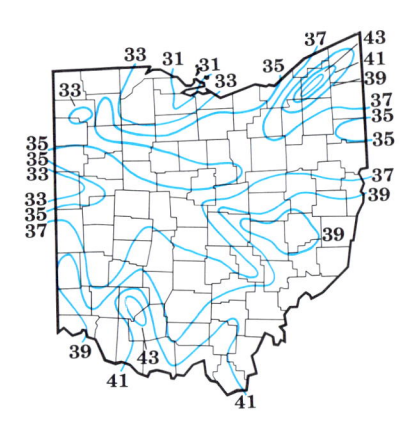

Average annual precipitation (inches)

continuous rain pelted the state for five days. Between March 23 and 27, eight to ten inches of rain fell, causing rivers and streams to overflow. Flood waters surged through flood plains, smashing houses, tearing bridges from foundations, and killing livestock. Downtown Dayton was completely flooded except for the tops of lamp posts sticking out of the water. Officials never learned exactly how many people died in the flood, but estimates range as high as 430, while damage ran to $300 million.

Flood control dams, reservoirs, and levees have been built throughout the state to control or prevent recurrence of the 1913 flood, but run-off from spring rains still overflows streams, causing minor flooding along their banks. Many homes built near streams around Dayton are raised on pilings.

High water levels in Lake Erie during the 1960s and 1970s have resulted in much flooding and beach erosion along the shoreline, especially in the northwest. This is the result of waves, pushed by sustained east and northeast winds across 100 to 200 miles of lake, piling up water in the western basin. The waves contain much energy. In addition to flooding adjacent lowland, the waves pound the shore, eating it away.

Lake Erie water is very slow to release its wintertime chill. After the seasonal low of 33 degrees in January and February, the water temperature rises into the forties in April, fifties in May and sixties by the end of June.

In early spring, even though warm air is covering the state, a sudden wind shift to north will often lower temperatures near the lake shore 20 degrees in a few minutes. It is not uncommon in early spring to find readings in the crisp forties along the shoreline, while only five miles inland the temperature is in the sixties.

This early spring effect of Lake Erie not only keeps northeastern Ohio cool, it also brings many days of clouds and showers. As a result there are few clear days in this corner of the state until late April or May. One good effect of the cold is to retard the blossoming of grapes on the Erie Islands and along the lake shore. This spares the grapes from sudden hard freezes in the spring and helps make possible Ohio's Lake Erie wine industry.

The northwest, central, and southern counties are often spared the spring weather miseries of the northeast. While spring may be just a rumor near Lake Erie, places like Columbus, Cincinnati, Zanesville and Marietta often bask in 80-degree weather. The Cincinnati Reds frequently enjoy balmy weather for their April baseball opener, while the Cleveland Indians are dodging snow squalls.

By June, the struggle between the warm inroads of spring and the cold remnants of winter has been decided. While June provides Ohio with its share of thunderstorms and tornadoes,the warm and hazy days of summer bring more stable weather.

Summer

While the weather systems that affect Ohio in summer come from as many sources and directions as in spring, the warming rays of the sun at this latitude weaken the cold fronts and slow their movements.

Summer in the northeastern counties of Ohio cannot be appreciated unless you have spent some time sweltering in cities like Philadelphia, Washington, and Baltimore. Although temperatures reach the eighties with regularity, and the humidity can reach uncomfortable levels in

Cumulus clouds

southern and central Ohio, winds blowing across cool Lake Erie behind weather fronts often provide an air-conditioning effect. The Lake Erie water temperature rises into the mid-sixties during July, reaches the seventies in August, and holds nearly steady well into September.

While prolonged 90-degree temperatures are uncommon in the northeastern counties, other sections of the state do not fare so well. Extended periods of 90-degree weather will occur. Ohio's warmest temperature on record (record-keeping began in 1871) was registered at Thurman (Centerville) in Gallia County. On July 21, 1934, the mercury reached 113 degrees.

The heat and humidity of an Ohio summer is only temporarily broken by weak cool fronts from the north and northwest. The arrival of a summertime cool front is often announced by towering cumulonimbus thunderstorm clouds. Torrential rains from such storms are possible anywhere in the state. However, on the average, southwestern Ohio counties suffer more than other regions, and Wilmington in Clinton County has more thunderstorms than any other location in Ohio.

Thunderstorms, like all storm systems, are low pressure areas in which the winds whirl counterclockwise. Thunderheads often tower many thousands of feet in the air, the result of the counterclockwise rotation of the air which forces air to the center of the circling winds, forcing the air mass higher and higher beyond saturation levels until it rains. Thunderstorms are much like small hurricanes and at times they can be very violent, bringing wind gusts of better than 70 miles an hour which rip off the roofs of homes and barns, topple trees and power lines, and deluge an area in brief but torrential rainfall. Although thunderstorms usually cover only a few square miles, they often occur in groups. Each storm yields intensive bursts of rainfall so a wide area can be drenched in a few hours.

The heaviest short-term rain in Ohio weather history fell at Sandusky in Erie County on July 12, 1966. From 2 a.m. until 9:30 p.m. a total of

Mean maximum temperatures of July °F

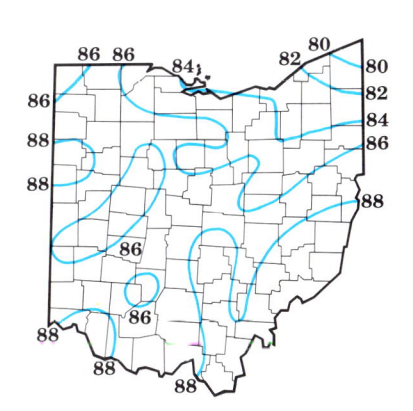

Thunderhead

10.51 inches came down. Between 3 a.m. and 11 a.m., 9.54 inches was recorded. The rainfall was so heavy for so long because towering thunderstorm clouds remained stationary over the area. Although lightning was visible far to the east in Cleveland, very little rain fell away from the target area. As an example of Ohio's often fickle weather, consider that nine and one half inches of rain fell within eight hours at Sandusky while rainfall for the entire month of July was less than one inch just to the east in Lake County.

The worst summer flooding in Ohio history occurred July 4-5, 1969, when thunderstorms drenched northern Ohio in four to 11 inches of rain. There was even a report of 14 inches of rain eight miles northwest of Wooster in Wayne County. Three years later four to seven inches deluged much of Ohio during gale-whipped rains from the remnants of Hurricane Agnes June 20-25, 1972.

Two unofficial reports of torrential rains are included in weather diaries. On July 16, 1914, at a point 2½ miles northwest of Cambridge in Guernsey County, seven inches of rain supposedly fell in a little more than an hour. An undocumented report tells of a 12-inch rain in 80 minutes near Canton June 24, 1888.

While hail is not uncommon during severe thunderstorms in Ohio, the frequency cannot compare with that of our hail prone midwestern states. The loss ratio for crop insurance in Ohio is one of the lowest in the nation. Twenty-three percent of all losses to insured crops have been to corn, 18 percent to vegetables, 11 percent to wheat, and 10 percent to tobacco.

Hail is formed when water condenses around dust particles which are then blown high in the air by rising air currents. The water freezes and the ice pellet drops, only to be repeatedly blown aloft again until the ball of ice is heavy enough to fall to earth. The size of a hailstone depends on the number of elevator trips skyward it takes. In Ohio, hailstones usually vary from pea to golf ball-size, and rarely baseball-size.

An interesting warm weather phenomenon is the fog which blankets the Ohio River Valley and many southeastern Ohio valleys in warm weather. In the evening when temperatures cool, air at the tops of hills sinks and collects in valleys. If the air temperature is near the dew point, then a temperature drop of only a few degrees produces heavy fog.

Except near Lake Erie, the surface winds in Ohio are relatively still during summer, especially in comparison with states farther west. The reason is that Ohio has more trees than many western states. As the wind blows over the trees, friction causes it to slow and frequently almost to stop. For example, at Columbus, 26 percent of the hours in a year have winds blowing at less than three miles per hour (the limit for dead air) compared with 11 percent at Cincinnati, and 2 percent at Cleveland. There is more wind at Cleveland and all along the lake because there are no trees to block a wind crossing Lake Erie from the west, north, or east.

On hot, sultry days in late summer and early autumn some Ohio cities suffer when still, hot air rises and traps a layer of cooler air near the ground. This is called a temperature inversion and problems arise when pollutants from factories, power plants, and other industries are trapped near ground, unable to be blown away.

Heavily industrialized areas in the Ohio Valley near Steubenville suffer from inversions more frequently than other parts of the state. When air pollution builds to a certain level, production in many factories must be reduced to lower the amount of pollutants spewing into the atmosphere. Cool fronts from the west or northwest eventually clear the air and improve conditions.

Autumn

For many Ohioans early autumn is the favorite time of the year. September is usually a pleasantly warm month, with mild days and refreshingly cool nights continuing into mid-October. This early fall period with its light winds results in a series of sunny, hazy days.

This weather usually is the most predictable and an Ohio autumn with its blaze of brilliant fall foliage is just about the only "typical" season in the state. The fair weather is caused by high-speed jet streams which originate in Japan and rush along at 150 miles per hour straight across the Pacific, North America, and right out into the Atlantic. The high altitude winds blow so fast the storms never have a chance to develop. The result is a stationary high pressure system which creates a long period of fair weather in October. This fair weather is especially good for farmers harvesting their crops, but when the same thing happens in the spring, it spells disaster, because it limits the amount of vital spring rain needed to spur crop growth in early summer.

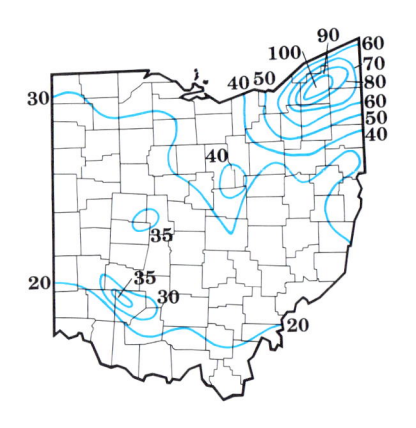

Average annual snowfall (inches)

The first killing frosts of the year will visit Ohio anywhere from mid-September to early November, and the first snow of the season, usually in the form of hard snow "grains" or soft snow "pellets," falls over northeastern counties about the third week in October. Sharp cold fronts in October are often followed by several days of moderating temperatures and calm weather. November, however, begins a new chapter in the Ohio weather story. The cold fronts are colder and more vigorous. It can be said that November brings the "cloud season" to the northern half of the state. As cold Canadian air crosses the still warm waters of Lake Erie, it picks up water vapor that quickly condenses into a thick cloud layer upon reaching land. It is because of this "lake effect" that November and December are usually the cloudiest months in northern Ohio. When Lake Erie is ice covered in mid- and late-winter, the lake effect is reduced or ends entirely.

The first heavy snows of the season can be expected over the extreme northeastern counties of Ohio by mid to late November. Sustained and gusty west by northwest winds can drop very heavy snows over the higher elevations east and south of Cleveland. This primary "snowbelt" is in Lake, Geauga, and Ashtabula counties and eastern Cuyahoga County. As cold fronts continue to strengthen in late November and December, the secondary snowbelt areas southwest of Cleveland are also hit by locally heavy snows.

The process that causes the heavy lake effect snow is called "orographic lifting." Winds crossing the relatively warm waters of the lake pick up water vapor and carry it inland. As the surface air is forced upward over the higher land elevations, the now-warmed and moisture-laden air collides with colder air aloft. This causes the water vapor to sublimate directly into ice crystals, i.e. snow.

A term often used by northeastern Ohio weather forecasters is "heavier amounts in the snowbelt," since judging lake effect snowfall is a shotgun affair at best. Even within the snowbelt accumulations may vary widely. In 1962, for example, no snow fell at the shoreline in Euclid, just east of Cleveland, while 19 inches piled up just one-half mile to the south. Lake Erie's water temperature falls through the sixties in September, the fifties in October, and the forties in November.

Any rise in land elevation can trigger local orographic snows, even without benefit of nearby lake waters. The rise in land elevations east of Cincinnati in Highland County, for example, results in a miniature snowbelt while another snowbelt is in west-central Ohio near Bellefontaine.

Winter

While some refer to Ohio's winter as invigorating, others believe it is interminable. Winter's embrace is usually lengthy. The decreasing sunlight in Ohio during winter not only causes the turn to colder weather, but also creates more cloudiness. Cold air promotes rapid condensation of water vapor into the microscopic water droplets that collectively make up the clouds.

Much of Ohio's winter weather originates in the cold valleys of Alaska, the Canadian Klondike, and over the snow-covered, wind-swept terrain of the North Pole. These dark, far-northern latitudes are source regions for the frigid cold fronts of winter. Huge mountains of bitter cold

Winter storm tracks

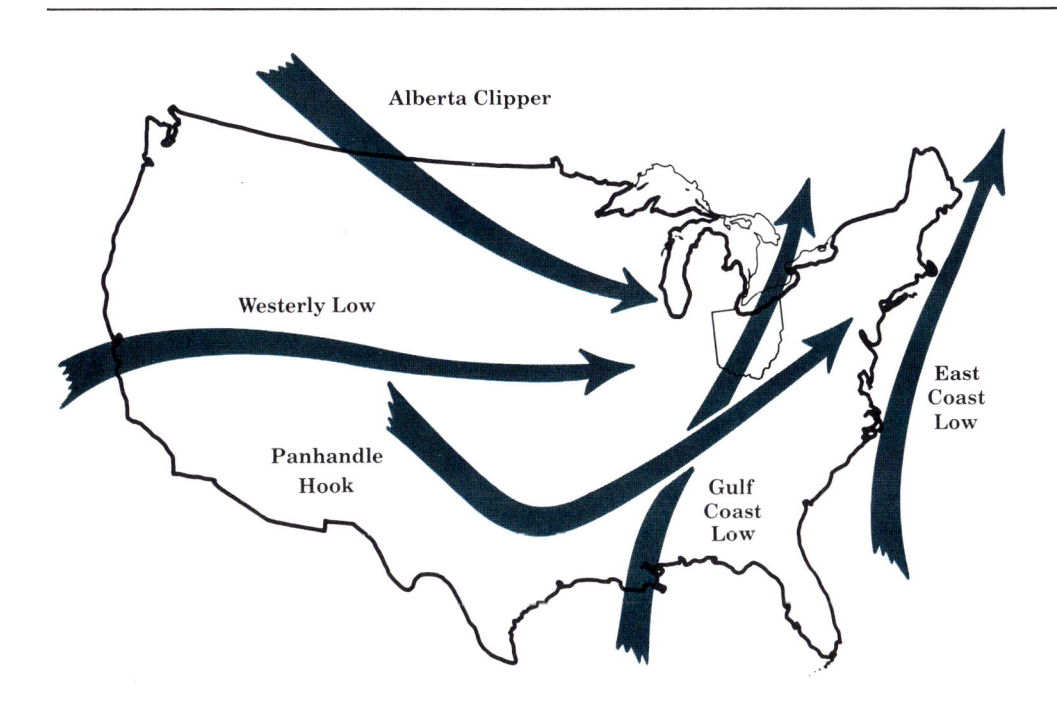

air are dislodged from the north by the winds and carried southeast, through Canada, and across the Great Lakes into Ohio. The record-breaking cold and snowy winters of 1976-1977 and 1977-1978 were the result of a northwesterly air flow that continued unabated throughout the winter.

Ohio snows come from six basic weather situations. The first is the lake effect previously mentioned. This condition prevails if Lake Erie water remains open to crossing air currents. By January and February the increasing ice in Lake Erie will lessen, or end entirely, lake effect snows.

The Alberta Clipper is a fast-moving storm center that forms east of the Canadian Rockies in Alberta. Traveling 30 to 50 miles an hour, the Clipper moves so fast in its cold, dry air environment that it usually results in only light snows of one to three inches. Small fry have difficulty making snowmen from this dry, light, easily-shoveled snow.

Another matter is the Panhandle Hook. This storm begins east of the American Rockies, drops through the Oklahoma Panhandle and then turns northeastward, drawing a considerable amount of moisture northward from the Gulf of Mexico. Panhandle Hooks put down a heavy, wet, hard-to-shovel snow. This storm pattern across Kentucky and West Virginia gives Ohio its heaviest general snowfall (heaviest snowfall is often to the north of the storm center).

Westerly Lows swing through the Great Plains, never coming close enough to the gulf to absorb much moisture. These storms usually are timid and poorly organized, and result in light, dry snows.

In contrast, Gulf Coast Lows bring Ohio rain or the wettest snow. These storms originate east of the Rocky Mountains and drop south, picking up moisture from the gulf. If this storm center moves northward from the gulf and passes west of Ohio, mild air on the east side of the storm results in rain. If the storm strikes just a little farther east, then heavy and soggy snows will fall on the colder west side of the storm path.

Finally, East Coast Lows can be counted on to blanket the big cities of the eastern United States with heavy snow several times each winter. Often developing along the Carolina coast, this deep storm feeds on the

The Ohio State University Marching Band brought a buckeye leaf to the 1950 "Snow Bowl" game between OSU and the University of Michigan.

unlimited water supply of the Atlantic Ocean as it speeds north-northeastward into New England and Newfoundland. The violent counterclockwise rotation of air causes the legendary "northeaster." But, only the most severe East Coast Low can bring snow as far west as Ohio.

The movement of the low pressure storm centers is dictated by the wind flow aloft. Strong, upper-level jet winds of 100 miles an hour or more snake across the United States from west to east during winter. These jet winds guide the storm centers and cause them to strengthen as they are carried across the country.

Snowfall totals vary widely in the state from an average of 106 inches at Chardon in Geauga County to 15 inches at both Ironton in Lawrence County and Portsmouth in Scioto County. Snowfall also varies widely from winter to winter. A most striking reversal came after the snowy winter of 1917-1918. The statewide average fall in that season was 46 inches, while a nearly snowless six-inch average followed in 1918-1919.

A look at the statistics for an Ohio winter indicates the state hardly ever has an average one, especially where snowfall is concerned. In 1901 a blizzard in eastern Ohio dumped from 12 to 31 inches of snow and the winds piled it into 10-foot drifts. In fact farmers reported that sheep were buried in the storm. Twelve years later a storm termed the "Great Lakes' Worst" blew for three days and put down from 10 to 24 inches of snow as far south as Cambridge. The Great Thanksgiving Day Storm of 1950 proved even tougher. This storm hit the state November 23 and raged for six days. Almost all of Ohio was affected and snowfall varied from 6 inches in the northwest to 40 inches in the extreme east. Steubenville, which received 36 inches of snow during a three-day period in the storm, still holds the single storm record for snowfall.

Most Ohioans do not have to remember the stories of their parents and grandparents for a winter storm story to tell their children. The winter of 1976-1977 was the coldest in weather history for Ohio and much of the Great Lakes. The winter of 1977-1978 saw record-breaking snows across Ohio.

During the early morning hours of January 26, 1978, a storm center that brought the lowest barometer readings in history passed from south to north over eastern Ohio. Winds that morning were blowing 40 to 60 miles an hour and gusting to 102 miles an hour near the Cleveland shoreline. Visibility was zero and hundreds of motorists were stranded in snow and hurricane-force winds. New snows of over one foot fell on top of heavy snow left by earlier storms. Drifts towered to 20 feet and many roadways in Ohio were impassable nearly one week after the storm. The Blizzard of '78 could truly be called a white hurricane. Thirty-seven people died and damage ran to hundreds of millions of dollars in one of Ohio's strongest storms in history.

The coldest temperature officially recorded in Ohio was 39 degrees below zero at Milligan (south of Zanesville) in Perry County on February 10, 1899. Until the hard and cruel winters of 1976-1977 and 1977-1978, the winters of 1898-1899, 1935-1936, and 1962-1963 were considered Ohio's toughest.

In most winters Ohio can expect the legendary January thaw. This usually arrives during the second and third weeks of the month, followed by an abrupt return to the snow and cold of winter.

Lake Erie water temperatures decline through the thirties in December, reaching a wintertime low of 33 degrees by early January. (Lake water temperatures are taken at a depth of about 30 feet, where ice formation does not occur, thus there is no reading below 33).

We have looked at what can be considered average weather conditions during each season in Ohio. Unfortunately, average weather in this state is somewhat like the "average person": You will probably never meet one.

Average annual lowest temperatures

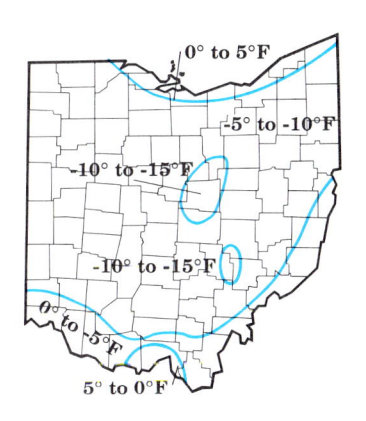

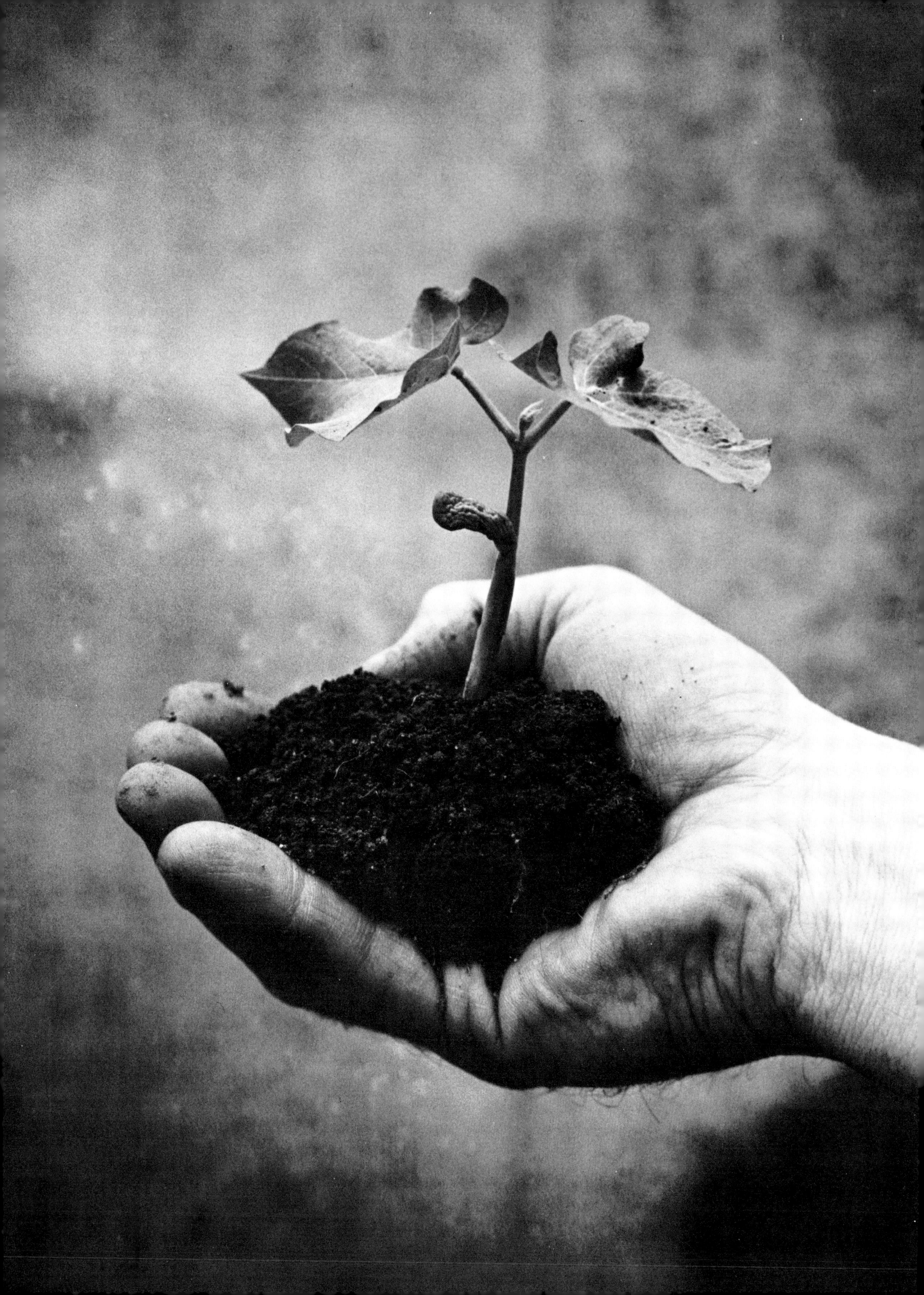

Chapter 6
Cradle of Life

SOIL is truly a cradle of life. Thousands of kinds of plants and animals live in it, on it, and from it. Countless bacteria and protozoans live in the soil in complex arrangements with other organisms. Roots from mighty forest trees penetrate the soil, branching here and there in an underground world fully as complex as that above the surface. Woodchucks, tiny mice, and many kinds of insects burrow through it. Virtually all organisms that live in it or on it, including humans, depend on the soil for their livelihood.

Soil is the uppermost layer, commonly several feet thick, of the earth's crust. It has been changed over time by the combined action of weather, plant growth and decay, and animal activity into a body of earth that provides plants with nutrients and support. Some soils form in material derived from rock and are referred to as mineral soils. Others form in thick accumulations of organic deposits such as peat and are known as organic soils. Hundreds of different soils are recognized in Ohio.

by Nicholas Holowaychuk

How Soil Forms in Ohio

Each of these hundreds of soils is the result of a different combination of climate (especially rainfall and temperature), organisms (plants and animals), parent materials (the materials in which soils form), and

Soil profile showing different "horizons"

topography (the lay of the land). A fifth factor — time — also is important since the length of time these processes have been active influences the degree or stage of soil development. Since the influence of climate and organisms are most pronounced near the surface, most soil formation occurs in a zone from the surface down to a depth of several feet or to bedrock if it is closer to the surface.

The combination of these five factors determines the kinds of chemical, physical, and biological processes that go on in a soil. As a result of these processes, a soil acquires certain characteristics such as color, acidity, and organic matter content to name a few. The characteristics appear in certain combinations in more or less horizontal zones called soil horizons within the vertical section of the soil. The entire vertical section of the soil from the surface downward is called a soil profile. In most soils the profile consists of three horizons. The custom is to designate the upper horizon as "A," the next horizon as "B," and the lower horizon as "C." Soils less than 20 inches deep are considered to be shallow while those over 5 feet are very deep.

Climate

Moisture and energy are the most important climatic factors in soil formation. Ohio's climate produces enough rainfall to percolate or drain through the soil, especially during winter and spring. The water leaches or washes out soluble minerals and some nutrient elements such as calcium, magnesium, and potassium. These alkaline elements are washed down more readily when the water contains organic acids formed by decaying organic matter, so Ohio soils are usually acid in the upper soil layers. Leaching also removes minute, suspended clay particles to lower soil zones. The result is that subsoil horizons are frequently higher in clay.

Temperature affects soil formation. Most soil-forming processes are faster and more intense at higher temperatures. Since climate is relatively uniform over the state, the differences between soils are due mostly to the effects of the other factors. Nevertheless, in the hill country of southeastern Ohio, differences in microclimates have caused major differences between soils in the same areas.

Organisms

Green plants provide the main pathway of the sun's energy into the soil. They convert solar energy into organic material which, during decomposition, provides the energy used by teeming populations of soil microbes and other organisms. Vegetation also is the main source of soil organic matter. In Ohio most soils formed under a forest cover in which leaves and other plant parts fell to the ground and were decomposed by microbes. The resulting organic residues were incorporated into the soil to a depth of several inches. In contrast, vegetation in prairie openings of western Ohio had a dense thick mat of fibrous roots below the surface. This has resulted in a thicker, dark surface horizon than found under forest.

Vegetation contains calcium, magnesium, and other mineral nutrients, and when it decomposes, these elements are recycled into the soil. Some vegetation is more efficient at recycling. For example, all through eastern and southern Ohio mixed mesophytic forest is interspersed with mixed oak forest. Since such trees as basswood and tuliptree of the mesophytic woodlands recover a greater proportion of these elements than do trees of the oak forest, the soils formed in the mixed mesophytic forests are usually less acid and more fertile than those of the mixed oak forests.

Parent Materials and Topography

Parent material is the substance from which soils develop. As such, it has a major effect on soil characteristics and distribution. In Ohio most parent materials are related to glaciation whether or not the material is within or outside the glacial areas. Glacial till, lake deposits, outwash, loess (fine, wind-blown dust), alluvial deposits, and materials from bedrock are all common parent materials.

The glaciers also controlled the eventual characteristics of the landscape — the topography. To a large degree topography controls the amount of water run-off. Some of the rainfall on hilly land results in run-off which may erode the soil and wash away nutrients. On lower, more gentle slopes or on nearly level areas, rainfall is more likely to be absorbed and run-off reduced. The result is that flat areas are wetter.

Wetness inhibits aeration and oxidation in varying degrees, favoring chemical and biological processes which require little or no oxygen. Almost any Ohio farm field in the spring reveals the effects of aeration. On slight rises of just a foot or two there is enough aeration so the color of the soil is brown or yellowish brown. In contrast, in depressions where there is too much water for too long a time, black colors in the surface and gray colors in the subsoil are common. In situations where good aeration alternates with poor aeration, a speckling of gray, brown, and yellowish brown, called mottling, results.

The topographic stability of a soil also influences soil formation. On the level ground such as in parts of southwest Ohio it is less likely parent material will be disturbed, thus allowing more advanced development of characteristics. In contrast, soil on sloping ground, although it may form in old materials, will likely have characteristics less well developed. Downslope movements and associated mixing not only lead to changes in parent materials, but also interrupt the soil-forming processes. This is especially important in eastern and southeastern Ohio. Here though the parent materials are derived from very old rocks, many of the soils show only moderate development. Only on the nearly level, relatively stable ridge crests and on less sloping portions of the materials filling the numerous old valleys do soils show strongly expressed characteristics.

Time

In evaluating the effect of time on soil formation, several conditions have to be considered. Have soil-formation processes been interrupted or changed? How old are the materials in which soils form? Do the materials occupy stable positions? How easily can these materials be altered during soil formation?

In Ohio, the oldest soils in glacial materials are those found in areas of Illinoian glaciation. On level ground the soils formed here have

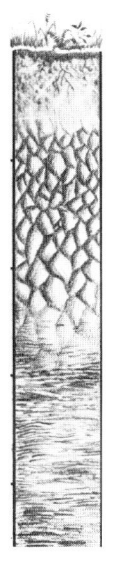

Generalized soil profile showing strong development with distinct horizons.

Generalized soil profile showing moderate development with less distinct horizons.

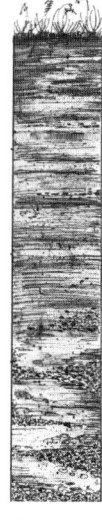

Generalized soil profile showing weak development without distinct horizons.

74 Ohio's Natural Heritage

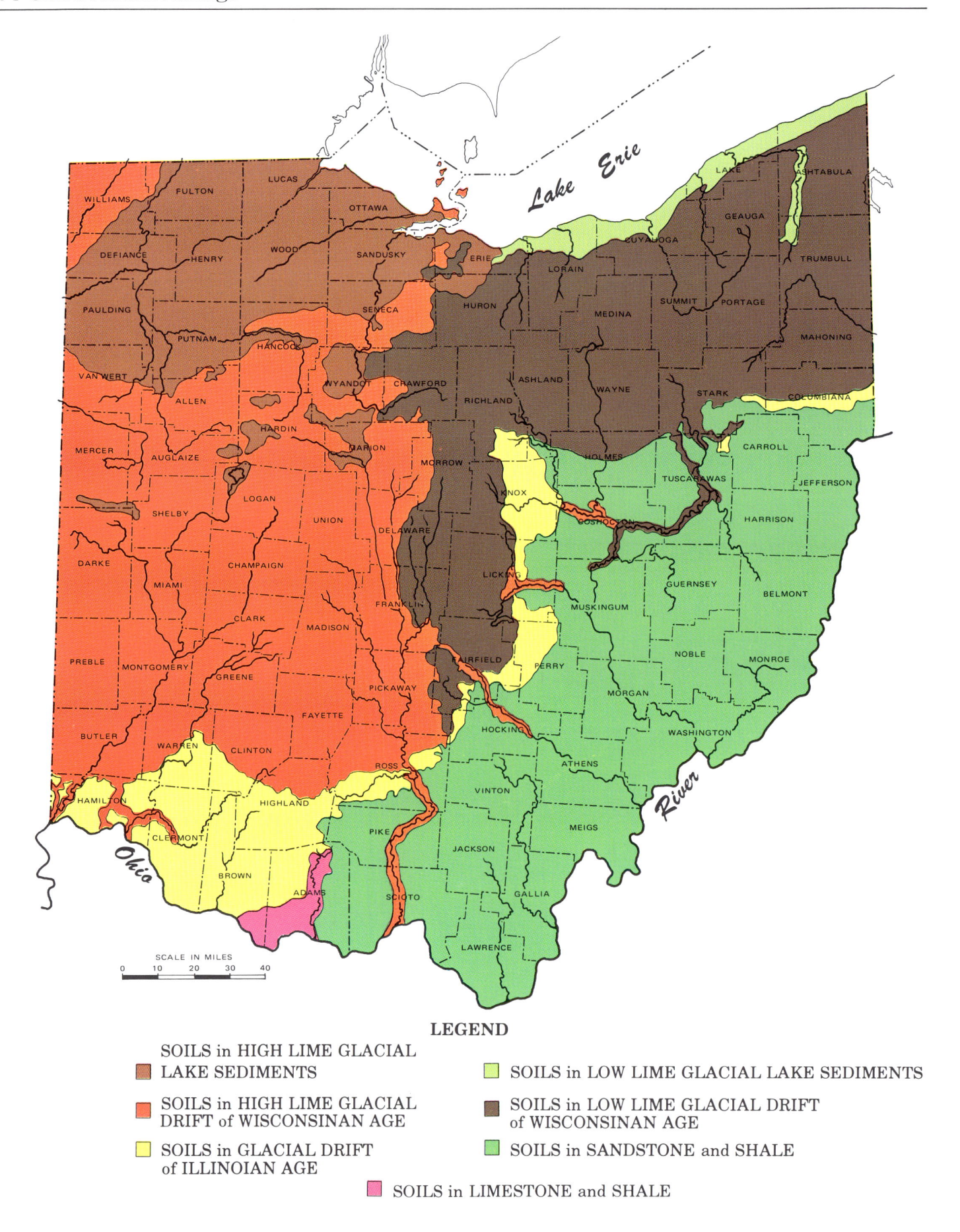

LEGEND

- SOILS in HIGH LIME GLACIAL LAKE SEDIMENTS
- SOILS in HIGH LIME GLACIAL DRIFT of WISCONSINAN AGE
- SOILS in GLACIAL DRIFT of ILLINOIAN AGE
- SOILS in LOW LIME GLACIAL LAKE SEDIMENTS
- SOILS in LOW LIME GLACIAL DRIFT of WISCONSINAN AGE
- SOILS in SANDSTONE and SHALE
- SOILS in LIMESTONE and SHALE

Ohio's Soil Regions

undergone leaching and other types of weathering down to about 10 feet. They developed other characteristics to similar depths. The oldest soils in the state are in southeastern Ohio. These are very acid and strongly weathered to about six feet. These soils have reached an advanced stage in soil development. In contrast, flood plain soils have weak characteristics and they represent very youthful stages of development.

Ohio Soils and Their Distribution

The integrated effects of the five soil-forming factors have resulted in many kinds of soils. To date nearly 400 soil series have been identified in the state. A soil series includes all those soils that are alike within narrowly defined ranges in their characteristics.

Despite the large number of soils, there are combinations of many of these soils that follow a systematic pattern of distribution in the state. This is due largely to certain geographic similarities in origin and characteristics of parent materials and in topography.

Lake Plain Soils

All Lake Plain soils of northwestern Ohio are derived from materials deposited in the ancient lakes that existed during the latter stages of Wisconsinan glaciation. It is an area of monotonously level topography and the lake sediments deposited over this area have resulted in large areas of very fertile but poorly drained soil. This is rich farm land and the principal crops are corn and soybeans. In northern Seneca and southern Sandusky counties there is a black soil area which produces tomatoes, cabbages, cucumbers, and other truck crops.

Much of the parent material in the western half of the Lake Plain, called the Great Black Swamp, consists of deposits laid down in the lakes and along the lake borders. Those laid down within the lakes are largely clayey sediments, while the deposits along the lake borders are sandy or loamy with varying amounts of gravel. In general, Lake Plain soils are very fertile, except for an area of gently undulating sand barrens called the Oak Openings in western Lucas and eastern Fulton counties. In addition to deposits associated with the lakes, there are very extensive, nearly level areas of glacier-laid calcareous clay that have been little affected by the lakes.

A large number of soil series occur in the Lake Plains but only a few are of large acreage. Hoytville soils are the most extensive. There are about 2.5 million acres of poorly drained, neutral, highly fertile soils in the Lake Plains. Much of the very poorly drained soils developed in lake-laid clay sediments.

Both the parent materials and the soils are much different in the long, narrow eastern extension of the Lake Plain. Apparently the wave action of the former lakes removed most of the water-deposited sediments except for sandy and gravelly areas along the beaches. As a result, the soils formed either in materials derived from the shale or from till exposed by the wave action or in the sandy and gravelly material. The soils on the latter are acid and well drained. Away from beach ridges, the soils are quite variable, but in general they are moderately deep, acid, and poorly or very poorly drained.

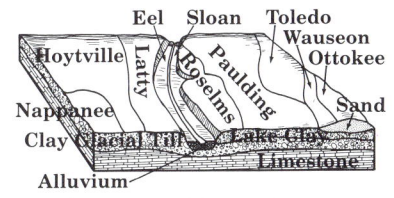

Northwestern Ohio soils in relation to parent material and relief

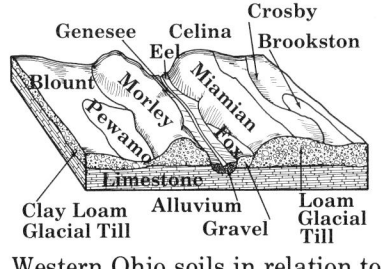

Till Plains Soils

Western Ohio's Till Plains are only slightly more rolling than the Lake Plains. What steeply sloping land there is occurs mostly along the larger valleys and some glacial moraines. Originally, most of this region was in deciduous forest, but there also were many prairie areas. Except for outwash along the larger streams and a scattering of former lake basins with clayey lake deposits, glacial till or glacial till covered by loess are the parent materials over the area. Topography is the most important element that influenced the formation and distribution of these soils.

In the northern portion of the Till Plains the parent material is mostly Wisconsinan high lime till. Blount, a somewhat poorly drained, moderately deep soil formed in clay loam till, is widely distributed. It occurs in nearly level or very gently sloping areas, and with 1.5 million acres, it is probably the most extensive soil in the state. Pewamo, the associated deep, very poorly drained, dark-colored soil of the flats, also covers a large area. To the south of the Blount soils are the Miamian, a well drained moderately deep soil that has been studied in detail. These and most other soils in this agricultural region are well suited for corn and soybeans. Several other soils, although of lesser extent, are of interest because they represent soils that developed under prairie vegetation. They are mostly deep, medium acid to neutral soils with thick, dark-colored surface horizons that are quite fertile. All of these soils are most prevalent in the neighboring states to the west where the prairies were much more extensive. To the east of the Till Plains, the parent material is low lime till of Wisconsinan age. Most soils are moderately deep and are somewhat more acid than comparable soils in the northern Till Plains.

In the southern Till Plains there is considerable contrast in topography and parent materials. Away from the valleys of the Ohio River and its tributaries, the upland topography is nearly level or very gently undulating. The parent materials in this case consist of loess-covered loam or clay loam Illinoian till leached free of lime to a considerable depth — in some places as much as 10 feet. Along the Ohio River Valley and its tributaries, the terrain is steep and hilly. Much of the original till deposits have been removed so the parent materials consist of either thin remnants of till or of residue derived from weathering of the uncovered interbedded limestone and shale bedrock. The soils on the nearly level to gently undulating uplands are very acid and strongly developed. Of these soils the most extensive in the nearly level land are the poorly drained Clermont and the somewhat poorly drained Avonburg. Rossmoyne, an extensive, moderately well drained soil, is found where the land is gently rolling. There is a greater variety of soils in the hilly land. Where the parent materials have been derived from weathering of limestone or the interbedded shale and limestone, most soils are moderately deep, well drained, and generally acid.

Western Ohio soils in relation to parent material and relief

Glaciated Appalachian Plateau Soils

Much of the Glaciated Appalachian Plateau is rolling and hilly. But there are also many sections, such as the broad divides between some of the streams, where the land is nearly level. Parent materials from the Wisconsinan glaciers cover most of the plateau, but there are also some

Illinoian age materials along the outer border (to the south). Much of the till has a loam or silt loam texture with varying amounts of fragmented sandstone, siltstone, and shale. Its content of lime is low and in places completely lacking. There are limited areas of low lime, clay loam, and clayey till as well. There are also clayey or silty lacustrine (lake-deposited) materials in former lake basins here and there and gravelly outwash deposits that contain little if any lime.

There are many kinds of soils in this area, a number of which also occur in eastern states. This variety is due to the wide range in topography, the variety of parent materials, and the large size of the area. In general, most of the soils are quite acid and low in fertility, and while they are deep, some have dense subsoil horizons called fragipans. Water percolates through these fragipans very slowly, and markedly reduces the permeability of the lower soil to water and roots.

Because of the hilly topography, more wheat and less corn is raised. In addition, there are a large number of dairy farms, and beech and maple forests are common.

Canfield and Rittman are moderately well drained, deep soils found on gentle slopes. Wooster is a well-drained soil occurring on more sloping land. Canfield, and to a lesser degree Wooster, occur extensively at the Ohio Agricultural Research and Development Center in Wayne County. Venango and Platea are somewhat poorly drained soils, commonly found on level or gently undulating sections in the eastern part of the area. All of these soils have a fragipan horizon in the subsoil. Hanover is a very deep, well-drained soil formed in loam till of Illinoian age, but it too has a fragipan subsoil. A common but not as extensive soil on loam till that occurs throughout the area is Loudonville. This is a moderately deep soil occurring frequently on upper slopes and shoulders of hills and ridges where the shallow till is underlain by bedrock near the surface.

In the former lake basins the more prevalent soils are Canadice and Fitchville. Both are deep and somewhat poorly drained, and they formed in clayey and silty lake materials. Outwash deposits are found throughout the area, most commonly as terraces along the drainage ways. The predominant soil on these materials is Chili, a deep and well-drained soil with gravelly subsoil.

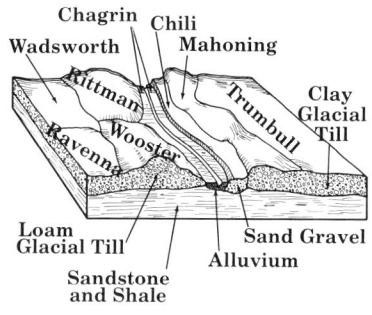

Northeastern Ohio soils in relation to parent material and relief

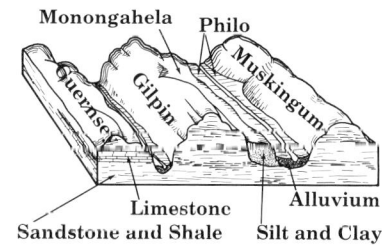

Unglaciated Appalachian Plateau Soils

The Unglaciated Appalachian Plateau is so hilly that what level ground there is occurs on the ridgetops or in the wider valleys.

The parent materials over the plateau are local in origin, derived from the weathering of sandstone, siltstone, shale, and, less frequently, limestone bedrock. Although each of the first three kinds of bedrock may occur as massive beds, they are usually thin. Since there is considerable relief, several kinds of these rocks may be found on a single slope. As a result, the parent materials present on slopes have seldom been derived from one particular kind of rock. Instead they consist of a mixture of material derived from the several kinds present on the slope. Furthermore, since considerable down slope movement (and mixing) of material occurs through soil creep and other mass-movement processes, the parent material at a particular location is very likely to have been influenced by rocks occurring upslope. These materials range from sand or sandy loam to clay in texture, depending on the nature of source rocks.

Southeastern Ohio soils in relation to parent material and relief

Cowdery Cemetery at Keno in Meigs County about 1935. Sheet erosion on adjacent farm land has removed about three feet of soil

Cowdery Cemetery at Keno in Meigs County in 1978. An additional three feet of soil has eroded from adjacent farm land during the past 40 years.

They are generally acid, but where some limestone or limey shale is present they may be neutral or mildly alkaline.

There are a few soils formed from lake sediments deposited in old glacial lakes. Also, a few soils along river valleys have formed from glacial outwash material. Remnants of this outwash and of earlier alluvial deposits occur as terraces along many of the larger streams. In addition to these materials, patchy remnants of loess over other materials are found throughout the area, seldom more then 30 inches thick. These remnants are mostly on level or gently sloping tracts where erosion or mass movement was minimal.

The unglaciated plateau has a tremendous number of soils — each the product of diversity of topography and parent material. Since the Appalachian Plateau crosses state boundaries, many of these soils also occur in West Virginia, Pennsylvania, and eastern Kentucky. Many of the soils also are acid, reflecting the influence of the materials derived from the acid sandstone and shales, and the heavy forest that covered the area. Nearly all the soils are well drained, many are stony, and because of the instability of materials on slopes have weakly expressed profiles.

Bluegrass Region Soils

Deciduous forest once covered nearly all the Bluegrass Region, except for a few places where prairie was dominant. The parent material is of local origin — weathered limestone dolomite and calcareous shale — and it varies in thickness, depending on the topographic position and kind of bedrock. It is generally clayey and sometimes contains quantities of rock fragments, especially where it is shallow. Loess of varying thickness apparently covered these materials, since remnants of it up to about 24 inches thick still persist on the more stable, gentle slopes.

Even this small area has many soil types, but there are several — Bratton, Eden, Opequon, and Lawshe — that are more common. Both Bratton and Eden are moderately deep, well-drained, clayey soils. Bratton, however, is derived from the clayey materials that had a shallow loess cover. This makes part of the soil silty. Also, since Bratton is more prevalent on more gentle slopes, it is somewhat better developed and is moderately acid. Eden soils also formed in clayey materials but lack the silty upper horizons. These soils are medium acid to neutral, occur on steeper slopes, and contain many rock fragments in the subsoil. Opequon is a shallow, clay soil underlain by limestone bedrock only about 20 inches beneath the surface. The common prairie soil in the Bluegrass Region is Lawshe. It developed under grass interspersed with red cedar in clayey material derived from calcareous shale. It has a thicker, dark-colored surface horizon and is neutral.

Flood Plain Soils, Bog Soils, and Lake Sediments

Flood plain or bottom land soils represent a significant area in Ohio. They occur along streams, and along some of the larger rivers they are extensive. Flood plains are subject to periodic, and in some cases, frequent flooding. The flood waters always bring deposits of fresh alluvium, which means the soils never develop much before they are

Celery growing in organic soil

covered over by fresh parent material. Since the alluvium is derived from erosion upstream, bottom land soils are strongly influenced by the kinds of soils and parent materials that occur in the headwater areas.

In general most flood plain soils are deep and have loamy, silty, clayey, or sandy textures. They are medium acid to mildly alkaline. And most important for Ohio farmers, they are very fertile and make good cropland where flooding is less frequent.

Organic soils are found in the bogs and marshes of the Till Plains and the Glaciated Plateau. Their main characteristic is that they consist almost wholly of black or dark brown organic material, depending on the stage of decomposition. Black color indicates a more advanced stage of decomposition. There are several series of organic soils differing mainly in the thickness of the organic material and the kind of mineral material underneath. Under natural conditions organic soils are wet and poorly aerated for long periods and the organic material decomposes very slowly. When these soils are drained, as they often are, aeration increases and the material decomposes more rapidly. This decomposition causes some loss of soil and in addition the soil becomes loose and light and is easily blown away by the wind. Organic soils also burn easily when dry and many areas have been damaged by fires.

Ohio is naturally blessed with a rich heritage in its soils. They not only provide a most vital resource to agriculture, forestry, wildlife, and recreation, but also offer an intellectual challenge because of their various characteristics and distributional patterns. The soils of Ohio, like many of the other natural resources, represent a meeting ground of the Midwest, the East, and the South. In agriculture, Ohio shares the high productivity potential of the corn belt to the west and the more varied pastoral and woodland pursuits common to the east and south. Soils reflect the integrated effects through the ages of the interactions of such natural components as climate, organisms, geology, and landscape. They carry a record of natural conditions that have existed in the past and they may help us predict what can be expected in ages to come. This should make us doubly appreciative of this rich heritage that took so long to develop.

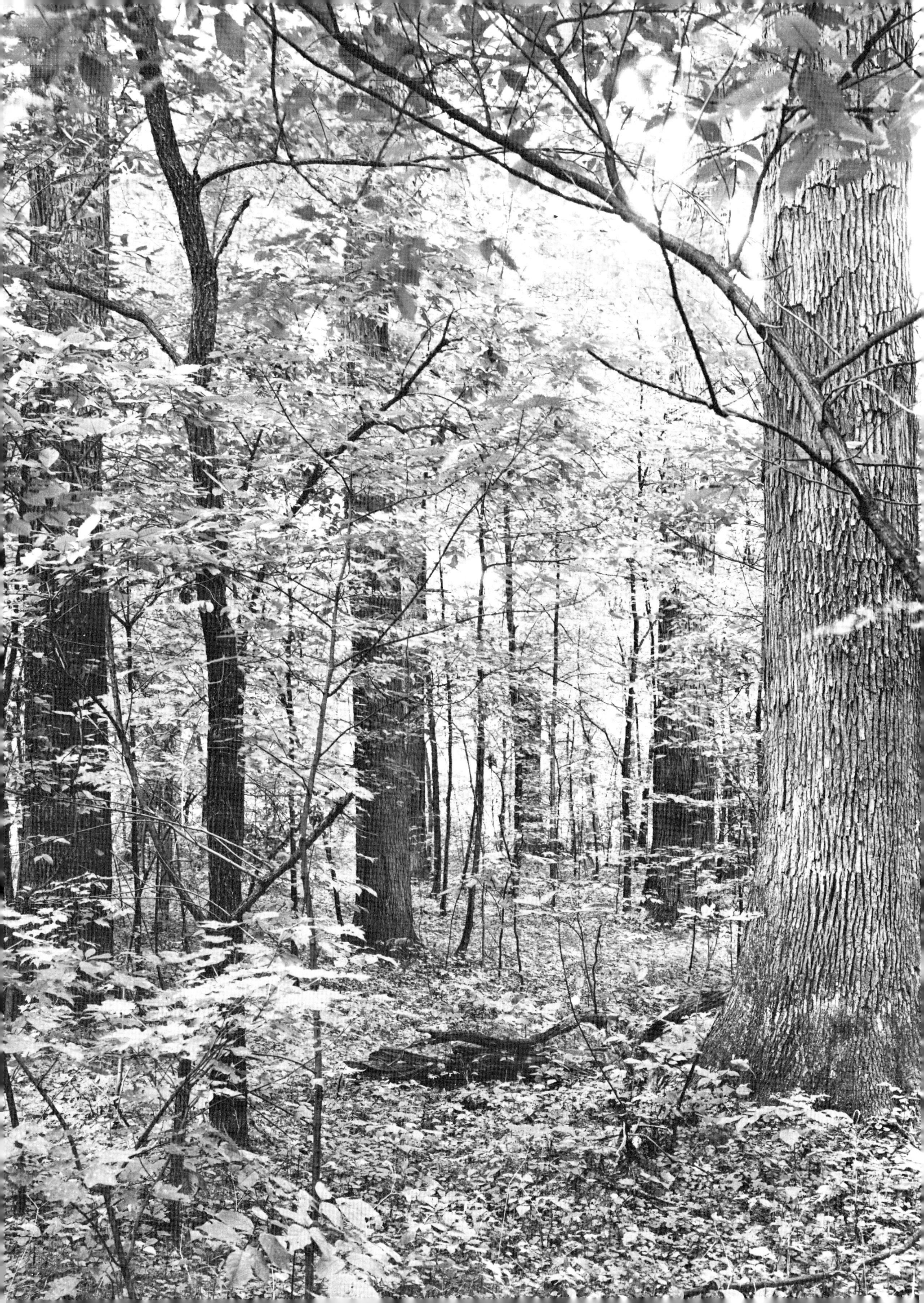

Chapter 7
Ohio Forests

A vast forest wilderness once spread across the middle of the continent from the Appalachian Mountains to the Great Plains. None of the world's temperate zone hardwood forests surpassed this one in variety and size of trees, and according to all accounts, early explorers and settlers heading west across the mountains were mightily impressed. The forest was at once a magnificent sight and an awesome challenge. Towering oaks and hickories, beeches and maples, tuliptrees, walnuts, elms, gums, chestnuts, and ashes, some over 150 feet tall, were evidence of the fertility of the soils and the good life awaiting those with the strength and determination to clear and till the land.

The territory of Ohio lay in the heart of this region. Its forests were as impressive and varied as those anywhere. Beech and sugar maple, dominant in the northeastern part of the state, were very important to the Indians who originally lived there and to the settlers who came later. Beeches provided heavy crops of nuts in the autumn. These were eagerly sought by many forest animals, that, in turn, provided food and clothing for humans. The maples were a source of syrup and sugar highly prized by both the Indians and the settlers.

In the rugged, unglaciated region of southern and southeastern Ohio, oaks were more prominent. On the dry ridgetops, chestnut, and black, scarlet, and white oaks made up much of the stand. On the slopes were mockernut and pignut hickories. Shagbark hickories occurred in

by Ernest E. Good

Beechnut

Sugar maple

Tuliptree

Red oak

Virginia pine

Chestnut oak

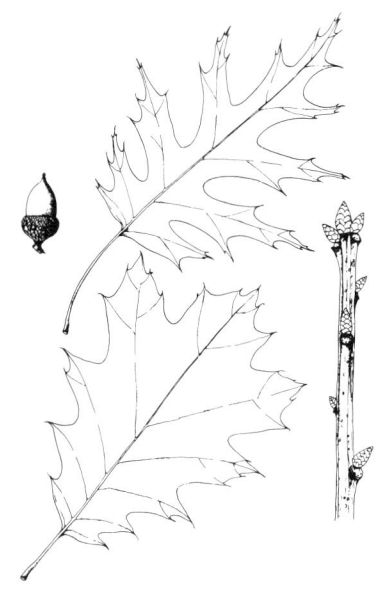

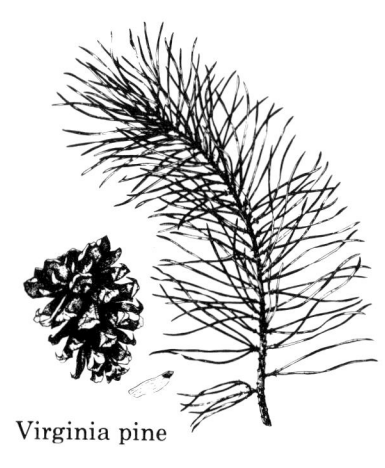

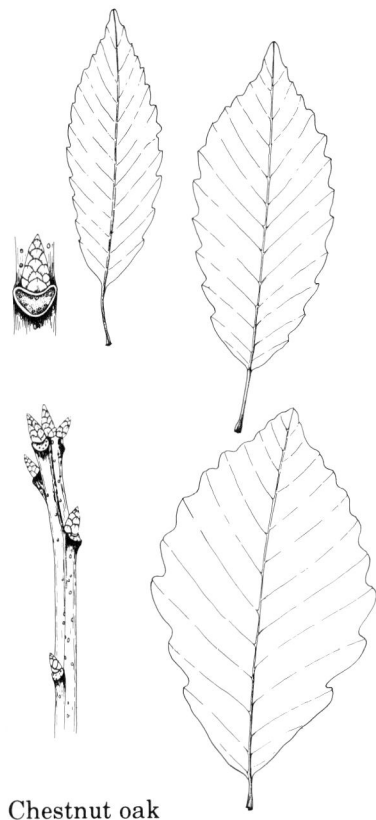

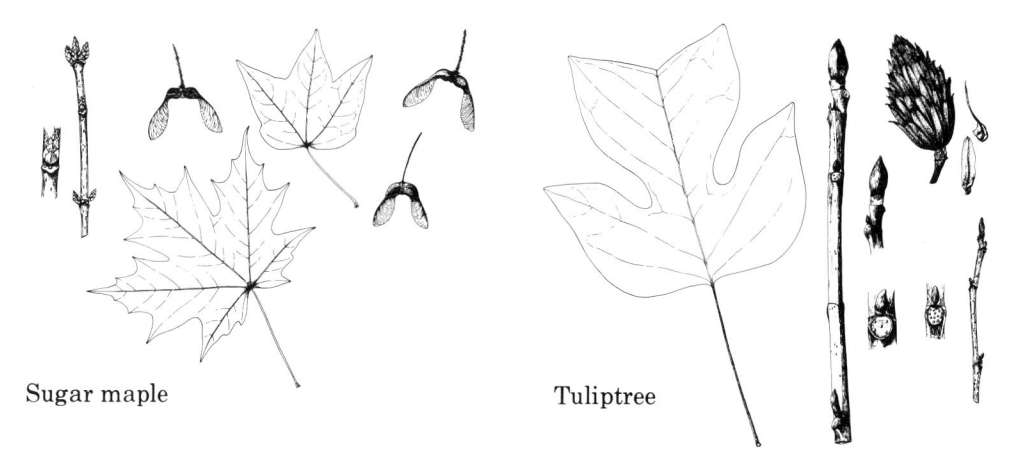

smaller numbers. Conifers included red cedar and pitch, short-leaf, and Virginia pines whose ranges extended into southern Ohio. With their ability to grow on infertile, dry sites they were, and still are, common pioneers, being among the first invaders on disturbed soil or abandoned farms. In some places where the soil is especially poor, these species may be dominant today.

But the soils were not all infertile. Nestled among the hills were protected coves where deeper soils, more moisture, and shelter from sun and drying winds made growing conditions especially good. Some of the largest trees and finest woods grew on these sites. Tuliptree, ash, red oak, blackgum, sugar maple, wild black cherry, and walnut were a few of the valuable species. Sometimes the first limb was 100 feet above the ground, and the trees towered up out of the coves, challenging the ridgetop species for a place in the sun. Others less common but useful were cucumber magnolia and butternut. Good quality furniture made from some of these woods is still in use and is eagerly sought by collectors. The quality built into these pieces is virtually impossible to duplicate today. When pieces come onto the market as antiques, they command prices unimagined by those who built them.

In western Ohio the forests were varied with much beech and maple. In the northwestern section due to poor drainage, there were vast areas of swamp forest with stands of silver maple, several species of ashes, American elm, pin oak, swamp white oak, bur oak, Shumard's oak, cottonwood, and other swamp species. In the spring much of this region was covered with standing water and was alive with mosquitos. It is easy to understand why this was the last part of the state to be settled. Today it is the most changed.

The Forest System

As the early surveyors and pioneers knew, the nature of the soils greatly influenced forest composition. Soil texture, especially as it affects drainage, is very important. On shallow, well-drained soils, the deep-rooted, drought-resistant species, like the oaks and hickories, compete most successfully. On deep, moist soils with good drainage, black walnut and tuliptree grow well. Pin oak, green ash, red or silver maple, and other swamp species survive best on heavy clay soils. Some trees are sensitive to soil acidity or alkalinity. For example, chinquapin oak, blue ash, hackberry, and red cedar are usually associated with alkaline or "sweet" soils, while stands of chestnut oak and sorrel tree (sourwood) grow on acidic or "sour" soils.

Topography also exerts an important effect upon the forest. South- and west-facing slopes are exposed to the direct rays of the sun and the prevailing winds. Thus they are warmer and drier than north- and east-facing slopes. This fact is plainly reflected in the species and growth rates of the trees and in the variety and abundance of ground cover. Air drainage also plays an important role. Frequently, valleys which drain cool air permit the southward extension of northern plants. Cool air trapped in depressions known as frost pockets also affects the plants which grow there.

These factors do much to produce the tapestry of autumn colors, and that season is perhaps the best time to understand the distribution of forest types. The ridgetops with the browns and rusts of the oaks contrast sharply with the bright splashes of red, orange, and yellow in the coves where blackgums, maples, and tuliptrees grow. In areas where limestone layers outcrop between beds of shale or sandstone, bands of pink across the hills in spring show how the redbud grows in the calcium layer. Old fields overgrown with red cedar also indicate a limestone bedrock not far below the surface.

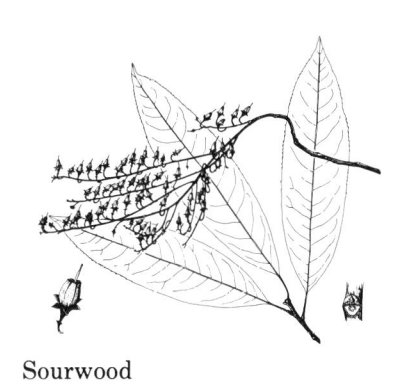

Sourwood

Predator and Prey

The forest is a remarkably efficient energy-conversion system. It is composed of much more than trees although they constitute its most conspicuous feature. One of the most interesting and important aspects of energy use and transfer is predation. All animals in the forest reproduce much faster than is needed to maintain their numbers, and it is the fate of the vast majority of these creatures to be killed and devoured by other animals. This occurs at all levels and has played a major role in molding the structure and behavior patterns of both predatory and prey species.

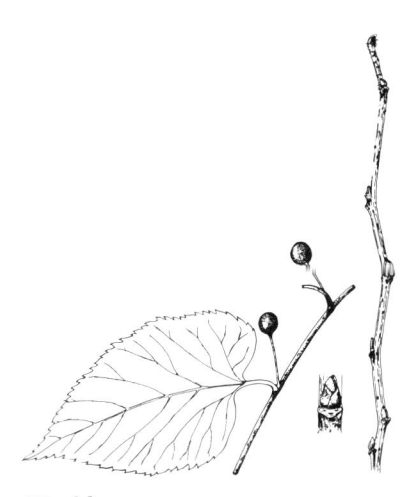

Over the years animals have developed adaptations such as concealing coloration, fleetness, and keen senses which help in capturing prey or eluding predators. Some prey species hide from predators. Other species flee. Some have noxious tastes or odors which protect them. Still others can defend themselves with hoofs, claws, or teeth. Some predators stalk their prey, while others capture their food on the wing or exert considerable effort to rout the prey species from its hiding place. Spiders construct elaborate traps and lie in wait. These attack and escape mechanisms must be in balance if both predator and prey species are to survive. In balanced systems survival is assured. Under the usual conditions found in nature no predator ever exterminates its prey.

Hackberry

Small forms usually reproduce more rapidly than do larger animals. Some insects produce thousands of offspring each season. Mice may produce dozens of young, deer but one or two. Balancing this, small forms usually have numerous predators while large animals have but few. Fitness does not guarantee survival for the prey, since fortune too plays a role. For the unfit, however, death is a swift certainty. Animals which are unwary, diseased, crippled, or otherwise handicapped are more easily captured and are continually weeded out. The result is a more vigorous, healthy, and alert prey population whose numbers are maintained at a level which the habitat can support. This level is called carrying capacity. While it is obvious that predators require prey in order to survive, it is less obvious, but no less true, that prey populations require predators to maintain their viability.

Kentucky warbler with larvae

Crab spider

The lacewing produces predacious larvae

Predators are commonly viewed as animals which prey on species requiring substantial effort to capture and kill. Most predators of this kind have obvious modifications such as strong, curved claws or talons, hooked beaks, or enlarged canine teeth which are used in capture and killing. These are usually carnivorous mammals (foxes and weasels) or raptorial birds (hawks and owls). There are many exceptions. An example is the whole group of insectivorous birds. These may rightfully be considered predators but, in this case, the capture of prey may require little effort. The effort is involved in locating the food supply and involves none of the conspicuous features commonly associated with predatory behavior.

All of these animal eaters are converters at least a step or two removed from the primary harvesters of solar energy, the green plants. Through photosynthesis, green plants, with the energy provided by sunlight, are able to convert carbon dioxide and water into simple sugars. These and other substances acquired from the soil are built into nutrients available to animals. When the plant is eaten by some animal, a process begins in which the energy is transferred from organism to organism, spreading it through the system. Seeds produced by a green plant may be gathered and eaten by a white-footed mouse. Later, the mouse may be eaten by a hunting weasel, and eventually the weasel may be caught and devoured by an owl. If it is a large owl it is unlikely it will be eaten by another predator so, except for the energy involved in reproduction, this ends the transfer of that energy until the owl dies. At that point the bird's tissues are returned to the soil where they are reduced to basic components which may be used by other organisms as the cycle begins again.

This transfer of energy from one organism to another is called a food chain and may involve one or several steps. When considered from the standpoint of species rather than individuals, such transfers may more appropriately be called webs, for each link is likely to be involved in several chains, making the whole a complex, interrelated system. The more diverse the group of organisms, the more complex the system. The more complex the system, the more stable it is, since the failure of a single link is less likely to add significantly to the stress of the entire system. Every organism is involved, and each plays a significant role whether or not that role is evident.

The Layer Cake

The forest is a layered system. The towering, dominant species stand above all forming the canopy. The giant oaks and tuliptrees have clear trunks and relatively small crowns. On good sites mature trees can sometimes be found measuring 100 feet or more to the first limb. Their crowns are the home sites of animals ranging from hawks to katydids. This canopy is the topmost layer in a series of strata in the forest, each of which has unique features and each of which plays an important role in promoting the efficient functioning of the forest energy system.

Below the canopy stand other trees, less tall and more shade tolerant. These are often sugar maples and they form a subcanopy or second layer. Their branches may appear to be the canopy when viewed from below, but it is through these that the trunks of the true canopy trees disappear.

The gray fox is a forest predator

The broad-winged hawk brings small animals to its young

The third layer is composed of shrubs and small trees. In dry forests, dogwood, maple-leafed viburnum, and, in some areas, mountain laurel are common. Where the soil is more moist, pawpaw, witch hazel, and musclewood may be prominent. In wet woods spicebush frequently is abundant. Its small yellow flowers bloom well ahead of the unfolding leaves and in the autumn its shiny red fruits, in spite of their strong spicy flavor, are eaten by many birds.

The fourth or lowest layer is the groundcover made up of herbaceous plants, vines, seedlings, mosses, and ferns. This layer has by far the greatest variety of species. It is here that the spring flowers and the summer and autumn fungi put on their shows, and it is the zone most quickly affected by grazing or other disruptive factors. All of the plants in the other layers were part of this layer when they were in their early stages.

The canopy receives by far the most light. Temperature fluctuations are greater and more rapid, and it absorbs the full force of winds and storms. It is the harshest of the woodland habitats. Each progressively lower layer receives less light and provides more protection from the elements. Those organisms that live in and below the leaf litter on the forest floor occupy the mildest and most stable environment.

A Dynamic System

The forest is a highly competitive place, with all of the plants using the available light, nutrients, and water. Slight changes in the availability of any of these or other factors may shift the advantage and are reflected in forest growth. The change is always toward the aggregation of plants and animals which will be the most efficient in using the energy present. When this combination is achieved, the forest ecosystem is said to be "climax" and will maintain a sort of dynamic stability. Unless there is a change in climate or a natural catastrophe, the general nature of the community will remain the same. However, amidst this relative stability there is constant change. The stability of the system cannot be maintained without it. All of the organisms present have limited life spans. Trees take years to reach maturity. Other organisms mature, reproduce, and die in a few months or even weeks, and the death of the organisms provides space for successors.

When a tree dies it no longer affects the space around it in the same way it did when it was alive. The space is quickly invaded by other plants, and almost immediately after death, it is attacked by a number of wood-boring insects. The larvae, in chewing their way through the wood, attract hungry woodpeckers, which in turn, excavate holes in the dead branches. In subsequent years these holes may serve as nesting sites for other birds or for flying squirrels or white-footed mice.

As the bark loosens, insects and other invertebrates move in, only to be followed by skinks and other lizards looking for food. A ring-necked snake may live here for a time. Eventually decay destroys the roots and the tree falls, effectively ending the bird nesting, but mice and chipmunks continue to use the old nest holes and other cavities. The log, if hollow, may serve as a den for a skunk, an opossum, or even a fox. If not, then a ruffed grouse or a turkey hen may make her nest close beside it. Decreased competition under the dead tree permits an abundant growth of young trees and shrubs. Thus when the dead trunk falls amid this growth, a male ruffed grouse may use the top of the log as a platform for his spring mating display. If so, it may serve this function for several years. All the while uncounted little plants and animals benefit in a thousand ways from the remains of the old tree. They eventually reduce it to humus in the soil where it continues in still another role.

Forest Succession

The forest provides excellent protection to the soil. In their zeal to civilize the wilderness, settlers cleared much land which could not maintain its productivity without more protection than agricultural crops could provide. This problem was especially severe in southeastern Ohio. Erosion, leaching, and the loss of organic matter reduced productivity to the point where farming was no longer economical. When this happened, the land was abandoned and began reverting to woodland. But the abandoned land was no longer suitable for the climax

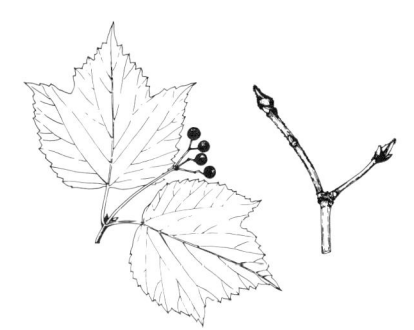

Maple-leafed viburnum

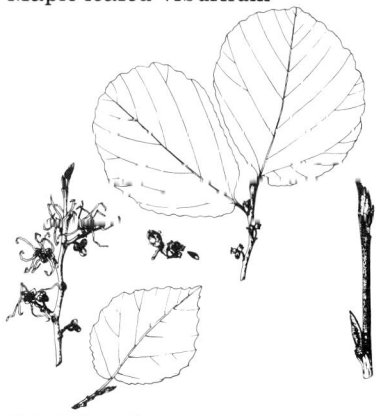

Witch-hazel

Galleries produced by elm bark beetles exposed on a dead branch

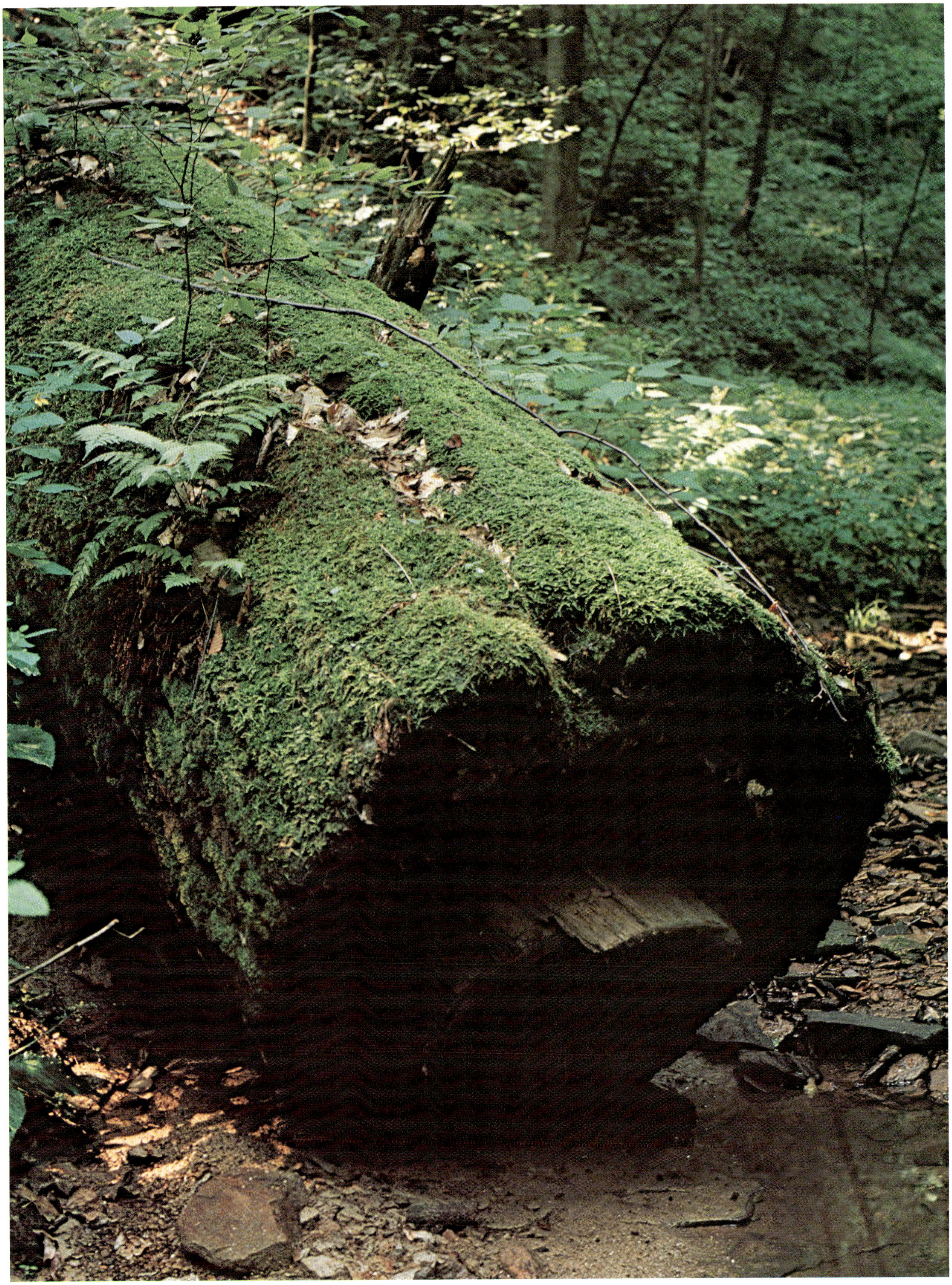

species since light levels and soil temperatures were high and nutrient levels in the soil had been reduced.

Fortunately there are a number of plants which are highly tolerant of these harsh conditions. They quickly invade fields or cut-over areas which are left unmanaged. No sooner are they established than they begin to alter the site. Because they are first, these plants are known as pioneer species. There are many plants of this type, and each has characteristics which adapt it to specific site conditions. Some germinate best on disturbed soil, some on recently burned areas, and some where livestock graze. If these characteristics are known it is usually possible to deduce the recent history of a landscape from the evidence provided by the plants growing there.

The sequence of events may follow this pattern. A crop field, eroded and depleted of nutrients, is finally abandoned. The first plants to invade are annual weeds such as foxtail grass, ragweed, and smartweed. A killdeer, vesper sparrow, or horned lark may nest on the ground where the cover is still sparse. The next year wild asters, yarrow, goldenrod, and other perennials will sprout, eventually crowding out the annuals. Broomsedge and poverty grass are often the first perennial grasses to grow. These species are indicators of poor soil because they cannot compete successfully on soils with a good supply of nutrients. Ground-nesting birds, which build nests in this heavy cover, may carry in blackberry seeds, and some briar patches may develop. Field sparrows will begin nesting and add their trill to the volume of spring bird songs. With the extra cover and the accumulating mulch on the ground, conditions favor the sprouting of some pioneer tree species such as dogwood, wild crab, hawthorn, sassafras, persimmon, and pine. In turn, yellowbreasted chats, brown thrashers, cardinals, towhees, goldfinches, and certain warblers are attracted to the trees.

Additional organic matter begins to accumulate in the soil. Since it is well shaded, summer temperatures are lower. The good cover present permits mice, chipmunks, and even squirrels to move about freely. They carry in and store seeds of the heavy-seeded forest trees, while light seeds are blown in by wind. Seeds sprout, seedlings of climax forest trees grow, and as they grow, soil conditions continue to change, and many years will pass before the relative stability of the climax forest is achieved. However, true forest conditions exist long before that time.

This type of succession is only a general pattern. There are many variations. The pattern is speeded up if seed sources are near and if grazing animals are kept away. Graze-resistant plants with spines or thorns such as hawthorn, wild crab, and wild rose are often common where pastures are reverting to forest.

In southern and eastern Ohio, pines are often the first species to invade old fields, while red cedar often invades old fields in southwestern Ohio. Pines and cedars grow in these fields because they can survive the low moisture and nutrient levels on such sites, and their high light requirement is adequately met. Nearly pure stands of pine sometimes grow, but pines will not reproduce in the dense shade, so, after many years the stand begins to thin. By that time the site is so altered that hardwoods (maple, oak, ash, hickory) are usually able to survive and, in time, they become dominant.

Old fields and other areas with harsh growing conditions are often planted to pines. This crop shortens the time needed to restore forest cover to the land because the earlier successional stages are bypassed. Pines have a higher commercial value than other pioneer species suited to these sites and are a quick source of income for landowners who want

A decaying log serves many functions (opposite page)

to harvest timber or Christmas trees. After harvesting, pine plantings normally revert to hardwood stands.

Pioneer species such as pine survive in climax stands only because of the dynamic nature of the forest. The mortality of trees and the long periods needed for regrowth assure that there are always places where the pioneers can survive and from which they can quickly spread as favorable sites develop.

Ohio was once more than 95 percent clothed in mature forest. Today most of this magnificent primeval growth is gone, sacrificed to the needs of an expanding population and a developing technology. Now about one fourth of the state is woodland. In some counties remaining forests cover as little as three or four percent of the land. Forest cover in hilly eastern and southern counties may be more than 70 percent, but virtually all present woodland has been considerably altered by human activities. For example, pioneer species make up much more of the stand and few trees approach mature size before they are harvested. These are subclimax forests. They cannot be maintained at the present stage without considerable management, although changes will be slow in any case.

Forestry practices in existing woodlots frequently increase growth and modify the species composition of the stand, enhancing the economic return. Cutting practices are especially important in this regard. Trees, like other organisms, have stages of growth. Growth is

Autumn colors help to identify plant species invading an old field

The brown thrasher nests in early stages of forest succession

rapid in young trees. It slows as the trees mature and the incidence of rot and other forms of deterioration increase with age. Therefore it is usually most profitable to harvest trees before the loss from deterioration offsets the gain from growth. If this practice is followed for each tree as it reaches optimum size, and defective or low value trees are removed on a continuing basis, it is called selective cutting, a policy expensive for the commercial timber harvester since more time, energy, and money are needed to harvest each tree. Another problem is that, in some situations, lower value, subclimax species may reseed the sites.

A more economical method of harvesting, called clear cutting, is widely used. Clear cutting involves the removal of all trees over two inches in diameter and allows a new stand to start from seedlings, sprouts, and advanced reproduction, resulting in an even-aged stand which may be harvested again after several decades. The length of this period of regrowth depends on productivity of the site, the tree species, and the product sought. The method is attractive to the lumber industry because of its economy and because the small timber produced is adequate for the market. However, clear cutting has created much controversy because of the devastated appearance of newly harvested areas, and because of alleged harmful effects on animals. These effects can be minimized or, in some cases, entirely avoided, if the clear-cut areas are kept small. Areas of three or four acres up to about 40 acres are least disruptive and are beneficial to some kinds of wildlife. For example, deer usually benefit because of the increase in cover and browse.

Larger clear cuts are disastrous to animals requiring relatively mature forest habitat. These include squirrels, large hawks, pileated woodpeckers, and a number of small birds. Because of the many years needed for regrowth, this practice is best suited to large corporate or public holdings. The small woodlot owner should seek professional help in developing a management plan.

Today timber harvesting is usually done before the trees have reached maturity. There are several reasons for this practice, the most important being that the forest products currently in demand can be produced from relatively young stands. In addition, if the trees are large, harvesting costs are higher, and it is more difficult to remove them without seriously damaging the site. Thus, both economic and environmental considerations make it unlikely that future commercials forests will ever resemble the virgin stands of 200 years ago.

There are a number of nature preserves and other forested tracts in Ohio, some of which include old stands of mature timber. Many of these are retained for aesthetic or educational purposes and the timber will probably never be harvested. In these, or in similar areas still to be preserved, we may yet retain remnants of Ohio's forest heritage. And as these develop, people may, like their ancestors, stand in awe of the grandeur.

The Life of the Forest

The forest is a place of constant change. It is not unique in this respect but the changes that occur in woodlands are often on a grand scale. They are obvious and occur suddenly with a startling spontaneity. There are slowly developing changes too, but the more spectacular ones are seasonal. They occur every year at about the same time but never in quite the same way. Vagaries of weather and other factors, frequently unknown, fill each season with surprises. In any case, whether things happen unfailingly or unexpectedly, the changing panorama is never dull.

The tufted titmouse is a year-round resident

The Forest in Spring

As winter wanes, days lengthen and warm, and the annual cycle begins anew. The first changes are hardly noticed. Now when a branch is cut or broken, sap oozes out — the first sign that the sugar, produced last summer is moving to the buds where it will fuel the coming surge of leaf and flower growth. These phenomena may be several weeks away for some species. Others, such as the red maple, may be starting to bloom as early as February.

The first true sign of spring is in early March, when from the margin of some woodland pool will come the clear whistled notes of a spring peeper, the ascending trill of a chorus frog, or the low clucking notes of a wood frog. These species breed in earliest spring and their calling lifts one's heart, for it surely signals the end of winter. A few more days of mild weather and the frog chorus will increase until, at night, it may seem deafening. Shortly the pools will teem with myriads of tiny black tadpoles. Cardinals, mourning doves, and tufted titmice also are affected by the lengthening daylight. In early spring they begin calling several weeks before the real dawn chorus of birdsong begins. The titmice begin singing during maple sugar time, so these birds are known locally as "sugar birds."

Skunk cabbage - one of the earliest wildflowers

The spring peeper's song is an early sign of spring

The first conspicuous change comes in early April when the forest floor erupts in a brief but spectacular show of spring flowers. In March, sometimes earlier, skunk cabbage and snow trilliums bloom. They lift the spirit, especially when the flowers poke through late snows that seem to have delayed warmer weather.

Close behind these earliest flowers come the hepatica, spring beauties, trailing arbutus, and bloodroot. Then comes the real show. In an explosion of color, a wide variety of flowers bloom and carpet the forest floor in what is certainly one of nature's most memorable events. Large-flowered trillium, foam flower, rue anemone, and toothwort are among the whites. Violets and Jacob's ladder represent the blues. Bellwort, ragwort, and celandine are yellow. Wild geranium and wood sorrel are shades of lavender. Firepink is red and moccasin flower is pink. This burst of bloom ends almost as suddenly as it begins when leaves burst from the swollen buds in the canopy. As they expand, the light on the forest floor dims and soon the foliage of the spring flowers, having harvested the energy which will produce next year's show, fades and dies.

By this time a second spectacular change is in progress. At dawn in early May the forest rings with a magnificent chorus of bird song. Coming north to their breeding grounds, migrants mingle with the resident species and all, stimulated by the onset of the mating season, provide a concert experienced only briefly once each year.

Insects have hatched and are busy feeding on the unfolding leaves. Flocks of wood warblers search among the treetops for the insect prey which makes up most of their diet. Some of these will stay to nest, but most migrate farther north. All will provide a chorus of songs and glimpses of color that are memorable.

Hepatica

Bloodroot

The white trillium is common in Ohio forests

Long-spurred violet

Other birds returning to nest in Ohio will join the year-round residents, and soon all the niches are filled. Most species are territorial, meaning that the males lay claim to a tract which is defended against others of the same species. They advertise their claims by singing or expressing other audible signals, usually from a prominent perch or other exposed position. Most are active during the day and many species have colorful markings or display behavior patterns which increase their visibility. Together, these characteristics make birds the most conspicuous animals in the forest. Mammals are usually much more abundant, but it is the breeding birds that we see. Two pairs of breeding birds per acre is about what may be expected in a well-forested area.

A number of species live at the lowest levels of the forest and nest on the forest floor. Largest among these are the turkey and the ruffed grouse. The turkey is a magnificent bird which disappeared from the state before the turn of the century. It was reintroduced in the 1950s and now lives in much of wooded southern Ohio. Through good management it is expanding its range and appears to be back to stay. Like the turkey, the ruffed grouse was once abundant over the whole state, but it is now found only in the more heavily wooded eastern and southern counties. During April males perform their mating display. They select a drumming site, usually a log, and beginning before dawn, drum well into the morning. Drumming consists of beating wings against the air, producing a hollow sound much like a small engine starting in the distance. There are a few slow thumps, followed by others in more rapid succession and ending in a roll of whirring sound. It is virtually impossible to see this behavior without erecting a blind and concealing oneself before daylight and awaiting the arrival of the grouse.

Another bird nesting on the forest floor is the whip-poor-will. This species is quite common in deep woodlands of the state, but is more often heard than seen. It begins singing at dusk, continuing through the night, and is a part of the charm of Ohio woodlands. The whip-poor-will does not actually construct a nest but lays its two attractive eggs on the dead leaves avoiding other ground cover. The incubating bird with its mottled brown plumage is so well camouflaged that it is practically impossible to find the nest without first flushing the bird. The young are equally well hidden against the background of leaves. Many smaller birds also nest on or near the forest floor. Some of the most characteristic include the ovenbird, and the Kentucky, the black and white, the worm-eating, and the hooded warblers.

A few species nest in the canopy. These include several of Ohio's birds of prey. One of the most common is the red-tailed hawk. These birds nest in March long before the leaves appear. The bulky nest of sticks is built high in the canopy and can be easily seen until the trees leaf out and incubation of the eggs has begun. The same nest may be used for several years. However the great horned owl, the largest of our owls, nests even earlier. As early as February, an owl may appropriate a red-tail's nest, forcing the hawks to build another. Broad-winged and Cooper's hawks also nest high in forest trees. Canopy-nesting species among the smaller birds include the scarlet tanager and the cerulean warbler.

The middle layers of the forest, the lower sub-canopy and the upper shrub layer, are the domain of a different group of birds. Acadian flycatchers, red-eyed vireos, and ruby-throated hummingbirds are species commonly nesting in the lower branches of subcanopy trees. The wood thrush also nests in the middle layers. Its flute-like song at dawn and dusk is one of the most delightful woodland sounds.

Where openings occur in the forest or along the edge of woods, the shrub layer is usually dense. The cardinal and the indigo bunting are two of the most colorful birds of this habitat. Both species are tireless singers and are usually favorites of those who know them. The female, as well as the male cardinal, is a talented songster.

The black and white warbler

The great horned owl - a nocturnal predator

A ruffed grouse incubates her eggs

Still other birds nest in holes in trees. The woodpeckers all do this, usually excavating in dead trunks or branches. They eat mostly wood-boring insects, many of which are harmful to forest trees and wood products. Additionally, abandoned nest holes are readily used by other hole-nesting species such as titmice, chickadees, nuthatches, great crested flycatchers, kestrels, or even other woodpeckers. Several species of woodpeckers live in every forest, and their nest cavities range in size from the chickadee-sized holes made by the little downy woodpecker to the big rectangular ones excavated by the pileated woodpecker. These latter ones are large enough for screech owls or squirrels in which to live.

Instead of singing, woodpeckers drum on dead trunks or branches. The sound echoes through still woods and can often be heard a quarter of a mile away. The beak is also used to excavate the nest cavity, and this may be in the same branch used for drumming. Even though the wood is rapidly cut away and chips fly, very little sound is produced.

Most Ohio forests harbor 12 or 15 species of mammals, and populations range from a dozen or less to scores of mammals per acre. Of course most of these are small like the shrew and the white-footed mouse. The deer is the largest native mammal commonly found in Ohio's forests. Deer provided much of the meat and hides for garments used by the early settlers and they are still hunted for meat and sport. During the late winter the bucks begin growing new antlers, which by spring appear as blunt knobs covered with a velvety growth. Does drop fawns by late May. If forest food is abundant, most births are twins.

Deer are adaptable animals and numbers tend to increase in many areas. However when there are too many, they can do damage to the forest, eating back what they can reach more rapidly than it can grow. This devastation leaves the canopy relatively unaffected, which in turn, cuts off the light and holds back regrowth in the understory, effectively reducing the ability of the forest to maintain a population of these animals. Deer disappeared when much of the land was cleared. They were absent from the state during the early part of the twentieth century, and their return is related to the regrowth of forest on abandoned farm land. The species is not typical of mature forest, but thrives best in a mixture of earlier successional stages. These animals have made such a successful comeback that there are probably more deer in Ohio now than before settlement.

One problem for deer is that population tends rapidly to outgrow the food supply. Since large predators, such as the wolf and cougar, have been extirpated from the state, deer have no population checks except those related to man's activities, disease and, perhaps ultimately, starvation. When deer exceed the carrying capacity of the woodland, they quickly strip foliage from trees and damage crops in nearby fields. When food runs short, starvation is inevitable. Thus good management is needed to maintain the herds at a level where the food supply is adequate.

Animals, plants, and energy — the forest community is bursting with activity in the spring. All of the processes which make the system work are in full swing at this time. Most will continue through the growing season, but it is in the spring that they begin. Beginings frequently call attention to themselves. A male bird sings to attract females and defend his territory. The pair carries food to the young and scolds loudly when the nest is threatened. Leaves are unfolding and enlarging, flowers are blooming, the forest is filled with the sounds and activity of life so that one cannot help being stirred to a realization of the magnitude of the change.

The pileated woodpecker

The distinctive rectangular shape indentifies the work of the pileated woodpecker

White-tailed deer fawn

The Forest in Summer

Growth slows and spring slips almost imperceptibly into summer. There is a succession of summer blooming flowers and a late summer burst of goldenrods, asters, and other composites. But the appearance of these species lacks the suddenness and striking contrast of the spring flowers. Seeds ripen. Young animals are weaned away from parental care. Energy is stored in roots and tubers and, in general, life activities are at a peak. Green is the color of the summer woods — not the pale virginal greens of new spring growth nor the bright, golden greens of open fields, but deep, rich green.

Cicada

Katydid

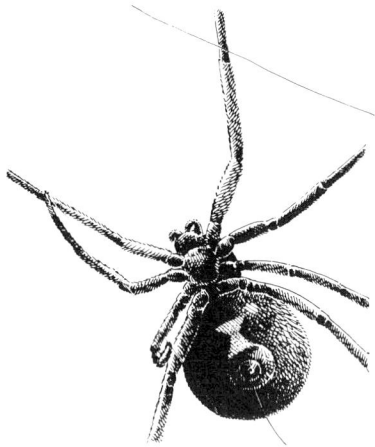

Black widow spider

The gray tree frog is often heard but seldom seen

By June many of the birds stop singing. In place of their songs, so prominent in spring, are the droning, buzzing, vibrant songs of the cicadas. Those that appear each year emerge from the ground in early July and leave their cast shells on posts and tree trunks. Only the males sing. The females, after mating, deposit their eggs in the twigs of trees, and this frequently causes the tip of the twig to die. In midsummer the brown of the dead leaves is conspicuous in the crowns of many trees. After hatching, the young nymphs drop to the ground, burrow into the soil, and feed on sap from the tree roots for several years before emerging and starting the cycle again. While they are active, their songs, grinding out through the heat of summer, are a constant reminder of the season.

At dusk there is another chorus. The katydids, tree crickets, long-horned grasshoppers and field crickets — the Orthoptera — are singing by the hundreds. The woodland is alive with insects. Millions of these little animals are active on every acre, eating leaves, sucking juices, devouring each other, and unceasingly reproducing. The larger and noisier ones are easier to see but they play a lesser role than the many smaller forms. They creep, fly, hop, and burrow, using prodigious amounts of energy, and they have a vital role in the functioning of the ecosystem.

Occasionally one finds a spring peeper, a toad, or a wood frog in the summer forest. They have long since ceased their frantic calling and left their breeding areas, now spending quiet, solitary lives amidst the relatively abundant food supply of the woodland. Tree frogs may still be calling from the trees at night, but high temperatures and low rainfall during this season are not the best of conditions for most amphibians.

Early litters of young squirrels are well-grown now, and these animals can be seen climbing about the trees carrying leafy twigs for nests. Some adult females are caring for second litters. Fawns have grown rapidly, and by midsummer no longer rely on hiding for protection. Their fleet legs quickly take them to safety when danger threatens.

Marks in the mud, like the prints of tiny hands, are evident along streams, ponds, and puddles. These are the tracks of the raccoon. Some prints are large, others small, which means females are taking their young on nightly hunting expeditions. They hunt for crawfish, frogs, and other small animals, fruit, or whatever they can find to eat, including the treasures found in garbage cans. Raccoons often hunt near water but are by no means confined to such areas. Few pools or nooks in the forest escape their sensitive, exploring paws. Almost everyone is familiar with these little masked bandits, but their nocturnal habits make them less visible than the many tracks they leave.

The most common mammal of all is one most likely to be overlooked. Short-tailed shrews live mostly beneath the leaf litter and many people have never seen one. In the woods on a warm, dry, windless summer day there is little sound except the faint humming of insects. A wood peewee or a red eyed vireo may call lazily among the branches overhead, or a chipmunk may cluck softly in the warmth. In this tranquil setting faint rustling among the dry leaves attracts immediate attention. The noise may be millipedes or beetles crawling around in their search for mates or food. However, mysterious movements under the leaves and tiny squeaking noises mean a shrew is near. The rustling and leaf shaking may be followed by a tiny head pushing up between the leaves, then peering about with nearly invisible eyes. Occasionally the little animal will emerge and briefly scurry about on the surface in search of prey.

A probing finger pushed into the leaf litter is almost certain to break through into one of the myriad shrew burrows which thread through the upper layers of the soil. It is normal for several of these tiny animals to live on each acre, and populations of a dozen or more per acre sometimes occur. Their burrows may be significant in enabling forest soils to absorb water rapidly.

Summer also is the season when butterflies and moths are most abundant. Swallowtails float about the canopy or visit summer flowers.

Raccoon

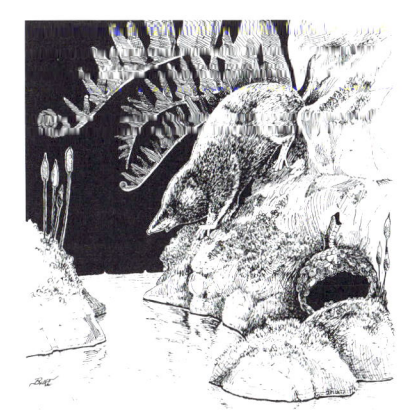

Short-tailed shrew

Tiger swallowtail

A skipper - one of a group of common butterflies

Male luna moth

Lichens on tree bark

White-footed mice and wild black cherries (opposite page)

Skippers flit over the forest floor. Leaves on every tree and shrub show the holes and notches produced by feeding larvae. Although one occasionally sees a hummingbird moth drawing nectar at a flower at midday, the moths usually are not active until night. After dark, the underwing moths, which have clung camouflaged on the bark of trees all day, take off. Giant species like the cecropia, the luna, the royal walnut, and the polyphemus fly about. These species, in spite of their size, are not often seen unless they come to lights. Sometimes detached wings show where a bat has had a meal. The larvae of several of these grow large and take fantastic science-fiction forms and colors. However they are difficult to find and can best be located by looking for droppings beneath the trees where they feed. Even the larvae of smaller forms are interesting because of their color patterns or their behavior.

A mild hazard of late summer walks in the woods is the myriad of spider webs which are constructed across forest paths. The spiny back spiders construct most of these webs, which are constant nuisances to hikers.

Food for forest animals is no problem during summer. For those that do not eat each other, the bounty of the woodland is evident. In every opening, raspberries are ripening and birds, raccoons, and foxes are making certain that nothing is wasted. Wild black cherry branches hang heavy with small dark berries. Thrushes, waxwings, woodpeckers, and other birds flock to the trees to feed. These same species move to the blackgums when their fruits ripen. Squirrels also share in the bounty. The large seeds of these fruits are cached by chipmunks or white-footed mice. Sometimes nearly a pint of wild black cherry or wild plum seeds may be found stashed in a hollow log or stump. Those eaten by the birds are scattered far and wide in their droppings.

One group of plants found in the forest at any time of year does not, at least to the casual eye, exhibit profound seasonal change. These are the lichens. They are not confined to the forest and are found almost everywhere; but they are abundant in woodlands and lend a subtle character to the scene. Lichens are primitive plants, and although they are considered to be true species, each consists of a fungus and an alga growing in close association. The alga carries on photosynthesis which produces food that both use. The fungus provides a matrix in which the alga grows and which provides protection. Neither the fungus nor the alga exists alone under natural conditions. Lichens exist in a variety of forms. Some called crustose lichens grow as a thin coating on trees, rocks, and soils. Others the fructose lichens, develop more or less conspicuous fruiting structures. These may be brightly colored as in the familiar red British soldier or uniquely shaped as in the case of the common pixie cups. The foliose lichens are sometimes seen on rocks and trees. These are leaf-like and some species grow to be several inches in diameter.

These plants are able to endure long periods of drying and will begin growing whenever moisture becomes available. A familiar lichen is the reindeer moss or reindeer lichen. When dry it is very brittle. But after a rain it absorbs much water and becomes rubbery. Similar forms make up a substantial portion of the diet of caribou in the Arctic.

Many lichens grow on tree bark. In fact, so many grow on trees that their bluish-green or gray colors lend a distinctive appearance to the forest. Several species of birds attach pieces of lichen to the outside of their nests and this may serve as camouflage. The blue-gray gnatcatcher and the ruby-throated hummingbird, which normally build their nests saddled on a tree branch, are outstanding examples of this

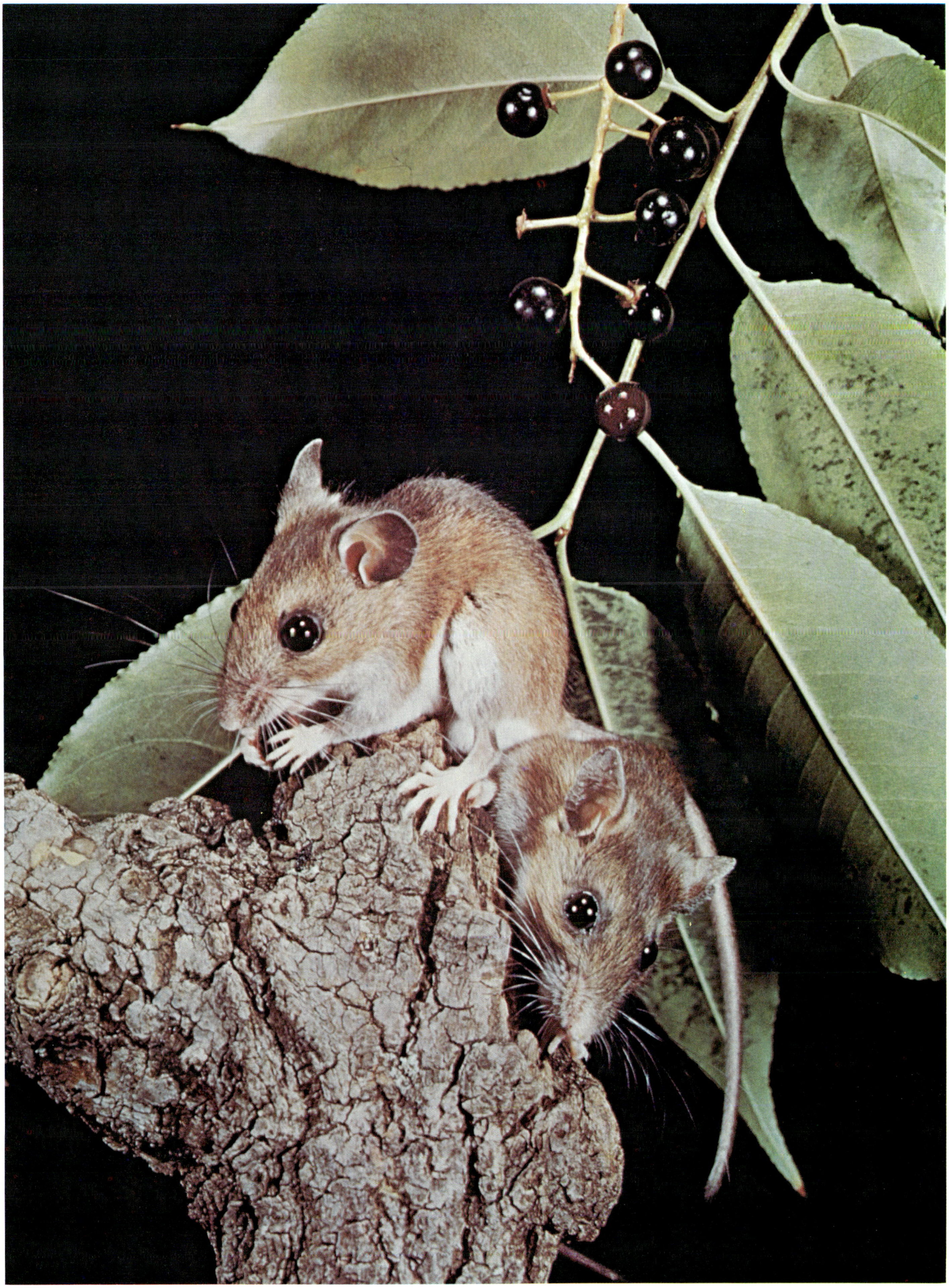

behavior. The lichen-covered nests are difficult to find since the tree branches used for nesting are usually covered with the growth.

The other plants of summer are there to stay at least until frost. They can tolerate the shade, in fact have made their growth since trees leafed out. One of those most common and conspicuous at this season is the white snakeroot. Although the white flowers are very attractive, the plant is highly poisonous. In the early days cattle grazing in woodlands frequently died after eating snakeroot. Humans who drank the milk also became sick with an illness known as milk fever. At present few people drink the milk from a single cow and the ailment is virtually unknown. The plant is still abundant and is a characteristic feature of the late summer scene.

Eventually flowers turn to seedheads. Airborne seeds drift across the landscape on summer breezes. Hickory nuts swell and squirrels turn their attention to the early mast crops. Young woodchucks born last spring now have their own burrows and are living much more solitary lives than they did earlier in the year. In general, life in the forest has settled into a comfortable routine, and the general impression seems to be that things can go on like this indefinitely. However there are signs that something is afoot. A branch on the blackgum tree turns a bright scarlet. Birds begin to molt and change their plumage. Summer is coming to an end. There are a few late broods of birds, a few litters of young squirrels still at the den trees but, except for the insects, it is a quiet time.

The Forest in Autumn

In autumn, days grow shorter, nights become cooler, and another major change is in the making. There is none of the bold noisy activity of spring. Now there is a scurrying and flitting about which, although quiet, implies urgency.

Leaves have formed sugars all through the season, but now they suffer a breakdown of the green chlorophyll. Bright yellow pigments previously hidden in each leaf are exposed, while reds and purples are synthesized in the fall. This change triggers what may be the most spectacular show of the year. In some years there can be little doubt of it. The colors exposed vary greatly in different species. Tuliptree and aspen show clear yellow. Sugar maple is usually some shade of orange. Blackgum, red maple, and scarlet oak show bright reds and sourwood is a deep maroon. In the mixed hardwood forest the colorful panorama is unforgettable. In October country roads are often clogged with traffic as people flock to view the breathtaking scenery.

In a few weeks the scene will be more somber. A cell layer at the base of each leaf begins to break down. Eventually the leaves drop and turn shades of brown. Few leaves are perfectly whole, for they have served as a food supply for hordes of insects since unfolding in the spring. However their function in the ecosystem is still not complete. On the forest floor they protect the soil, provide cover for some animals and nourishment for many others. Nearly a ton of leaves and debris is deposited on each acre of hardwood forest every fall.

Almost immediately the leaves begin to break down and disintegrate. Here again there are great differences between species. Some leaves such as those of the maples, are thin and will be virtually unidentifiable by spring. Others, such as black oak, may be intact after several years. The decay is promoted by bacteria and other micro-organisms, by insects, and by fungi.

Fall color

The fungi are best known. These are the familiar mushrooms, pore fungi, earthstars, and puffballs. Slender, thread-like, microscopic structures called mycelia grow over and through the dead leaves and other organic matter. These rapidly break down the leaves, extracting nutrients essential for growth and releasing the remainder, which may be recycled by other members of the community. Periodically when conditions are favorable, fruiting bodies develop from the mycelia. These are the portions easily seen, but it is the mycelia that break down the organic material and release the nutrients.

In addition to decomposing leaves and other plant materials, fungi have a vital role in forest tree growth. Many species of fungi grow in a symbiotic relationship with the roots of pine, oak, birch, and other species by forming mycorrhizae (fungus roots). The fungi apparently absorb mineral nutrients which diffuse into the tree roots, and in turn, the fungi live off the carbohydrates stored in the roots. Some mushroom species are very specific about their hosts and will not grow unless they are associated with the roots of a particular species. For example, some species of *Suillus* which are fleshy pore mushrooms, are never found outside the root zone of white pine. And the yellowish-white or reddish-orange fly mushroom, a species of *Amanita*, is found in association with birch, pine, or spruce (although spruce does not grow naturally in Ohio).

The best time to see mushrooms is when temperatures are still warm and autumn rains begin. Then the warm days, moist soils, and high humidity cause the fungi to fruit. The enormous variety and quantity of these plants are amazing. Their colors and forms are so varied that it is easy to compare the summer and fall fungi show with the early spring wildflowers. Of course fungi can be found at nearly any season and some species are gathered as food by people who have learned what delicacies are there for the picking. Wild animals also eat fungi. Many species from deer to insects avidly seek out and devour most species of mushrooms. Even some of the most deadly to humans are eaten by box turtles and other animals without harm.

By early autumn the fruits and seeds of other plants have developed and are now ripe and ready for the harvest. For most forest animals this is the season of plenty. Year-round residents must either store much of this, or if they hibernate, eat it and store it as fat which will sustain them during the long winter ahead. Fruit and nuts are produced in quantity nearly every year. In the aggregate this food supply is termed "mast." Of course the amount produced varies from year to year depending on the weather. Normally enormous quantities are produced — enough so that settlers turned their hogs into the woods to fatten in the fall. The oaks produce tons of acorns. Those such as pin, shingle, and chinquapin oaks produce small fruits taken by jays, woodpeckers, crows, grouse, turkeys, and wood ducks. Squirrels and deer eat all species. Hickory nuts and walnuts are favored by squirrels, and even mice may hoard them. Hazelnuts are gathered by chipmunks and mice. Beechnuts are a staple in some areas in some years. Good crops may cause some birds which normally migrate to remain through the winter. These small, three-cornered seeds are eaten by many woodland species from woodpeckers to bears.

The fleshy fruits are eaten on the spot, and early stages of forest succession produce some especially good ones. Persimmons, which in late summer are unbearably astringent, are now soft and sweet. They hang on the tree for a long time and, especially after frost, are among the most delicious of fruits. This fact is not lost among the foxes, raccoons, and opossums in persimmon country. Droppings of these animals,

Earthstar fungus

Puffballs

Poisonous fly mushroom

Red oak acorns

Flowering dogwood brightens the woods in early May

Dogwood fruit is important wildlife food

which may be found in the field at this season, will usually contain great numbers of the large, flat, brown seeds. In fact this is the way persimmon is dispersed. The various species of hawthorns and wild crabs provide abundant fruits, and the sour little apples growing on the crab are eagerly eaten by deer, even after they have fallen to the ground and look thoroughly rotten.

All through the forest, wherever enough light penetrated the canopy, the white flowers of dogwood bloomed in the spring. Now in the autumn, clusters of bright red berries grace the branches and supply a favorite food to squirrels, grouse, and many small birds. The fruits hang on the branches for some time and, even after they drop to the ground, they are still eaten when forest creatures find them among the leaves. The single seed in each fruit is thick-shelled and hard. Grouse pass these through their digestive tracts with germination unimpaired, thus spreading the species to new openings. Cardinals can crack these seeds in their heavy beaks, and chickadees and titmice have been observed gleaning bits of the seeds dropped by feeding cardinals.

These and many other species make life in the autumn forest an easy time for other animals and an interesting time for us. During this colorful period one of the most conspicuous animals is the chipmunk. The low, clucking notes or the high-pitched chittering of this little ground squirrel are among the most familiar sounds of the autumn woodland. Chipmunks are active during the day, scampering about gleaning seeds and fruits which they cache in their underground burrows. They have internal cheek pouches where they store great amounts of food for transport. Much of this is gathered from the forest floor, but in the fall they are often seen high in the trees gathering acorns and other fruits directly from the branches. Food gathered now will be used in the brief active periods during the winter.

Chipmunk

Gray squirrel

Tree squirrels also cache food which is used in the winter. Since they do not hibernate, enough must be gathered to last until spring. Fox and gray squirrels bury nuts and acorns where they find them. Obviously they will not remember the locations of all of these fruits, but their keen sense of smell enables them to find the caches even through several inches of snow. Now while busy collecting and storing, these little animals are surprisingly quiet. Usually only the sound of a nut dropped among the dead leaves or the sound of a hard shell being cut indicates activity.

Another mammal, less well-known but equally abundant, is the flying squirrel. This is our only nocturnal squirrel and it is seldom seen unless driven from its den by disturbance during the day. It cannot truly fly; but, by means of furred membranes along its sides, it can launch itself into the air and glide long distances — occasionally a hundred feet or more between trees. Flying squirrels do not hibernate. In winter, nests may be shared by many individuals. Sometimes at night their high-pitched twittering can be heard as they run and glide among the treetops.

Autumn is the breeding season for the deer. Bucks, with necks swollen and newly-grown antlers polished, roam the woods searching for mates. Many young trees fall victim to their zest as they rub the plants with their antlers, stripping the bark from the trunks. Many such "buck rubs" are evident in deer range at this season.

Although birds are no longer singing much, the trees are often alive with activity. Warblers and others migrating south stop to rest and feed in Ohio. There is little left of the brilliant color so evident in the spring. For the most part, they are now rather drab little creatures with obscure markings. They go quietly about their business of gathering food during the day, presenting a challenge to birders attempting to identify them. At night they may launch themselves across the darkened sky on another leg of their hazardous journey to a climate where they can survive the winter.

People who hike in the autumn forest are well aware that many forest plants produce seeds with hooks or barbs. When a passing animal brushes a plant, seeds will frequently attach to its coat and be carried to a new site, thus providing for the dispersal of the species. Among the common clinging seeds are those of bedstraw — tiny, globular seeds produced near the ground. Agrimony is most often noticed as rows of small burs aligned across trouser legs. Tick trefoils are probably the best known of all because of the abundance of small flat triangular seed pods which stick tightly to clothing. Others with clinging seeds include black snakeroot, enchanter's nightshade, wooly sweet cicely, and beggar's-lice.

The witch-hazel blooms in October along with some of the asters and a few late goldenrods. In November, except from some of the oaks and beeches, most leaves will have fallen. Numbers of late migrants dwindle, and the mast, which may still be present, is the kind which holds little attraction for wildlife. In late autumn the forest is winding down. It is a slow but inexorable process and, of course, is as essential to woodland life as any other in the year.

White-breasted nuthatch

The wood duck nests where forests border streams or ponds

The Forest in Winter

After the glorious, colorful, busy days of autumn the forest becomes more somber. Woods which were alive with the sounds of chipmunks and insects in October are silent. The glowing colors of autumn leaves fade and everything seems muted. Winter is a period of resting but it is far from a lifeless time. Most of the little animals are still there waiting, in some stage, for the return of spring. Some insects have disappeared completely, leaving only eggs to hatch in the spring and start a new generation. Other insects spend the winter in the naturally quiet, pupal state. In some species the larvae, nymphs, or adults hibernate. The animal is torpid in this inactive stage and very little energy is needed to maintain life. All of the cold-blooded forms — the toads, frogs, salamanders, snakes, lizards, and turtles — are hibernating below ground.

Chipmunks also have retired to their burrows. They have stored quantities of food and, when aroused by spells of mild weather, nibble this before resuming their hibernation. They will not be truly active again until the first warm days of spring. Woodchucks, fattened on the lush growth of late summer, have their energy stored as fat. They also will remain torpid in their dens all winter. Sometimes it is said that these animals sleep through the winter, but this is not true. The torpor of hibernation only superficially resembles sleep. In hibernation the bodily functions are remarkably slowed. The metabolic rate drops so much that the heartbeat may be imperceptible and the breathing rate is frequently only a few times per hour. Under these conditions very little energy is used and the animal can live for months on stored body fat.

For those mammals which do not hibernate, snug dens are very important. Some may use woodchuck burrows while others find hollows in trees or under rock piles. These are generally lined with leaves or grass which provide protection during the cold weather. During especially cold weather most small mammals stay in their dens. They can remain for up to a week or, in some cases, much longer. Animals thus inactive are not truly hibernating although they may show a reduced metabolic rate. However they are easily aroused.

Squirrels and mice make frequent visits to caches where food was stored in the autumn. The fox and gray squirrels, after having buried their food where they found it, must now rely on their keen sense of smell to find it a second time. Although it seems this could be more difficult since the first time the mast was on the surface, it poses no problem. Midwinter is the breeding season for these animals. The success of their matings will in part be determined by the supply of nourishing food available. Raccoons and foxes also breed in the winter only a little later than the squirrels.

Shrews show no slackening of activity at this season. Burrowing deeper in the soil when the surface freezes, they actively seek hibernating insects or other prey at all hours of the day.

Several species of birds winter in Ohio forests. Some of these may feed partially or entirely on seeds, but most search for hibernating or quiescent insects. Chickadees, nuthatches, kinglets, and brown creepers are among those that search beneath the bark or in crevices. Woodpeckers still seek insects in all stages as well as the fruits that persist on the poison ivy, viburnum, and dogwood.

With the coming of the first major snowfall, conditions change again. The white flakes drift down and provide an insulating blanket on the forest floor. This prevents deep freezing and reduces stress on both

The downy is the smallest of Ohio woodpeckers

plants and animals in the soil. The shrews are given an extra measure of protection from predators and are assured of more unfrozen soil in which to forage for their food. If the snow is deep, the grouse, which have roosted at night in greenbrier tangles or in trees, plunge under the snow for extra protection from the cold and from predators. But for the small animals who must feed and carry on their other activities on the surface, the snow provides additional exposure to both winged and mammalian predators. The brown bodies stand out starkly against the white snow. Then there is little protection from the owl which can watch and strike suddenly and silently from above.

A hiker in the woods after a snow will be rewarded by an interesting story of the activities of the animals there. The whole account is preserved in full view until the next warm spell. It is easy to see who was up and about and what it was doing. Tiny tracks of white-footed mice go from tree to tree or disappear beneath the snow. Fox tracks, neatly aligned and purposeful in appearance, contrast with seemingly aimless meanderings of an opossum. Here a squirrel has dug unerringly for a buried acorn. There a grouse has flushed leaving wing marks in the snow. Fascinating hours can be spent deciphering the recorded messages.

Even though winter is the season of dormancy for the plants, roots continue to grow. Some species which are evergreen are most conspicuous in winter. A number of ferns, wintergreen, partridge-berry, mountain laurel, and even the leaves of a few species of orchids, add green splashes here and there among the dead brown of the fallen leaves.

Trees are no less interesting after they have lost their foliage. The color and texture of the bark and the form of the bare branches against the sky are frequently as distinctive as the shapes of leaves or autumn colors. The smooth, silvery bark of the beech contrasts sharply with the dark, deeply fissured trunk of the chestnut oak. The close bark of the tuliptree, the long loose strip of the shagbark hickory, and the little black flakes of the wild black cherry are all easy to identify. The bare twigs of the hop-hornbeams are slender and numerous. Those of the mockernut hickory are nearly finger-size and the crowns are open. Oaks are round-topped, tuliptrees are cone-shaped, and American elms, where they still exist, have vase or fan shapes. It is not difficult to identify trees in winter and their various shapes and shades add character to the landscape.

Pines and hemlocks, which were obscured by the verdant foliage of the hardwoods during the growing season, now stand out as bold, green masses against the background of grays and browns. They add a touch of color to the landscape and provide welcome protection to the animals which stay through the winter. During daylight hours, owls find the dense foliage to be good protection from the weather and from flocks of marauding crows. Small birds sit snug among the branches at night, safe from snow and wind. In some years northern finches come down in numbers, and seed from the cones provides an attractive food for some of these.

Winter is the season of greatest stress. As summer and autumn were seasons of relative ease and plenty for forest animals, late winter is a season of tension and scarcity. Food supplies dwindle and each period of bitter cold causes more damage. Many animals will not survive until spring, but this is not a waste. Each organism fulfills its function in the system whether its life is long or short. The effects of winter stress are frequently seen in population levels and productivity during the

Shagbark hickory has distinctive bark.

Cottontail tracks in snow

following spring and summer. However, there is a continuity which, in the long run, is served by the severity of the winter.

The transition from winter to spring, although eagerly anticipated by most of us, is not without its dangers. A few warm days in late winter may bring some organisms out of hibernation prematurely. Then the inevitable relapse to wintry weather poses an extra threat. Some plants may break dormancy too soon and buds may be killed during the next hard freeze. This changing season is a period of uncertainty, the most hazardous of the year. However, like all periods in the forest, it passes quickly and spring comes on apace, beginning the annual cycle anew and reaffirming the belief that, if not abused, the system is immortal.

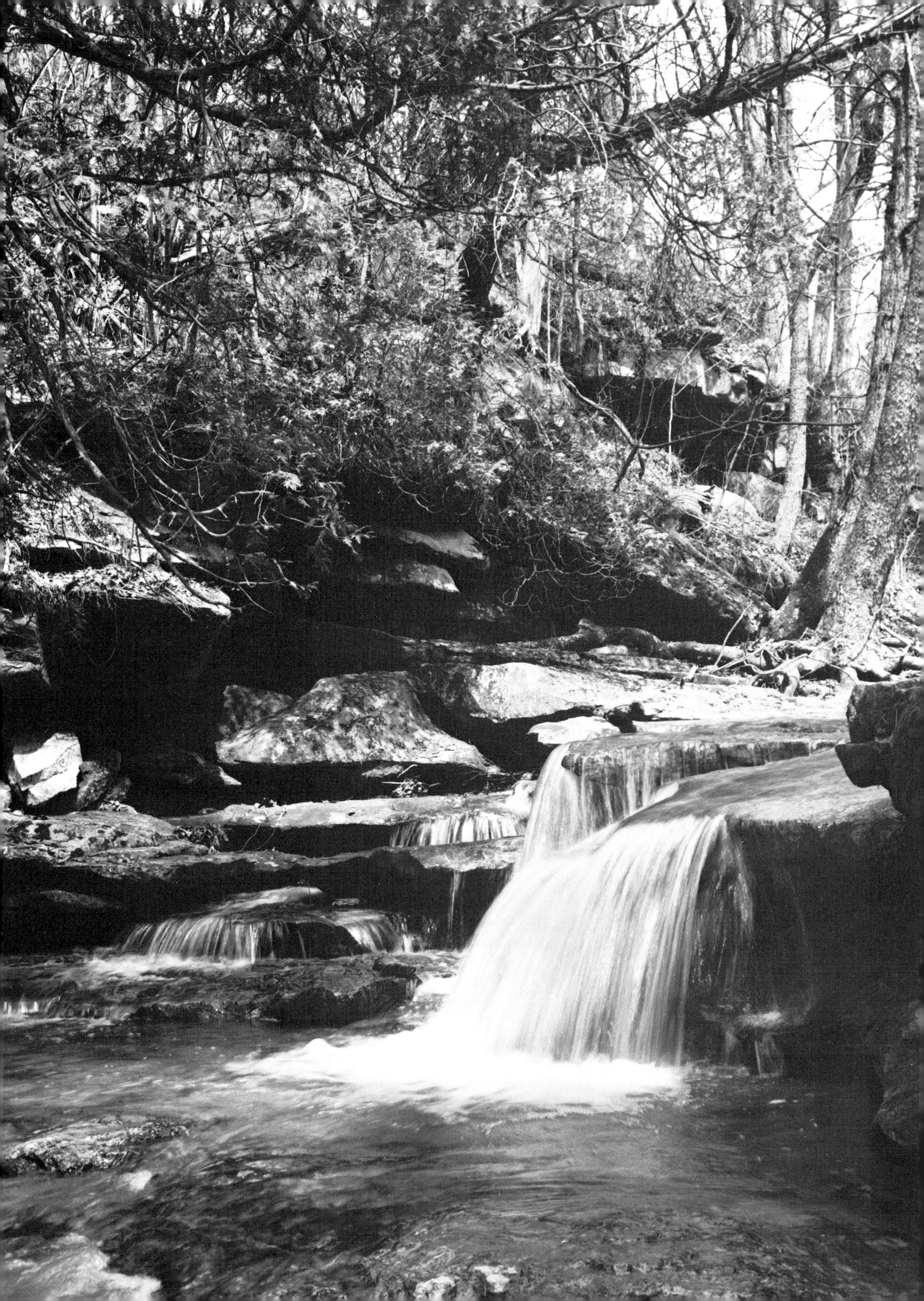

Chapter 8
Ohio Waters

WATER may be found flowing in streams, standing in ponds and lakes, crystallized as snow cover or hoarfrost, drifting as mist, fog and clouds, falling as rain and snow, moving through subterranean aquifers as ground water, or flowing forth as a bubbling spring on a hillside. Ohio has been blessed with an abundance of water and our uses of water seem without end. In addition to drinking, washing, and other domestic and industrial uses, we use our water resource for swimming, fishing, boating, and agriculture. And we all admire its natural beauty.

Without water Ohioans, of course, would be seeking another place to live — a place that had water. Life cannot exist without water. Living plants and animals are, in fact, composed mainly of water. Ohio's waters support a modern industrial and agricultural state in addition to an impressive number of wild species, nearly all of which were Ohio residents before humans arrived.

In Ohio there is an abundance of water in more than 3,300 named streams, and probably at least as many unnamed tributaries. The combined length of Ohio streams is over 44,000 miles — almost one mile of stream for every square mile of land. There are about 50,000 lakes, ponds, and reservoirs (over 200,000 acres of water) in the state in addition to the two and one half million acres of Lake Erie. All this is surface water and does not include the billions of gallons of ground water in Ohio's rich underground aquifers.

by David H. Stansbery
Michael B. Lafferty

Water has been an integral part of this planet since its beginning. For at least three billion years water has played a vital role in the development of life. It has been a primary factor in producing the kinds of plants and animals in the state today as well as the habitats in which they live.

Water—A Modern Miracle of Ancient Origin

A miracle is defined as "any wonderful or amazing thing." But the abundance of water on the earth's surface and the continual use of this resource by people has rendered it less amazing than otherwise. Several of its characteristics are not only unique but largely responsible for its importance on earth. For example, water has a tremendous capacity to retain heat. It absorbs heat and releases it much more slowly than does air. Thus, although the air temperature may change rapidly, the temperature of a deep lake changes much more slowly, sparing the aquatic plant and animal life the trauma of severe temperature changes. In contrast, the water temperature in a shallow pond is much closer to the temperature of the air above it. Streams which are constantly flowing and mixing with the air exchange heat with the atmosphere much more readily than do deep, quiet rivers, lakes, and flooded quarries.

Water becomes lighter or heavier, depending on the temperature. It is heaviest (most dense) at four degrees Celsius (39° F). As water cools from four degrees to its freezing point at 0 degrees, it becomes progressively lighter in weight. At the freezing point ice forms at the surface, and, being lighter than liquid water, it floats, serving as an insulator keeping heat in the water below. This characteristic, plus the large amount of heat retained by a relatively small volume of water, is the reason only shallow ponds freeze to the bottom. Natural waters are transparent to translucent, so sunlight penetrates most streams, ponds, and lakes. This light is used by green plants in photosynthesis. The growth of all green plants, from microscopic algae to submerged rooted macroscopic plants, is dependent on the sun as a daily source of light.

Oxygen, needed by nearly all life forms on earth, is soluble in water. Many minerals, also necessary for plant growth, dissolve in water and may be absorbed by plants growing there or may be transported downstream to other environments.

Nearly all of our universe is either flaming gas or frozen solid. The biosphere of the earth is largely the way it is because the temperature of the earth guarantees that most water here will exist as a liquid. Protoplasm — the stuff of life — is more than 80 percent water. Drying is dying, and life as we know it cannot exist without water. To be sure, some organisms do not need much of it to live. Lichens (tiny algae and fungi living together) live on cliff faces, tree bark, barren rocks, and other dry inhospitable places. Nevertheless, some water is still needed and the lichens would turn to dust without it.

Organisms sometimes benefit from what people consider too much or too little water. Droughts and floods help some organisms survive. Certain Australian fish reproduce only during annual floods. Some species of mayflies would never hatch if the water level of Lake Erie did not fall in winter. Because of reduced winter inflow, the water level of Lake Erie drops about three feet every winter. This drop exposes large

Clear Fork in Mohican State Park

Scud

areas of lake bottom near shore which freeze. The mayfly eggs on the bottom apparently require freezing if they are to hatch in the warming waters the following spring.

These periodic extremes are apparently just as necessary for the continued existence of certain aquatic species as is occasional burning of prairie areas in the case of some plant species. Even in severe droughts, water continues to flow in many streams. Although the gravel and cobbles of the stream bottom may be parched and dry, water may be flowing a few inches below the surface through the buried gravel of the streambed. That water will contain life — crustaceans, mollusks, annelid worms, aquatic insects, and other organisms most of which will survive until rains fill the stream again.

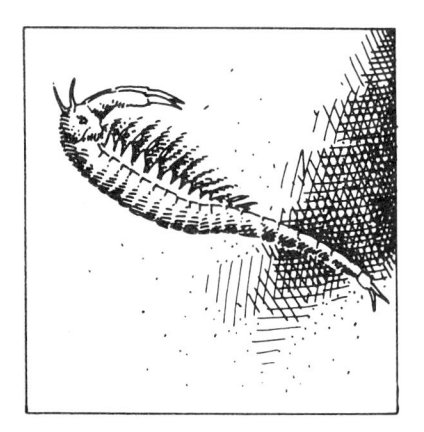

Fairy shrimp

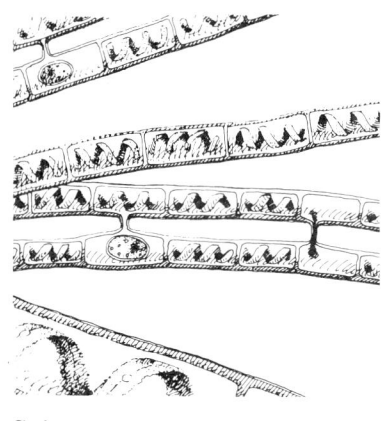

Spirogyra

A combination of two extremes — annual drying and freezing — is apparently necessary for tiny fairy shrimp to survive in the temporary ponds of Ohio. Fairy shrimp apparently hatch only after the pond water in which the eggs have been laid evaporates in summer, allowing them to dry, and then freezes during the next winter. The eggs of these little animals are especially common in roadside ditches and ponds in springtime. The long filamentous alga, *Spirogyra,* reproduces sexually only when ponds and other small bodies of water dry, or when the shoreline retreats leaving the alga temporarily high and dry.

Ohio Water—Origin, Nature, and Destiny

There is as much water on the earth now as there was one billion years ago. Our water circulates in complicated cycles. In Ohio, summer storms typically bring water-laden clouds from the Southwest. Water condenses and falls as rain. When it strikes the ground much of it soon evaporates back into the atmosphere. Some of it percolates into the soil and is absorbed by plants, and some forms rivulets that converge, becoming the headwater tributaries of our river systems. Tremendous quantites of water move through plants from the soil to the atmosphere by the process of transpiration. If an animal eats any part of a plant, the water may become part of the animal's body. This water in turn may be exhaled or excreted by the animal or, if the animal dies, it may pass to the bacteria and fungi of decay before returning to the non-living part of our environment.

Water not evaporating back into the atmosphere, not absorbed by plant roots, or flowing directly into a stream, may sink deeper into an underground aquifer. Even there, it does not stop moving. In aquifers of loose gravel and cobbles or jointed limestone it flows relatively fast, but in fine-grained sandstone aquifers where the particles of rock are much closer together, a century or more may be required for the water to move only a few feet.

Yet, the water is moving. About the only time water is not moving is when it is bound as ice in winter. Even then the water is only temporarily halted, and when temperatures rise in the spring, the ice melts and the water once again resumes its never-ending journey.

As the water flows through soil and rock, it dissolves soluble minerals. Water in nature is not just hydrogen and oxygen. Water includes a complex mix of dissolved minerals, suspended sediments, and, in most places today, fertilizers, pesticides, domestic sewage effluent, and industrial wastes. Water in Ohio also varies from alkaline in the glacial till plains of western and northern Ohio, to acidic in the sandstone, shale, and coal measures of the southeast. Natural waters have a tendency to be slightly acidic due to the formation of carbonic acid from the combination of carbon dioxide and water. Additional acidity comes from the decomposition of organic remains yielding humic and other organic acids. Limestones and dolostones neutralize some or all of this natural acidity, but it persists in regions lacking these buffering bedrocks. Thus the chemical nature of the soils and bedrock through which waters flow can alter their capacity to support various types of living organisms. Each tributary changes, more or less, the chemical composition of a river. Evaporation from the surface can increase concentrations during dry seasons while spring thaws may dilute these concentrations during times of high flow. The water chemistry of a river is never quite the same from place to place nor from time to time at any one place.

The Licking River in Licking and Muskingum counties, for example, has its headwaters in rich agricultural land in an area of glacial till. Although the surface soils are acidic, the underlying till contains small amounts of limestone which makes the headwaters alkaline. Water running into the Licking carries some soil sediment from the fields as well as nitrates, phosphates, and other farm fertilizers and pesticides. When the Licking flows through more heavily forested country farther east, just before it enters the Muskingum River it picks up less soil sediment and nutrients because the land, not suited for agriculture, has fewer farms and more forests. The run-off water is released more slowly from the heavily wooded slopes than from the farm fields up stream. Also, the impoundment of Dillon Dam acts as a settling basin, trapping sediments and their associated nutrients and pesticides. The river may also receive acid effluent from coal mines in the eastern portion of its watershed. Although its headwaters are in an area of low-lime glacial till in the Glaciated Appalachian Plateau, the lower reaches flow through unglaciated Ohio, and when its waters reach the Muskingum, they are less alkaline.

The constantly changing composition has a tremendous influence on aquatic life. Large amounts of acid will prevent many organisms from living in a stream. Fish from the acidic lakes and streams of eastern Ohio are frequently smaller and fewer in number than the same species from western Ohio. Some species of crawfish, mollusks, and other animals live only in certain stream systems. For example, crawfish in the upper Ohio Valley are still largely distributed according to pre-glacial drainage patterns, even though continental glaciation rearranged streams over a million years ago. These distribution patterns may be determined by water chemistry which is largely a product of bedrock and soils.

Water is rarely 100 percent pure. Even rain water contains minerals and acids. Sometimes we find the dust from windstorms occurring hundreds of miles away from the source, and we have detected radioactive fallout from nuclear explosions halfway around the world.

Problems may arise when the nutrients flowing into a stream or lake are excessive. An excess of certain nutrients can produce algal blooms — population increases far above normal. These plants, vital in normal concentrations, may deplete the available oxygen supply during warm summer nights, resulting in their deaths and that of other aquatic life before morning.

One of the greatest sources of excessive stream nutrients is raw sewage or the effluent of sewage treatment plants. Columbus, for instance, has had a tremendous impact on stream life in the Scioto River. Numerous species of naiad mollusks (mussels) lived in the Scioto River below Columbus in the early nineteenth century, but not one living specimen has been found between Columbus and Circleville in nearly half a century. The only apparent exception is not an exception at all. Living naiades were discovered in recent years just above Circleville. A careful investigation of what seemed to be a population of pollution-tolerant naiades showed that all were found living just downstream from the mouth of Big Darby Creek. They were living in creek water within the banks of the Scioto River but before the creek and river water had become mixed.

Old mollusk shells are easy to find in the river below Columbus. They dissolve slowly because the shells are lime-based and the river water,

Northern leaf shell, a naiad mollusk formerly found in the Scioto River but now extinct

Ulothrix algae

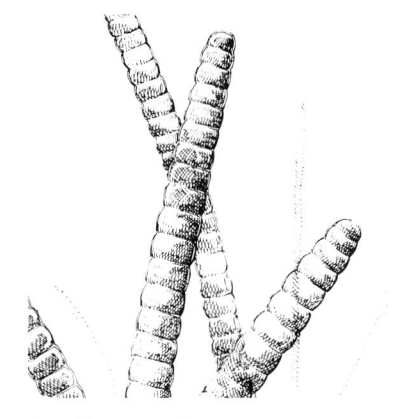

Oscillatoria algae

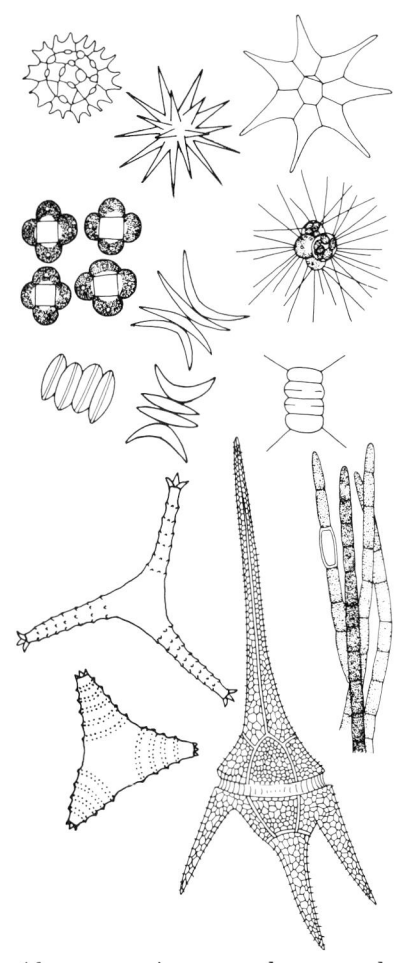

Algae come in many shapes and sizes

however polluted, is still alkaline. Historic accounts reveal that these mollusks have been dying in the lower Scioto since before 1858. The reasons are apparently too much organic sediment and clays from land clearing for early agriculture combined with the excessive nutrients from brewery slops, slaughter house offal, sawmill waste, sewage, and other pollutants generated by a developing city. What seems to have been a convenient means of waste disposal for a growing Columbus has been disastrous for much of the life of the river.

Sediment from poor farming practices, stripmining, and carelessly managed construction sites constitutes one of the worst pollutants. An excess of clays and silts can kill aquatic life just as surely as too many nutrients. Annually, many millions of tons of top soil erode into Ohio streams. The result is not just unattractive, muddy water. This turbidity blocks life-giving sunlight, keeping submergent aquatic plants from growing and thus reducing the supplies of food and oxygen required by both aquatic plants and animals. The silt may also cover eggs laid on the bottom by a host of animals, resulting in a great reduction or entire loss of the next crop of these species. The all too frequent reduction in reproduction of walleyes and certain other valuable fish may be explained (either directly or indirectly) by silt smothering the eggs of smaller fishes and other animals upon which they depend for food.

Water Life

If a stream has an ample supply of nutrients, oxygen, carbon dioxide, sunlight, and varied habitats it will usually support a rich variety of plants which, in turn, support a variety of animal species.

In Ohio, as elsewhere, the forms of aquatic life which make the food are the algae, other microscopic green plants, and higher green plants. These are the primary harvesters of solar energy and food producers — the plant life on which the animal life in a stream is based. Algae have been called the "grass of many waters," and rightfully so since these are the most abundant primary producers within the river. In the standing water of ponds and pools, tiny, thread-like strands of *Spirogyra* may be present, while masses of the alga *Cladophora* will be anchored to rocks where the current is swift. The algae exist literally in thousands of different forms from isolated cells in a bewildering variety of geometric forms — circles, triangle, ovals, crescents, and stars — colonies of long chains or filaments of cells, or the tiny spheres of fused cells. Some of these algal cells, known as diatoms, are among the most abundant of all forms of aquatic life. Despite their small size, collectively they add up to millions of tons in Ohio waters alone. Within the green chloroplasts of each cell, photosynthesis, powered by the light of the sun, transforms carbon dioxide and the hydrogen of water into simple sugar and oxygen. Research has demonstrated that photosynthesis under optimal conditions is the most efficient means of binding significant quantities of solar energy yet discovered, up to 30 percent conversion efficiency.

The plant life of a stream or pond is not distributed at random. While some species of algae are found throughout a pond or stream, each species is most abundant in that habitat where the conditions of living and reproducing are nearest to optimal. While many of the factors determining plant distribution are still unknown, a number of patterns reappear so often as to be predictable.

For example, close to a pond shore, the cattails and other rooted plants emerge from the water as much as several feet, while a little farther out grow water lilies and other rooted aquatics such as spatter dock, characterized by their floating leaves. Generally distributed in both of these zones is the duck weed, a free-floating plant, which frequently covers large areas in still water.

Beyond the water lilies in deeper water are the pondweeds characterized by species of *Potamogeton*. These plants are completely submerged except during blooming when a tiny white flower floats at the surface attached to the main plant by a slender stalk. The pondweeds are usually the last zone of rooted plants. Beyond them the water is usually so deep that not enough light reaches the bottom to support the growth of rooted aquatics. The deeper center of the pond contains free floating algae in open water.

Land plants can also play an extremely important role in supporting aquatic life in Ohio waters. This assist comes from literally millions of tree leaves as well as flowers, fruits, and seeds that fall or are blown into the water each autumn. The smaller streams are shaded bank to bank by tree branches, and each autumn thousands of tons of leaves fall into the streams where they decompose during the following winter, spring and summer. These leaves are important food for certain insects, crawfish, mollusks, and other aquatic animals. The shade is also important in shielding the water from the sun, thus keeping the stream temperature within the tolerance of the aquatic species present. Clear-cutting stream banks or flooding valley floors with dams destroys this important natural control.

Whether food is produced by plants on the banks or on or beneath the water, animals are the principal consumers. Herbivores feed directly upon the plants themselves. Examples include aquatic insects, annelid worms, mollusks, certain fishes, and amphibians, as well as some reptiles, birds, and mammals. Fish are the best known aquatic

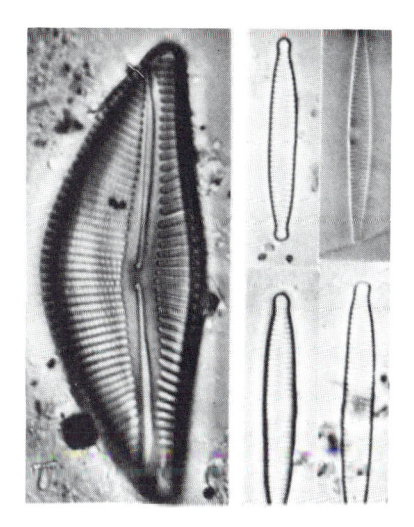

Diatoms

Backswimmer

Pond snail

Pumpkinseed sunfish

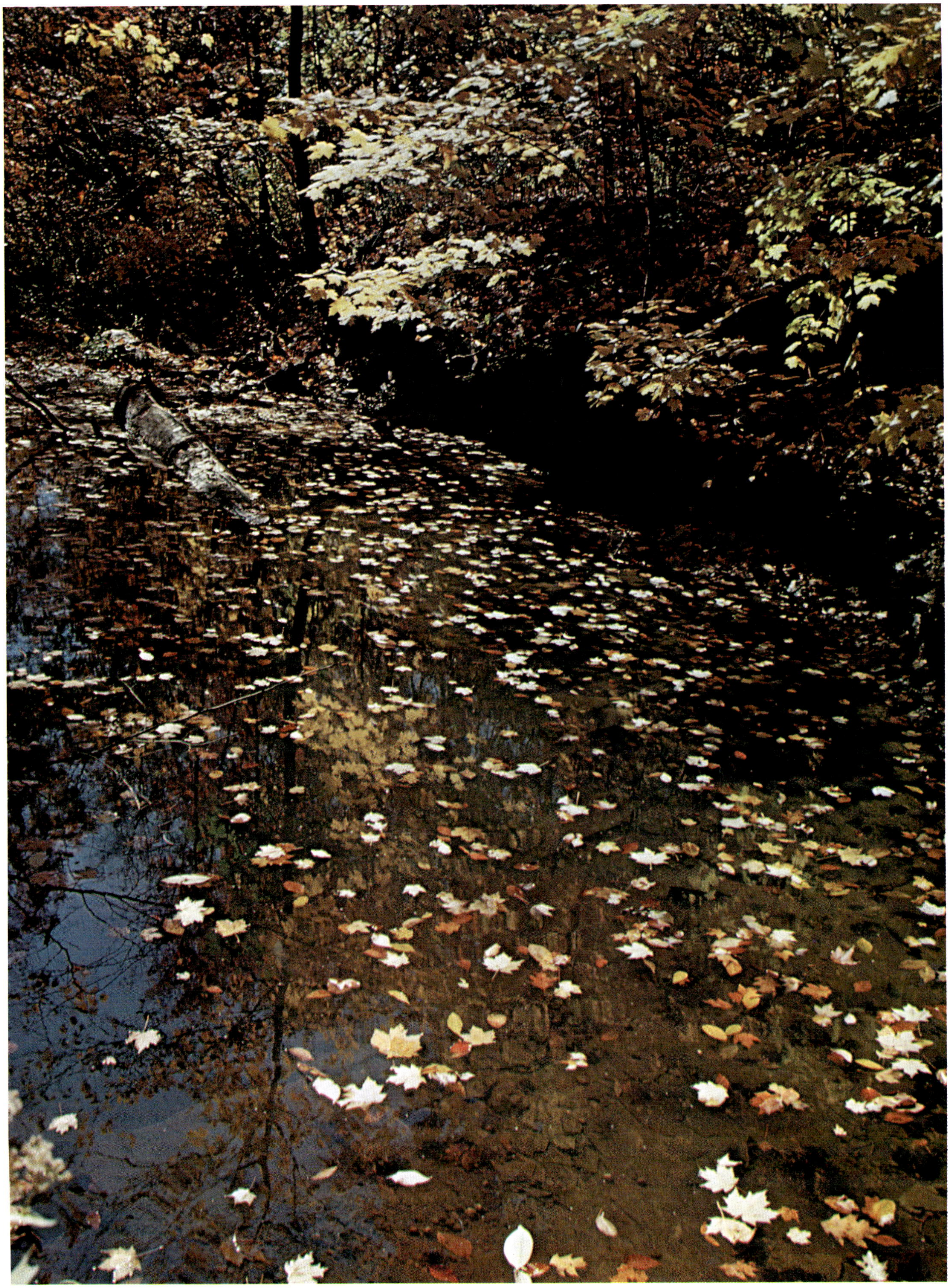

consumers. Some, such as the central stoneroller minnow, are essentially herbivores and feed mainly on algae and diatoms. Others such as the smallmouth black bass are carnivores and eat smaller fishes and other aquatic animals such as crawfish and insects.

The crawfish is a good example of an omnivore which is able to feed largely on what is readily available. Any animal tissue available gets first priority, but plant material is typically far more abundant; and, being non-motile, it is far more available, making the crawfish a functional herbivore. These 10-legged crustaceans can grow from hatching to mature, reproducing adults in a single summer, thus making them one of nature's most rapid means of transforming green plants into fish flesh. It becomes obvious that if we wish to maintain numbers of harvestable fish, attention must first be given to plant production and invertebrate production of the kinds necessary to support the carnivores desired for the table. Fish production thus involves much more than just fish.

In most natural bodies of water only a small fraction of the matter and energy bound up as living organisms is utilized for human food. These organisms are of far more value to people in other ways.

Although the substance of many of these plants becomes herbivore which eventually becomes carnivore, much is "lost" along the way since not all organisms become the food of other creatures. But, regardless of the pathway taken, the organic compounds that make up the body of every organism are eventually reduced to the simple inorganic compounds used by plants in making new protoplasm. Thus the material elements of each ecosystem are continuously recycled through what have come to be called biogeochemical cycles. Although the substance of this cycle may remain largely or entirely within the system, the energy needed to make the machine go is light. This energy is bound up by green plants at the energy harvester or food producer level and converted into other energy forms as it is transferred from level to level through the food web of the community. The second law of thermodynamics operates here just as it does in machine systems designed by humans. The light energy from the sun becomes the heat energy of the ecosystem by the time the molecules carrying it are reduced once again to carbon dioxide and water, the raw materials of photosynthesis.

If it were not for the small but essential bacteria and fungi of decay, the world would be filled with the undecomposed bodies of all those plants and animals that have gone before us. The natural resource of one or more materials required for new life would have been depleted, and all life on earth would have ended. The agents of decay are equally important if the producers of our biosphere are to continue to function properly.

The processes of food synthesis and energy conversion — photosynthesis, ingestion, digestion, assimilation, metabolism, growth, death, decay, and recycling — are part of the continuing dynamics of every ecosystem on earth. Algae grow and are then eaten by herbivorous insects which are consumed by a hungry darter. Or, the plant may die and be broken down by fungi or bacteria. A young bass may eat the darter which ate the insect which fed upon the algae and, in turn, be eaten by a mink or other mammal. The eggs of a common shiner may make a meal for a crawfish who will be eaten by a queen snake which becomes part of the diet of a great blue heron.

Above the water, an adult dragon fly may be feeding in flight on mosquitoes, which escaped the roving bass when they were larvae, only

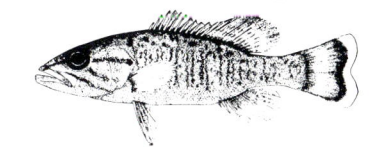

Northern smallmouth bass

Crawfish

Water snake preys on a frog

Dragonfly

A large amount of organic matter including leaves annually falls into streams. Through decay and direct feeding this material is incorporated into the food web of the stream (opposite page).

Bull frog

to be delivered to the gullet of a hungry bull frog if the dragonfly flies too low. It can all seem very confusing until each organism is fitted into its place (or places) in the community food web and viewed as one point of many along the pathway of a number of biogeochemical cycles.

Water Environments— The Aquatic Systems

Aquatic biologists have divided freshwater systems into two large groups, depending upon whether the water is standing as ponds or lakes or flowing as creeks and rivers. Although the combined length of all our flowing systems is great, Ohio has far more water as ponds and lakes. Human efforts to transform parts of streams, at least temporarily, into bodies of essentially standing water have added greatly to Ohio's resource of flat water. However, this has been done at the expense of free-flowing streams and the great diversity of aquatic life they contained.

Streams

Look at the stream map of Ohio and it is easy to see certain similarities in the various stream systems which drain the state. The strongest impression is the tree-like branching characteristics of most streams. The main river forms the trunk of the tree. Other, smaller streams flow

Surface Water Resources In Ohio

into this trunk and a maze of small brooks flow into these tributaries. As more and more tributaries join the main river, the volume of water increases. As the flow increases, the water cuts a wider and deeper channel accomodating the increased volume of flow.

A river which has been flowing over a stabilized land surface for a long period of time is one of the few things that can be young, middle-aged, and old at the same time. Rivers grow toward their sources, so the headwaters are the youngest part of a stream, typically flowing rapidly through steep sided, v-shaped valleys. Farther downstream, the river widens and flows in gentle curves through broader valleys. In its lowest reaches near its mouth the river is oldest and widest. Here the water flows in sweeping meanders through a nearly flat plain down a broad-floored valley where the surrounding hills are nearly worn away by erosion.

Most Ohio streams do not demonstrate this typical pattern of development throughout their length because most have been affected by glaciation rather recently in their geologic history. Not enough time has elapsed since the ice melted for them to have developed fully the typical river pattern although sections of most Ohio rivers do show various stages of this development.

Headwaters. In southwestern Ohio, the main stem of the Little Miami River flows south for 105 miles through rich farm land and wooded hills to the Ohio River east of Cincinnati. This stream is one of the most attractive in Ohio. The 64-mile reach from Foster in Warren County to Clifton in Greene County has been designated as Ohio's first national scenic river, and the entire river is a state scenic river.

The Little Miami has a complex geologic history with some sections occupying pre- and inter-glacial valleys while other sections occur in valleys carved by the stream during post-glacial time. It rises in Clark County northeast of Clifton as a series of springs which create brooks draining small watersheds in the surrounding low hills. Here the river is really a dendritic pattern of small creeks none of which is over a few feet wide. The gradient is relatively steep near the headwaters but soon becomes gradual as the meandering waters flow over a bottom of glacial deposits containing considerable gravel. The water is clear and cool and supports a variety of organisms. Water pennies, small flat insect larvae, are found under rocks in the riffles, while mayfly nymphs, stoneflies, crawfish, chubs, and darters provide food for game fish including smallmouth bass and rockbass. The plant life is primarily diatoms, other algae, and water willow.

At Clifton, about 15 miles below the headwaters, the Little Miami plunges into a deep narrow gorge which widens somewhat and continues for about four miles through John Bryan State Park. In the gorge just below the most narrow section, the river resembles a mountain stream with long runs—stretches of fast flowing water unbroken by rocks. The bottom of a run is covered with coarse gravel and sand because the water is flowing too fast for much silt and other fine particles to be deposited. Algae are the principal water plants in the gorge but there are more kinds of fish and other riverine animals.

Below the gorge, the runs give way to a riffle-run-pool sequence. More emergent aquatic plants grow along shore. Cattails may be found here as well as arrowhead and water plantain. However, these plants are not particularly common as they are often washed away in the spring after heavy rains send water cascading through the gorge. The animal life also is more varied. In the pools and riffles largemouth bass and spotted bass may be found feeding on food which washes down in the fast water.

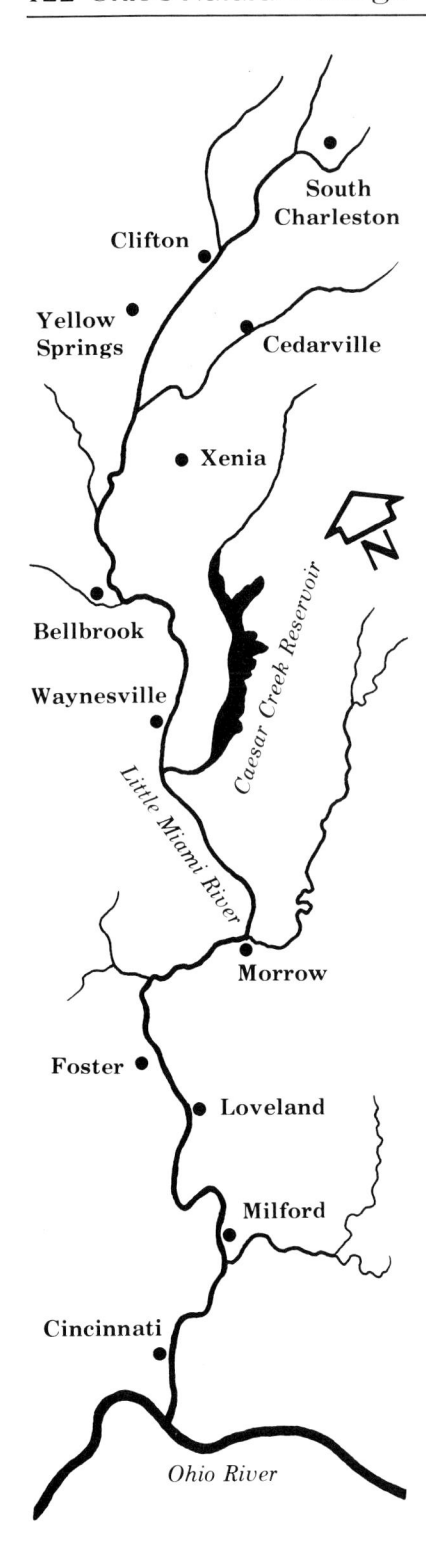

The Little Miami River in southwestern Ohio

Stonefly

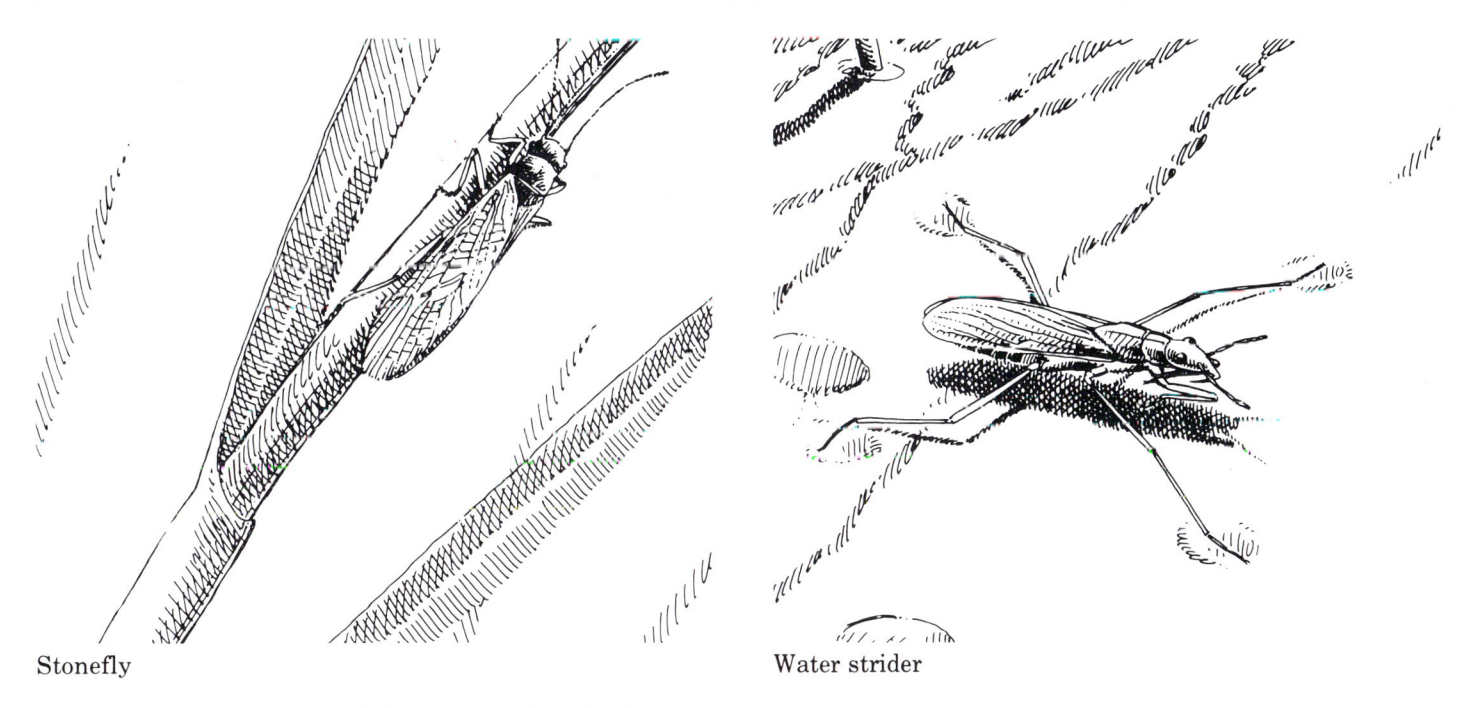

Water strider

Larger fish such as catfish are found in the larger pools which may be as much as 20 feet deep.

Middle Reaches. With the exception of "The Narrows" just west of Xenia and the steep wooded slopes east of Bellbrook, most of the country between the lower end of the gorge and Waynesville is gently rolling farm land. The river with a wider channel flows in broad lazy curves in a valley which is a mile wide in many places.

The river here contains long stretches of runs interspersed with elongated pools and riffles. Water in riffles is typically shallow and flows rapidly over cobbles and gravel, mixing freely with the air. Water below a riffle is usually rich in oxygen. The bottom of a riffle is typically composed of larger sediments such as boulders or cobbles because the water flows too fast for many fine sediments to settle. However, some silts and fine sands may be found in the quiet water beneath and between the boulders and cobbles. As the gradient lessens and the water slows, sands and gravels are deposited forming bars and beds on the river bottom. Peak diversity of animal life in a river is usually found associated with the larger riffles and runs, and this is the case in the Little Miami.

From the mouth of Ceasar Creek in northeast Warren County to Loveland in northwest Clermont County, the valley narrows considerably and in some sections forms a gorge.

Lower Reaches. Near Milford, the Little Miami flows into an area where there is seemingly no movement at all. Short stretches of faster water do exist between Milford and the Ohio River, but most of the river here is a series of long pools formed where the gradient is almost nonexistent. Pools may be large where the higher riverbed downstream acts as a low dam, or pools may be small deep holes in the river bottom. The deepest portions of a river do not contain the greatest diversity of life in the stream, but the pool margins of the lower Little Miami do contain a variety of emergent plants which serve as cover for the larger fishes.

Water is frequently muddy in the lower reaches of the river. Silt from farm land and construction sites upstream is washed into the system and settles to the bottom of quiet pools. This accumulation of sediment may smother those benthic (bottom-dwelling) animals not able to work

The Little Miami River Gorge just west of Clifton

Snapping turtle

Leech and hydra

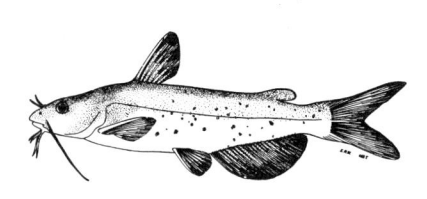

Channel catfish

their way to the surface of the ooze. The oxidizing of organic sediment also reduces the amount of free oxygen available to the living animals present. However, some forms with broad tolerance such as certain leeches, crawfish, catfish, and carp, may thrive in the new habitat. They thrive largely because of increased food and habitat which were previously used by those species which can no longer exist under these adverse conditions.

River impoundments. The Little Miami joins the Ohio River east of Cincinnati. Master stream for a portion of southwestern Ohio, the Little Miami is itself a tributary of the master stream of the east-central United States. The Ohio River at Cincinnati is in an intermediate stage of development. During settlement time, there were several rapids in this huge river at Cincinnati and Louisville. Flatboats could only pass over them during high water.

As river commerce became more profitable, a system of dams and locks was constructed enabling barges to use the Ohio year-round. These dams changed the nature of the river. After the dams were closed, the Ohio was transformed from its natural characteristic of riffle, run, pool to a series of continuous pools. Today, the Ohio River is a series of elongated pond-like impoundments which have fewer river characteristics.

The broader and deeper a river impoundment is the more like a large pond or lake it becomes. Yet, perhaps the most critical difference between river and lake is the strength of the current. The current of a free-flowing river mixes, aerates, and transports its water in ways only feebly duplicated by most lakes. Lakes on the other hand have the capacity to trap sediments and their associated organic nutrients in the substrate for long periods of time, while any one section of a river may loose all or most of this material with each season of high flow.

Both our long-lived rivers and our ephemeral lakes and ponds have value. In our modifications of these waters we should carefully assess the duration of these changes, basing our decisions not only upon present costs and benefits over the next few decades but upon those which will affect our descendants for hundreds and even thousands of years in the future.

Lakes and Ponds

Streams are constantly cutting down their beds, staying young in the headwaters and becoming older downstream at the same time. But the same cannot be said about lakes and ponds. Once formed, these totally enclosed bodies of water begin a transformation, filling gradually with silt and plant-animal debris until their open waters become a bog, marsh, or swamp, and finally a low damp place in the earth. In some regions where the rate of filling is relatively rapid the eventual "death" of a pond can be completed in the span of a human generation or two. In colder climates, hundreds or even thousands of years may be needed.

A true lake, in the strict sense of the term, is completely enclosed by land and has no outlet. Streams may flow into a lake, but the water leaves by evaporation from the surface or by transpiration through its emergent vegetation. Ohio has very few bodies of water which meet these criteria. Most natural bodies of water, such as Nettle Lake in Williams County and the Portage Lakes in Summit County, have characteristics of a true lake yet remain part of a stream system. Most of Ohio's "lakes" have been made by damming streams and most "ponds"

An Ohio pond

are constructed farm ponds. Lake Erie is not a true lake but may be more accurately thought of as a wide pool in the main stem of the St. Lawrence River system.

Ohio has relatively few natural ponds, although they are more numerous than its lakes. Hydrologists do not agree on the definition of a pond, but in Ohio, ponds are best thought of as small lakes.

Ohio's true lakes and ponds were nearly all formed by the glaciers which once covered most of the state. The true lakes and ponds were formed during the glacial retreat when large blocks of ice, some weighing millions of tons, broke off the retreating glacier and were surrounded or even covered by glacial outwash and till sediments. The ice melted, producing a pond called a "kettle."

Small kettles dot glaciated Ohio, especially in the northeast. Today many of these ponds have aged to the point where they are bogs, swamps, or marshes. Some have filled completely. All that remains to document their existence are low, moist depressions where the soil is

White crappie

Red-winged blackbird

dark with humus and the higher, greener vegetation reflects the rich store of nutrients and abundant water in the soil below.

New ponds have open water with little or no obvious vegetation. However within a short time, the ponds become very lively places with both submergent and emergent vegetation invading.

A pond disappears over the years but always from the shore towards the center. As the years pass, a pond slowly fills with silt and organic debris. Some of this organic debris may decompose, turning the pond bottom to muck. The more the pond fills, the more land plants encroach. After a few years, red-winged blackbirds perch on cattails where once only water-lilies grew, and the water-lilies in turn are found farther out where once only the crimped-leaf pondweed was found. Eventually shrubs and saplings are growing where once there was water.

True ponds and lakes age in this fashion. Lake Erie and other large bodies of water which have current also age like this, but the anology goes only so far. Lake Erie is really more a connecting river between the upper Great Lakes and Lake Ontario. It has a current flowing generally west to east, downhill from the upper Great Lakes to the St. Lawrence River. As the lake ages, it will likely follow the classic pattern until after some thousands of years, the filling will have decreased the cross-section of flow enough that the current becomes strong enough to carry away the sediment presently being deposited. Lake Erie will never completely fill up but will become a meandering river flowing across a broad flat plain.

In addition to the relatively few lakes and kettles left by glaciation, Ohio has more than 50,000 farm ponds. These ponds were constructed as catch basins to provide water for livestock, recreation, and fire protection. Farm ponds have provided many farm families a first-hand view of pond succession literally at their doorstep. The ponds, if left unmanaged, would have the same fate as our glacial kettles. There is a point in pond succession where use of the pond for fishing, boating, swimming, and as a water source is maximal. Owners usually wish to perpetuate or at least prolong this highly productive stage. This calls for management techniques which will stop or reduce siltation and filling. This means reducing the silt-concentration in the incoming water as well as reducing those types of vegetation which accumulate faster than they are recycled through decomposition. Controlled harvesting of the fish populations, fertilizing, restocking, water-level adjustment, and a host of other techniques have been used to extend the time of maximal productivity and to transform a near-natural pond succession into a continuing experiment in productive pond aquaculture. While we may mourn the loss of marsh and swamp species that the farm pond may have supported, we also benefit from the open pond species and the associated benefits produced when succession is slowed to a minimum at a relatively young state. Ohio needs both pond types for many reasons, and ideally each farmer will understand the benefits of each.

The advent of interstate highways brought an upsurge in the creation of "borrow" or "barrow" pits where road builders obtained fill materials for road grading. Since the water table in these areas is usually fairly high, nearly all of these pits filled with water and became ponds. Most of these ponds are only several acres in size. Nevertheless, they contain many of the same plants and animals found in natural ponds, and they provide an excellent opportunity to see pond succession in action.

In addition, Ohio has several large lakes which were once part of the State's transportation network but now serve as important recreational areas. These impoundments are the old canal lakes such as Lake St. Marys, Indian Lake, Lake Loramie, Guilford Lake, and Buckeye Lake. Once large kettles, they were ideal to dam because they were near the Ohio River-Lake Erie divide and could supply water to the canal system. The lake water was used to maintain the water levels in the state's canal system in the early nineteenth century. Today the approximately 25,000 acres in the five lakes are maintained for swimming, boating, fishing and other recreation. These canal lakes are all extremely shallow and aging very rapidly. Silt-laden streams enter from the surrounding rich farm land and the silt settles out in the ponded lake water, so the lakes must be dredged constantly or else become marshes.

Lake Erie borders most of the northern margin of Ohio and is the only body of water in the state which has (or did have) truly big lake fish species. Erie gained fame as the site of the richest freshwater fishery in the world, and it may well have been. The flow of nutrients into the lake in the form of domestic sewage, agricultural runoff (supplemented by farm fertilizers in more recent years) increased this productivity of highly desirable food fishes (whitefish, cisco, blue pike, and walleye) until the capacity of the lake to dilute the incoming nutrients was overwhelmed. Many species of fishes and other aquatic animals are now either extirpated from the lake or reduced to their lowest levels in history. Other species, having wider ranges of tolerance, have not only been able to survive but have greatly increased in number. The productivity of Lake Erie as measured in pounds of fish per acre per year may well be at an all time high. What has been lost in species diversity

Diving beetle

A planarian

Painted turtle

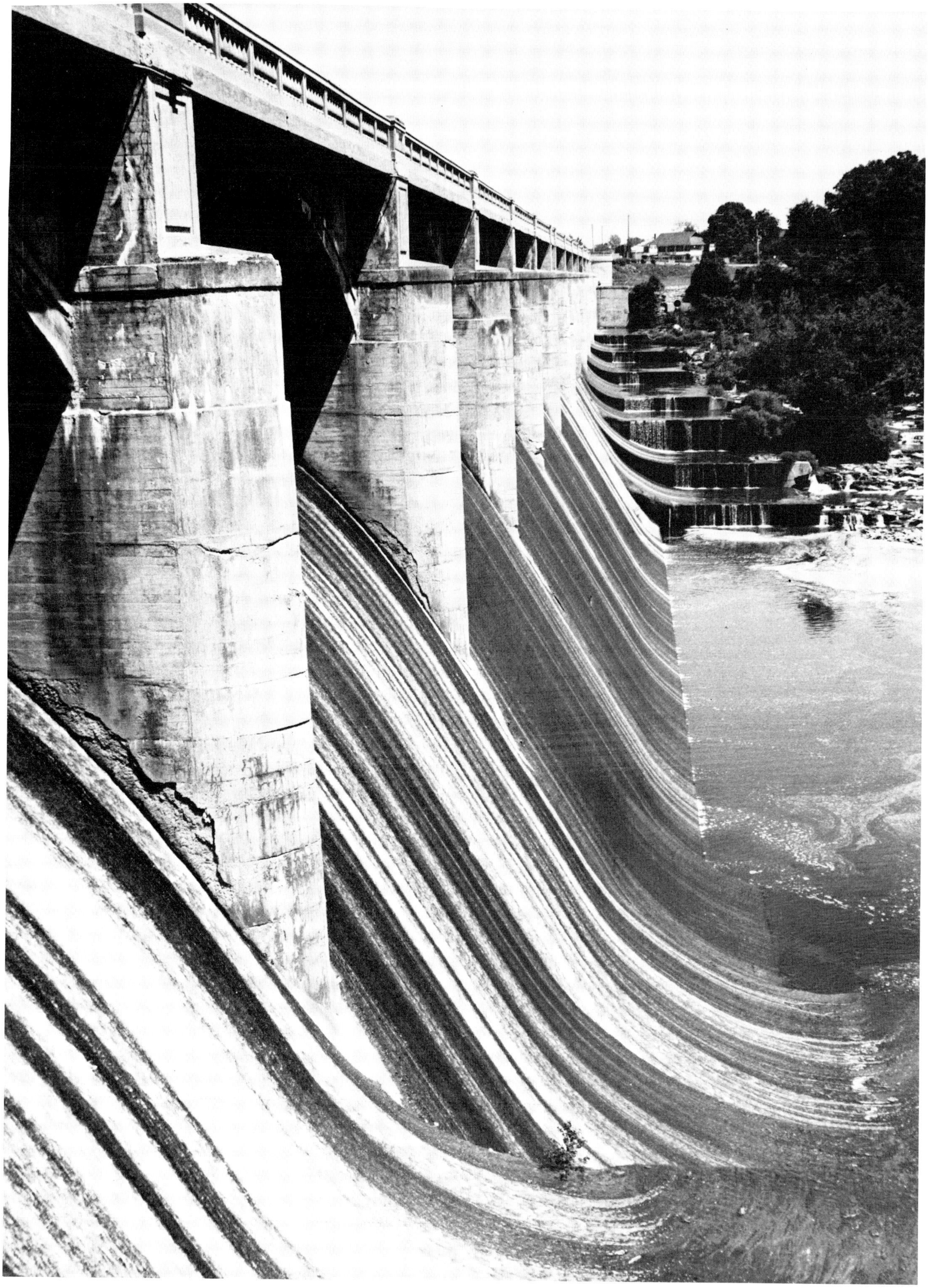

appears to have been replaced by increased numbers of those species which find the present habitat more suitable than that which existed previously.

Changes in Aquatic Habitats

The Ohio waters found here by our pioneer ancestors several centuries ago have been greatly changed by the growing and industrious generations which followed. Society's goal has been largely one of devising more and more efficient means of transforming the seemingly endless supply of natural resources into processes and products of immediate benefit. These resources included rivers, creeks, lakes, and ponds. Somewhere in *Green Laurels* Peattie expresses the essence of this attitude by noting that it was the ambition of every pioneer woman to make 10 tall sons grow where only one Native American had been before. This we have done and more! We have benefited enormously from technological ingenuity. But we have also paid a price that we are only now beginning to realize.

The natural development of our streams seems certain to continue despite the temporary human modifications of channelizing, impounding, and polluting. The Tigris and Euphrates rivers of Mesopotamia have been canalized, impounded, and otherwise modified by a series of civilizations, and yet they continue to flow much as they did in prehistoric time. Such gains as were secured by the river modifiers were paid for later by those who lived through the periods of recovery initiated by eroding dams and silt-filled canals and impoundments. But points of "no return" were not passed insofar as the hydraulic characteristics of the rivers were concerned. The rivers did recover. Physically and chemically they closely resemble their historic namesakes. But what of the species that once lived in these streams? Perhaps our greatest concern should be of passing points of no return in the extinction of aquatic species.

Most of the search by humans among wild species for forms which might be of benefit to society has been centered upon those plants and animals which were sought out and used when people survived by hunting and gathering. Some of these species have been domesticated. Most are large forms of rather obvious use. These include many trees, and a number of larger mammals and birds.

Through genetic selection humans have "improved" those plants and animals already brought into domestication, but the search for additional benefits from other wild species has scarcely begun. There are only a few hundred domesticated forms, compared to over 300,000 species of wild plants and well over a million species of wild animals. Each of these is a potential resource. Each is unique. The extinction of any one of these is a point of no return. Whatever benefit they may have had for people is gone forever if they become extinct.

The primary cause of extinction in both aquatic and terrestrial species is generally agreed to be habitat destruction. This becomes particularly important when we note that only two percent of the earth's surface is fresh water, and the number of different species living in freshwater habitats is far greater than the number living in the oceans. Most of the freshwater is lake habitat lacking most stream species. Note also that our rivers and streams are almost without exception the recipients of domestic sewage, treated and otherwise; industrial sewage containing a wide variety of toxins; and agricultural run-off rich in fertilizers,

The O'Shaughnessy Dam near the Columbus zoo on the Scioto River (opposite page)

The redside dace is restricted to small clear streams with bottoms of clean gravel, sand, or bedrock. Such habitat must be maintained for this species to survive.

pesticides, and silt. Our rivers, indispensable as a source of water, are very susceptible to degradation (a pollutant upstream can foul the river for many miles below that point), and have been indiscriminately used as sewers for both liquid and solid refuse. Many species have been eliminated from many Ohio streams. Although this problem has long been recognized only in recent years has any effective remedial action been taken.

The recovery of species diversity in Ohio streams depends almost entirely upon habitat restoration. This restoration, hopefully, will be accomplished through technological and social advances which will modify population patterns and lead to land uses which will utilize and preserve the environment rather than deplete it. For example, populations need to be distributed so that one area is not overburdened with more people than its carrying capacity. Techniques should be developed which will enable water to be stored underground with a minimum of physical structures. Building on flood plains should be controlled and these areas should be used for parks, nature preserves, and farming. Waste should be recognized as a resource material and should be recycled for continued use. Farming techniques minimizing loss of humus-rich topsoil into streams should continue to be developed and used.

These are only a few of the opportunities to improve Ohio waters that are available to this and future generations. No generation in the past has possessed such extensive knowledge that can be put to use preserving, restoring, and wisely using our rivers, ponds, and lakes for the benefit of humans and other creatures of the biosphere.

Our present problem is not so much one of learning how to preserve, restore, or modify; it is one of determining what to preserve, what to restore, and what and how much to modify in what ways. Ohio has a great many people and each may have a somewhat different idea of what should be done with each body of water. A large part of our responsibility is insuring that our individual and collective needs are met and that our wants are dealt with justly and wisely.

The efforts of Ohioans to preserve aquatic habitats have been far more successful in the case of ponds, bogs, swamps, and marshes than in the case of rivers. The Division of Natural Areas and Preserves of the Ohio Department of Natural Resources has made a start in setting aside samples of Ohio's various standing-water habitats for posterity. Though sometimes difficult, it is usually possible to purchase or obtain an easement on the land surrounding a marsh and, through ownership or legal agreement, to prevent its being either drained or prematurely filled.

A river, however, extends in long dendritic patterns over many meandering miles of countryside. Its resources may, in some degree, be the property of many tens, hundreds, or even thousands of landowners who reside along its banks and who may not be inclined to share the wealth to which they claim title. There is a common saying having some basis in fact that what is public property is frequently treated as nobody's property. Ohio's Scenic River Program in the Division of Natural Areas and Preserves provides a necessary first step toward the protection of the natural values of selected rivers.

The river transport of sediments to the sea is a wholly natural process. Neither was it initiated by humans, nor can people halt it. What we can do is change its rate but, hopefully, only where a consideration of all long-term values indicates that this is wise. Too many solutions have produced far greater problems than the original problems they were designed to solve. We need to apply more of our available knowledge to future problems than did those who came before us.

Stream dredging for industrial aggregate or for ease of barge traffic also destroys much of the stability of the stream substrate. The resulting loss in bottom-dwelling (benthic) organisms may persist for decades after the disturbance. It is frequently reflected in decreased populations of those free-swimming forms that depend upon benthic species as a food source. In too many instances these plants and animals have never returned. We must decide, in each instance, where the greater value lies.

Ohio's natural landscape, including its rivers and lakes, is the result of the interaction of a number of major factors over an unimaginable span of time. *Climate*, acting upon *bedrock* and *glacial deposits,* has, in conjunction with *plant* and *animal* life, produced the present *soils* and *waters*. All seven factors should be taken into consideration during the planning process for the future of Ohio's waters. People may obtain benefits by modifying parts of natural systems — domestic water supplies are a good example. Other benefits can only be obtained by maintaining some bodies of water in a natural state. Our eagerness to modify rivers in the past led to the extirpation of many aquatic species from Ohio and to the extinction of several others. These extinct species will forever stand as a reminder of what can happen if we become overzealous or complacent again.

Our opportunities are great because of the wealth of the water resources that remain, because of our knowledge gleaned in large part from experience itself, and because or our greater appreciation of the range of values offered by Ohio's natural waters.

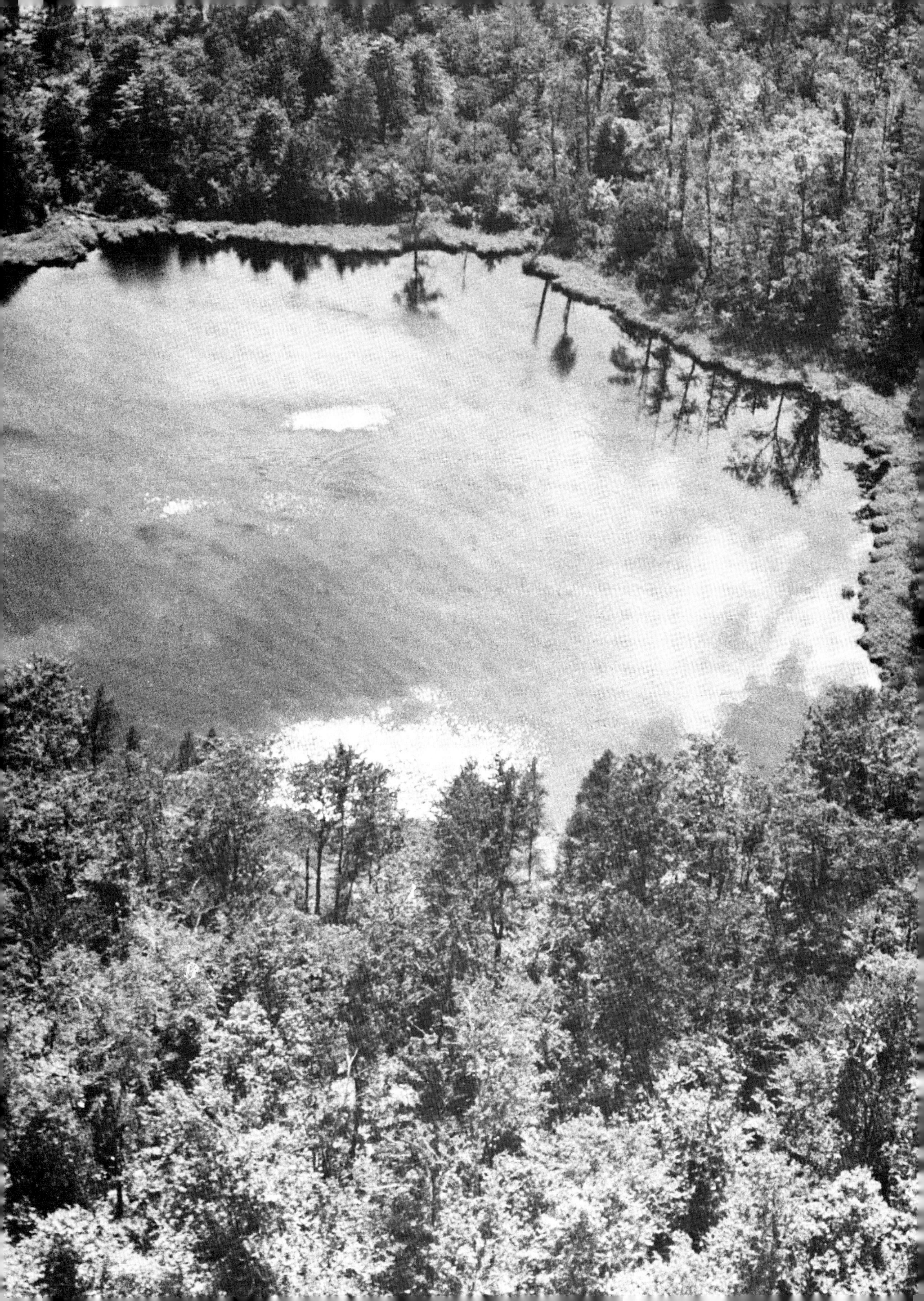

Chapter 9
Relicts of the Past

THE forest is the dominant natural community of Ohio's landscape. But scattered here and there are prairies, bogs, and caves — natural jewels which add tremendous diversity to the pool of plant and animal life.

Ohio's prairies, product of an ancient, dry climate, are the farthest eastward extension of the grasslands which blanketed North America from the foothills of the Rockies to the eastern deciduous forest. Bogs are water-logged relicts of the Ice Age which contain many northern species and add immeasurably to the diversity of the outdoors. Caves too are products of ancient weather and geologic processes, and the unique features and life within them are aspects of Ohio's natural heritage that most people never see.

by
K. Roger Troutman
Guy L. Denny
Roger W. Brucker

Prairies
K. Roger Troutman

In pioneer times, there were more than 300 grass-dominated, treeless prairies in Ohio, mostly in the western half, ranging in size from a few acres to more than several townships. They were really small versions of the more extensive grasslands in the West. In Ohio there were about

1,000 square miles of prairie encompassing about two and one half percent of the land area.

Settlers considered Ohio prairies unsuitable for farming reasoning that land incapable of supporting trees must be infertile. Furthermore, fuel and building materials had to be transported from the surrounding woods. Wet prairies often became impassable quagmires during heavy rains. During dry periods, fire sometimes swept the landscape, destroying animals unable to outrun the flames or find refuge underground. During fall and winter the tall, thick or matted grass made travel difficult, and early attempts to plow the soil were thwarted by the thick, tough prairie sod. Only after drainage systems were perfected, fires controlled, and the steel plow invented, were the prairies conquered and settled.

Gray-headed coneflower

Origin of the Prairie Ecosystem

Mid-American prairies began forming 25 to 50 million years ago after the Rocky Mountains uplifted. The mountains interrupted the flow of humid ocean winds blowing east, and through the eons, plants which were adapted to the drier climate replaced the ancient forests. The seemingly endless sea of grass which succeeded the woodlands covered more than a million square miles and extended from the foothills of the Rockies in central Texas, north to Alberta, then east until the rains from the Gulf of Mexico moderated the climate in the Ohio River basin.

The interior North American grasslands are of two basic types. Mixed prairies are characterized by annual rainfalls of less than 25 inches and lie mostly west of the 98th meridian. The dominant grasses are sparse and seldom grow higher than 18 inches. To the east are the tallgrass or true prairies. Two hundred years ago, this type covered about 400,000 square miles. Grasses along the eastern tallgrass boundary are especially impressive with big bluestem often gracefully waving at heights up to 10 feet. The extensive root systems of these giant grasses and the constant addition of organic matter from dead plants, made the soils in this region deep, dark, and among the most productive on earth. This eastern portion extends into Ohio and is part of the prairie-forest border or tension zone. Within this zone before settlement, the grasslands increased in area during droughts, only to be reinvaded by forests during wet periods.

No one knows when prairies first developed in Ohio. They may have existed in unglaciated Ohio before or between the glacial advances. It is certain that the climate became warmer and drier following the end of Wisconsinan glaciation, and that oak and hickory forests succeeded spruce and fir throughout much of eastern North America. The warming trend continued and about 4,000 years ago when semiarid conditions prevailed in what is known as the Xerothermic Period, prairies expanded eastward into the state. This extension, known as the Prairie Peninsula, covered an area generally east of the Missouri River, south of the Great Lakes, and north of the Ohio River. Edgar N. Transeau, a botanist at The Ohio State University, mapped the Prairie Peninsula and popularized the term in 1935.

In time, the climate became more humid and the forest advanced west once more. By the late 1700s, the continuous prairie had retreated to the Indiana-Illinois border, leaving isolated pockets called outliers in Ohio, Indiana, and Michigan. Today, eastern prairie exists only where one or

Indian grass

more environmental factors such as periodic fire, high evaporation rates, seasonal flooding, dry soils, or extreme topography prevent the growth of trees.

Few presettlement prairies survive in Ohio and most prairie remnants have been invaded by woody plants and Eurasian weeds. Tallgrass prairies are now found mainly on sites that are frequently very wet or very dry such as marsh borders, river bluffs, steep slopes, railroad and highway rights-of-way, and abandoned cemeteries. Even these areas are no longer exempt from modern management practices. Good prairies continue to disappear because of drainage changes, soil disturbances, overgrazing, herbicide use, and long periods without burning. Considering the amount of tallgrass prairie that existed less than 200 years ago, this ecosystem is probably the most endangered natural system in Ohio if not in all of North America.

One of the largest prairies still existing in Ohio is located in Resthaven Wildlife Area just west of Castalia in Erie County. A small but significant prairie in the Darby Plains of northern Madison County is the Bigelow Cemetery State Nature Preserve near Chuckery.

The Tallgrass Prairie

At first glance a prairie looks much like an old field, meadow, or weed patch. However prairies are distinctly different. Meadows and old fields undergo rapid succession and invasion by alien weeds and trees, but prairies are diversified, fire-adapted communities. Unlike many herbaceous plants, most native prairie plants live for decades and are seldom, if ever, aggressive weeds in croplands. An undisturbed prairie will not have any, or at most only a few, alien species.

Grasses are the dominant plants of the prairie. Although they comprise less than 10 percent of the prairie plant species, grasses comprise more than 90 percent of the total plant biomass. Most Ohio prairie grasses are not limited to prairies but are most successful in the prairie environment.

Big bluestem, Indian grass, and other warm-season grasses grow slowly in spring, more rapidly in early summer, and then bloom from mid-July through frost. Unlike cool-season species, they remain green all summer. Some species, especially big and little bluestem, slough grass, and Indian grass have beautiful fall coloration. Wet site species often form thick sods where growing conditions are good, while on drier sites they form patchy clumps. Dry site species are nearly always clump or bunch grasses. The major warm-season grasses from wet to dry sites are bluejoint, slough grass, switch grass, nodding wild rye, big bluestem, Indian grass, little bluestem, and sideoats grama grass. Cool-season grasses such as June and porcupine grass break dormancy in early spring and grow rapidly until they bloom in May or June. By midsummer their seeds mature and the grasses become dormant.

Forbs make up the rest of the macroflora of the prairie. These are the herbaceous, ungrasslike prairie wildflowers that add color, texture, and variety to the landscape. Beginning in early spring with the violets, there is a virtually unending parade of flowers. As the seasons pass, five to 15 species will be blooming at any time with each succeeding group being taller. For example a person standing in a prairie in April will be ankle deep in flowers, knee deep in June, waist deep in July, and head deep or more by August.

Big bluestem grass

Sneezeweed

Prairie dock

Little bluestem grass

Killdeer Plains prairie in Wyandot County (opposite page)

The composition of prairie vegetation depends on the amount of moisture. Wet prairies are depressions in the land in which water collects during the spring, but dries up during the summer. The prairies at Killdeer Plains Wildlife Area in Wyandot County are of this type. Soils are deep and dark and contain much clay. Plants such as bluejoint, slough grass, and dense blazing star are found here. Prairies of medium wetness are known as mesic. These prairies were once found on sloping or rolling land, but are now found mostly in old cemeteries and along railroads such as the Claridon Prairie in Marion County just east of Marion. There are few mesic prairies left because their rich, loamy soils have been planted to corn or soybeans. Fire is important in maintaining plants on these sites. Indian grass, big bluestem, prairie dock, and Sullivant's milkweed are common. Dry prairies are found on well-drained sites such as steep slopes and cliff tops. The prairies of the glacial moraines and the unglaciated cedar glades of Adams County including those of Lynx Prairie and Buzzardroost Rock Nature Preserves are of this type. More common plants include little bluestem, butterfly weed, and round-headed bush clover. Soils here tend to be thin and low in organic matter.

Many other habitats contain prairie plants, sometimes in large numbers. Although they are often locally called prairies, communities such as oak openings and barrens that contain many woody plants, and fens, bogs, and sedge meadows that are permanently wet, are not in the strictest sense prairies. Other habitats such as cliffs, roadsides, and old fields often support many prairie species. However they are seldom dominated by prairie grasses and should not be considered as true prairie.

Life on the Prairie

A prairie community is beautiful and complex — especially in mid-to-late summer when flowering is at its height. However one must stop and study the prairie to appreciate fully some of the plant and animal survival adaptations in this relatively harsh environment.

More than two thirds of the typical prairie plant is underground, compared to one half or less for most forest trees or grass in a bluegrass lawn. The large amount of root area compared to leaf surface allows the prairie plant to survive during dry periods. Grass roots tend to dominate the upper soil horizons while forb roots flourish beneath the grass roots, sometimes to a depth of 10 feet or more. This stratification reduces competition for moisture.

Many prairie plants have finely divided or slender leaves, while others have compound leaves arranged like venetian blinds. Finely divided leaves improve air circulation, lower air temperature, and decrease evaporation. In addition, "venetian blind" leaves allow air circulation but shade lower leaflets. The leaves of other plants are close to the ground, so only the flower heads are raised into the drying winds. Other mechanisms which reduce water loss include vertical placement of leaves (less exposure to direct rays of the sun), fuzzy or hairy leaves (reflect light), and rolling of leaf blades when dry (reducing leaf surface exposed to circulating air).

Many short species complete their life cycles early in the growing season and are dormant the rest of the year when water is in relatively short supply. Some plants have hard-coated seeds which prevent

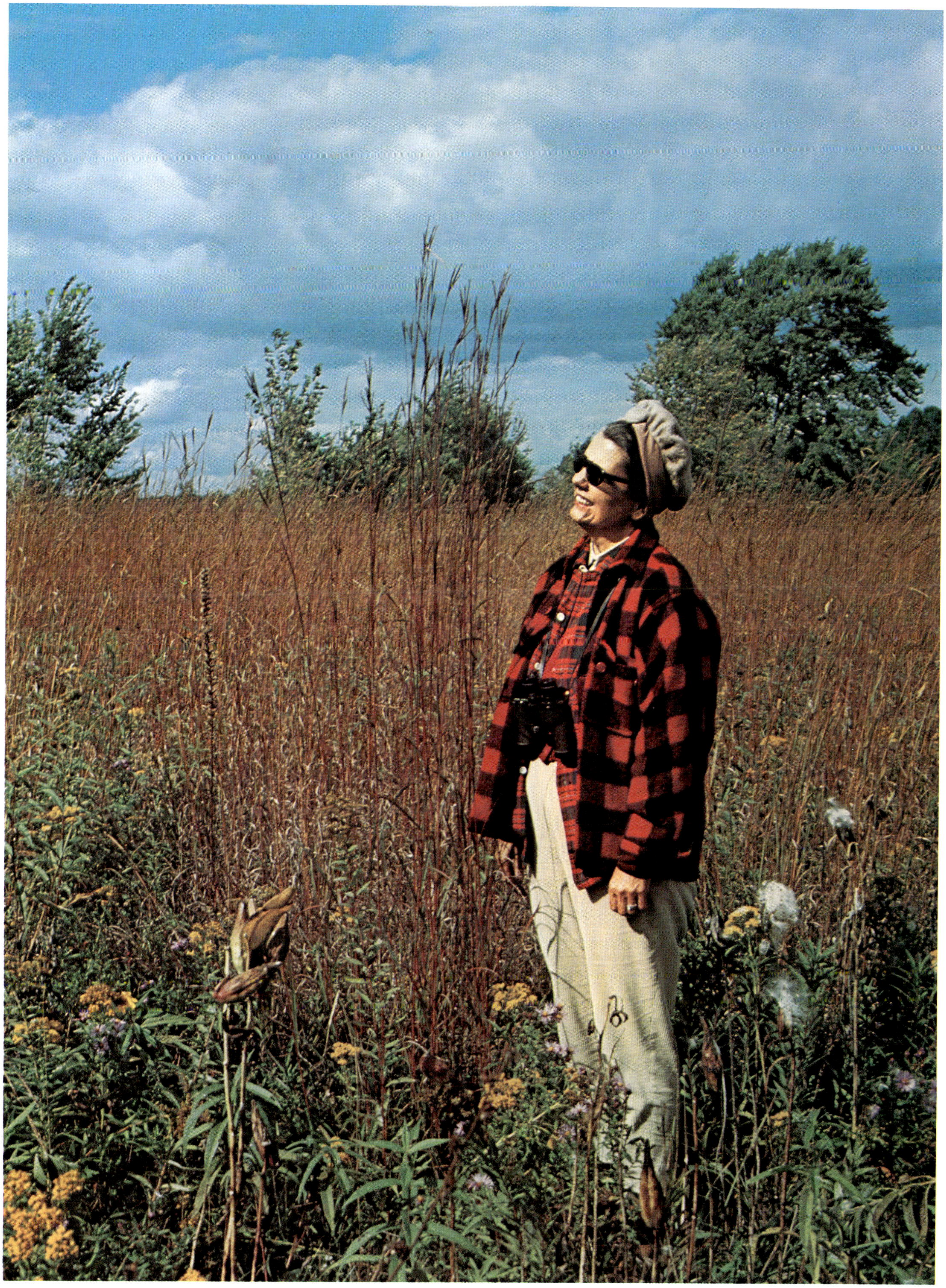

Prairie burn

germination except during periods of high moisture. Since most prairie plants are long-lived perennials, failure to reproduce in drought years is not critical. If moisture is critically low before blooming, flowers do not develop and the plants just vegetate throughout the growing season.

One of the most important characteristics of a prairie plant is its ability to withstand fire. Prairie plants have their crowns (where roots meet shoots) at or beneath the soil surface. Thus a fire, sometimes exceeding several hundred degrees a few feet above ground, will pass overhead without killing the plant, except possibly during the growing season. Prairie fires accomplish several beneficial things. They reduce competition from woody or unadapted plants; they "lengthen" the growing season by allowing the blackened, litter-free ground to warm sooner in spring; and they release essential nutrients that would otherwise take years before changing to usable forms.

Prairie Animals

Animals play many important roles in the prairie community. One of the most important is their ability to recycle plants or each other within the ecosystem and eventually make nutrients available to the myriads of small or microscopic decomposers. Woody plant seeds are spread (for better or worse) into the prairie community by many birds and mammals. Browsing animals, both large and small, in turn tend to reduce woody plant competition, thus preserving the treeless environment. These browsers, along with the burrowing mammals, ants, and crawfish, create bare areas where plants, especially annuals, can become established.

Insects, although small in size, probably outweigh the mammals on a per acre basis. Insects, especially beetles, bugs, flies, hornets, and bumblebees, are vital for the pollination of many prairie plants. Ants often burrow into the soil three to four feet deep, stirring and loosening the soil in the process. They often carry below the surface plant and animal parts which eventually become available for plant use. In the prairie ecosystem, chewing insects such as grasshoppers and crickets

Oxeye

convert the abundant herbaceous vegetation into insect tissue, which in turn, becomes a diet staple of many small or medium-sized vertebrates.

Elk and bison were once part of the Ohio landscape, but these large animals were virtually extirpated (exterminated) before statehood and little is known about their numbers, habits, and habitats. However, Ohio and the other states along the prairie-forest border have many medium-sized mammals capable of living in treeless areas. In fact many of these mammals may be more common today, living in and near pastures, crop lands, and vacant fields, than they were two centuries ago in the relatively few treeless openings. These mammals (larger than a mouse but smaller than a deer) may have been rare in the prairies where the threats of fires or floods were ever present, and the dense, tall grasses with a nearly impenetrable sod made both ground level and underground travel quite difficult. Early records of mammals this size are quite few (what explorer would write about rodent-sized critters when he was surrounded or threatened by fires, floods, bison, or Indians?). Thus we can only guess about the former status of animals such as the badger, groundhog, fox, coyote, and 13-lined ground squirrel. However both badgers and ground squirrels have increased both their range and numbers during the present century.

The badger is one of our rarest and most interesting mammals. This multi-colored, low-slung, broad-shouldered cousin of the mink and weasel, with its long teeth and claws, is one of the most feared animals on the prairie. Besides using jaws and claws to capture a great variety of prey from the size of grasshoppers to groundhogs, the badger is quite capable of defending itself against aggressors many times its size — people included. If cornered in soft dirt a badger can dig itself out of sight in a matter of seconds. Normally, the badger uses its digging capabilities either to excavate a den system, three to four feet deep and 30 to 40 feet long or to dig out rodents, rabbits, or other small mammals. Badgers, although fearless, are shy creatures. Even where they are

Liatris or blazing star

Badger

Eastern plains garter snake, an Ohio endangered species

common, they are seldom seen except along roadsides where they have all too often been killed trying to defend their vehicle-killed food against the wheeled, mechanical beasts of humans.

The prairie is an excellent place to live for both meadow and prairie voles. Surrounded by a nearly constant supply of food and sheltering grass, they often reach prodigious numbers. These mice, living either below ground in holes or in grassy nests above ground, are well equipped with a specialized set of teeth which both cut and grind the abundant vegetation or small insects they may find. Underground, moles with their huge, spade-like front feet tunnel hither and yon in search of grubs, earthworms, and other tasty morsels.

One of Ohio's rarest snakes, the eastern plains garter snake, is an inhabitant of prairie sloughs and wet areas. The beautiful, dark snake is limited in Ohio to Marion and Wyandot counties. The closest population of this snake, whose range coincides with the Prairie Peninsula, is northwestern Indiana. The snake, which shares nearly the same habitat as the common garter snake, spends much time in crawfish holes and eats a variety of food including insects and small frogs.

The bird most commonly associated with prairies in Ohio was the greater prairie chicken. This member of the grouse family, with its communal courtship dances and eerie booming sounds, disappeared from the state about 1900, a victim of habitat destruction and overhunting. Marsh, water, and shorebirds were probably extremely abundant on the Ohio prairies of yesteryear. These aquatic birds used the wet or flooded treeless landscape of the Ohio prairie to rest, feed, or nest upon after their long northward migration over the forested mountains. Ironically, the land birds which inhabit treeless areas, such as kestrels, horned larks, meadowlarks, bobolinks, and several sparrows, are probably more common today than they were before the destruction of the prairies. These birds quickly adapted to the Old World crops and pastures of the settlers and probably increased rapidly in numbers until modern agricultural practices again destroyed much of their habitat.

In a short span of 150 years with the help of cow, plow, and drainage tile, people have nearly eliminated an ecosystem that developed over millions of years. What was once over a thousand square miles of prairies has been reduced to a remnant thousand acres or less. Only through people's understanding and desire to preserve what little is left of Ohio's prairies, will future generations of Ohioans be able to see rather than just read about their natural prairie heritage.

Bogs

Guy L. Denny

Bogs are gifts of the ice age. Yet, unlike the mute remains of fossilized bone and wood, glacial grooves, and glacially deposited earth, bogs are exciting living links with our glacial heritage.

Ohio's bogs originated during the last ice age. As the climate warmed and the glacier retreated, Canadian-type vegetation along the margin of the ice sheet colonized the newly exposed glacial soils and countless lakes and ponds left by the slowly melting wall of ice. Later, as the climate continued to become warmer and southern deciduous forests began replacing the spruce and fir forests, many of these Canadian plants were able to survive only in a few sites where special environmental conditions existed. Today more than 13,000 years after the final retreat of the Wisconsinan glacier, bog communities of fascinating and highly diversified Canadian plants remain as living tributes to that age so long ago.

In Ohio there are two kinds of bog communities: those that occur in acid, peat-filled depressions and those that occur on spring-fed alkaline mineral soils.

Sphagnum Peat Bogs

As with all lakes and ponds which eventually fill with sediments, glacial basins were doomed to disappear from their very beginning. By the time the first settlers arrived in Ohio thousands of shallow peat deposits had filled to such an extent that they had been recolonized by marsh plants and swamp forests. Sphagnum bog communities have survived only in the deepest of kettle hole lakes. These deep lakes were formed when huge blocks of ice broke away from the glacier. Later they were buried by sand and gravel outwash. As the climate warmed, the ice melted and left a deep kettle hole filled with water surrounded by glacial deposits.

Marsh plants have not successfully colonized bogs because of the harsh growing conditions found there. The predominant vegetation in

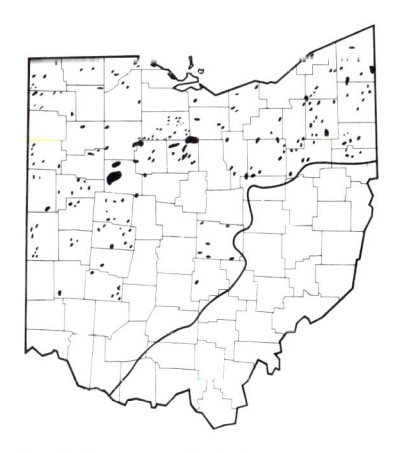

Peat deposits of Ohio

an acid bog is a very intriguing plant called sphagnum moss. As it grows this moss releases acid into the water — accounting in part for bog waters often having a pH of less than 4.0. Under such extremely acidic conditions many plants seem to have great difficulty absorbing water even though their roots may be submersed.

Furthermore, bog lakes are typically oxygen deficient. They often have neither well defined inlets nor outlets, so the water is usually stagnant. Non-flowing, highly acid water minimizes the presence of microscopic organisms which normally decompose dead plants. As a result, dead vegetation, primarily sphagnum moss, builds up and compacts into peat rather than decaying and enriching the water with nutrients. What decomposition occurs is incomplete and results in the release of humic acids which further lower the pH and produce a brown or tea-like color in the water.

Sphagnum also has an unusual cell structure which enables it to hold many times its own weight in water. On hot summer days it acts like a giant sponge, evaporating large quantites of water, cooling the bog surface while at the same time maintaining a high humidity — a condition absolutely critical for the survival of many bog species. This thick, spongy covering of sphagnum also acts like a huge blanket of insulation, keeping summer temperatures below the surface of these deep, cold waters significantly lower than those above. Even on hot summer days, temperatures at root level within a bog mat frequently are 10° to 15°F cooler than surface temperatures. Not only does this dramatically affect seed germination, it also means that bog plants have a greatly reduced growing season as compared to species on adjacent uplands.

The Bog Mat

Kettle hole sphagnum peat bogs are usually characterized by distinctive, somewhat concentric zones of vegetation. From open water to bog forest, each zone marks the inevitable march of plant succession which ultimately changes bog lake into swamp forest.

One of the first invaders of open water is often swamp loosestrife. It has the unique ability to grow out over bodies of open water. Where the tips of its gracefully arching branches touch water, air-filled tissue develops causing the stem to swell several times its original size thus enabling that segment of the stem to float. New branches develop from these small "rafts" and repeat the process again and again. Finally an intertwining network of stems is projected well out over the surface of the pond.

Within this protective framework and around the base of each floating cluster of stems, sphagnum moss becomes established, creating small floating hummocks of vegetation. It grows year after year until hummock finally merges with hummock forming an extensive, floating sphagnum mat. Leatherleaf and other shrubby plants can now become established on the mat, and as their roots add strength, it eventually will be able to support even the weight of a person. As one walks on this mat, it quakes like a giant water bed — hence the name "quaking bog."

Some of the most fascinating and beautiful bog plants live on the floating bog mat. Although spring comes late to this frigid seedbed, one of the first wildflowers to appear amid the sphagnum moss is bog buckbean with its delicate, translucent flowers appearing almost as if

Calopogon or grass-pink orchid

made of spun glass. By early June the mat is graced by the presence of rare and lovely calopogon and rose pogonia orchids. Dainty long-billed flowers of the cranberry are also now abundant among the sedges, rushes, and ferns on this sphagnum carpet. Yet the most unusual of all bog plants are those that are able to digest insects, thus compensating for the lack of available nutrients within the bog environment, especially nitrogen.

The pitcher plant is the aristocrat of the bog community. It has a single maroon flower perched at the end of a long stem rising out of a rosette of unique pitcher-shaped leaves. Insects attracted by these colorful leaves soon find themselves trapped. Coarse, downward-pointing bristles around the upper inside portion of the leaf direct the unsuspecting insects downward. Beyond the bristles, yet just above the liquid contents of the pitcher, victims encounter an exceptionally glossy, smooth surface on which most quickly lose their footing and plunge into the basin below. Once drowned, their bodies are digested by enzymes secreted from special glands in the wall of the pitcher. Interestingly, however, other insects such as *Wyeomyia* mosquitos and a certain species of midge complete their larval development in this same watery graveyard.

The delicate little sundew has a rosette of club-shaped leaves which covers an area scarcely larger than a half dollar. Each leaf is covered

Cranberries

Sundew with entrapped ant

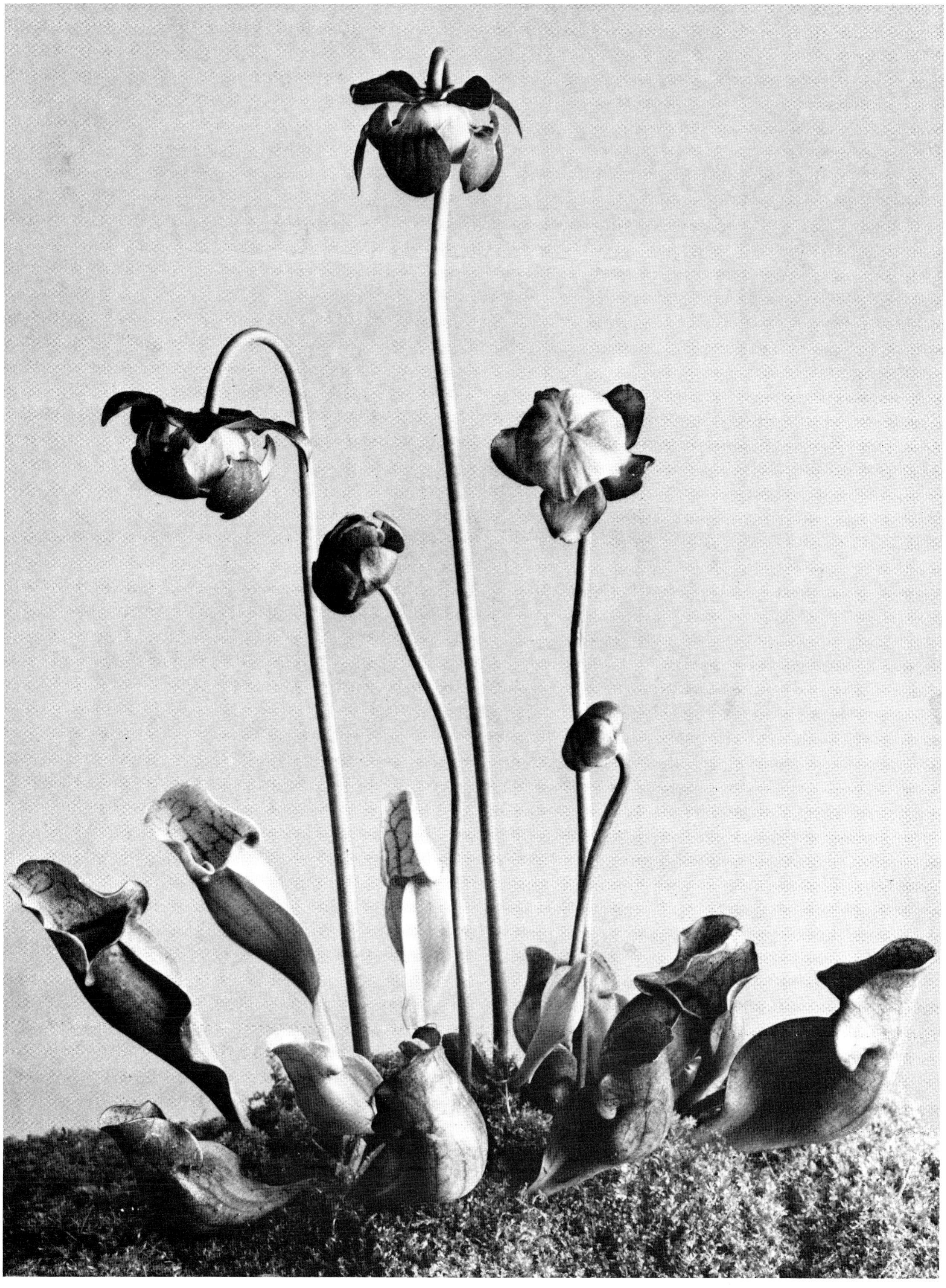

Winterberry

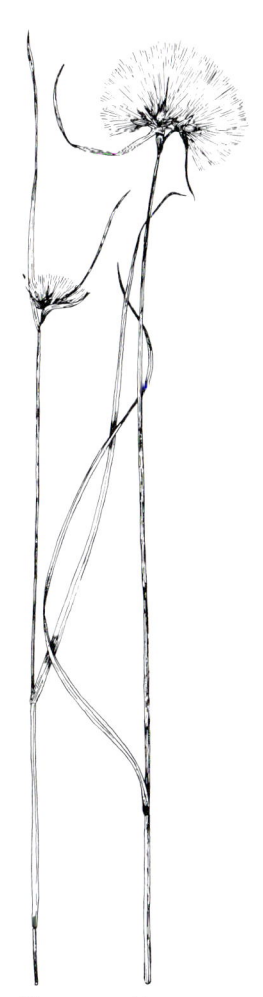

with glistening tentacles tipped with sweet, sticky droplets. Insects attracted to this bait are soon hopelessly entangled; the more they struggle, the further entrapped they become. As they die, the leaf, over a period of many hours, slowly folds around and digests its prey.

Many other plants needing full sunlight also live on the mat, especially grass-like plants called sedges and rushes. The most striking of these is the tawny cotton-grass, a sedge which stands a foot tall and is capped by a fluffy, tawny-white tuft of cotton-like material. Cotton grass, like many bog plants, ranges all the way north to the Arctic Circle. Many ferns also may be present. They include marsh, cinnamon, and royal ferns. In scattered clumps throughout the mat, we may also encounter a few kinds of marsh plants whose invasion of the bog is very limited because of the severe environmental conditions. These often include arrowhead, cattail, arrow-arum, and spatter-dock.

Tawny cotton-grass

The margin of the mat most distant from the open water usually is composed of a dense zone of low-growing shrubs, primarily leatherleaf in Ohio, but also including Labrador tea, bog rosemary, and bog laurel in those bogs farther north. This low shrub zone in turn blends into a dense, almost impenetrable thicket of tall bog shrubs and small trees—the tall shrub zone. Especially conspicuous is high bush blueberry with its distinctive, tasty, blue fruits, and winterberry and mountain holly with their bright crimson berries. Other common plants found in this zone include poison sumac, alder, black huckleberry, arrow-wood, and chokeberry. All provide excellent food and shelter for a large number of song birds which visit such bogs.

The Bog Forest

Finally, as we approach the oldest and therefore driest portion of the bog where the peat is most firmly compacted, we enter the bog forest zone. Within this zone, trees such as red maple, blackgum, and yellow birch replace the shrubs.

In a number of less-disturbed bogs in northern Ohio, tamarack may also be present. Tamarack is a representative of the original boreal

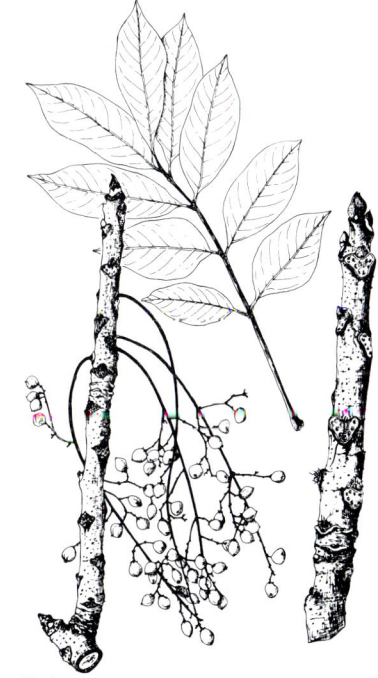

Poison sumac

Pitcher plant (opposite page)

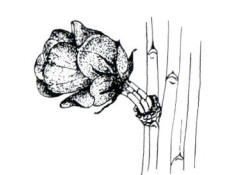

conifer forest. It is an elegant, conical-shaped tree with silky, soft tufts of green needles. This is one of only two types of deciduous conifers native to North America. In late September and early October its needles turn a beautiful golden-yellow before falling to the ground. Few tamarack remain in Ohio, for they are very susceptible to both flooding and fire, two major destroyers of bog communities.

In time, the bog forest stage will close in over the entire basin as the kettle depression fills with peat and becomes drier and firm enough to support that community. But whether occupying the entire basin or merely the extreme margins of the bog lake, the bog forest has its share of rare and beautiful plants. Shade-tolerant sphagnum covers the forest floor like a luxuriant, light-green carpet that is broken only by hummocks of tall ferns, especially cinnamon ferns. Around the trunks of many of the trees, particularly growing on the thick layer of needles beneath the tamaracks, flourish Canada mayflower, partridge-berry, hispid dewberry, star-flower, and goldthread.

Ultimately even the bog forest stage will be replaced by a swamp forest community more typical of these latitudes. Yellow birch and tamarack are northern trees whose seedlings cannot survive in the dense shade of their parents. Eventually they are replaced by elm, ash, and different species of wetland oaks. Even the sphagnum carpet will be obliterated by a heavy covering of leaf mulch. In the end, only the presence of peat, well-concealed by forest litter, will reveal that the bog ever existed.

Tamarack or larch

Alkaline Bogs or Fens

While most of Ohio's sphagnum peat bogs are located in northeastern Ohio, especially in Summit and Portage counties, the majority of

Showy lady slipper orchid

Cedar Bog, south of Urbana in Champaign County

alkaline bogs occur in western Ohio, particularly in Champaign, Logan, and Clark counties. Perhaps the best known of these alkaline bogs is Cedar Bog, located in the Mad River Valley of Champaign County four miles south of Urbana.

Although both acid and alkaline bogs have traditionally been referred to as peat bogs, ecologists use the term fen or calcareous bog to distinguish bogs that are alkaline from those that are acid. Although each type shares a glacial origin and a few of the same plants and animals, each is a distinctively different plant community. Acid sphagnum bogs usually develop in kettle holes within major end moraines and around glacial lakes formed by ponding. Alkaline bogs typically occur on sites adjacent to, on, or at the base of somewhat porous gravel ridges or hilly terminal moraines where springs supply clear, cold ground water.

Instead of highly acid water, springs and brooks in a fen are at the other extreme — highly alkaline. Their pH often ranges from 8.0-9.5 because the glacial deposits through which the water percolates contain large amounts of limestone-rich gravel. As ground water moves through these highly permeable deposits, it dissolves the limy materials and becomes charged with calcium and magnesium bicarbonates. The impact of this highly alkaline water on plants is similar to that of acid bog water in that few plants can survive such extreme pH conditions. Once again, water absorption seems to become a problem for many fen plants. Furthermore, ground water is typically oxygen deficient. This, in association with high alkalinity, significantly reduces the numbers of microscopic organisms that normally decompose dead plants. Therefore, here too we find an accumulation of peat. Consequently fens also tend to be about as deficient in nitrogen as are sphagnum peat bogs.

Sedges and grasses, not sphagnum, make up the bulk of peat formed in alkaline bogs. Since sedge peat decomposes more than sphagnum peat, it is usually darker in color, weighs less and is only slightly alkaline to slightly acid in reaction.

The cold, flowing water also cools fen temperatures below ground level in summertime. And just as in kettle hole bogs, this cooling shortens the growing season and affects seed germination of fen vegetation.

Fens are also characterized by extensive accumulations of marl, a grayish-white, lime-rich mud which develops when calcium carbonate precipitates out of the ground water. Certain places within the fen may quake just like the floating mat in a kettle lake bog. However, this quaking mass of peat is usually not floating over deep water. Instead it is supported on shallow, high volume springs.

The Marl and Fen Meadows

Plant zones are also evident within alkaline bogs but they are not as regimented as in acid bogs. The earliest stage in fen development is represented by the marl meadow. These meadows exist where springs flowing continuously out of the ground have the greatest impact on fen development. Here the waters are the coldest, least oxygenated, and most alkaline. The marl meadow zone may be several acres in size but more often can be measured in square feet. It is characterized by shallow puddles and brooks situated on a well-exposed marl soil where the water table is at or above ground level. Here vegetation is sparse and consists of short sedges and rushes as well as a variety of unique fen plants. Among these are calopogon orchid, false asphodel, bunchflower, marsh violet, Kalm's lobelia, grass-of-Parnassus, tuberous Indian plantain, and chara. Cotton grass also grows here but it is an earlier-blooming species than that which grows in acid bogs.

Some alkaline bog species are the same as those encountered in acid bogs. For example, round-leaf sundew grows on both the floating sphagnum mat in kettle hole bogs as well as in the marl meadows of many Ohio fens. Stranger still is the presence of pitcher plant, typically an acid peat species growing directly upon marl in at least two different fens in northern Ohio.

By autumn the marl meadow offers a marvelous floral display of Ohio goldenrod, Riddell's goldenrod, purple gerardia, ladies-tresses orchids, and perhaps the most beautiful of all, fringed gentian.

Farther away from the springs, the marl meadow makes a gradual transition into the fen meadow stage. It is characterized by an increase in both height and numbers of sedges and rushes, the accumulation of marly peat, and the appearance of hummocks dominated by low-growing shrubs such as alder buckthorn.

The predominant member of this zone is shrubby cinquefoil which often forms extensive, dense patches among the knee-high grasses, sedges, rushes, and clusters of marsh ferns. Shrubby cinquefoil is a low-growing shrub common to the northern regions of North America, Asia, and northern Europe.

The slightly drier portions of the fen meadow often support a combination of prairie species, relicts of the post-glacial Xerothermic Period. Chief among these prairie fen relicts are Indian grass, prairie cord grass, big bluestem, queen-of-the-prairie, nodding wild onion, prairie dock, spiked blazing star, and sneezeweed. Unchallenged by trees and common field vegetation, these relict species have survived in fen meadows for thousands of years. Scattered patches of tall shrubs, supported by slightly elevated, and therefore drier hummocks, are also a major feature of the fen meadow. These include swamp birch, ninebark, poison sumac, alder, nannyberry, and several species of willows.

Within this fen meadow zone another relict community may be found. Where sufficient peat has accumulated and where a seed source is nearby, acid bog plant communities may become established on top of and among the fen plants. The result is a fascinating mosaic of acid and alkaline bog plants growing side by side. The pH of the sphagnum may be 4.5 while just a few inches below, in the marly soil, the pH may be a sharply contrasting 8.5.

Finally, at a distance from the alkaline springs where the ground water has been substantially warmed and diluted by surface water and has absorbed ample oxygen, the boreal fen community abruptly gives way to marsh plants and swamp forests. These communities, in turn, mask all traces of the fen community except for the high marl and peat content of the soil.

Queen-of-the-prairie

Conifers in the Fen

Immediately after the glacier retreated, the original fen communities probably included arbor vitae and tamarack. However these gave way to marsh and swamp forest as the climate warmed. Remnants of these alkaline bog communities survived only on those sites fed by cold, highly alkaline springs in climatic conditions that approximated those shortly after glaciation.

Even though arbor vitae, also known as white cedar, may have been present in many of Ohio's fens, today the only fen in which it remains is Cedar Bog where it flourishes. Scattered seedlings and young trees occupy the fen meadow, while dense stands of mature trees occupy the outer limits of the meadow. The thick layer of fallen leaves beneath the larger trees has created an acid ground cover which supports many of the same wildflowers found in the acid bog forest, such as Canada mayflower and star-flower.

In a few of the alkaline bogs in northeastern Ohio, tamaracks still grow around the outside margins of the fen meadow. Unlike arbor vitae, which requires limy mineral soils, tamarack can thrive in either acid peat or alkaline mineral soils.

Bog lemming

Animals of the Bog

Bogs do not support a great diversity of animal life. But they do provide habitat for several interesting species. Some animals commonly encountered are also found in many other habitats in Ohio — raccoons, mink, small rodents, wood ducks, painted turtles, green frogs, ribbon, garter, and water snakes, as well as a number of song birds such as catbirds, red-winged blackbirds, and thrushes.

Just as tamaracks and pitcher plants are relicts of more northern climates, so too are animals such as the massasauga (swamp rattler) and the spotted turtle. The massasauga, also known as the swamp rattler, is a small snake which formally abounded in the wet prairies of glaciated Ohio. However, extensive farming and draining of these areas drastically reduced its numbers. Today, a few massasaugas are still found in bog meadows and wet prairies in northern and western Ohio. Elusive, secretive snakes, massasaugas, if encountered, make little attempt to bite unless thoroughly aroused. The bite is seldom if ever fatal to adults because the highly toxic venom is not injected deeply by the snake's small fangs.

Spotted turtles show a preference for bogs, fens, and wet meadows. This handsomely marked turtle has a black shell spotted with bright yellow dots. It is most often seen during spring basking adjacent to shallow water in bog meadows. Like the habitat in which they are found, both the spotted turtle and the massasauga have become extremely rare in Ohio.

Swamp rattlesnake or massasauga

Caves

Roger W. Brucker

Caves, or caverns as they are sometimes called have always intrigued people. Humans early ventured into caves to see where the passages went. Sometimes they camped in them to avoid extreme rain or snow, or extreme heat or cold. Indians used only a few Ohio caves for shelter, and most Ohio caves were first entered by humans in historic times.

Ohio caves are small as caves go. The longest is about three-fourths of a mile long, in contrast to the 200-plus-mile length of the longest known cave in the world, Kentucky's Flint Mammoth Cave System. Still, Ohio caves have some notable features. One cave contains the largest celestite crystals known in any cave. Another contains such pure-white spelothems (formations) and colorful minerals it is known as one of the most beautiful in the United States. One cave is an earth crack that permits a unique view 140 feet into the ground.

Most Ohio caves are confined to a 40-mile-wide belt running north and south from Put-in-Bay in Lake Erie, through Adams County on the Ohio River. They are found mainly in Silurian age limestones and dolomites and in Devonian rocks of the Columbus and Delaware Limestone.

Cave explorers are very fussy about defining a cave as any natural opening beneath the earth's surface into which a person can move back into total darkness. Caves are voids formed from water trickling through soluble rock and then draining out again. The sandstone "caves" in Hocking County are generally excluded, as they are better described as rock shelters which seldom permit penetration to total darkness. They were formed by water which remained on the surface and eroded or undercut the rock.

Location of Ohio caves

Formation of Caves and Cave Formations

Four things are necessary to form limestone caves: rainfall, rocks with cracks and openings, rocks that dissolve (except in rare cases), and a place to drain away the water, such as a stream. The absence of any one will prevent a cave from forming.

In limestone areas, sinking rain water trickles through organic matter such as rotted leaves and weed fragments in the soil, becoming a weak carbonic acid solution on its way downward. This moving carbonic acid attacks the limestone, dissolving the calcium carbonate and carrying away a little of the insoluble material along with calcium bicarbonate. The larger the cracks become, the more water trickles through, which in turn, erodes the cracks even more. Over long periods of time, caves will be formed.

Sinking ground water may reach the roof of an air-filled cave or cavern where it may lose its accumulated load of dissolved carbonate mineral. As the carbon dioxide is lost to the cave air, the dissolved mineral may be deposited in a variety of forms. Stalactites are spelothems that resemble icicles and hang from the ceiling of some caves. Where the water drips to the floor and conditions are right, mineral may be deposited on the floor, first as a mound and then as a stalagmite.

Stalactites and stalagmites do not always form at the same rate. Some rocks dissolve and redeposit more readily than others; the amount of rainfall may vary from year to year; and significant changes in climate can halt or accelerate spelothem growth. Except for Ohio Caverns in Champaign County, caves in the state are not highly decorated with speleothems. Overburden that covers the limestone keeps mineral-charged water from trickling down into most of the caves.

Cave Life

Caves combine an utterly dark environment with fairly constant temperature and high humidity — conditions attractive to a variety of animals. Bats, small aquatic animals, and insects are the principal animals found in Ohio caves. Some animals known as *trogloxenes* (cave guests) visit a cave but do not live there permanently. Examples include bats, which may stay in a cave or rest there in daylight hours in the summer. Raccoons, mosquitos, and even people are other examples of animals that do not spend their life cycles entirely in caves. Some salamanders and beetles prefer darkness, and caves serve them very well as homes, although they could live elsewhere. Other animals called *troglobites* live nowhere else except caves. These animals permanently live in the darkest reaches of caves. They are highly adapted to caves and often have no color pigment, very small eyes, or no eyes at all. Blind cave fishes, flatworms, and salamanders are examples. However, few highly adapted cave animals live in Ohio caves — possibly because glacial outwash material sealed caves, thus keeping out surface animals which might have entered and become adapted to the darkness over thousands of years.

Cave animals utilize food much more slowly than surface forms. Their behavior is much less energetic and seems more directly related to

Bats are common cave inhabitants

searching for food. It may be that the sparse food supplies washed into the caves by water favor the survival and adaptation of animals better able to find food and conserve energy.

Diversity of cave life is related to pollution. In polluted caves a few species of animals multiply rapidly, and the variety among members of the cave community is quickly reduced.

Lake Erie Caves

Ohio has about 150 caves, and some of the most interesting are on the Lake Erie islands. South Bass Island contains about 50 caves, most hardly larger than one or two rooms in an average home. In the heyday of cave exhibiting from 1900 to 1940, as many as half a dozen caves were open to visitors.

Crystal Cave, near the center of the island, was discovered in 1897 when a water well was being dug. The cave is about 40 feet underground and covers an area as large as a living room. It appears to be the inside of an immense geode with crystals lining the void in the rock. Most geodes are grapefruit-sized, but in Crystal Cave some of the crystals are that large and larger. They average an inch across near the bottom of the chamber, and five inches across near the roof. There are even bigger crystals. The largest measures 24 by 18 by 10 inches and weighs about 300 pounds.

The crystals are strontium sulfate, a bluish-white mineral called celestite. Crystal Cave, like other island caves, shows no evidence that an underground stream enlarged its chambers. Instead some geologists have concluded that circular-shaped pockets (called lenses) of anhydrite were part of the bedrock. Cracking opened pathways that allowed ground water to seep into the anhydrite, and the mineral expanded, like popcorn being popped, forcing up a bulge on the surface. Continued seepage along other cracks washed away the anhydrite, leaving the empty cavities.

Other geologists think that gypsum lenses were present in the rock. Gypsum dissolves readily and can also leave voids. Some of the cavities collapsed at the center, leaving crescent-shaped fragments of caves at the perimeter, and Crystal Cave may be such a fragment. Strontium sulfate is 30 times less soluble than anhydrite. If it were present along with other minerals, it could have been left behind.

Crystal Cave's crack system may have been tiny or may have become plugged so that stagnant water in the cavity became supersaturated with the celestite mineral. Crystals began growing in the supersaturated solution, and over a very long time the geode became completely lined with crystals. Sometime before the well was dug, the water drained from the cavity.

Just across the road from Crystal Cave is Perry's Cave. According to legend, Commodore Oliver Hazard Perry used the cave to store gunpowder and cannon prior to his victory in the Battle of Lake Erie in 1813. But this story is unlikely since the cave would have been the wettest storeroom on the island.

Perry's Cave, the largest cave on South Bass Island, consists of a single chamber 280 feet long, 165 feet wide, and 7 feet high at its highest point. The cave is about 50 feet underground. At the eastern end of the cave is a crescent-shaped pool of water. Its level rises and falls with the level of Lake Erie, evidence that a connection exists.

Stalactite forming beneath Perry's Victory Monument at Put-in-Bay.

Stalactites and stalagmites are only one or two inches long, although drops of water splash from the ceiling all over the room. The formations are probably tiny because the Bass Island Dolomite is very resistant to solution attack. Dripping has occurred only in the last 10,000 years. Before that the Bass Islands were below the surface of the lake. So, the spelothems have formed within the last several thousand years as a result of the rain water which dissolved calcite left in cracks of the dolomite after the glacier retreated. Other caves at Put-In-Bay, although very small, have interiors that resemble Perry's Cave.

The Blue Hole and Seneca Caverns

Cold Creek at Castalia attracted Indians before white settlers arrived. From a large pond (now called Duck Pond) five artesian springs rise forming a creek whose waters remain ice-free in winter, and clear and cold in summer. This stream has red algae growing in it — one of the few locations in Ohio where this occurs. In 1812 a miller built a dam on the creek to drive his mill wheel, but the dam changed the underground water flow route, and in 1820 the Castalia Blue Hole broke out on the surface.

The Blue Hole is an artesian spring about 75 feet in diameter and 45 feet deep that discharges an average of 7,500 gallons of water per minute, or about 11 million gallons per day. Water temperature varies from 46° to 51°F.

Water is supplied to the Blue Hole from a series of underground drainage ways which underlie about 40 square miles of terrain in the Castalia area. The terrain, called karst topography, shows few surface streams. Most drainage is underground.

Seneca Caverns is near the Blue Hole and connected to it through the underground water passages. The caverns are on low, rolling land where broad, shallow sinkholes capture the rainfall and runoff and drain it underground. The cave is popularly known as an earthquake

Seneca Caverns in northeast Seneca County

crack. It is not possible to tell whether it was produced by an earthquake, but it certainly is an earth crack. Adjacent blocks of Columbus Limestone have moved or slipped about 12 feet. A path leads down a zigzag course from one end of the 250-foot-long opening to the other and back several times, permitting close examination of about 140 feet of bedrock. It is possible to see exactly where the walls and floors fit with other walls and ceilings before the movement. Cross joints can be lined up by eye. At the bottom of the cave is a slow-moving stream containing tiny amphipods, shrimp-like crustacean troglobites about one-half inch long.

In winter the water level falls about 30 feet. Heavy rains can cause it to rise as much as 80 feet and remain at the same high level for many days.

One dramatic example shows why people need to understand caves and karst processes. For many years the city of Bellevue disposed of its sewage by injecting it into the underground drainage system. When dye tracing indicated that pollution was emerging diluted but untreated from the springs around Castalia, people began to notice. But what really shocked them was a deluge of rain that far exceeded the capacity of the crack system. Underground drainage backed up through sinkholes flooding the low-lying areas in and around Bellevue. Unfiltered raw sewage backed up also.

Bellevue now treats its sewage in a modern wastewater treatment plant. Because of regional pollution it is not safe to drink untreated water out of natural springs, either in caves or on the surface in any cave area of Ohio.

Indian Trail Cave and Zane Caverns

Other important caves in northwestern Ohio are the Indian Trail Cave near Carey in Wyandot County and Zane Caverns near Bellefontaine. The Indian Trail Cave descends about 45 feet and leads 100 feet through a passage four to 10 feet wide.

Zane Caverns is a single joint in the crystalline Columbus Limestone enlarged by solution. A path leads 800 feet between walls three to 15 feet apart. The cave is still enlarging, and water brings in mud and calcite that is deposited as stalactites.

A pool in Zane Caverns contains a nest of cave pearls. There are over 100 of these spherical concretions, resembling white and gray moth balls. They originate in cave pools that are saturated with calcium carbonate which precipitates on sand grains or rock fragments. Excess mineral coats the floor around the pearls and builds up the walls of the "nest." Depending on how crowded they are, the pearls are free to move. Such pearls are rare, but by no means unique.

Cave pearls in Zane Caverns, Logan County

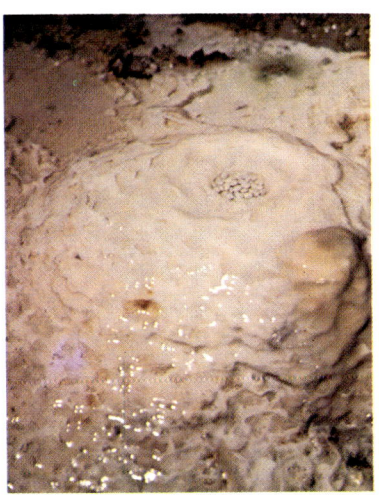

Ohio Caverns and Olentangy Caverns

The largest and most highly decorated cave in Ohio is Ohio Caverns, four miles east of West Liberty. In 1897 a boy poked in a sinkhole and followed a cool draft of air. His exploration led to a long passage partially filled with mud. Elegant white spelothems were discovered when the entrance passage was dug out in 1925. As a background to the formation, walls and ceilings are naturally stained with iron and other minerals in colors ranging from yellow through orange, red, dark red,

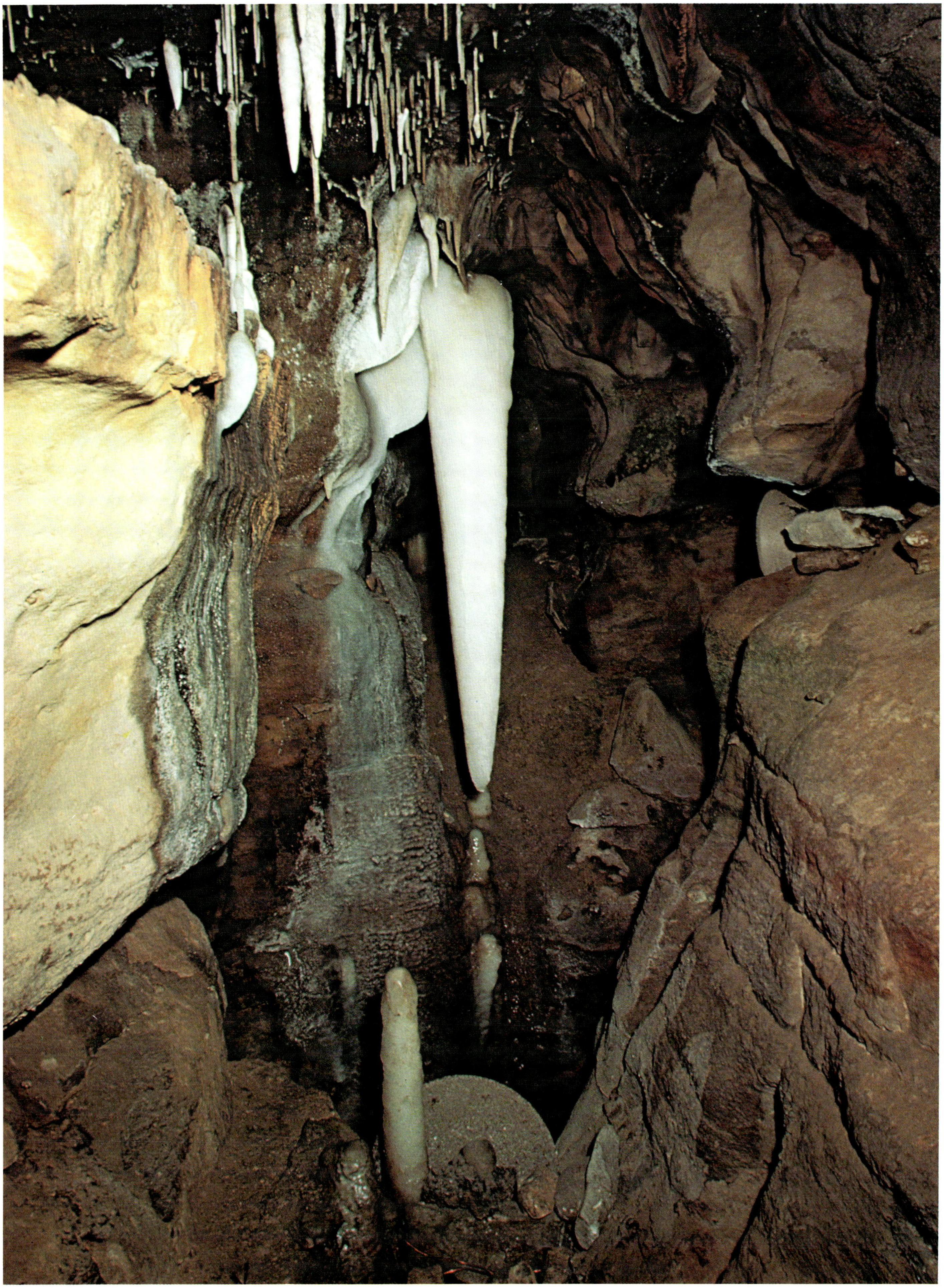

and violet. The result is one of the most spectacularly colorful caves anywhere.

The origin of Ohio Caverns is not known beyond the general processes already described. Like most caves, it is probably only one fragment of a larger system of underground drainage that was extensive enough to produce at least one other cave in the same area.

Olentangy Indian Caverns is the largest of a number of caves found in the Delaware Limestone north of Columbus. Wild caves near Dublin are reached through small cracks in sinkholes in farm fields. The caves sometimes serve as dens for raccoons and other animals, and sometimes for old bedsprings and other junk. Olentangy Caverns is two and one half miles north of Powell in Delaware County. A 30-foot-diameter, 30-foot-deep sinkhole leads through a crack down 55 feet into a passage 75 feet long, about five feet wide, and six to 15 feet high. Passages off the main room pinch or are mud-filled after a few feet. The cave is formed by solution along joints in the limestone. It is said that it is possible to work one's way down to a stream.

The Seven Caves

On Ohio Route 50 between Bainbridge and Hillsboro is a remarkable group of caves located along Rocky Fork and its tributary, Cave Run. The Seven Caves (actually eight caves) are developed at the same general elevation, about 50 feet above the nearby streams. They are in the Cedarville Dolomite of Silurian age. All of the caves open onto paths. Wet Cave is the largest of the group. Its entrance is about 30 feet wide and 15 feet high, and the cave is about 315 feet long. The main cave leads to a room 18 feet wide and 15 feet high. Here a small passage extends about 200 feet northwest where it pinches shut.

The exposure of these caves is locked in the history of Rocky Fork gorge. The gorge, only about 25,000 years old, was dammed by the Wisconsinan glacier. The ice caused the preglacial Rocky Fork to reverse its flow and cut its present 75-foot-deep gorge. The rock offered little resistance to the erosive force of the water which cut down through the rock leaving tributary valleys stranded 40 feet above Rocky Fork. In the mouth of one such valley, large blocks in the stream bed appear to have once belonged to a cave ceiling. Cave Run itself may have been such a cave with some of the present-day caves tributary to it.

There are scores of other caves in Ohio. Many are in Ross, Highland, and Adams counties. There are also caves, or rumors of them, in Pike, Miami, and Shelby counties, and elsewhere. Nearly all of them are tiny, muddy, wet, and not so impressive as most of those that are exhibited to visitors. There are a few exceptions, and their locations are closely kept secrets to prevent them from being vandalized.

Because they are so rare now, great care must be taken to protect Ohio's remaining prairies, bogs, caves. They are truly relicts of a bygone age. They awaken, at least in some, a kinship with wild, untrodden places where Ohio's biologic, geologic, and glacial past survive. Agriculture and marl mining have damaged prairies. Plant succession, draining, and economic exploitation have devastated bogs and fens. And irreparable harm has been done to Ohio caves by people who take stalactites and other flowstone features, or by persons who disturb bats and other cave life. With each passing year, more and more of this heritage is lost. What remains is ours to explore, enjoy, and protect.

Crystal King stalactite in Ohio Caverns, Champaign County (opposite page)

Part II
Natural Regions

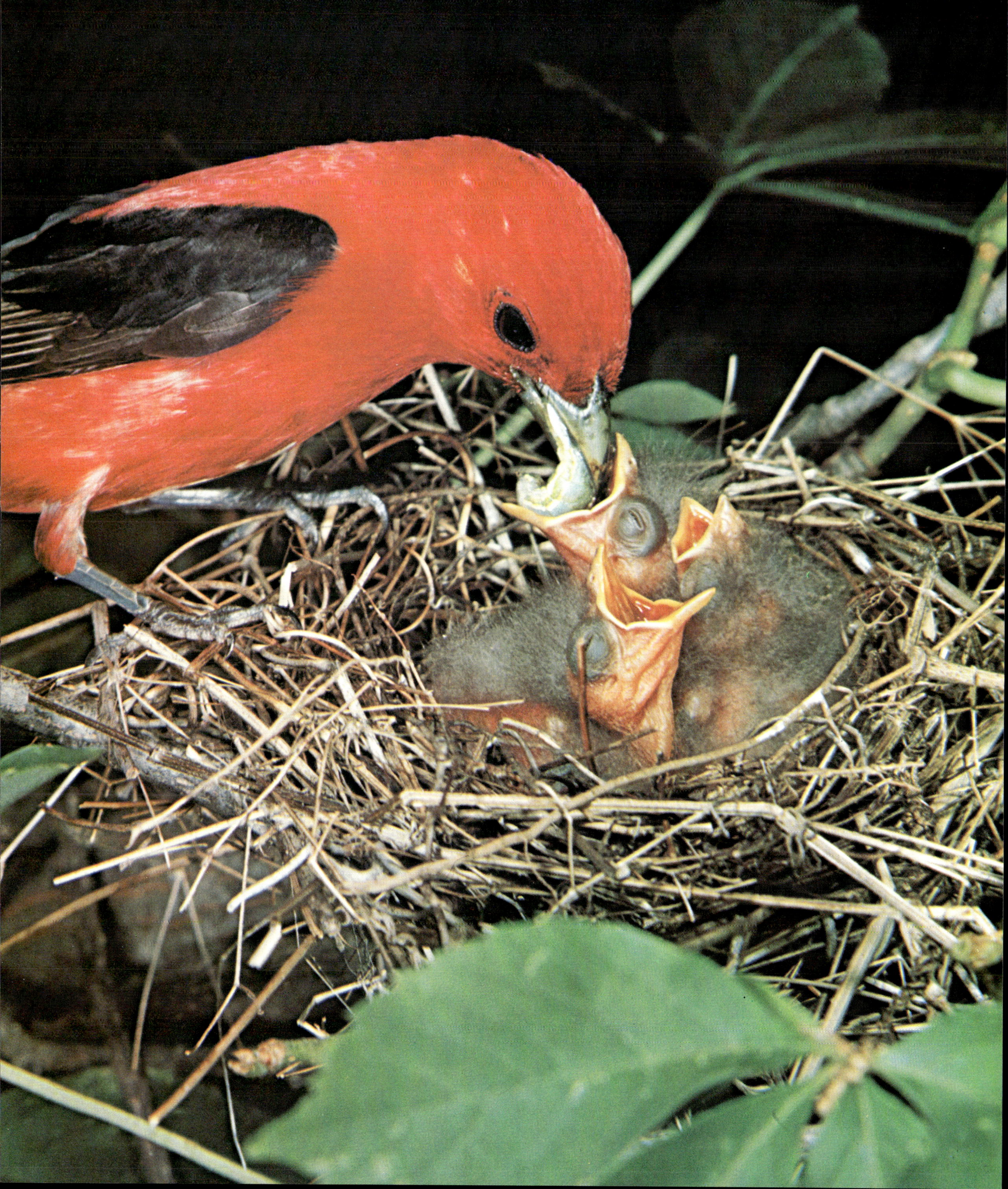

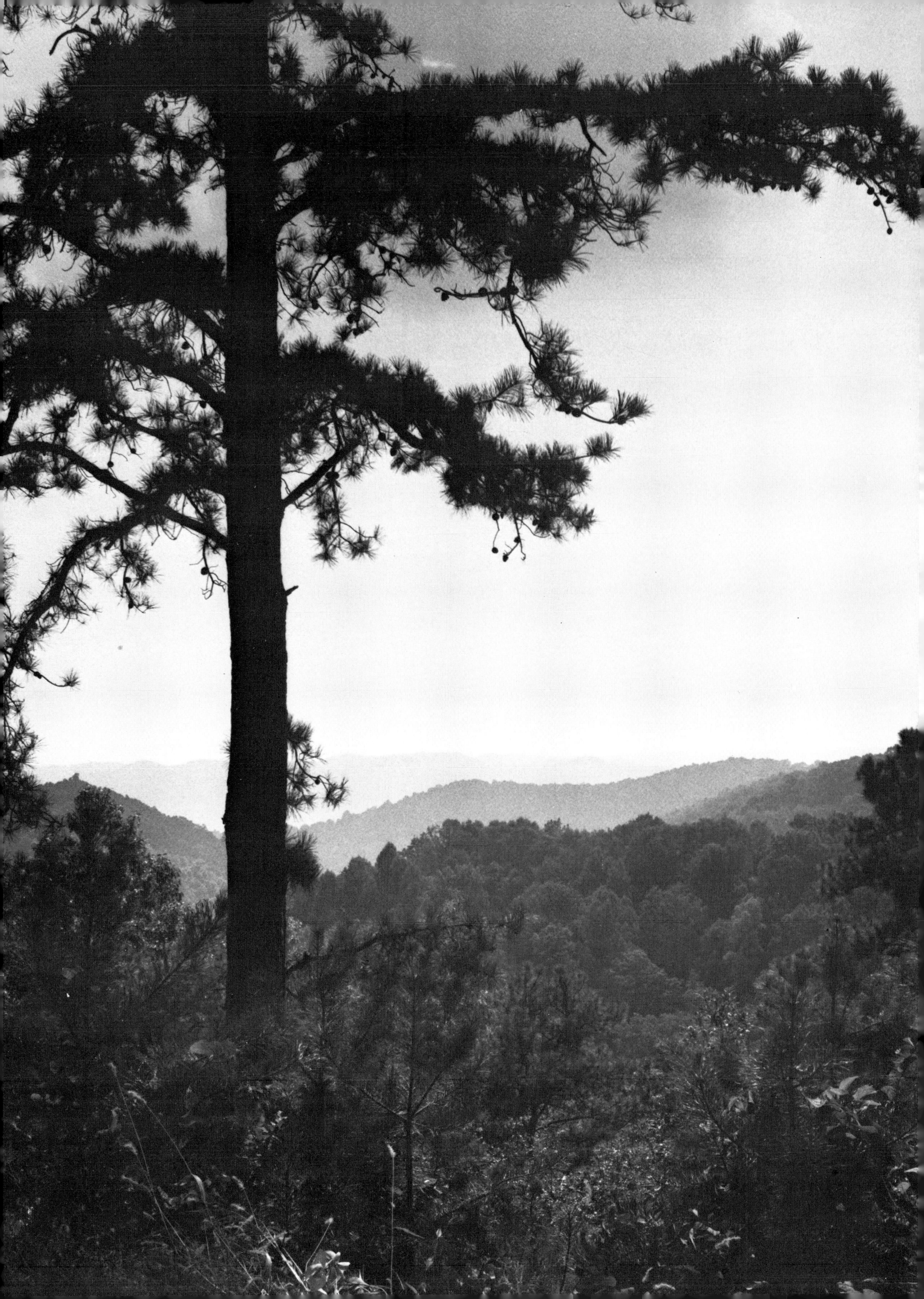

Chapter 10
Hill Country

THE rugged and scenic hill country — the Unglaciated Allegheny (or Appalachian) Plateau in the southeastern and southern part of the state—is Ohio's oldest landscape. Much time has passed since the region was first uplifted from the ancient sea allowing for the development of many different habitats. Probably more kinds of plants and animals live here than in any other part of Ohio. Massive oaks tower from the hillsides. Stately tuliptrees grow tall and straight out of the rich, moist soils in coves between cliffs and hills. In the air, vultures trace lazy circles. Whip-poor-wills call from distant ridges on summer evenings, and deer bound nimbly through stony woods.

Pioneers first settled areas in the hill country, and the original forests, covering virtually all the land, soon fell to ax and fire. Corn, wheat, and apples replaced oaks, hickories, and tuliptrees. Cattle, sheep, and horses replaced bison, wolves, and bears. About an acre of forest a day was cut and burned for charcoal, especially in the southern portions, to feed each of the 40 or more hungry iron furnaces of the early and middle nineteenth century. Farmers found that the shallow upland soils, which eroded readily, would not continually support crops. Many hillside farms were abandoned as were the ironworks. Coal mining, however, increased to supply fuel for even hungrier industrial furnaces and power plants. As coal mining expanded, the accompanying piles of mine wastes and spoil banks increased, and streams stained yellow-orange

by Charles C. King

Persimmons

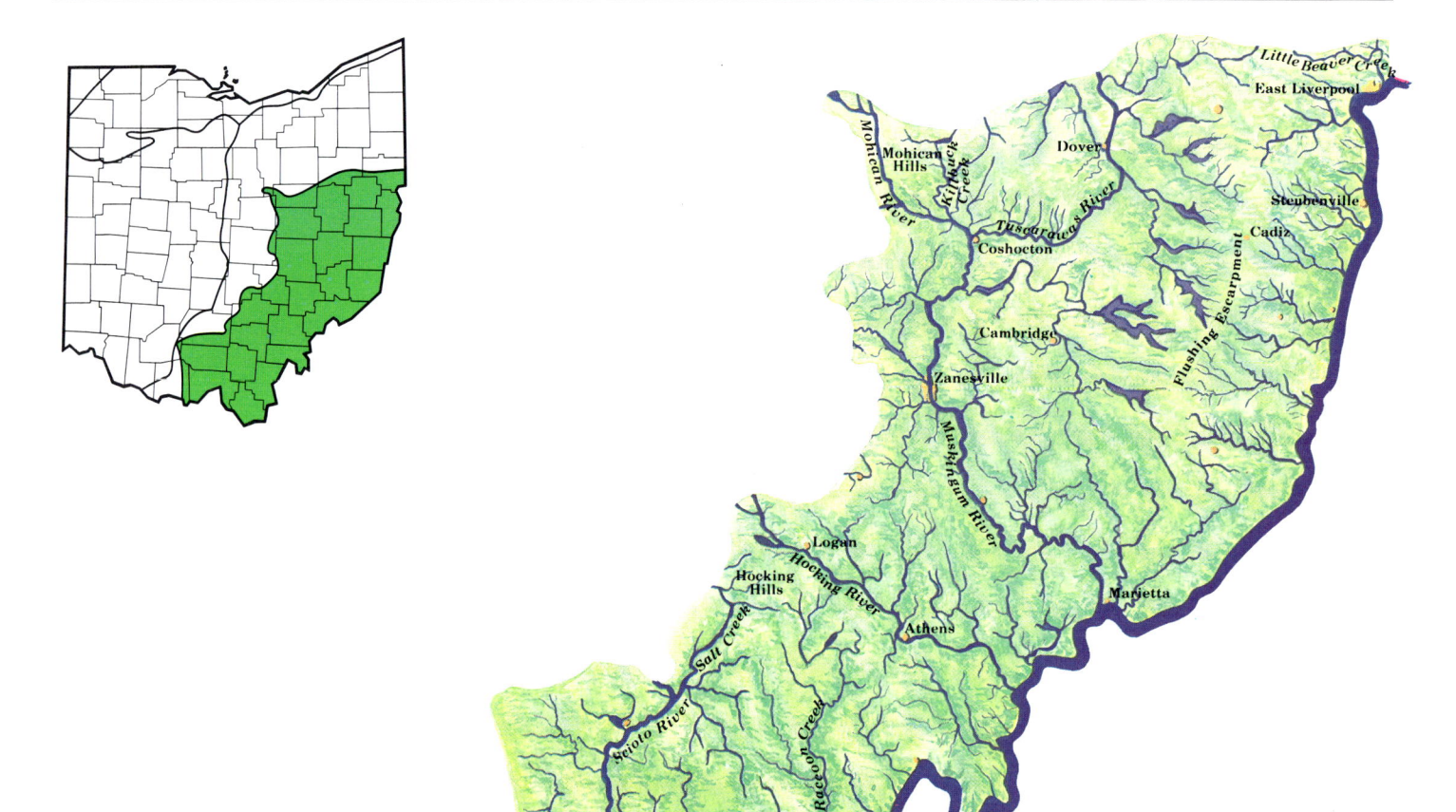

became common. Today much of the forest has regrown and covers more than 70 percent of the region, far more than in any other part of Ohio. However, some old wounds persist and may never heal, and some new ones are being developed. Yet, the hill country, with its hills and valleys, streams, cliffs, gorges, waterfalls, rock shelters, and natural bridges, provides the stage upon which its forests and abundant wildlife present some of the most fascinating dramas of Ohio's natural heritage.

Setting the Stage

These hills are part of the Appalachian Highlands. They have been developed from rock layers which dip gradually to the east or southeast. Most of the rock layers are middle to late Paleozoic acidic sandstones, shales, and coals with an occasional limestone member. Where the tops of the hills are erosion-resistant sandstones, the hills are higher and steeper. Where the softer shales predominate, the hills are lower and more rounded.

Knobs are predominant features in the eastern tier of counties near the Ohio River from Columbiana County south to Monroe County. Another group also occurs near the Allegheny (or Appalachian) Escarpment on the southwestern border of the hill country from

Fairfield County south to Adams County and into Kentucky. Just east of these latter knobs is an intermittent band of sandstone cliffs which are best developed in the Black Hand Sandstone in the Hocking Hills (at Old Man's Cave and at Conkles Hollow), and in the Sharon Conglomerate in western Jackson County. Other cliffs occur locally throughout the region, usually in association with a major stream.

The streams that for millions of years carved the landscape over the southern three fourths of the hill country were part of the old Teays River system, draining to the Gulf of Mexico or its predecessor. Two other northerly-flowing stream systems which drained to the Atlantic Ocean were at work in the northeast portions, those of the old Dover and Steubenville rivers. These basins were separated from the Teays system

A view from the cliffs above Conkles Hollow in the Hocking Hills.

Doughty Creek entering Troyer's Hollow in Holmes County

by a major continental drainage divide extending through Monroe County northwesterly to Holmes and Ashland counties and beyond. They were separated from each other by another divide, the Flushing Escarpment, extending northward from Monroe County to Columbiana County and beyond.

Although the hill country was not covered with ice, the entire area was nevertheless dramatically affected by the glaciers. All three major preglacial streams draining the area and many of their tributaries were sooner or later blocked by the advancing ice sheets. Lakes were created in the valleys into which considerable sediments were deposited.

The major end products of some rather complicated drainage rearrangements over long periods of time were the elimination of all natural lakes in the hill country and the creation of a new master drainage system of the region — the Ohio River. The old Steubenville River and portions of the Teays River and its tributaries were reversed, widened, deepened, and incorporated into the Ohio River. Divides in Monroe County, Adams County, and elsewhere were breached in the process, and the Ohio River was formed essentially in a canyon running through the Allegheny Plateau. The most rugged areas in the hill country are located near the sites of these breached divides where differences in elevation between the river and nearby hilltops are between 600 and 800 feet. In the Shawnee Hills near the Adams-Scioto county line, a difference of just over 800 feet exists, the largest in the state. An area of steep slopes in Monroe County which was originally settled by Swiss immigrants is aptly called "The Switzerland of Ohio." The Ohio River now separates otherwise closely related portions of the Allegheny Plateau in Ohio from similar landscapes in neighboring portions of West Virginia and Kentucky.

Numerous divides were breached as the Muskingum River system was formed. The old Dover River south of Akron was reversed and became a major segment of the present Tuscarawas River. The Walhonding and Licking rivers and tributaries developed over rearranged landscapes.

Doughty Creek, near Charm in Holmes County, breached a major divide, and in so doing, it created the narrow and scenic Troyer's Hollow. As a result of such rearrangements, the Muskingum basin includes a considerable amount of glaciated landscape as well as portions of the old Teays drainage system.

Because of such glacial reversals, the existing drainage patterns in the hill country are unusual in that many of the major streams originate in the low plains and then flow into areas of higher hills (e.g., Scioto River, Paint Creek, Salt Creek, Clear Creek, Hocking River, Licking River, Kokosing River, and Mohican River). These newly created streams became outlets for torrents of glacial meltwaters. Large deposits of glacial outwash, primarily sands and gravels, are located in these broad, flat valleys in the hill country, sometimes long distances from the glacial border. These deposits frequently occur as terraces along these streams and strongly affect the type of biological communities present today. Also, the chemical constituents of the water in these streams are different from the usually acidic water of streams originating in the hill country. In streams originating in the plains where limestone is more common both in the bedrock and the overlying glacial deposits, the water is usually somewhat alkaline. Fish, mollusks, and other aquatic life characteristic of these streams reflect the differences.

The border between the hill country and the plains to the west does not have a "fall line" where waters fall from the hills onto the plains as on the slopes east of the Appalachian Mountains between the Piedmont and the Atlantic Coastal Plain. Rivers that flow across that eastern fall line provided a major source of water power to the people in the eastern states and, indeed, there developed the major early cities and industrial centers from New England to Georgia. Such was not the case in Ohio because of the glacial reversal of the major streams in the hill country.

Local surface features greatly affect the local properties of climatic air masses that move across the region. Since cold air drains down slope, on some still mornings certain valleys are much colder than adjacent ridges. Valley frost pockets, like one near Waynesburg in southeastern Stark County, frequently record the coldest temperatures in the general area. On the other hand, if the valley has a large stream that moderates the system, the valley may remain warmer than the surrounding territory. The Ohio River and its famous valley fogs moderate the temperatures there. Portsmouth, Ironton, and a few other river localities enjoy on the average about 180 to 190 days of a frost-free season while most of the hill country has such a season of only 150 to 165 days.

Surface features and direction of slope (aspect) of the land surface greatly affect not only surface temperatures and the amount of sunshine but also the amount of wind, humidity, and evaporation at a site. The classic pioneering study demonstrating the important implications of small-scale climates in the functioning of natural communities was conducted in the 1940s at Neotoma Valley by John N. Wolfe and several of his associates from The Ohio State University. A tributary of Clear Creek in the Hocking Hills flows through the valley, which was named "Neotoma" because it was an early collection site in Ohio of the eastern wood rat, a species of *Neotoma*. From three years of concentrated research in that small valley, the study showed that the length of frost-free periods in different habitats varied from 124 days in a frost pocket, to 190 days on the upper slopes, to 209 days on the ridge tops, to 276 days in protected ledges and crevices. These and other records demonstrated

Rosyside dace are limited in Ohio to the upper reaches of several preglacial Teays River tributaries, especially Sunfish Creek in western Pike County. These populations may have become isolated from others of their species in Kentucky and West Virginia when the Teays became altered by glacial advances.

that the Neotoma habitats and specific microclimates had greater variations than those that were published for the entire state. The Ohio hill country landscape contains many microclimates where conditions differ greatly from those reported by the local weather service.

The combination of numerous variations of land surfaces, soils, and microclimates has provided a medley of biological habitats which supports the diverse plants and animals living today in the hill country. Species that survived in the area for a long time were joined by eastern and southern species via the Teays River corridor. Northern species retreated south in front of the ice sheets, and western species migrated eastward during warm, dry inter- and postglacial periods. The settlers brought many kinds of plants and animals with them, some on purpose but many by accident. A few species from other parts of the world are still being introduced in the same way. Liberty Township in western Jackson County contains many types of habitats and microclimates, and probably has more different kinds of vascular plants than any other area of similar size in Ohio. Primarily through the efforts of Floyd Bartley and Leslie Pontius, over 1,100 species, or about 40 percent of the state total, have been collected from its 42 square miles.

White oak

Chestnut bur surrounding the nut

Plant and Animal Communities

Many biological communities occupy the lands and waters of the hill country. No two are identical because of complex variables such as soils and microclimates. Nevertheless, similar communities can be grouped in associations for convenience. Three generalized associations predominate in the hill country: upland mixed oak forests, mixed mesophytic forests, and lowland forests.

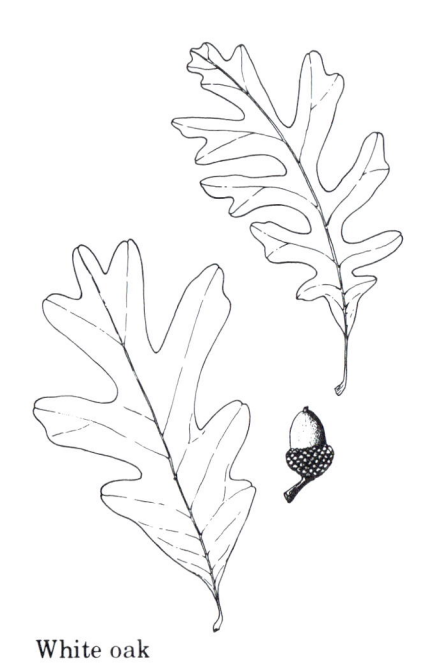

Upland Mixed Oak Forests

These are the most widespread forests in the hill country. They are developed best on south- and southwest-facing slopes and on dry, sandstone-capped ridges and knobs, although they also completely cover many of the lower hills. White oak, usually the dominant species, is probably the most common tree in the hill country, and in some areas grows in almost pure stands. However, few of the magnificent original trees over 100 feet high remain. Dysart Woods near Centerville in Belmont County, one of the finest old-growth forests in the hill country, contains, among others, excellent specimens of original white oak.

Oak-hickory communities are probably the most prevalent type of the mixed oak forests in the hill country. They are especially common on the lower hills. White oak is dominant and black oak and shagbark hickory are common associates. Pignut, mockernut hickory, red oak, sugar maple, and in the south, post oak, are somewhat less common. Frequently on north and northeast-facing slopes where moisture is more readily available, tuliptree is abundant.

The canopy cover of oak-hickory and similar forests is rather loose and open in contrast to other forests of the region. A moderate amount of sunshine penetrates to the forest floor causing moderately high evaporation rates which, coupled with good drainage, keep the woods relatively dry most of the time. Organic matter does not decompose readily but remains as a well-defined matted layer on top of the usually strongly acidic soil. The general environment of the forest floor is rather severe. As a result, the diversity of wild flowers and other ground-cover plants is relatively low, and individual plants are usually widely spaced. Woodrush, fire pink, bluets, pussytoes and, in the southern portions, the fragrant dittany with clusters of lavender flowers are common. The small purple pink flowers of beggar's-ticks develop into triangular seeds which frequently become fastened to clothing in the fall. Rattlesnake plantain is a common orchid with small white flowers on a spike less than a foot high in summer, but its distinctive green and white leaves remain year-round. Tangles of thorny greenbrier frequently force hikers to detour in these woods.

Smaller trees under the canopy include sassafras, serviceberry, and dogwood. The leaves and stems of sassafras are very aromatic when crushed, and the roots, which taste like root beer, have long been used for a tonic tea. The leaves provide one of the primary foods for the large green caterpillar of the promethea silk moth. In late summer the caterpillar spins a silken cocoon wrapped inside a leaf and attached by silken threads to the twigs. These leaves are the only ones remaining on the sassafras tree in winter. Although quite prominent, birds find the swinging coccoons difficult to destroy. In late spring or early summer the adult moths emerge but do not feed. Eggs are laid on sassafras, wild cherry, or a few other species shortly after mating, and the cycle continues.

In very early spring, the shaggy white blossoms of serviceberry mark the scattered distribution of these small gray-barked trees on leafless hillsides. Their sweet and seedy fruits provide abundant bird food in early summer. More common southward is persimmon. Its reddish-yellow fruits the size of small plums are sweet and nutritious to humans and wildlife alike, especially opossums, but an astringent shock awaits those who nibble before the fruits are ripe.

The tops of many dry, sandstone ridges and knobs were covered originally with a chestnut oak-chestnut type of mixed oak forest. Most American chestnuts were killed in the early decades of the twentieth century by chestnut blight, an introduced fungus disease first discovered in New York City in 1904. The fungus probably gained access to the United States on nursery stock from the Orient where it is not a destructive species. This valuable lumber and nut-producing tree was almost limited in Ohio to the Allegheny Plateau. Stump sprouts still appear, but they rarely live for more than a few years before being eliminated by the same fungus disease.

Although the chestnut is gone, chestnut oak remains with black oak, blackgum, and, in the southern portions, sourwood as common associates. Chestnut oak in Ohio is almost entirely limited to the strongly acidic and dry soils of the Allegheny Plateau, and it is more frequent southward in the state. This forest type is common along the tops of the Mohican River and Little Beaver Creek gorges, and in the Hocking and Shawnee Hills. Usual ground-cover plants are members of the Heath Family—several kinds of blueberries and huckleberries, wintergreen, the very fragrant trailing arbutus, and frequently mountain laurel, an evergreen shrub with showy white and pink blossoms in May. More rarely, the delicately scented orchid, pink moccasin-flower, can be found.

Several species of small to moderately-sized native pine trees occasionally grow in mixed oak forests especially on dry bluffs and ridge tops in the southern half of the hill country. Virginia pine is a crooked,

Promethea larva

Promethea cocoon

Promethea adult male

Trailing arbutus (left)

Mountain laurel (right)

White pines and mixed oaks in the Mohican Hills

Broomsedge, or "poverty grass," is a common invader of old fields in the hill country. It is an accurate indicator of infertile and worn-out soil.

irregularly branched small tree and is commonly called scrub pine. Yellow pine is similar, and pitch pine is somewhat larger. These pines are especially prominent in the Hocking Hills, in Jackson and Vinton counties, and in areas of the Permian shales in portions of Washington, Meigs, and adjacent counties. Pines also grow on the bluffs on the Ohio and lower Scioto rivers, and at Black Hand Gorge State Nature Preserve in eastern Licking County.

White pine is a much taller and more highly prized lumber tree than the three previously mentioned species. Natural stands are restricted to somewhat more moist sites in the northern portions. These tall, stately sentinels form characteristic silhouettes above neighboring oaks in the Mohican Hills and, including the Little Beaver Creek gorge, at a few locations east of the Flushing Escarpment from Columbiana County south to Monroe County. A few acres of majestic original white pines and hemlocks still survive in the Mohican River gorge in southern Ashland County. These native pine species, which do not reproduce in their own shade, perpetuate because of naturally occurring disturbances, such as fire, windstorm, and erosion, that periodically open up areas of the forest. Since they readily colonize eroded and worn-out soil in old fields, these pines are probably more abundant today than at the time of settlement.

In addition to the rather local distribution of naturally growing pines, others, primarily the North American species—white and red pine—and Scotch and Austrian pines from Europe, are planted throughout the hill country for reforestation and soil conservation purposes or for Christmas tree plantations. The former plantings usually provide excellent "nurseries" for native oaks and other hardwoods. Many eroded slopes adjacent to the lakes created by the Muskingum Watershed Conservancy District, for example, Leesville, Clendening, Atwood, and Tappan reservoirs, were planted to pines in the 1940s and 1950s. The original success of these pine plantings and the subsequent hardwood encroachments have helped stabilize the soil and added beauty to the countryside around the lakes.

The mixed oak forests and especially the oak-hickory communities are the great acorn and nut-producing forests of the hill country. These provide food and shelter for many animals. Gray squirrels are relatively common in these woods but their populations fluctuate, partially in response to variations in the nut crop. Open woods are the home of the larger, but less common, fox squirrel, an invader from the West within the last century. The small flying squirrels are common but seldom seen since most of their acrobatics and gliding are done at night. Another nocturnal and abundant, but seldom seen, animal is the white-footed mouse. This little seed, nut, and berry eater is active all year, even on the coldest nights, as tracks on morning snow indicate.

Hairy-tailed moles burrow through the soil searching for insects and worms, leaving their characteristic ridges and mounds as evidence of their presence even across the compacted earth of woodland trails. This species in Ohio is limited almost entirely to the Allegheny Plateau. Another common small insect- and worm-eater of the forest floor is the short-tailed shrew, which consumes up to three times its own weight each day. It may be the most abundant native mammal in Ohio. On the other hand, a very rare shrew and the smallest mammal in the western hemisphere lives in these woods. It is the pigmy shrew — only three to four inches long including one and a half inches of tail. Several mature adults from Ohio have weighted only one and a half to two grams. It would take 14 of the heavier ones to make an ounce! A specimen was reported from Zanesville in 1857, but no other was taken in Ohio until the winter of 1975-76, when three were recorded for Zaleski State Forest in Vinton County.

Acorns provide part of the diet for the eastern wood rat which, according to an early record, ranged as far north as Ashland County but now is apparently restricted to cliffs and outcrops in eastern Adams County. Like its more notorious close relative, the western pack rat, the eastern wood rat collects just about anything not nailed down. Bones, feathers, corncobs, coins, wire, flashlight batteries, shotgun shells and many other items have been found in their middens. Wood rats are very secretive animals, carry no human diseases, and are not harmful to humans. Unlike the Norway rat, the common rat of dumps and back alleys, they do not adapt to intrusion by man. In fact, disturbance of the animal's rocky and rugged habitat may have contributed to its decline.

The large animals of these forests did not survive settlement. The bison, which from early reports had trails "like wagon roads" leading to salt licks in the hill country, was virtually eliminated from Ohio by 1800. The last one was reported shot in 1803 near the present site of Vesuvius Furnace in Lawrence County. By 1850, bobcat, black bear, elk, and gray wolf were gone or nearly so. Sightings of bobcat and black bear are still reported occasionally. In most cases these probably represent migrants from adjacent states rather than members of established, resident breeding populations. White-tailed deer were gone from Ohio by 1904. They were restocked in Scioto County in 1936, and natural migration from other states added to their numbers. With the abandonment of many farms, ideal habitat of one-third forest, one-third brushland, and one-third cropland within blocks of about 2,000 acres was very common in the hill country. Deer populations increased dramatically all over the state, but the hill country today supports the major portion of the Ohio deer herd.

Most of the mammals, such as raccoons, opossums, skunks, woodchucks, weasels, mice, bats, cottontails, and gray foxes, have survived the demise and recovery of the forests. Cottontails have probably even increased as their brush habitat has increased. The gray fox is a forest dweller and is more common than the red fox which moves in more open areas. The red fox was unknown in the hill country before much of the land was cleared. As a forest animal, the gray fox is adept at climbing trees, something the red fox cannot do.

Turkey vultures and the much less common black vultures soar for miles over hill-country forests in search of meals of carrion. The black vultures which nest in the Sugar Grove area of the Hocking Hills may be the only breeding population in Ohio of this southern species. The fence lizard, or swift, with its bright blue belly and darting movements, is common in the dry, upland mixed oak forests of the southern half of the hill country. The less common large-headed skink is found on cliffs and dry hillsides or in trees, generally in the same area. The marbled

Flying squirrel

Woodrat

Gray fox

Opossum

Black vulture

Copperhead

salamander, quite unlike most salamanders, is frequently found on dry, wooded slopes where it hides under logs and rocks.

The hog-nosed snake, or puff adder, is usually found in the dry woods in the southern part of the hill country. Although it is harmless, it puffs itself up into an alarming position and emits a threatening hiss if disturbed. When annoyed sufficiently, it may roll over on its back and "play dead." However, when rolled over on its belly, it promptly rolls on its back again. Too often this fierce act is convincing enough that people kill this harmless snake. Other non-poisonous snakes in these woods are the keeled green snake, black racer, and black rat snake.

The poisonous copperhead, although not abundant, is generally distributed throughout the hill country and worthy of caution. Sawdust and slab piles from previous sawmill operations frequently provide protection for this snake. The timber rattlesnake is also poisonous and doubly worthy of caution, as it is potentially the most dangerous snake in the state. In the hill country, it is limited to the southern portions and occurs primarily in the Shawnee Hills. There, in the largest contiguous stand of forest in the state, the snake is not pressed too hard by civilization. Woods and streams of the Shawnee Hills probably support the largest reptile populations in Ohio.

Mixed Mesophytic Forests

Plants which grow in areas with average water supply are called "mesophytes." Certain forests of such plants in which dominance is shared by a large number of tree species are called "mixed mesophytic forests." E. Lucy Braun, the eminent botanist from The University of Cincinnati, coined this term in 1916 when reporting about forest types near Cincinnati, and popularized it in 1950 in her classic book, *Deciduous Forests of Eastern North America*.

About 20 to 25 species of large trees are characteristic of these forests. However, no single forest community is likely to have all of even the more common species, and composition varies considerably from place to place. Frequent members of this type of forest in the Ohio hill country are white and red oak, tuliptree, sugar maple, beech, wild black cherry, white ash, blackgum, red maple, shagbark hickory, bitternut, white basswood, black walnut, in the northern portions cucumber tree, and in the southern portions, yellow buckeye. Hemlock, an evergreen, is less generally distributed and is usually limited to ravines and steep, north-facing slopes.

Mixed mesophytic forests have developed on hill country sites where climate is moderate, commonly on north- and east-facing slopes, or less commonly on lower south- and west-facing slopes. The moist but well-drained and crumbly soils are only moderately acidic. Considerable amounts of well-decomposed organic material such as leaves and other plant parts enrich this soil and, especially in the upper layers, give it a very dark color. When compared to the more rigorous environmental conditions of the mixed oak forests, these conditions are quite moderate, which is the primary reason so many species survive in these habitats.

Mixed mesophytic forests are renowned for their plant diversity. Literally thousands of species live here including ferns, clubmosses,

Timber rattlesnake

Generalized forest associations and geology in the hill country

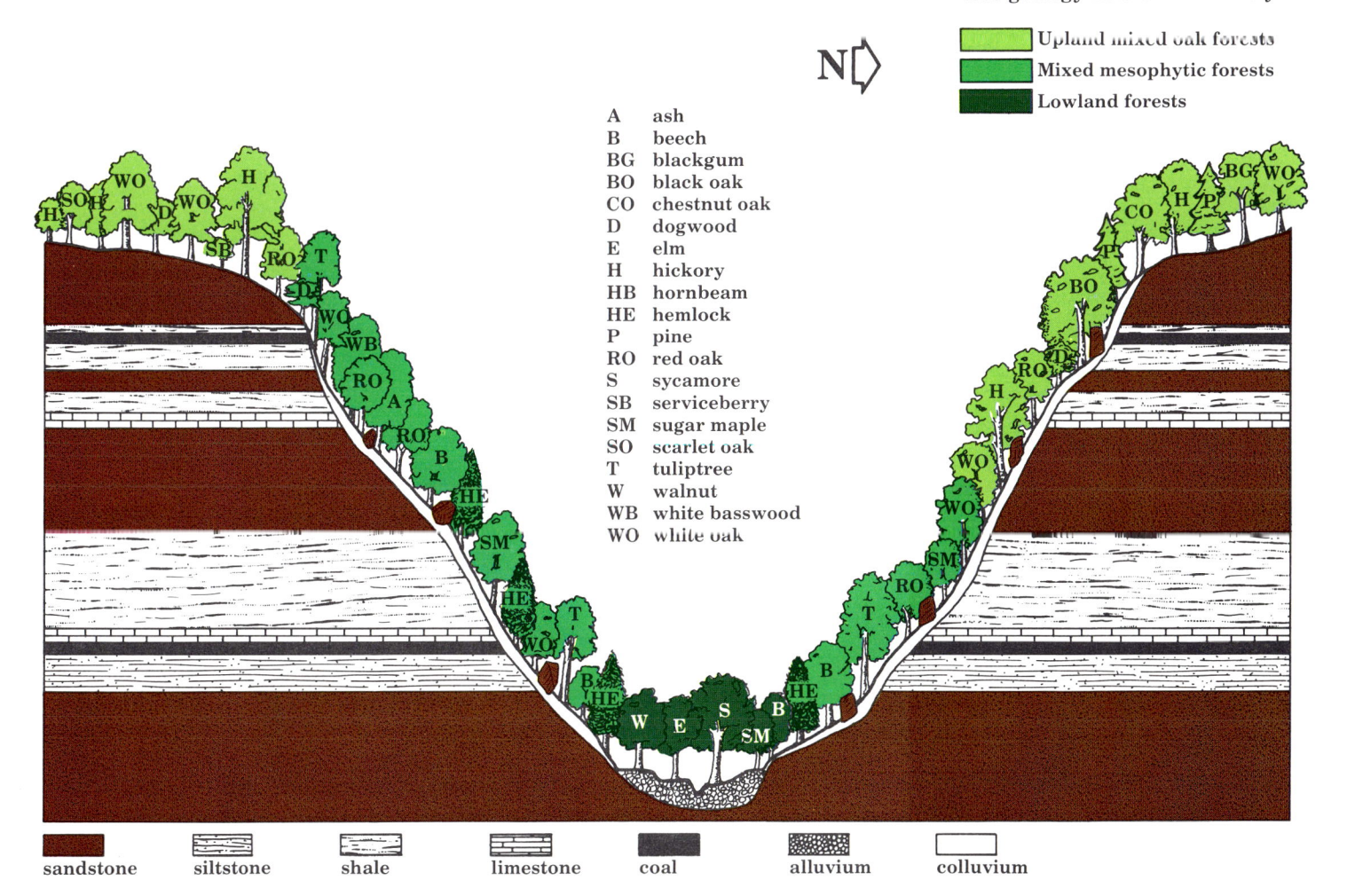

- Upland mixed oak forests
- Mixed mesophytic forests
- Lowland forests

A	ash
B	beech
BG	blackgum
BO	black oak
CO	chestnut oak
D	dogwood
E	elm
H	hickory
HB	hornbeam
HE	hemlock
P	pine
RO	red oak
S	sycamore
SB	serviceberry
SM	sugar maple
SO	scarlet oak
T	tuliptree
W	walnut
WB	white basswood
WO	white oak

sandstone, siltstone, shale, limestone, coal, alluvium, colluvium

Virginia polypody ferns (left)

Pawpaw leaves and fruit (right)

Zebra swallowtail butterfly

Doll's-eyes or white baneberry

mosses, algae, fungi, and lichens, which in turn provide support for many species of animals. These forests are in some ways the most ecologically exciting in the state because there are so many species to interact. Although good examples of mixed mesophytic forests occur in many locations in the hill country, the best examples are in the Sharon Conglomerate area of Jackson County such as along Rock Run in Lake Katharine State Nature Preserve, and in the Hocking Hills State Park at Rock House. Most of the few remaining stands of original hemlock in Ohio are in mixed mesophytic forests in the Hocking Hills where several specimens tower 135 feet or higher above the forest floor.

There are numerous small trees under the canopy in these forests. The sinuous and twisted trunk of the hornbeam (or musclewood) is very common. Its wood is so tough it is also called ironwood. Others include dogwood, redbud, and, especially in the southern portions, pawpaw, which in autumn bears yellow fruit shaped somewhat like a banana. Pawpaw leaves are the primary food of caterpillars of the zebra swallowtail butterfly. This beautiful insect lives most commonly where pawpaw grows, and in southern Ohio both are quite common.

Vines of Virginia creeper and wild grapes tangle in the tree tops and produce blue-colored berries that are prime food of turkeys, grouse, chipmunks, deer, and many other woodland animals.

Spring sunshine not only brings small, inconspicuous flowers in many tree tops but also turns the forest floor into a beautiful wild flower garden. The show begins in April with hepaticas, anemones, spring beauty, bloodroot, Dutchman's breeches, violets, trilliums, and Jack-in-the-pulpit, and continues into May with mayapple, foamflower, wild ginger, blue phlox, showy orchis, Solomon's seal, baneberry, and wild geranium, to name but a few. The delicate fronds of the beautiful maidenhair fern unfold at this time also. Rapidly expanding foliage in the tree tops replaces the flowers of most of the forest trees, and the canopy curtain is quickly closed. The floral display wanes rapidly as many of the species set seed and virtually disappear by mid-June. A few remain with foliage and seed much of the summer. Jack-in-the-pulpit produces a cluster of bright red berries in late summer, while white baneberry, or doll's-eyes, develops enticing, but poisonous, berries in autumn.

Summer-blooming species are definitely limited. The small paired flowers of partridge-berry bloom in June and July. Scarlet berries, edible but rather tasteless, develop in autumn and remain through winter and spring. One of the most unusual summer flowers is the Indian-pipe, a parasite on soil fungi which form mycorrhizae (fungus roots) with the roots of trees. The fungi provide an energy link between the green trees and the non-green Indian-pipes. Fluid from the stems of Indian-pipe was used by the Indians as a lotion to ease eye irritation.

The rare *Sullivantia* blooms with small white flowers in mid-summer from moist cliff faces of dolomite and sandstone. It is restricted almost entirely to the hill country of southern Ohio with only very limited records from northern Kentucky and southeastern Indiana. This species was originally collected in 1839 from the Paint Creek and Rocky Fork gorges in Highland County by William Starling Sullivant, an outstanding early Ohio botanist and the son of the founder of Columbus, Lucas Sullivant.

These forests have several southern species which probably arrived in Ohio via the Teays River system. Bigleaf magnolia has the largest entire leaf of any native Ohio plant (up to three feet long), and also the largest flower in the state (up to 15 inches across). It grows in Ohio only in the Sharon Conglomerate area of Liberty Township, Jackson County. Umbrella magnolia, a close relative, lives in four southern counties and is also quite rare. Others include sourwood, flame azalea, and great rhododendron.

Northern species, which probably migrated southward in front of advancing glacial ice, include Canada yew, red-berried elder, and mountain maple. These grow at several sites, not necessarily together but frequently with hemlocks as in the Hocking Hills, the Mohican River gorge, or the Little Beaver Creek gorge.

Many animals that live in other types of habitats in the hill country also live in the mixed mesophytic forests. Deer, gray squirrels, raccoons, skunks, weasels, bats, black rat snakes, box turtles, wild turkeys, ruffed grouse, and great horned owls, to name but a few, readily move between various forest types and habitats in search of food and shelter. Many others, especially the myriads of smaller forms, have narrower environmental tolerances. Their movement may be restricted either by the limitations of their body forms or by food and shelter needs. For instance, some insects, such as leaf miners, live only in leaf tissue of specific plants. Others, such as the immature forms of some small flies,

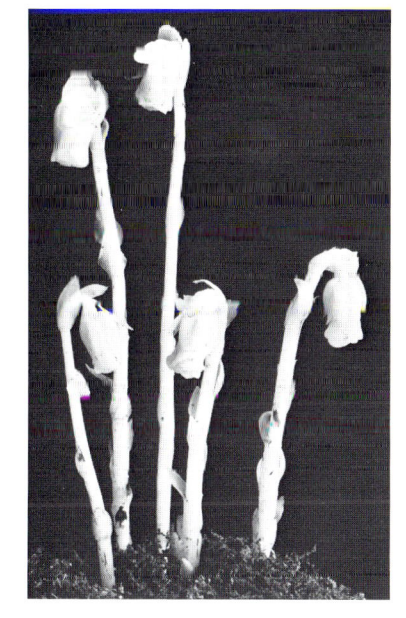

Indian-pipe

Sullivantia

Box turtle

Wild turkey gobbler

The cecropia moth is the largest moth in the United States with a wingspread up to six inches.

This native predacious mite (highly magnified), by feeding on other mites which infest apple trees in the hill country, offers potential control of these pest species.

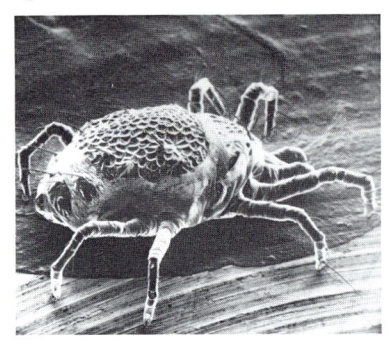

are restricted to the pockets of water that collect in tree holes, those rotted cavities of dead limbs in tree trunks. Certain insects parasitize only specific hosts and are in turn parasitized by other specific parasites. Enormous numbers of many different kinds of animals without backbones live almost unnoticed in these forests: spiders, mites, ticks, millipedes, centipedes, sowbugs, segmented and unsegmented worms, rotifers, and protozoans. Many species undoubtedly are still unrecorded. Many provide the primary food supply for larger forms. Each performs specific functions in the complex ecological network of checks and balances of the forests of the hill country.

Species which require continually moist environmental conditions may be better adapted to mixed mesophytic forests than to the drier mixed oak forests. The smoky shrew, for instance, makes its underground runways in the moist, loose, and organically rich soils of hemlock and beech woods. This northern species, which is limited in Ohio to the Allegheny Plateau, is considerably more restricted in its distribution than its near relative, the short-tailed shrew.

Most of the salamanders of the hill country require the moist habitats of woods and ravines. Common species are the northern dusky, ravine, two-lined, and very colorful long-tailed salamander. Less common is the stout-bodied northern red salamander which is limited in Ohio to the Allegheny Plateau. The green salamander is a southern species and in Ohio occurs only on several cliffs near the Ohio River in Lawrence and Adams counties.

Many birds live in the mixed mesophytic forests of the hill country. Some are permanent residents such as the red-tailed hawk, screech owl, barred owl, pileated and downy woodpeckers, Carolina chickadee, and tufted titmouse. Others are common summer nesting residents such as the eastern wood pewee, wood thrush, blue-gray gnatcatcher, red-eyed vireo, cerulean warbler, ovenbird, Louisiana waterthrush, Kentucky warbler, American redstart, and scarlet tanager. Many other birds, especially the numerous warblers, migrate through these woods in the spring and fall, frequently feeding on the insects that are usually abundant. Rare sharp-shinned hawks in turn prey upon many of the resident and migrating songbirds.

Lowland Forests and Streams

Forests of low bottom lands and flood plains are considerably different from those of slopes and ridges. Here species must survive periodic flooding and siltation, poor drainage, high water tables, and poor soil aeration. Fewer plant species are adapted to these conditions than to the conditions of the upland sites. However, those species that can survive usually grow rapidly and attain a large size because of the abundant moisture and nutrients of the alluvial soils carried by streams from the uplands. As drainage increases and flooding becomes less frequent on the higher bottom lands, more species grow. On some of the best drained sites, the diversity approaches that of mixed mesophytic forests.

Black willow, the introduced white willow, and sycamore grow along most water courses in the hill country. Sycamores with characteristically irregular white and tan bark patterns on upper limbs are the largest trees by girth in the eastern United States. The largest Ohio sycamore on record was 42 feet, 7 inches around at 4½ feet above the ground, and grew along the Muskingum River in northern Washington County. According to early reports, some old hollow specimens were so large that the pioneers would occasionally live in them. One tree near Waverly in Pike County had a cavity over 10 feet

Sycamore

Sharp shinned hawk

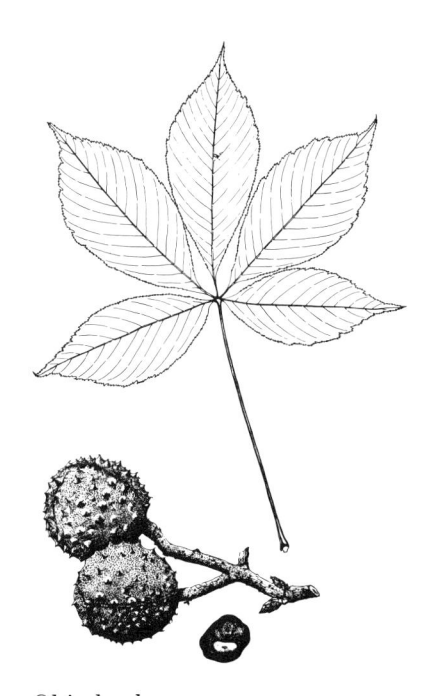

wide and was used as a blacksmith shop for a time. In the southern counties, river birch with its curly, salmon-colored bark is common along many smaller streams, but not the larger rivers. In stark contrast to most other species, it thrives along many streams polluted with acid mine drainage.

Flood plains and low terraces which contain limestone deposits either from local bedrock sources or glacial outwash commonly support cottonwood, silver maple, and box elder. Ohio buckeye, the state tree, occasionally is found on the moderately well-drained sites except in extreme southeastern areas where it does not occur naturally.

The origin of the name "Ohio Buckeye" is traced to the writings of the botanist Francois Andre' Michaux in 1818:

> It is unknown in the Atlantic parts; I have found it only beyond the mountains and particularly on the banks of the Ohio...where it is common. It is called "Buckeye" by the inhabitants, but as the name has been given to the Yellow Buckeye (*lutea*) I have called it "Ohio Buckeye."

There is common agreement that the name "buckeye" for both species originated from the close resemblance of their seeds to the eye of the buck deer. The details, however, as to how Ohioans originally became known as "Buckeyes" in pioneer days are not so generally agreed upon. By 1840, in any case, the buckeye as an Ohio emblem and nickname became thoroughly established nationally during the successful presidential campaign of William Henry Harrison. He used the light and easily worked wood for buckeye cabins and walking sticks as campaign gimmicks on his way to being elected the first President of the United States from Ohio. Although generally accepted for many years, not until 1953 did an act of the Ohio General Assembly officially declare Ohio buckeye as the state tree.

The two species of buckeyes do not usually grow together. Yellow, or sweet, buckeye generally grows on better-drained sites than those which support Ohio buckeye. Although yellow buckeye appears in both kinds of forests, it is more characteristic of the slopes of mixed mesophytic forests than of lowland forests. Yellow buckeye is almost entirely restricted to unglaciated areas, and, except for slopes of Ohio River tributaries westward to Cincinnati, it is limited to the central and southern hill counties. Ohio buckeye is more common in the glaciated till plains and is generally limited in the hill country to limestone derived soils in relatively few valleys. Although yellow buckeye grows into a much larger tree, the two species frequently appear enough alike to be confusing. However, the hulls enclosing the seeds are distinctly different—prickly and warty on Ohio buckeye, but smooth on yellow buckeye.

Increased drainage of bottomland soils provides suitable conditions for additional species including butternut, tuliptree, black walnut, red oak, shagbark hickory, bitternut, and American elm. On a terrace of the Muskingum River in Marietta grew the Rathbone Elm, reputed to have been the largest American elm in the world. At six feet from the ground, its girth was 48 feet. It was 99 feet tall and had a limb spread of 150 feet. Unfortunately, in 1959, it succumbed to Dutch elm disease.

The best drained sites support beech and sugar-maple communities similar to those which covered large areas of glaciated Ohio. In the preglacial valleys of the Teays River and larger tributaries in southern Ohio where Minford silts and other heavy clay lake deposits occur, the poorly drained depressions now have pin oak, red maple, and less commonly sweet gum, a southern species. Most of these areas before settlement were forests of oak and hickory.

Minks, muskrats, beavers and rarely, river otters, live in and along hill country streams. Beavers had been eliminated from Ohio by 1830. In 1936, they reappeared in Belmont and Ashtabula counties and have been gradually moving westward and southward along water courses ever since. Frequently their dams and lodges are built on streams severely polluted with acid mine drainage. They cut a wide variety of trees, the most frequent being alder, aspen, red and silver maple, musclewood, and wild black cherry. Some unlikely species such as oak, dogwood, beech, tuliptree, and Virginia pine are occasionally cut also.

A large variety of waterfowl and other birds may be seen along the streams, especially during migrations, but there are relatively few nesting species. The phoebe usually nests under bridges, and the belted kingfisher lays eggs in a burrow along the bank. Wood ducks, the principal breeding waterfowl species in Ohio, are common along hill country streams. Such has not always been the case. About 1920 the species had been almost eliminated from the state. However, with legal protection, substantial restoration of its habitat, initiation of nesting box programs by the Ohio Division of Wildlife and other interested organizations, the wood duck has made a remarkable recovery. Formerly, the wood duck nested almost exclusively in hollow trees in mature, undisturbed woodlands, but since its recovery, the species nests in areas much closer to human habitation.

The pugnacious but nonpoisonous northern water snake lives in many hill country streams as elsewhere in Ohio. A close relative, the queen snake, is smaller and generally more frequent in the northeastern portions. Almost any non-polluted stream or pond is a possible home for the secretive snapping turtle, the largest turtle species in Ohio. Specimens up to 40 pounds have been captured. A smaller, more conspicuous turtle is the painted turtle which lives in a wide variety of wetland and aquatic habitats. The brown soft-shell turtle is a large river form and in Ohio is almost entirely limited to the Scioto and Muskingum rivers. The rivers and larger streams are also home to the hellbender, a large aquatic salamander which is quite harmless in spite of its size and grotesque appearance.

Of the many fish that inhabit the waters of the hill country, probably none is more spectacular than the mighty Ohio muskellunge. An early account describes a specimen of nearly 100 pounds and about six feet long taken from the Muskingum River. Weights up to 40 pounds were not unusual. This species was referred to as "the king of fish in the western waters" and was once very abundant in the Muskingum River and its major tributaries. The largest populations lived in long, deep, and narrow pools in the lower reaches with considerable vegetation, sandy bottoms, and clear water. There are now few remaining streams with adequate water quality to support this magnificent fish. Hatchery-reared Ohio muskies and hybrids are stocked in several reservoirs including Leesville and Piedmont lakes. Some individuals grow to be sizeable fish at five to 20 pounds. Hooking into one of these provides an unforgettable experience for any Ohio angler. Unfortunately, however, there is virtually no natural reproduction of muskies in these lakes, and a continual stocking program is required.

The Muskingum River and its major tributaries with headwaters in areas of low lime glacial deposits, have long supported large and diverse populations of fresh-water mussels. Dissolved limestone in these streams provides the essential calcium compounds used by the mussels in constructing their shells. These naiad mollusks, some of which may live for 40 years or more, were an important food source to the Indians

Beaver

Red-backed salamander, the smallest woodland salamander in Ohio, rarely goes to water but frequents flood plains.

Ohio muskellunge

Scraps of mussel shells accumulated around this button factory near Manchester in Adams County in the 1930s.

Knobbed rock shell mussel, long used by the button industry but now seriously depleted

and pioneers alike. Samuel P. Hildreth of Marietta made important collections of the mollusks in southeastern Ohio in the early 1800s. Victor Sterki of New Philadelphia collected more extensively about 1900.

Buttons were made from the shells in the early decades of the 1900s, and millions of Ohio naiad mollusks were used for such purposes. Upon the development of the cultured pearl industry in Japan, the fresh water mussel is again an item of commercial interest. When a bead of mussel shell is inserted into an oyster, the oyster will secrete a veneer of pearl over the bead, thus producing a cultured pearl in only a fraction of the time required to produce a pearl in the natural manner.

Pollution of the rivers has eliminated some species entirely from the hill country and badly affected the survivors. The Muskingum River system has the last remaining Ohio populations of the cob shell, the knobbed rock shell, the long solid, the common bullhead, and the butterfly shell.

Natural Treeless Areas

Although treeless areas in the hill country resulting from human activities are abundant, naturally occurring treeless areas are very uncommon. Where they do occur, unusual habitat conditions are present, such as unique soil features, cliffs, or standing water for much of the year.

A few small prairie communities are isolated within the forests of the hill country. One of the most interesting is Buffalo Beats near Buchtel in northern Athens County. On a dome of calcareous clay soil of less than half an acre grow prairie plants including big bluestem, rattlesnake master, stiff goldenrod, and blazing star. These species are more typical of prairie openings 70 miles to the northwest. The small size and old age (as great as 300 years) of the surrounding white and post oaks on the same soils indicate that the forest has been encroaching the prairie for a long time but at a very slow rate. In spite of the name, there is no evidence that buffalo (bison) actually stomped the ground here and eliminated the trees. Bison, however, may have carried in some prairie seeds which germinated and survived on this favorable site.

On a hillside in central Lawrence County, another unique assemblage of prairie plants occurs. The most noteworthy species is compass plant, a tall sunflower-like plant, here at its eastern limits and more typical of the tall grass prairies 500 miles west. It has deeply cut, vertical lower leaves which tend to line up in a north-south direction, giving rise to the name.

Interesting treeless areas of very small size occur on several exposed Black Hand Sandstone cliff tops in the Hocking Hills. These three- to six-foot-wide strips are situated right next to the oak-pine forest on south to southwest exposures. This habitat has been called a "miniature tundra" since it superficially resembles the great tundra of the north. The cliff edge is bare rock with only a few patches of lichens and possibly a few sterile moss plants. Just behind this zone grow a few taller species of lichens which are close relatives of the well-known reindeer lichens of the north. Several other short mosses, sedges, and grasses add to the tundra appearance. As soils become deeper farther back from the cliff edge, heaths, pines, and oaks encroach the lichen zone. This community is exposed to the strongest winds and storms, highest temperatures, lowest chill factors, and most sudden changes that the local weather can

Wood thrush

deliver. Although it survives these rigors, this small community is really quite fragile and is quickly eliminated under the trampling of hikers' feet.

Marshy places where water stands more or less throughout the year are the most abundant natural treeless areas in the hill country. These occur primarily along streams, in abandoned channels, and along the backwaters of the numerous ponds and reservoirs constructed in the areas. The tall shrubs—alder and buttonbush—dominate with sedges, rushes, and cattails. One of the finest old natural marshes in the hill country is located along Stillfork Creek near Specht in northern Carroll County. It contains typical plants of the area in addition to many

"Yellowboy" in a stream indicates pollution by acid mine drainage.

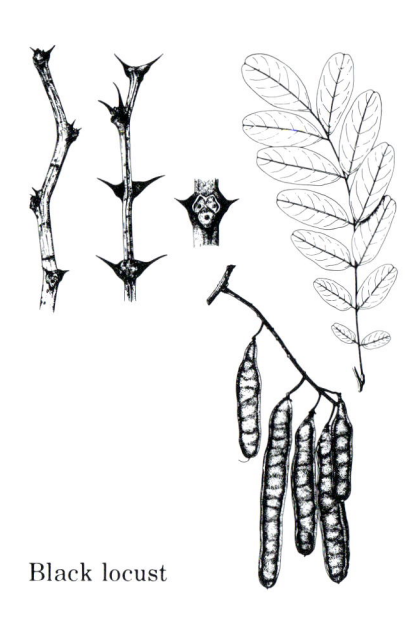

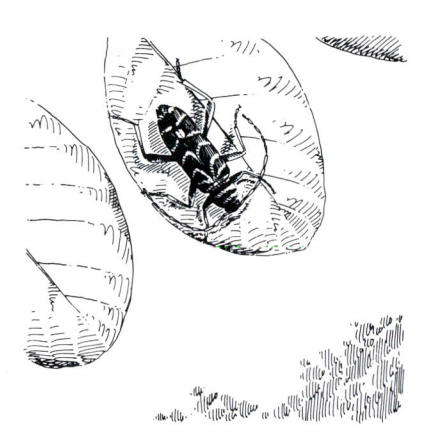

Black locust

Adult locust borer beetle

northern species. Also it has the only record for the rare spotted turtle in unglaciated Ohio. Other sizeable natural marshes are located in southeastern Jackson County in the upper Symmes Creek basin.

Mining Implications

Many areas of the hill country underlain by Pennsylvanian age rocks have been greatly changed since settlement because of the activities related to mining for coal and clay. Deposits of both these valuable minerals are usually closely associated with compounds of sulfur and other potentially hazardous elements. Iron pyrite, or fool's gold, is the common sulfur-containing mineral which causes most of the environmental problems.

Nineteenth century mining was done in many small drift mines entering a hillside on the level, and in larger deep mines at fewer locations. Piles of waste material ("gob piles"), when sufficiently large, ignited spontaneously and produced sulfurous gases which killed or stunted almost all the vegetation in a local area. Waste water from these mines also contained sulfur and iron compounds. Upon contact with the air, acids were formed in addition to the characteristic yellowish-orange and brown iron precipitate, locally known as "yellowboy," that forms in stream beds. Small amounts of these materials were naturally present at some springs in the hill country before mining, but mining greatly increased production.

Streams which receive this mine drainage are stained with "yellowboy" and do not support the plants and animals they once did. Certain sulfur bacteria and algae thrive, but virtually all the higher forms are eliminated. Few streams in mining areas in the hill country have escaped the devastation of mine drainage. Some streams recover if the mine drainage is abated, but since abatement in many instances is a very difficult and costly process, other streams may never recover.

With the development of larger machinery and increased mining technology in the twentieth century, deep mines became larger and drift mines were replaced by stripmines. Early stripmining efforts were small-scale. One of the first, before World War I, near Dundee in northern Tuscarawas County, used a power shovel which was surplus from the digging of the Panama Canal. As equipment increased in size, the depth of mineable overburden increased to over 100 feet. The acreage of spoil banks greatly increased also.

Many coal seams were covered by a layer of shale or clay with high sulfur content, which was usually left on the surface after the coal was extracted. This was unfortunate, since this material, if left unburied, remains as a source of acid to adjacent land and streams for decades after the mining operation.

Reclamation efforts were meager or non-existent until after World War II. As public concern increased and reclamation technology developed, more stringent laws were passed which required a higher degree of reclamation. It was found that black locust, a native legume which adds nitrogen to soils, could survive on all but the most acidic spoil banks. Many acres were planted to this tree with apparent initial success. Within a decade, however, the young trunks were attacked by the locust borer which devastated thousands of trees in these pure stands. The epidemic outbreaks of borers occurred because of the abnormal abundance of the host plant in the spoil bank monocultures. Numerous other tree species were introduced to provide variety and stability of the reclaimed areas, with varying success. Some of the more successful include European black alder, cottonwood, white ash, white pine, tuliptree, Virginia pine, pitch pine, and sweet gum. Crown vetch, another legume which adds nitrogen to the soil, was first planted extensively on spoil banks in Harrison County in the early 1950s. It is now found along many roadsides as well. Coltsfoot, a dandelion like flower from Europe, has invaded many stripmine areas and roadsides, especially the talus slopes of highwalls and road cuts. It is one of the first to bloom in the spring and the white fluffy seeds are readily blown around by the wind. Red maple, elm, sassafras, wild black cherry, and other trees are also revegetating spoil banks. Some mined sites after half a century or more still have virtually no vegetation. Other areas, however, have recovered very well and support good populations of fish, wildlife, or livestock.

Coltsfoot

An Apple Family from the Hill Country

In 1817, Alanson Gillette, a farm boy of Rome Township near Proctorville in Lawrence County, was given an apple seedling by his father. It was reported to be the runt of the lot of about 100 apple tree sprouts that Mr. Gillette had ordered from Marietta. Little did Alanson realize that the tree he planted near the Ohio River would originate a variety that would make apple production a very profitable business in southern Ohio and surrounding areas. Not long after the tree came into bearing about 15 years later, the size, color, and cooking and keeping qualities of the apple became widely known. Friends and neighbors avidly sought grafting twigs. By 1848, when the name "Rome Beauty" was officially recognized for this new variety, thousands of these trees had been planted in southern Ohio and elsewhere. The original patriarch tree was washed away by the Ohio River sometime before the Civil War, but the popular variety has been carried into apple-producing areas around the world.

Rome Beauty apple

A few years later and a few miles north in Clay Township, Gallia County, a seedling from Rome Beauty began producing quality fruit. This new variety was called "Gallia Beauty" about 1865. Although not as popular as its parent, it too has been distributed world wide. In 1932 at the Ohio Agricultural Research and Development Center in Wooster, an experimental cross pollination between Gallia Beauty and Red Delicious resulted in "Ruby" a third commercial variety in this family.

Pageants of Color

Each spring ushers in colorful pageants of the hill country forest communities. Gently changing pastel tones cover the hillsides as buds swell and forest trees bloom. Soon these soft colors give way to summer greenery, the sunshine harvester, whence comes most of the energy expended in community operations. Autumn foliage turns to brilliant yellows, oranges, and scarlets, and later to more subdued lavenders, maroons, and russets. Winter snows highlight evergreens against leafless hillsides. The yearly cycle is complete, and another spring provides renewed opportunities for development of old, yet always new, natural dramas in the Ohio hill country.

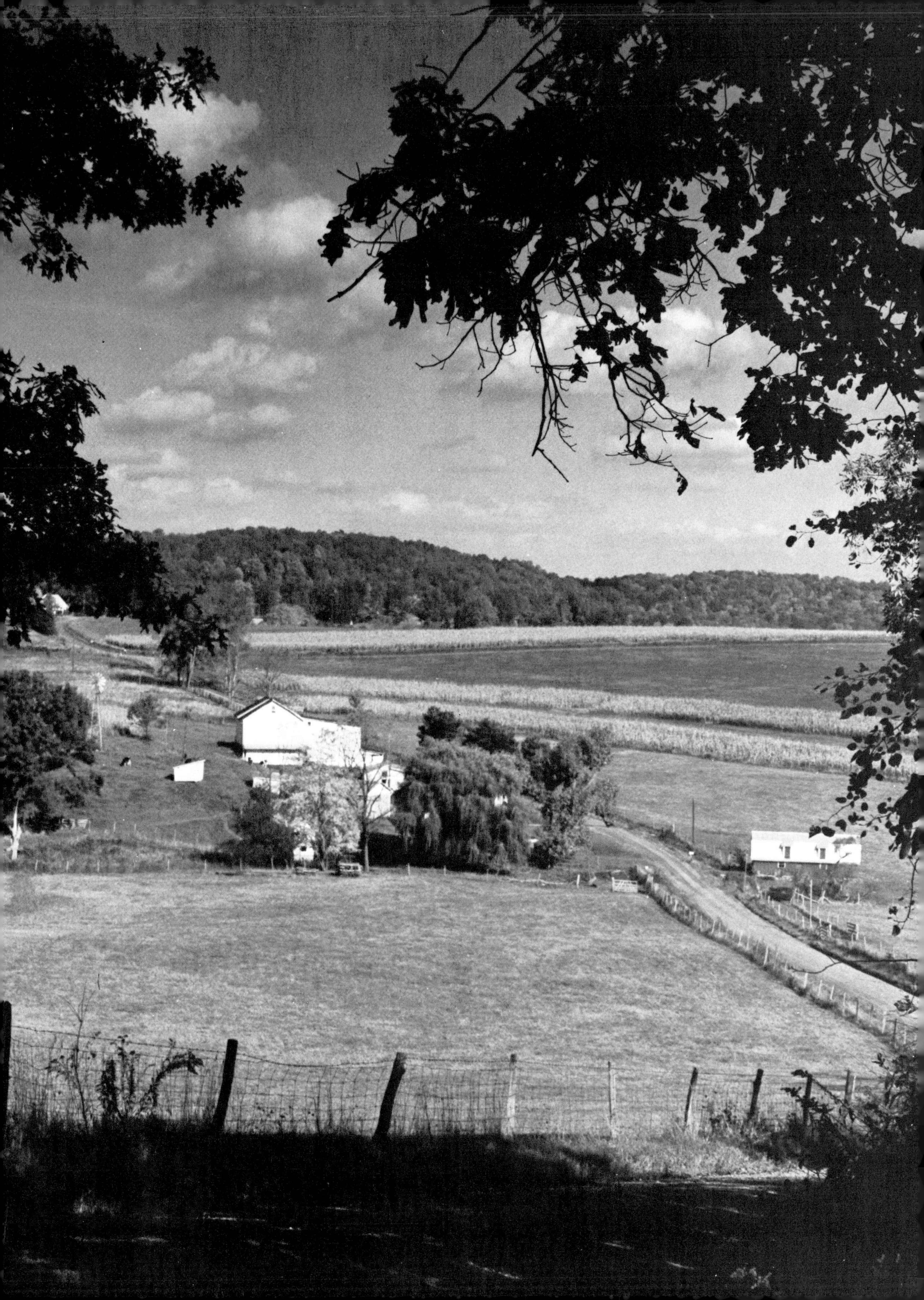

Chapter 11
Glaciated Plateau

THE Glaciated Appalachian (or Allegheny) Plateau stretches nearly 300 miles from Ashtabula County to Ross County and encompasses more people and industry than any other region in the state. Ironically, it also contains a great variety of plants, animals, and natural habitats. The plateau's rolling hills are interspersed with cities, villages, and dairy and grain farms — each surrounded with a rich diversity of forests, bogs, old fields, streams, and lakes. Natural systems have survived with human systems because of the physiography of the plateau. People have congregated in the valleys and the few level spots and to some extent have left the rest to nature. So today northeastern Ohio produces both steel and wood, milk and rabbits, and grain and deer.

by James K. Bissell
Glenn W. Frank

Geology

Travelers can learn much about the bedrock of the plateau without ever leaving their automobiles. Shale, limestone, sandstone, conglomerate, and coal are all exposed in roadcuts. The oldest rocks are shale formed in Devonian times 375 million years ago. Above these are shale and sandstone, formed during the Mississippian Period 330 million years ago, and finally, limestone, shale, sandstone, conglomerate, and coal from the Pennsylvanian Period about 300 million years ago. These rocks form the surface bedrock — outcrops, bluffs, and cliffs — wherever it is not covered by much younger glacial till.

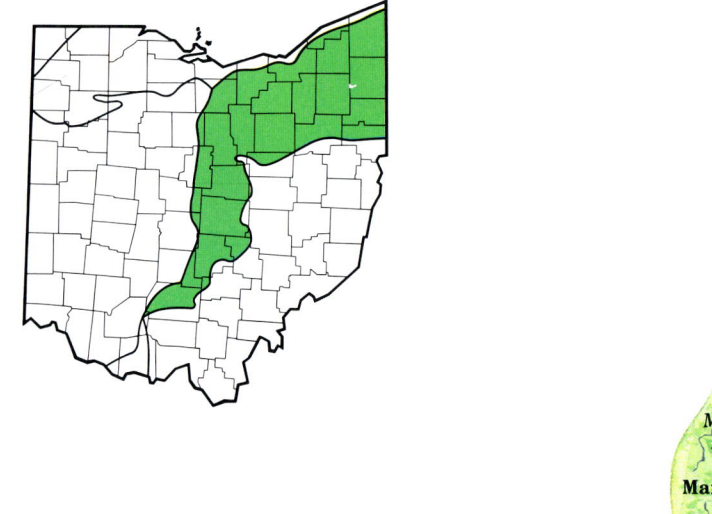

The Devonian and Mississippian rocks were formed from muds deposited in shallow seas, while the Pennsylvanian rocks were formed from deposits laid down in broad sediment-loaded streams and swamps. One of the most common Devonian shales is the Chagrin Shale, a blue-gray rock that can be seen at Chagrin Falls and in many bluffs along the Lake Erie shore. Devonian shales erode easily — today by streams and 25,000 years ago by glaciers which covered the plateau.

Devonian bedrock surfaces in a broad band through central Ohio. This band curves east when it reaches Lake Erie and generally borders the lake within the Lake Plain. Devonian rocks are exposed mainly in Ashtabula County and in bluffs along the Cuyahoga River.

In contrast to the Devonian shales, Mississippian rocks are exposed over more of the plateau. These Mississippian sandstones are exceptionally hard and resist erosion. When the underlying rock is eroded, the sandstone sheers off forming a cliff. One of the best known

Mississippian rocks is the Berea Sandstone, which forms spectacular 75-foot cliffs along Tinkers Creek in Cuyahoga County and smaller bluffs in the ravine of Rocky Fork northeast of Gahanna in Franklin County.

Pennsylvanian sandstone and conglomerate are exposed in the eastern half of the plateau — mostly in Columbiana, Mahoning, Portage, and Stark counties. These rocks, also very resistant to erosion, form high cliffs and fracture forming "ledges" in many state and municipal parks.

Sharon Sandstone and Conglomerate, a rock composed of cemented pebbles, form the extensive cliffs and rock formations around Nelson-Kennedy Ledges State Park in Portage County. One hundred-foot bluffs of the Sharon formation also overlook the gorge of the Cuyahoga River south of Cleveland and at Virginia Kendall Park in the Cuyahoga Valley National Recreation Area near Akron.

Plateau bedrock is of very high quality and much of it is quarried. In addition, clay and shale are used to make brick, pottery, tile, and drain pipe. Brick plants, with their large, dome-shaped kilns and open-pit mines, are found through the countryside. Limestone is quarried for construction and for cement. Tall smokestacks dot the countryside, and their white smoke plumes are often telltale signs of cement plants.

Sandstone is an excellent building stone when it is well cemented. Quarries at South Amherst in Lorain County, the largest and deepest in the world, produce Berea Sandstone for grindstones, curbing, retaining walls, home facing stone, and bridge abutments. Sandstone from northeast Ohio also is used for cement blocks, glass, and ferro-silicon products.

Fossil fuels are also important. Ohio's major coal-mining area is in the unglaciated plateau, but the mineral fuel also is mined in glaciated Mahoning, Columbiana, Stark, and Perry counties. Oil and gas are produced in every county of the glaciated plateau. Since the bedrock slopes toward the southeast, the oil-bearing bed may be at quite different depths, depending on the ground elevation and the location of the well. For example, oil is pumped from the Knox Dolomite in Morrow County at between 2,900 and 3,500 feet. In Licking County, oil is produced from Berea Sandstone 700 feet deep, and from the Clinton Sandstone 2,900 feet down.

Layered rock salt underlies a number of counties east of Lorain and Wooster but nowhere is salt exposed at the surface. The salt was evaporated in Silurian times about 400 million years ago along the margin of an ocean similar to the Persian Gulf. Individual beds, from a few inches to 50 feet thick, range in depth from 1,200 feet at Cleveland to 2,400 feet in Stark County 50 miles away. The same beds are even deeper toward the southeast. Salt plants in the glaciated plateau are located at Akron, Rittman, and Barberton; and Cuyahoga Falls has a salt well for use in its municipal water treatment plant.

Layers of sediment and soil overlie the bedrock. This sediment was carried and deposited primarily by glaciers and has been weathered to soil. It is especially important for agriculture, and the type of vegetation often reflects the composition of the soil. In addition, as the glacial ice melted, sand and gravel were washed into the river valleys and today these deposits are mined to provide raw material for concrete and other construction products. They are also important sources of ground water for cities and industries.

Glaciers and Landscape

Glaciers have had a profound effect on the drainage system and landscape of the plateau. Before the glaciers moved south, the plateau was hilly and very similar to the steep Appalachian foothills of southeastern Ohio. As the ice moved forward, propelled by its sheer mass, it deeply eroded the soft shale in the northern plateau, scouring the eastern basin of Lake Erie and the broad valley of the Grand River, north of Warren. Farther south, the ice encountered the harder and higher rocks of the Appalachian Plateau. Following paths of least resistance, the ice moved forward more easily in the valleys between the hills. Where it was thick enough to ride over the plateau, hilltops also were eroded into the broad, flat-topped terrain familiar to interstate-highway travelers today.

In the southern glaciated plateau, large quantities of water from the melting ice scoured parts of the valleys of the ancient Teays River and its tributaries. In some places the Teays was scoured 200 feet deeper than before the ice invasion.

As the ice flowed south, rocks from the north were deposited as part of rolling hills and long ridges. Most of the glacial material probably was not transported more than a few miles by the ice; however, near Lancaster in Fairfield County, granite pebbles originating from the Canadian Shield in Canada have been found on top of Mount Pleasant.

The glaciers alternately advanced and melted back as the climate fluctuated. Each time the ice advanced, new stream patterns formed. Some stream valleys were buried completely by glacial till, while others only were blocked by ice, soil, and rock. These natural dams forced streams to flow southward, and they did not flow north again until the Wisconsinan ice melted into the Lake Erie basin about 12,000 years ago. When the ice finally retreated for the last time it exposed a major water divide separating water flowing to the Gulf of St. Lawrence from water flowing to the Gulf of Mexico. Portage Lakes south of Akron is one place where only a short distance separates the headwaters of the north-flowing Little Cuyahoga River and the south-flowing Tuscarawas River.

Torrents of glacial meltwater carried millions of tons of soil, sand, and gravel southward. As the water eroded the landscape, the coarser sand and gravel was deposited in the stream valleys, forming the basis of northeastern Ohio's sand and gravel industry. This glacial outwash is very porous and ground water flows freely through it, providing a good place to drill for water. In some valleys more than 500 gallons of water per minute can be pumped. Canton, Cuyahoga Falls, and Kent are among many cities which draw municipal water supplies from glacial outwash. However people living in most of the plateau are not so fortunate and they must draw their water from aquifers yielding from five to 25 gallons of water per minute.

Natural lakes are also a feature of the glaciated landscape. All are very small and many are old and more properly classed as bogs or marshes. These bodies of water were formed by huge chunks of ice which broke off the retreating glacier and melted in depressions forming kettle lakes. These lakes received the fine clay outwash. For a time ice blocked the Cuyahoga River, backing up water and forming a lake extending southward to Akron. Clay and silt settled out of the still water and partially filled this valley. This action makes bridge, highway, and building construction in the valley difficult because the deposits are so unstable. Landslides are common, even under natural conditions. People's carelessness compounds the problems. Farmers grow vegetables in these old glacial lake regions that were filled with sediment and black, organically-rich deposits.

Plants and Animals of the Plateau

To the traveler on the road in the glaciated plateau, the predominant characteristic of the region is woodland — not the thousands of acres of continuous forest of southeastern Ohio — but the thousands of woodlands varying from an acre or two to one or two hundred acres. In the central plateau in Medina, Summit, and Cuyahoga counties, the woodlands are adjacent to the highway rights-of-way. In summer, they dot the hilltops like many green toupees as far as the eye can see. Cleveland is renowned for its woodlands around the city protected in a string of large metropolitan parks called the Emerald Necklace.

Plants of the Plateau

Naturalists roaming the forest remnants of northeast Ohio during the nineteenth and twentieth centuries often pointed out that the plateau is a major meeting ground between northern Allegheny and central Appalachian forests. Ridgetop forests south of Cleveland contain much white oak, just as do ridges in the central and southern Appalachians. But northeast of Cleveland, ridgetops and valley bluffs are covered with forests similar to northern hemlock forests of Allegheny woods in Pennsylvania and New York. The tension zone aspect of the glaciated plateau is most obvious on rugged uplands or wetlands. Oak woods on rough, broken topography and swamp woods on wetlands originally made up a minor percentage of the glaciated plateau, while beech-sugar maple forests were widespread.

Amish buggy near Burton in Geauga County

Sugar camp near Burton in Geauga County

Maple sap "drop"

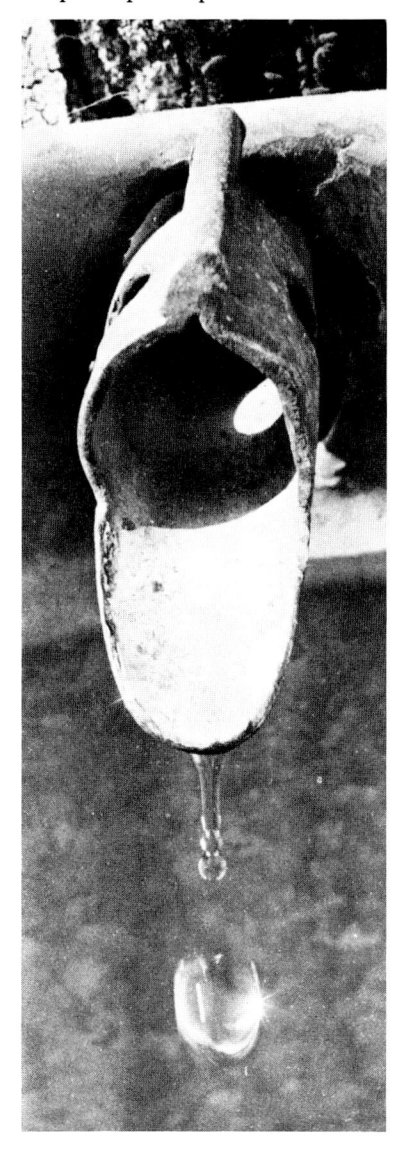

Northeastern Ohio is known as Ohio's dairyland, even though this type of farming has declined drastically in the twentieth century. The forests through which deer and beaver now roam are mostly regrowth secondary forests on abandoned farm lands. Today's plateau forests are different from those of virgin woodlands. Secondary-growth forests have red maple, tuliptree, white ash, wild black cherry, oaks, and hickories, while virgin forests are rare, but do occur in isolated stands throughout the northeast.

Three forest types on the glaciated plateau stand out as strongholds of southern and northern species such as shinleaf, trailing arbutus, round-leafed violet, columbine, or roseshell azalea. The associations of northern species and/or southern species which inhabit these localized vegetation types are ecological "islands" or "peninsulas."

Surrounded by beech-sugar maple forests, these rare plant islands tend to be on steep valley bluffs, ravine slopes, bedrock cliffs, and wet flats. Soils on these sites are shallow and poorly developed although each area is adjacent to a sea of relatively deep, well-developed soil.

The glaciers left a deep deposit of till across the northern plateau which originally supported the widespread beech-sugar maple forests. In pioneer times, the beech-maple belt was very extensive and stretched across the plateau from Mansfield to Pennsylvania.

Farther south the till deposits are thinner. Steep valley bluffs and bedrock cliffs poke through the shallower parts and often form bedrock corridors to the adjacent Unglaciated Appalachian Plateau to the south. This thin glacial cover, combined with stream cutting, has produced a steeply rolling, often rocky landscape known as the White Oak Hills. Forests of mixed oak are common here and white oak is most common of all. A lobe of the White Oak Hills extends north along sand-gravel hills in Geauga, Portage, Summit, and Stark counties. Mixed oak forests also extend north along the slopes of the lower Cuyahoga River Valley.

Soil moisture is very important for plants growing on the habitat islands; however, high or low rainfall causes little change in the surrounding beech-sugar maple forests growing on deep glacial till, because the water holding capacity of a deep soil is greater as compared to shallow soils. During dry periods, plants in beech-sugar maple forests obtain water from the deep internal soil network. Swamp-like conditions seldom develop in beech-sugar maple forests because rainwater runs off the sloping ground.

Because beech-sugar maple forests have dense, closed canopies, the limited light which reaches the ground affects growth there. Relatively little light reaches the forest floor after leaves mature in early summer, and few tree saplings and shrubs other than beech and sugar maple can tolerate the dense shade.

The long life spans, shade tolerance, and competitive root systems of beech and sugar maple account for their widespread distribution on the glaciated plateau. Widespread distribution of sugar maple means the glaciated plateau is a prime area for maple-syrup production. Much of this production is centered in Geauga County. The sugar maples are tapped in late winter when the sap begins to rise in the tree trunks. This sap is collected and boiled down for syrup. Much of the watery sap needs to be collected since sap from a good sugar maple only contains about one percent sugar, and a top yielding tree only has about four percent sugar in its sap.

Beech and sugar maple trees grow slowly compared to many less shade tolerant, shorter-lived trees such as red maple, white ash, and tuliptree. If not for forest fires, windstorms, and other natural disasters,

Christmas fern "fiddleheads"

beech and sugar maple probably would be about the only trees around. But after a windstorm, seeds sprout and the seedlings of wild black cherry, white ash, red maple, and cucumber magnolia once established on openings, quickly outgrow companion seedlings or small saplings of beech and sugar maple. Natural disasters, especially windthrow, are most common on rocky valley bluffs, ravine slopes, bedrock cliffs, and wet flats.

The only section of Ohio where beech and sugar maple are found on very dry sites is within the northeastern Ohio snow belt. Perhaps the reason is that this area has more cloudy summer days, cooler summer temperatures, and more winter snow cover as compared to the rest of Ohio.

The habitat islands or peninsulas discussed in this chapter are unsuited for typical closed canopy beech-sugar maple forests; consequently, movement of northern species southward or southern species northward could possibly occur on these habitat islands or peninsulas. Furthermore, the habitat islands and peninsulas apparently provide refuge to plants lagging behind after the climate changed during and after glaciation.

Many eastern mountain species such as clubmosses, blueberries, and pink ladyslipper (or moccasin-flower) are known to be more or less restricted to acid soils. Acid soils over most of northeastern Ohio make up a corridor extending eastward on the main divide into the highlands of northeastern Pennsylvania and western New York. In essence, an unbroken line of acid soil extends along the ridgetops of the Alleghenies into Ohio. In strong contrast, floodplains and lower slopes throughout the glaciated plateau have soil reactions similar to the alkaline soils of western Ohio. Perhaps the acid soil uplands between one river valley

Blueberries

Moccasin flower or pink ladyslipper orchid

Wintergreen or mountain teaberry

and the next in northeastern Ohio serve as barriers preventing or slowing the northeastward postglacial movement of many rich-soil Mississippi Basin species so common on the alkaline soils of western Ohio. Ohio buckeye, hackberry, sessile trillium, and nodding trillium are just a few Mississippi Basin species rare or absent within the primary snowbelt.

Northern Allegheny species such as star flower, Carolina spring beauty, hobblebush, mountain maple, and northern fly honeysuckle grow in the snowbelt probably because of heavy snow, steep slopes, acid soils, a corridor into Pennsylvania, and reduced competition from beech and sugar maple. To the south, the factors promoting mixed oak forests probably include light snow cover, less beech-maple competition, steep slopes and rocky ridges, acid soils, and a corridor into the unglaciated plateau. The wide geographic barrier that separates the hemlock-hardwoods in the northeast from the White Oak Hills in the south is the beech-sugar maple belt. A continuous corridor allows white oak-mixed oak forest and other mixed forests to extend north across the beech-maple belt on the steep slopes of the lower Cuyahoga River Valley from Akron to Cleveland. One of the best places to see this mixed-oak forest is in Cuyahoga Valley National Recreation Area north of Akron. The area protects about 22 miles of the Cuyahoga, and connects several metroparks of the Cleveland and Akron metropolitan park districts. The recreation area is really a kind of microcosm of northeastern Ohio. Farms, villages, private homes, and various public facilities such as the Blossom Music Center are interspersed among forests, steep-walled gorges, and fast-flowing tributaries of the river. Despite the several million persons who live near the recreation area, people and nature are in uneasy balance.

From the Cuyahoga Valley eastward along the northern rim of the Allegheny Plateau, the geologic features are prime for the further extension of the White Oak Hills and mixed forests. However the heavy snows and summer cloudiness in the snowbelt apparently favor the hemlock-beech forests on the steep bluffs northeast of Cleveland. White pines occasionally grow among these hemlock-beech woodlands.

Indian Signal Tree, a bur oak in the Cuyahoga River Valley just north of Akron off Peck Road. It is thought that the Indians shaped it to mark a trail between the Cuyahoga-Tuscarawas Portage and Cuyahoga Falls.

Painted trillium

Purple trillium or Stinking Benjamin

Forests on the thousands of wet flats across the glaciated plateau are especially distinctive. Water does not run off rapidly from flat land so the first trees to grow on the flats were probably American elm, white ash, red maple, silver maple, pin oak, and swamp white oak which can survive periods of water above their roots. But swamplands promote shallow rooting which makes swamp trees easy targets to topple in windstorms. Pools of water collect where large root balls pull free from the soil. When the roots decay, the soil that was attached to the roots is left in piles. What trees can grow here? Beech and sugar maple — but not very well.

Northern species which migrated south as the climate cooled before the advancing ice sheets can still be found in many northeastern Ohio swamp forests. Yellow birch, a component of hemlock ravine forest, is a common member of glaciated plateau swamp forests, especially in or near the snowbelt. Hemlock is common on wet forest flats in the extreme northeastern corner of the state. Most of these upland swamp forest flats contain patches of partially shaded or open ground after frequent windfall of many shallow-rooted canopy trees. These forests support a wide variety of wildflowers. One of Ohio's rarest and most beautiful wildflowers, painted trillium, occurs in only one woodland in the northeastern corner of the state. The petals of painted trillium are white streaked with thin, rose-pink lines of color as if painted with a brush.

Purple trillium, also known as Stinking Benjamin for its ill-smelling flower, is a northeastern mountain trillim more common within ravines and swamp forests of the glaciated plateau than anywhere else in Ohio. Ranges of three other trilliums reveal a common pattern of species shift from southwest to northeast across the glaciated plateau. Large white-flowered trillium is generally found in many forests throughout Ohio. But two other more southern trilliums, nodding trillium and sessile trillium, are common on rich stream bottoms in the western and southern regions of the glaciated plateau. Both these latter trilliums are rare or absent across the northeast corner of the glaciated plateau from eastern Cuyahoga County to Ashtabula County.

In addition to trillium, during April and May forest floors throughout the plateau are carpeted with spring beauties, anemones, Dutchman's breeches, purple cresses, and other spring wildflowers. All these latter-named wildflowers are known as spring ephemerals. Spring ephemerals do all their evident growing, flowering, and fruiting in the short period between the end of winter and leafing out of the forest canopy. By the time the canopy is in full leaf, most spring ephemerals have disappeared. Underground storage organs enable them to remain dormant beneath the ground until the following spring. Spring ephemerals are especially abundant in beech-sugar maple forests. Very little flowering activity occurs in the dark understory of a beech-sugar maple forest once the canopy has completely leafed out.

Some spring wildflowers such as trilliums, hepaticas, and bloodroot retain their leaves well into the summer in contrast to the spring ephemerals. Wildflowers such as zigzag goldenrod and wood aster cover the ground in fall where spring beauties and Dutchman's breeches carpeted the ground in spring. The evergreen leaves of hepatica can often be found amid stands of woodland asters and woodland goldenrods in the fall.

The open crowns of oak forest and swamp forest, in contrast to beech-sugar maple canopies, permit more light to reach the forest floor. Many summer bloomers such as wintergreen, partridge-berry, and false

Marsh marigold

Mayapples

Wild phlox in spring woods

foxglove inhabit the open oak woods. In summer, one of the most beautiful forest flowers is the pipsissewa. This delicate, fragrant white flower is found chiefly in dry oak woods from the southern reaches of the glaciated plateau into the unglaciated plateau.

Eventual drainage of swamp forest depressions and erosion of glacial till deposits will take place over thousands of years. As streams cut new ravines into the gently rolling beech-sugar maple belt, new shallow soil slope and ridgetop habitats will develop. Over thousands of years, the glacial till will be eroded and the beech and sugar maple forest probably will be replaced by the northern Allegheny and central Appalachian species. In contrast, most northern relicts will stay trapped on the cool, ever-deepening, north-facing ravine and valley walls. But for the present time, Ohioans are gifted with a tremendous north-south diversity.

Animals of the Plateau

When settlers first arrived in northeastern Ohio, the land was populated with such deep forest species as wolf, elk, bear, and mountain lion. Today these species are gone. Animals that were not shot outright were chased away when the forest was destroyed. Instead, species more suited to open areas and the edges between woodland and field are common today. Cottontail rabbit, red fox, raccoon, opossum, skunk, and the ever-present robin all have thrived.

Good wildlife habitat is available along the fence rows and in the corners of the fields that are maintained and used. Not only do these areas offer food and cover, they serve as excellent travel lanes from one field to the next for all sorts of small animals such as rabbits and foxes.

Today, people are probably more aware of birds in the glaciated plateau than any other animals. Many birds live on or migrate through the plateau, including the robin, wood thrush, many species of warblers, pine siskin, ruffed grouse, several species of hawks and owls, eastern phoebe, and tree swallow. These species also live in other parts of the state. There are a few birds that nest in Ohio or live primarily in the glaciated plateau. One of these birds is the veery, a thrush with an extremely beautiful song, which nests in northeastern Ohio and in the Oak Openings near Toledo. Other species include the ring-necked pheasant, common locally in western Ohio and more common in the northeast; the yellow-bellied sap-sucker, a migrant in most of the state which nests in Ohio only in the northeast; and the hairy woodpecker, a robin-sized, black and white bird rarely found away from the woods. Hairy woodpeckers are found rarely throughout Ohio, but are most common in the northeast. Of course all of these birds thrive in the edge areas between forests and fields where food is abundant and cover is near.

The woodcock is another bird more common to northeastern Ohio than other regions. However this robin-sized game bird is seldom seen because of its secretive habits and its excellent brownish protective coloration. Not a handsome bird, a woodcock has short legs, a short neck, large eyes, and a long beak; and it waddles when it walks. Not only are these small birds hard to see, they also hide their nests very well. A nest is usually no more than a depression in the grass, and a female woodcock will often remain on her nest until an intruder comes to within a few feet. Any closer and the bird suddenly leaves — zigzagging into a nearby thicket or clump of marsh grass.

The mating behavior of the males is one of the most interesting habits of this bird. On early spring evenings a male will strut around making indelicate peeping sounds similar to a Bronx cheer. Then he will fly up and circle high in the sky causing a melodious whistle to come from his wing feathers. Then, he drops quickly, almost dives, while making a twittering noise, and returns to his take-off spot. All of this activity serves to attract a mate, and a male woodcock will defend this area against all of his competitors.

Many mammals live on the plateau. Mammals common in other regions of the state are also found here including woodchuck, both red and gray fox, opossum, raccoon, skunk, cottontail rabbit, and white-tailed deer. Several species of bats also live on the plateau including the little brown bat, big brown bat, and red bat.

Like many species of birds, some mammals have benefited from the gradual reversion of farm fields to meadow and forest. This process has increased the cover for animals such as the red fox, woodchuck, muskrat, long-tailed weasel, and white-tailed deer. Always on the hunt for food (small rodents, young rabbits, and other mammals), foxes are themselves frequently hunted by humans — either in fox chases for sport, or by farmers who believe a fox may be preying on chickens.

Woodchucks are most common along the gravelly mounds which mark the southern boundary of the ice sheets, although they are common throughout the state. The digging is easier near these glacial deposits, and woodchucks frequently build extensive tunnel systems 25 to 40 feet long. Occasionally several rooms and hallways will jut from the main tunnel. The woodchuck eats small grains, fruit, and sometimes garden vegetables, and usually lives near a good food supply. Thus these animals are found right up to the city limits. Woodchuck burrowing in fields sometimes results in injuries to cows and other livestock that step in the holes, but, when burrowing is limited to fencerows, drainage ditches, and other out-of-the-way places, there is little damage.

Woodcock

Bluebird (opposite page)

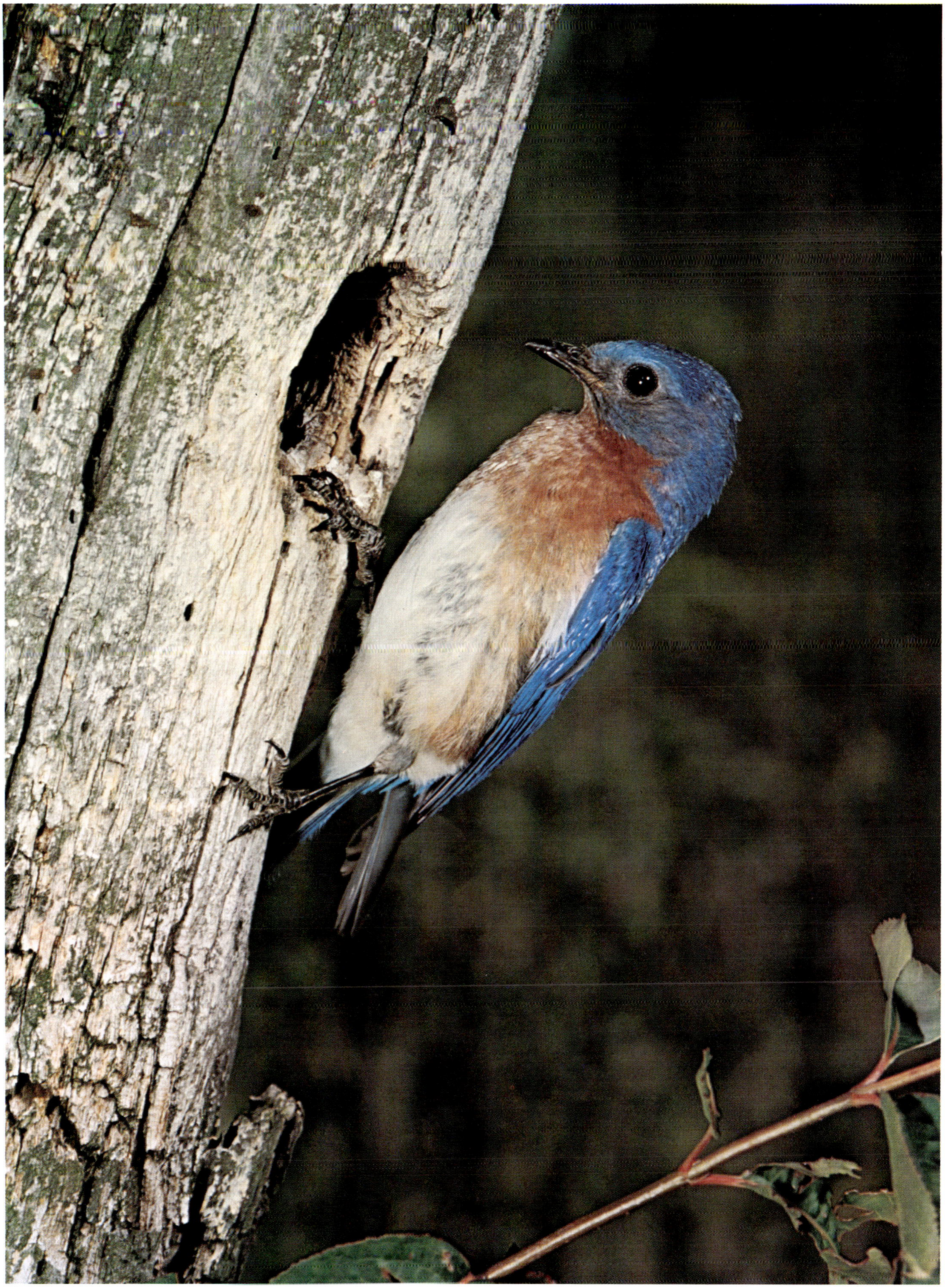

Weasel

Saw-whet owl targeting a white-footed mouse

In contrast to the woodchuck which is a vegetarian, the weasel is a carnivore. Its major food is mice and other small rodents. Weasels are small, slender animals that can follow mice into their tunnels and kill them with swift bites to the neck. Thus they are among the best mousetraps found in nature. Savage fighters, weasels can kill animals several times their own size. However they also are prey to hawks, owls, and even black snakes, which eat young weasels.

Another carnivore is the mink. Powerful, aggressive, and crafty, minks swim fast enough to catch fish. However one of the mink's favorite foods is muskrat, a slow, plodding animal that has little protection. After a kill, minks usually carry prey to dens where they eat or store the food. Some dens have been found with 10 muskrats and one or two rabbits. On the plateau, as in other parts of Ohio, minks usually live near water where they range the shores of reservoirs, bogs, or streams searching for food.

One of the mammals growing fastest in numbers on the plateau is the beaver. Once extirpated from the state, beavers migrated into northeastern Ohio in 1936 and by 1961 populations had become large enough that a five-day trapping season was initiated in Ashtabula, Columbiana, and Mahoning counties. The favorite food of these aquatic mammals is the bark of aspen trees, but they also eat willow, birch, wild black cherry, and many other hardwoods. Their sharp, chisel-like teeth enable them to cut trees for dams. Beavers also live in dens in pond or stream banks. When water backs up behind a dam and floods fields, farmers quickly tear down the dam. The beavers make repairs almost as

Beaver

quickly, and this tearing down and rebuilding goes on until the farmer gives up, resorts to a gun or trap, or requests the Ohio Division of Wildlife to trap and relocate the animals.

There are few small mammals found only on the glaciated plateau. The ermine or short-tailed weasel resembles the common long-tailed weasel except for the length of the tail. The star-nosed mole, the red-backed vole, and woodland jumping mouse also are found here.

Reptiles common to the glaciated plateau include the midland painted turtle and northern watersnake. The red-bellied snake, which has an orange belly, lives in moist wooded areas of northeastern Ohio.

Among amphibians, the dusky salamander, a small brownish animal living near streams, is common throughout eastern Ohio, while the Allegheny mountain dusky is found mostly in the northeast.

The landscape is actually better suited to more animals today than before the settlers arrived. The reason is the great variety of habitat on the plateau. The thousands of woodlands have lots of "edge" and each forest edge is next to a farm field, meadow, pasture, or bog. Wildlife habitat also increased after farmers discovered planting some of their marginal glaciated fields was not profitable. They allowed these fields to revert to pasture or woodland, adding thousands more acres to available wildlife habitat and insuring a place for wild things in the heavily populated plateau.

Garter snake

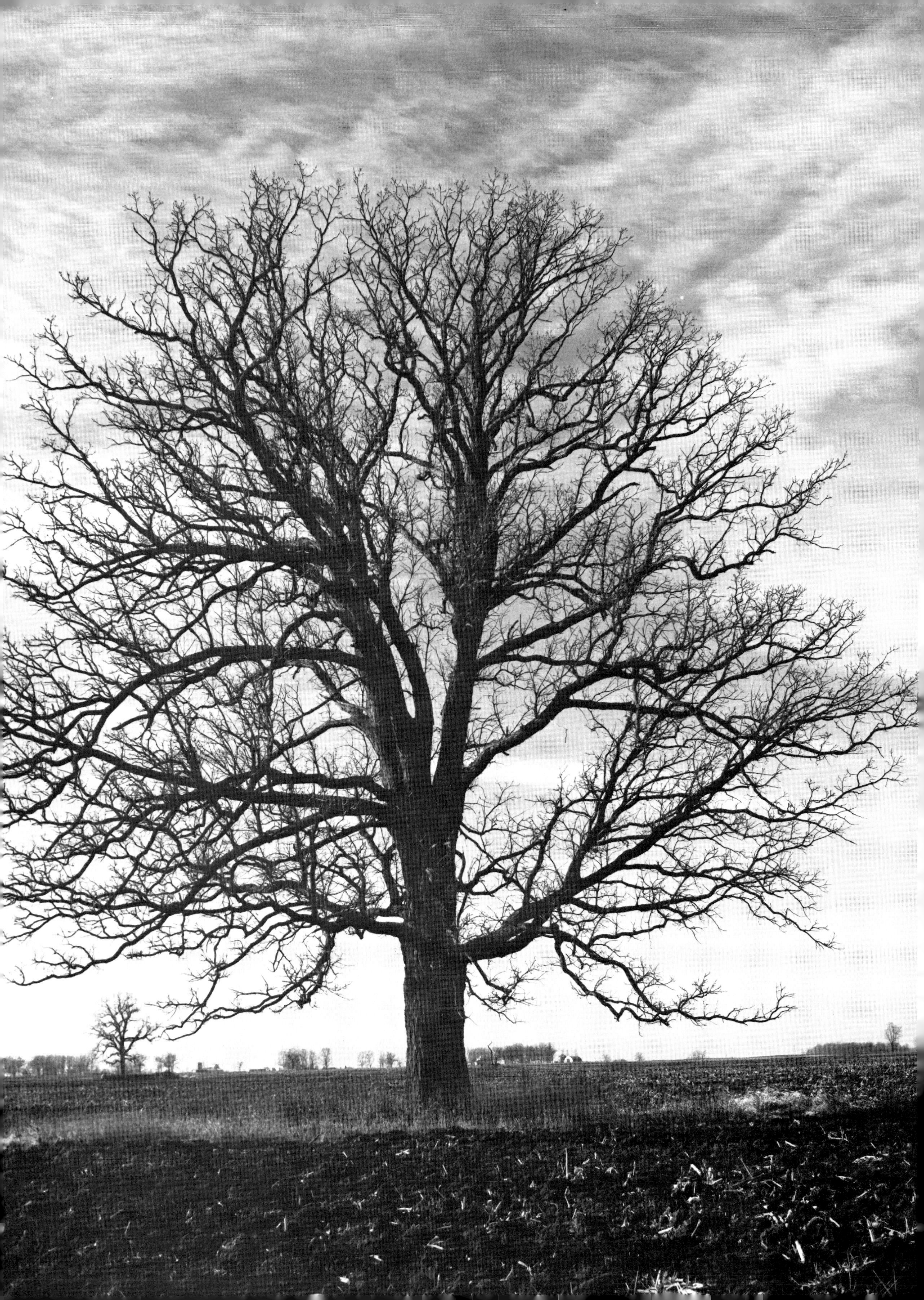

Chapter 12
Till Plains

by Jane L. Forsyth

OHIO'S Till Plains are her rich western farmlands. It was here that America's early pioneers first found fertile agricultural land, as they headed west, and here that many settled, beginning a way of life that is still one of the most important in Ohio.

The settlers did not find the open fields of today. Except for a few small prairie openings, the region was covered with dense woodlands, with trees growing thickly in response to the same rich soils that would later support corn, soybeans, and wheat. These soils, in turn, were products of the natural breakdown of the basic geologic materials of the area — the glacial clays and gravels and the underlying sedimentary bedrock. Even these materials, the glacial deposits and the bedrock, reveal a part of the history of Ohio that is an essential part of the heritage.

Bedrock Geology

Beneath the almost continuous cover of glacial deposits lies sedimentary bedrock, which, in the Till Plains, is mostly limestone, with a little shale. Much of this limestone is the magnesium-bearing form called dolomite. All these rocks are of early Paleozoic age (Ordovician through Devonian), approximately 500 to 350 million years old, and many contain fossils of ancient marine invertebrates, such as corals, brachiopods, clams, snails, cephalopods, crinoids, and trilobites. In fact,

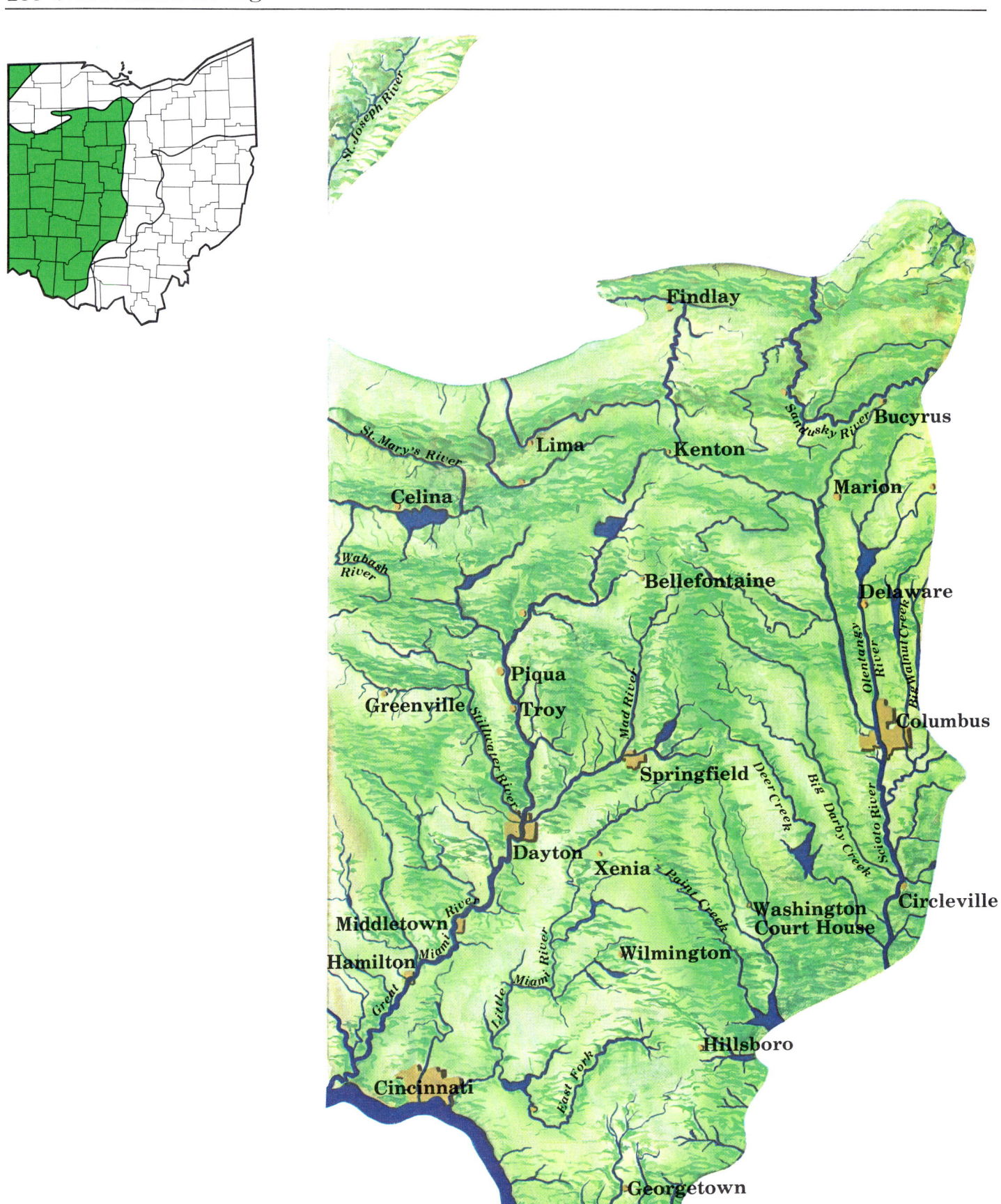

the Cincinnatian (Ordovician) rocks contain so many fossils of such diverse species, many weathering out loose, that they have become very famous and, since the early 1800s, have drawn people from all over the world to come and collect them. In places in the younger (Devonian) rocks, obscure fossilized fragments of primitive fish can be found, but higher forms of life are unknown in these rocks since such forms had not yet developed. These rocks, with their fossils, indicate the presence of a broad, shallow sea that flooded Ohio for about 300 million years. Lime precipitated from the water accumulated on the bottom and recrystallized forming the limestone bedrock.

The youngest rocks of the Till Plains, which lie on top of the limestones and dolomites, are shales. These form a narrow north-south belt through central Ohio, extending eastward into the plateau and eroded away to the west. They, too, tell a story, for they represent the consolidated remains of the first extensive muds to have been washed out into the ancient Paleozoic ocean in Ohio from rising land to the east. This eastern land was beginning to rise as a result of the first of the forces that would, 150 million years later, create the Appalachian Mountains. As the land rose, it was being eroded by streams that washed this sediment westward into the Ohio seas.

When the Appalachian Mountains were formed, all the different limestone and shale layers, or rock formations, of Ohio were bowed up into a low arch, the Cincinnnati Arch, the sides of which slope very gently at angles of less than one degree. Extensive erosion of these arched rock layers took place throughout Ohio, but the erosion cut deepest where the Arch stood highest, in western Ohio. Thus it is Ohio's oldest rocks (limestones and dolomites) that form the bedrock in the Till Plains, with the younger shale lying on these older rocks on the eastern side of the arch. A slight bulge in the crest of the Arch at Cincinnati caused erosion to go deepest there, thus exposing the famous fossiliferous Cincinnatian rocks.

The bedrock of the Till Plains may be observed mainly in quarries, road cuts, and stream banks. However, such places are quite limited in most of the Till Plains, because the glacial cover there is almost continuous and locally quite thick. An exception to this is the famous "Bellefontaine Outlier" in Logan County, where a remnant of the eastern shale rises up and protrudes as rocky hills. Immediately beneath the shale is the Columbus Limestone which, due to its purity, here contains caves — the Ohio Caverns and Zane Caverns. This is the same rock formation that occurs in the Marble Cliff quarries of Columbus and the huge quarry on Marblehead Peninsula, and in which the famous Kelleys Island glacial grooves were cut.

Erosion of all these rocks took a long time. The erosion began as sediment deposition ended and the seas drained away, about 200 million years ago, and continued until the first advance of the Ice Age (Pleistocene) glaciers about two million years ago. Thus, though the glacial materials lie directly on the early Paleozoic bedrock in the Till Plains, they are very much younger than the rock; the surface on which they lie is simply the final surface left by all that erosion. All the younger sedimentary rocks of Ohio, even those of the eastern plateaus, were once present in western Ohio, before they were eroded.

All of this erosion was done by streams. The glacier could not have removed this rock and soil because it came too late and the ice was much too thin. The main stream at that time was the Teays River, a major stream which had its headwaters in the Appalachians in the present valley of the New River. The Teays flowed northwestward across Ohio from east of Portsmouth to Celina and westward into Indiana. This river lasted from about 200 million years ago until its demise when the first of the Ice Age glaciers blocked and buried it, diverting its flow into a newly created ice-marginal river, the Ohio River. The only evidence of this

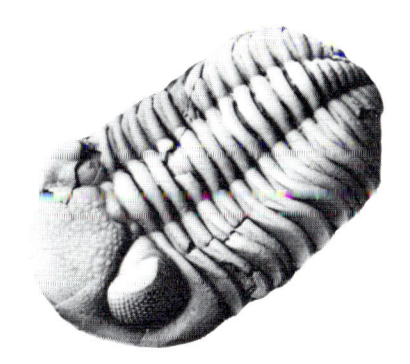

Devonian trilobite

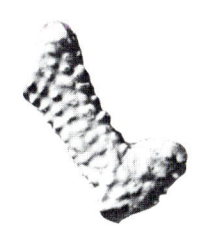

Ordovician bryozoan

Silurian brachiopod

earlier famous, long-lived river in the Till Plains is its abandoned valley, now deeply buried by glacial deposits.

This valley is deepest (400 to 500 feet) near the Shelby County town of Anna. Here the Teays cut so deeply that soft, older (Ordovician) shales and limestones are present all along the bottom of the valley, while harder, younger (Silurian) dolomites form the ancient uplands, all now buried by glacial materials. Anna also is famous because, of all the earthquakes that have been recorded for Ohio, more than half have occurred near here. None of these earthquakes was large and none is known to have had a value of more than 4 on the Richter Scale. Nonetheless, such a concentration of earthquake sites at this one location in the Till Plains is intriguing. It has been suggested that minor movements along faults in the underlying Precambrian crystalline rock may have caused these earthquakes, which were centered near Anna because the faults intersect here. It is also possible that the presence of the band of weak Ordovician shales along the buried Teays Valley may have helped to concentrate the earthquake activity here.

Glaciation

The Ice Age glaciers advanced across the Till Plains several times. Deposits of four major ice advances are recognized, each differentiated on the basis of soils, geographic distribution of materials, and stratigraphic relationships. Smaller differences in these same factors also have been used to identify five different retreatal phases of the last ice advance. Of all the main ice advances, only the last, the Late Wisconsinan, has been dated extensively by radiocarbon means, so that it is known to have reached its farthest point south about 20,000 years ago. Other glacial advances — Illinoian and Kansan(?) — are dated by other, less precise means at about 125,000 and 700,000 years ago, respectively.

In all these advances, the ice moved generally southward across western Ohio. It was divided into two lobes by the Bellefontaine Outlier, the Miami Lobe to the west along the Miami River Valley and the Scioto Lobe along the Scioto River Valley south through Columbus. At a later stage, when the ice was thinner, it was diverted toward the southwest by the Lake Erie Basin, creating a southwest-oriented lobe, the Erie Lobe.

Each glacial advance created many different stream diversions. Most famous of the diversions, of course, was that of the Teays River system, when it was blocked and diverted westward by the first of the Ice Age glaciers in Ohio, the Kansan(?), creating the Ohio River. No other diversion affected so great an area. Most of the other more famous stream diversions took place in the hills east of the Till Plains.

On the flatter land of the Till Plains, drainage changes are less striking than in the eastern plateaus. Probably most famous are the changes in the courses of the Ohio River and its tributaries in the Cincinnati area. The newly formed Ohio River, which initially flowed northwestward through Norwood, was diverted to the south, into its present course, by the Illinoian glacier, cutting through a preglacial divide and creating a "narrows" at Anderson's Ferry, west of Cincinnati. The Little Miami River was overrun by the Late Wisconsinan glacier in two places, east and south of Lebanon, diverting the river in both places into new courses along which it cut deep bedrock gorges. The old valley east of Lebanon is now filled with till and the pre-Wisconsinan valley southwest of Lebanon is partly filled with lake

Interbedded till and gravel

sediments and kames. Even a minor diversion southward of a small stream near Sharonville, also produced by the Late Wisconsinan glacier, resulted in the cutting of a small but spectacular bedrock gorge in what is now a city park.

Each ice advance left several kinds of deposits composed of either till or gravel. The most extensive deposit left by the Late Wisconsinan glacier is ground moraine, which appears as generally flat land underlain by till of a varying thickness. Located across this broad area of ground moraine are more than a dozen end moraines, appearing as belts of low hills or rolling, hummocky land. These end moraines overlap each other at every interlobate position, such as near Bellefontaine and Mansfield. Indeed, the end moraines accumulated to such a thickness on the Bellefontaine Outlier that they create the highest point in Ohio, Campbell Hill, with an elevation of 1,549 feet. This high point is located about a mile northeast of the city of Bellefontaine and is composed of over 350 feet of glacial material piled on top of the bedrock hills of the Outlier.

Gravel deposits are more scattered. In all major south-going valleys, flat outwash terraces are present. Outwash terraces are especially extensive in the interlobate area between the Miami and Scioto lobes, where three well-developed levels of outwash, representing three different stages within the Late Wisconsinan history, are present. Because the two higher levels occur in "one-sided" valleys, which open to the west, the glacier itself must have formed the west wall of the valley when the outwash was being deposited. The highest of the three levels, the Kennard Outwash, can be traced south to the head of Clifton Gorge in Greene County, at the upper end of John Bryan State Park. Clearly it was glacial meltwater, about 16,000 years ago, that cut this gorge. Broad deposits of outwash also occur near Newtown, in Cincinnati, where they

Clifton gorge and ice

Three levels of glacial outwash in the Springfield area.

are extensively mined for gravel and from which many teeth and bones of mastodon and mammoth have been recovered.

Kames and eskers, hills composed of gravel, occur in localized groups, the most extensive areas being in western Logan County and the region between Dayton and Springfield. In places, some of these deposits are covered by till — evidence for a readvance of the ice after these deposits were formed.

The detailed history of the Late Wisconsinan glaciation in Ohio, well documented by radiocarbon dates, is mainly recorded in the Till Plains. The older tills, deposited by a glacial advance dated from incorporated wood of spruce trees overrun by the advancing glacier, are overlain to the north by younger, wood-free tills that represent several major readvances of the retreating Late Wisconsinan glacier. Different ages of these younger, more northern tills are identified by different soils, generally shallower to the north (Russell, Miamian, Blount, and Hoytville soils). Beneath these Late Wisconsinan deposits, under a famous soil exposed near Sidney, is Early Wisconsinan till, material which is found in Ohio only below younger deposits.

Illinoian deposits occur mainly in a broad band south of the Wisconsinan boundary, but are also occasionally identified below surface Wisconsinan deposits in road or stream cuts or in well drillings. These deposits are recognized as Illinoian because of the deeply weathered (Cincinnati) soils developed in them. These soils are normally seven to nine feet deep, in contrast to Wisconsinan soils that are only two to five feet deep, and are much more strongly weathered.

The dominant Illinoian deposit is ground moraine, which, in the Till Plains, is flat and poorly drained. The Illinoian till is commonly capped by two to six feet of loess of Illinoian and/or Wisconsinan age, which increases the flatness and poor drainage of the land. Illinoian outwash is preserved locally as high-level terrace remnants in the Cincinnati area and along the Ohio River Valley, but such remnants are not common. These terraces are identified as Illinoian by their great height above the valley bottom and the very deep soil (10 to 12 feet deep) developed in them. An interesting area of Illinoian lake deposits and

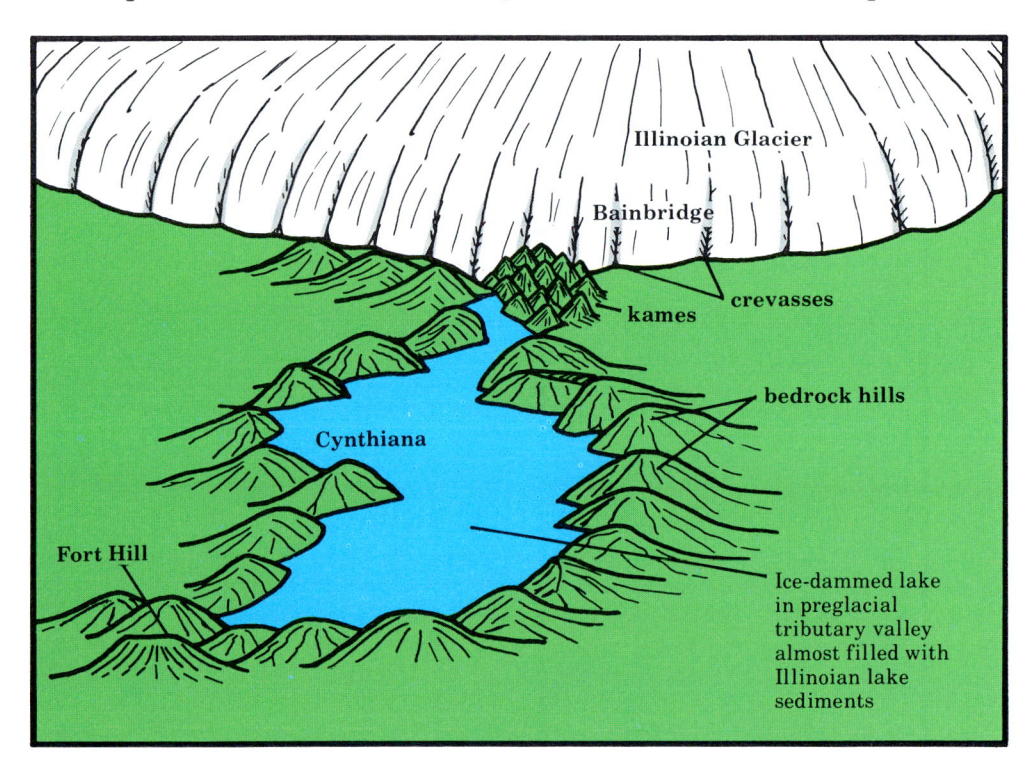

Ice dammed lake south of Bainbridge in Ross County

kames occurs a few miles southwest of Bainbridge in Highland, Pike, and Ross counties, along the edge of the Till Plains, where the Illinoian ice blocked the northward flow of a small southern tributary to Paint Creek. The lake deposits were formed in the tributary valley when the glacier blocked this stream, forming a lake there, and the kames were formed in the crevassed marginal ice of the Illinoian glacier.

All glacial deposits contain erratics, or rocks of a composition foreign to the local bedrock. In Ohio, these erratics are commonly pebbles or boulders of igneous or metamorphic rocks brought from Canada. Most erratics are boulder sized, two to four feet in diameter. In places they occur in special abundance along end moraines, and are called "boulder belts." The largest erratic in Ohio, however, is far bigger and occurs in eastern Warren County. Here a huge piece of Silurian Brassfield Limestone, about 45,000 square feet in area, was shifted about three miles westward from its outcrop in western Clinton County by the Illinoian glacier. Indeed, it was so big that a quarry, the Heidi Quarry, was cut into the rock in the early 1900s. Although much of the rock has been removed and the quarry has long been abandoned, Silurian limestone may still be observed lying on Illinoian till over older Ordovician shale and limestone.

Glacial deposits older than the Illinoian occur in only one part of the Ohio Till Plains, in western Hamilton County. Here, beyond the Illinoian glacial boundary, local areas of very deeply weathered till occur in scattered road cuts and stream banks, among abundant outcrops of Ordovician bedrock. Nowhere is the thickness of this ancient till more than 17 feet, and in all places the entire section of till is weathered. Clearly, this till is considerably older than the Illinoian, but whether it is of Kansan or Nebraskan age is not known. This till differs from the Illinoian till in another way. It is found only on the uplands, whereas Illinoian till occurs both on the uplands and in the valleys. Thus deposition of this Kansan(?) till preceded major valley cutting in western Ohio. This means the glacier that deposited this till must have been the same one that, by blocking the Teays, created the Ohio River, the first major stream to flow westward through the Cincinnati area, thus causing such dissection.

Soils of the Till Plains

The Till Plains of Ohio are famous for the extensive and detailed study of soils, now called Miamian. These soils which were originally simply called Miami soils have been subdivided into two different types. To the south are the Miamian soils developed in loam or clay loam till. To the north are soils developed in clay-rich till, for example, Blount soils. The extra clay in this till is believed to have been deposited in a temporary lake formed during glacial retreat and to have been picked up and incorporated in the till subsequently deposited by the readvancing ice. The Miamian and Blount soils are both found in late Wisconsinan high-lime tills, the high-lime characteristic being a result of the influence of the Paleozoic limestone-dolomite bedrock of the Till Plains. Farther east, in the areas of shale (and sandstone) bedrock, are low-lime tills in which soils called Alexandria were formed. Soils developed in the Illinoian tills of southwestern Ohio are deeply weathered (seven to ten feet deep) Cincinnati soils which, as mapped, also include some areas of Eden soils where bedrock has been exposed by erosion.

The two main factors affecting the nature of the soils formed in western Ohio tills are the age of the deposit (time) and nature of the till (parent material). Of the other three soil-forming factors, climate is the same throughout the areas, and the effects of topography and organisms simply produce variations in these main soils (catenas). Overall, soil differences based on the ages of the deposits are most important in controlling soil differences. However, many of the contrasts in the soils developed in Late Wisconsinan tills, most of which do not vary greatly in age, are due to variations in till characteristics, such as amount of lime, amount of clay, or thickness of silt cap, if present. Anyone with a meaningful understanding of how these factors can affect soil differences not only comprehends soils better, but will find soils a most useful tool in interpreting the glacial story of western Ohio, as well as contributing to a better understanding of the distribution of plants and animals there.

Plants of the Till Plains

Most of the vegetation characteristic of the Till Plains today is corn, soybeans, and wheat. Extensive stands of natural vegetation are found only on poorer land and along stream valleys. Even in these areas, in most cases, the vegetation is brushy and second growth. Locally a few remnants of the original woodland remain. Examples of these are Hueston Woods State Nature Preserve near Oxford, Culberson (Villars Chapel Woods) State Nature Preserve near Wilmington, and Cedar Bog State Memorial near Urbana. Many of these remnants, fortunately, are now being preserved by the Ohio Department of Natural Resources, The Nature Conservancy, and the Ohio Historical Society.

The original vegetation of the area, before its destruction by settlers, was mostly woodland, composed entirely of species adapted to the local environment. With clearing, draining, and cropping, the environmental conditions have been changed and many of the species that were originally common now occur only locally, having been replaced by crops and weeds. Because roughly 95 percent of the Till Plains is now in farmland or urban areas, the only way the nature of the original vegetation can be determined is by observing limited remnants of that early vegetation and by studying early land-survey records, in which surveyors identified sites by their locations relative to specific adjacent trees.

The kinds of trees growing in the original woodlands varied from place to place in response to differing environmental conditions, as determined by the glacial deposits and the soils developed in them. Beech-sugar maple forests occupied most of the Till Plains, though some areas were a little drier and had stands of oak-sugar maple. Extensive wet areas supported either swamp forest or mixed oaks (wet), and generally also included some wet prairies. Farther south, along the dissected bluffs of the Ohio River, were a few stands of a mesic type of forest called mixed mesophytic, composed of many different types of trees requiring good soil moisture and good soil aeration.

Beech-maple forests still are the characteristic woodland type on Ohio's Late Wisconsinan Till Plains. Dominated by American beech and sugar maple, this mesic woodland type also generally includes red oak, white oak, shagbark hickory, shellbark hickory, white ash, and

Morel mushrooms

wild black cherry, and occurs on flat to gently rolling till plains, on both ground and end moraine, throughout western Ohio.

Oak-maple woods, in contrast, occur where the land is a little drier, due to somewhat steeper slopes or drier substrates (such as gravel). Oak-maple woodlands are very similar to beech-maple, but lack beech, which requires continuously moist substrates and does not easily withstand the periodic late-summer droughts encountered with this forest type. Growing with sugar maple in this woodland type are black maple, red oak, white oak, and black walnut.

Where the ground is particularly flat and poorly drained, these forests are replaced by wetter woodlands--either swamp forest or mixed oaks. Swamp forest woods are dominated by American elm (now mostly dead), black ash, red and/or silver maple, blackgum, and shagbark and shellbark hickory. Pin oak is present in places, especially where the soils contain much clay, and swamp white oak is found in the wettest sites. Such woods occur on poorly drained uplands, not on floodplains (where sycamore, cottonwood, American elm, honey locust, wild black cherry, green ash, and willow are found). Unfortunately, the Dutch elm disease and phloem necrosis have decimated the American elm, so that live specimens of this species are becoming increasingly less common.

Wet, mixed-oak woodlands are dominated by pin oak, swamp white oak, bur oak, shagbark hickory, and, where the soil is less wet, by white and red oaks. Both swamp forest and mixed-oak woods may occur on wet sites, and it is not known what determines which of these two woodland communities will be present at any one site, though the mixed-oak woods seem more likely to occur where the land is wetter and the soils have more clay.

Prairies, or treeless areas, occurred in association with all the more extensive stands of mixed-oak woods, wherever conditions were too wet to permit growth of trees. In these areas, the principal plants were wet grasses and sedges, species such as giant reed grass and bluejoint grass generally dominating and producing what are known as "wet prairies." In areas that tended to become drier toward the end of the summer, other species, considered to be typical of western prairies, were present including: queen-of-the-prairie, purple coneflower, prairie dock, and big bluestem grass.

Of special interest are several areas of wet prairies associated with mixed-oak woods or groves that occurred as "islands" within the extensive beech-maple woods in the northern part of the Till Plains. In the Marion-Wyandot County area (Killdeer Plains) and in northeastern Seneca County, local clay-rich soils produced poorly drained sites that supported such wet mixed-oak woodlands interspersed with prairies. A similar, larger area of wet prairies and mixed-oak woodlands occurred in western Pickaway, Madison, and eastern Champaign and Clark counties, where flat, poorly drained till plains are also underlain by unusually clay-rich tills.

One of the most famous wet areas is Cedar Bog, Ohio's only white-cedar wetland, located southwest of Urbana. Here, where spring water wells up through glacial outwash, is an open sedge meadow surrounded by white cedars.

To the southwest was a large area of oak-maple woodland that occurred on the extensive area of outwash and kames present between Dayton and Springfield. Soils in these gravels were apparently too dry to support beech trees, and oak-maple woodland was dominant on these soils. Cutting diagonally southeast through this oak-maple area, in

Pin oak and early spring pond in Illinoian Till Plains of Clermont County

Bur oak grove interspersed with prairie in southwest Crawford County near Monnett

northeastern Warren and west-central Clinton counties, was a striking band of beech-maple woods. These trees grew on the Cuba Moraine, where increased soil moisture in the silt-capped tills permitted growth of beech. Farther southwest, on poorly drained Illinoian ground moraine capped by equally poorly drained loess, was swamp forest. Where valleys were cut into this flat surface, resulting in the development of better drainage with adequate soil moisture, beech-maple woodland was present.

To the south, along the Ohio River, was found mixed mesophytic woodland. This is a highly diverse community composed of mesic tree species requiring continuously available soil moisture and good soil aeration. The hills along the Ohio River Valley are composed mainly of Ordovician bedrock, though both till and gravel are also present in places. In addition, many different microclimatic differences occur, created by variations in slope and soil conditions along the dissected slopes of the Ohio River Valley. Also, in this southernmost part of the Till Plains, many southern species reach the northern limits of their ranges and thus grow along the river bluffs in Ohio. As a result, with such a diversity of habitats, substrates, microclimates, and ranges, a great many different species of plants are present here, including sugar maple, American beech, white oak, red oak, chinquapin oak, hackberry, white ash, shellbark hickory, basswood, tuliptree, cucumber magnolia, Kentucky coffeetree, and sweetgum.

These were the types of forests found in the Till Plains by the early settlers, but they were quite different from the woodlands present there when the glacier first retreated. In those cold, early postglacial days, the forests were mainly spruce (white spruce on the higher land, and black spruce on the lower, less well-drained land) and fir. At that time, in response to a general climatic warming about 10,000 years ago, these species were replaced, first by pine, then by oak and hickory, and ultimately by the many deciduous trees occurring in the Till Plains today.

As the climate continued to become both warmer and drier (the Xerothermic Interval), the prairie species invaded, creating the Prairie Peninsula, remnants of which are found as the wet prairies (occurring with the wet mixed oaks) and dry prairies of the Till Plains described earlier. Such prairies have long been interpreted to represent the migration eastward of western prairie species during this warm, dry period, but recent evidence suggests that the distributions of many of these "prairie" species are as much eastern as western, so some reevaluation of this classic picture is needed.

All this vegetation grew mainly in the rich deep soils of the thick glacial deposits. Where the limestone-dolomite bedrock was exposed or lay close below the surface, different, "lime-loving" plants were present. It may have been the high-lime character of the substrate, or the somewhat drier conditions provided by cracks and dissolved openings in the limestone, or perhaps a combination of these two (or other) factors that caused the plants to grow here. Species characteristic of these sites include trees and bushes such as blue ash, chinquapin oak, hackberry, fragrant sumac, red cedar, and redbud; and herbs such as snow trillium, wild geranium (herb Robert), nodding thistle, and some sedges.

Wildflowers abound in the fields and woodlands of the Till Plains. Many of these species are common throughout the state, but are perhaps at their best in the rich Till Plains soils. In spring, common flowers are Dutchman's breeches, rue anemone, trillium, spring beauty, and bloodroot. Wild ginger, the roots of which were collected by settlers and

New England aster

ground as a source of ginger spice, is also present, as is mayapple, the fruits of which were eaten by the early settlers. In summer, thimbleweed, American columbo, wild lettuce, jewelweed (with either yellow or orange flowers), and daisy fleabane are some of the common flowers. In autumn, the most abundant flowers are asters, goldenrods, and chicory, the latter plant more common in limy areas and whose roots were used by settlers to make a coffee-like drink.

Animals of the Till Plains

Animal life in the Till Plains is as varied as the vegetation and geology. However, the diversity here is much less than that of the wooded hills of eastern Ohio, because of the intensity of farming and urbanization and because of the destruction of essential habitats here in the west. The best-known animals of the Till Plains include fish, amphibians (frogs and salamanders), reptiles (snakes and turtles), birds, and mammals. Also important in the Till Plains but not discussed here are the great numbers and varieties of invertebrates.

Many streams of the Till Plains maintain relatively high sustained flows of water which support good fish populations. Extensive areas of permeable glacial deposits in their watersheds supply the streams with copious amounts of cool ground water year-round. The Mad River with its persistent flow of cool water from such broad deposits east of Bellefontaine is one of the few streams in Ohio capable of supporting a naturally reproducing population of brook trout. Apparently trout were not native to the Mad River but were introduced into the watershed in the late 1800s. The Mad River and tributaries (especially Kings Creek northeast of Urbana) also support the largest Ohio population of the rare and endangered tonguetied minnow (chub).

Monarch on milkweed

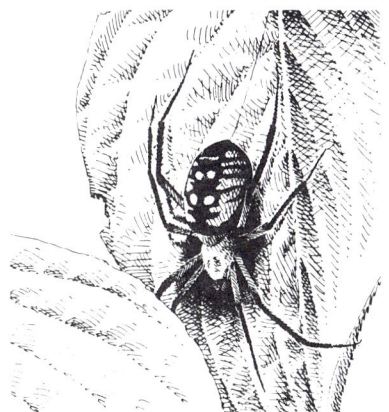

Garden spider

Kestrels (or sparrow hawks) are frequently seen on utility lines or hovering over fields in the Till Plains.

Rainbow darters inhabit clearwater streams with moderate or high gradients and bottoms of sand and gravel.

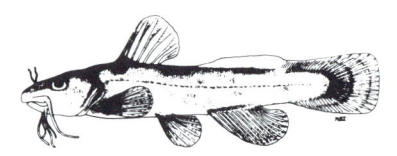

The Scioto madtom, a small catfish, has been found in no other stream in the world than Big Darby Creek in Pickaway County.

Cave salamander

Blue racer

Red-tailed hawk

Big Darby Creek, west of Columbus, has probably the most diverse group of fish species of any stream of similar size in Ohio. One hundred of the 166 species of fish recorded for Ohio have been found here with 86 coming from one 1000-foot stretch (Trautman's Riffle) near the village of Fox in Pickaway County. Species range in size from small darters to the longnose gar and paddlefish which may measure up to three feet and four feet, respectively. Milton Trautman, who has collected fish from this stream every year since 1922, claims that more species of darters (13) have been collected in a day at the riffle which bears his name than at any other place in America. The darters have been called the warblers of the fish world because of their small size and their brilliant breeding coloration which is most spectacular during the winter and spring. Another small fish, the Scioto madtom, was discovered at the riffle by Trautman in 1943. He collected this endangered species at the same site in 1945 and in 1957, but this species has never been recorded by anybody else from any other place in the world.

Amphibians with ranges centered in Ohio's Till Plains are the striped chorus frog and two salamanders, the small-mouth and tiger salamanders. Other species, such as spring peepers and red-backed salamanders, are also present because of their widespread ranges in Ohio. Many more species of amphibians are found in eastern Ohio, because the abundant hillside springs and the deep moist wooded valleys there provide the continuous moisture required by these animals. In contrast, the flat, cultivated, sun-baked clayey plains of western Ohio contain only a few scattered areas moist enough to permit preservation of amphibians. Even then, migration from one moist area to another is almost impossible, and the animals must tolerate occasional droughts. Some creatures, such as the tiger salamander, last through dry spells by burrowing into the ground.

These dry, open plains are only partly a product of climate and substrate. Mostly, they are a result of the clearing of the original forests. Thus it is very likely that many of the eastern frogs and salamanders were present in the original Till Plains woodlands. Only the species dependent on a habitat of rocky cliffs would have been absent. Now however, about the only species present are those that are able to survive on such dry open plains. An interesting exception is a very rare but strikingly colored salamander, the cave salamander, which lives in the damp twilight zone at the mouths of limestone caves. This endangered species has been found in Ohio only in Hamilton and Adams counties.

Of the many reptiles found in Ohio, only a few have their ranges dominantly in the Till Plains. Most of these are snakes. These reptiles are the eastern garter snake, Butler's garter snake, eastern plains garter snake, the blue racer, northern copperbelly, the eastern massasauga (or swamp rattler), and the spotted turtle. Reptiles with wide ranges in Ohio, which also occur in fair abundance in the Till Plains, include the queen snake, the common (or northern) water snake, the snapping turtle, and the painted turtle. The fence lizard and the copperhead, two species of reptiles found in eastern Ohio, also live in southwestern Ohio, but only in the deeply dissected hills along the Ohio River Valley. However, poisonous copperhead snakes are rare there now, just as records for the once-common massasauga rattler are rare elsewhere in the Till Plains.

Many species of birds are found in the Till Plains. Open plains with brushy margins or forested floodplains provide a natural diversity of habitat which attracts birds and makes available cover, food, water, and nesting areas. Relatively common birds of the Till Plains inlude the eastern meadowlark, horned lark, red-headed woodpecker, cowbird, savannah sparrow, song sparrow, and woodcock. Until recent years, the upland plover, boblink, dickcissel, and vesper sparrow were common, but lately these have declined in numbers. Most of these are birds characteristic of open fields, so they would have been uncommon in the days before the prehistoric western woodlands had been cut. In addition, a number of species are present because of humans, either having been introduced or maintained, intentionally or not, by human activities. Such species are the house sparrow, starling, pigeon, purple martin, barn swallow, chimney swift, robin, eastern bluebird, house wren, catbird, and ring-necked pheasant.

The Till Plains lie along one of the country's major migration routes. Migrating birds may be observed at any major body of water, such as Indian Lake or Grand Lake. These reservoirs were constructed to provide water for Ohio's canal system in the early 1800s, but today are state parks. Water birds using the lakes as resting stops include Canada geese, ducks, grebes, swans, egrets, and herons. Certain ducks, Canada geese, and herons also nest here. One of the largest heron rookeries near Grand Lake once had 175 nests in only 39 trees. Bald eagles also used to nest near this reservoir by the hundreds before 1900, but this magnificent bird is now probably gone, last being reported in the area in the 1960s.

Some northern species spend portions of the winter in the Till Plains, e.g. snow buntings, Smith's longspurs and short-eared owls.

Mammals present on the Till Plains today are mostly small. Larger forms require more extensive territories and thus compete, generally unsuccessfully, with people. Mammals common on the Till Plains include red fox, red squirrel, thirteen-lined ground squirrel, deer (locally), raccoon, opossum, woodchuck, skunk, rabbit, eastern mole, short tailed shrew, weasel (long-tailed and least), muskrat, little brown bat, white-footed mouse, deer mouse, meadow vole, and prairie vole. Most of these animals are found in scattered wooded areas, and some

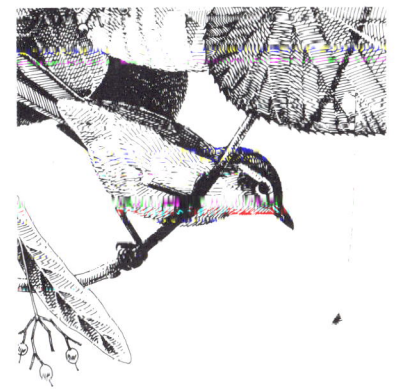

Red-eyed vireo

Ring-neck pheasant

Killdeer

Upland plover, formerly common but now a rare bird on the Till Plains.

Meadowlark feeding young

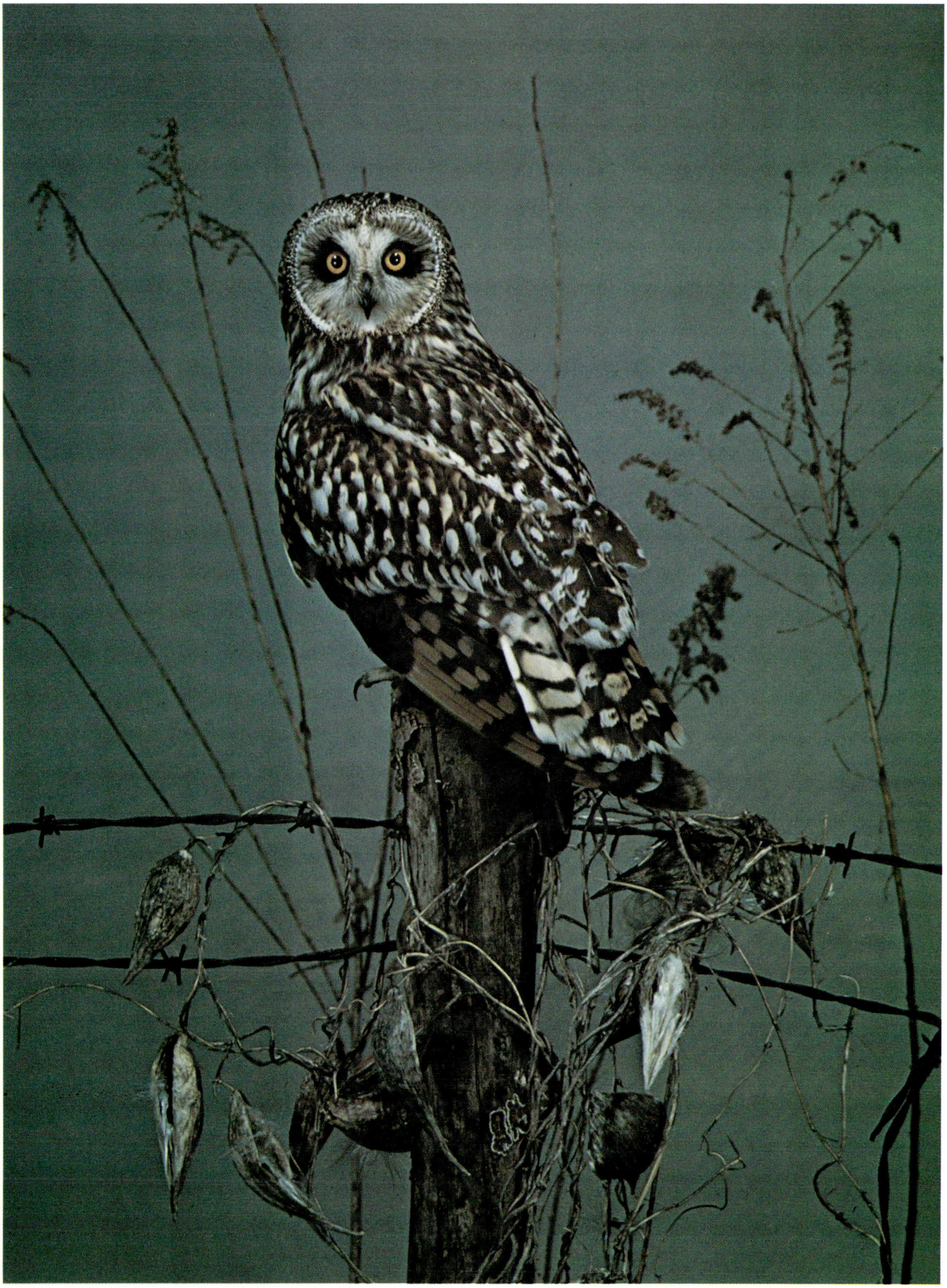

Red fox

live in open fields where cover (in burrows or hedges) is available and where human disturbance is not prohibitive. Even where the effects of urbanization are great, two species of mammals normally also occur, the house mouse and the Norway rat. Two species normally found only in eastern Ohio woodlands, the gray squirrel and the chipmunk, are also found locally in the Till Plains, but only in wooded parks.

Several mammal species present in the Till Plains have readily identified analogs in the plateaus. One example is that of the squirrels. In the woodlands of southeastern Ohio, it is the gray squirrel that is common, whereas in the open lands of western Ohio, it is the fox squirrel and the red squirrel that are dominant. The same is true of foxes. The gray fox lives in the eastern woodlands, and the red fox is more common on the plains of western Ohio. Before the destruction of the Till Plains forests by the pioneers, the eastern species of both the squirrel and the fox extended all across Ohio, and the western species did not exist in the state at all. Only since the clearing of the western woodlands have the fox and red squirrels and red fox invaded western Ohio. Another example is the ruffed grouse, a woodland bird that once occupied Ohio's forests from east to west. With the clearing of the western forests, the range of the grouse has been restricted to eastern Ohio, while an introduced species, the ring-necked pheasant, has now become relatively well established on the western plains.

All the species listed above are found on Ohio's Till Plains today. However, like the vegetation, different species of animals lived here in the past. During postglacial time, mastodon, mammoth, ground sloth, and giant beaver were present on the Till Plains, though all of these became extinct about 10,000 years ago. At the time of the earliest settlers, large animals living in the Till Plains included bear, wolf, bison, elk, deer, mountain lion, bobcat, lynx, otter, porcupine, and beaver. None of these species lasted long after the settlers arrived. Some were killed for meat, and some were killed because they preyed on farm animals or ate crops. In addition, the passenger pigeon, which had been present in Ohio in great numbers previous to settlement, also was eliminated, not only in western Ohio but throughout the world.

Cottontail rabbit

The short-eared owl is a frequent winter resident in certain areas of the Till Plains. (opposite page)

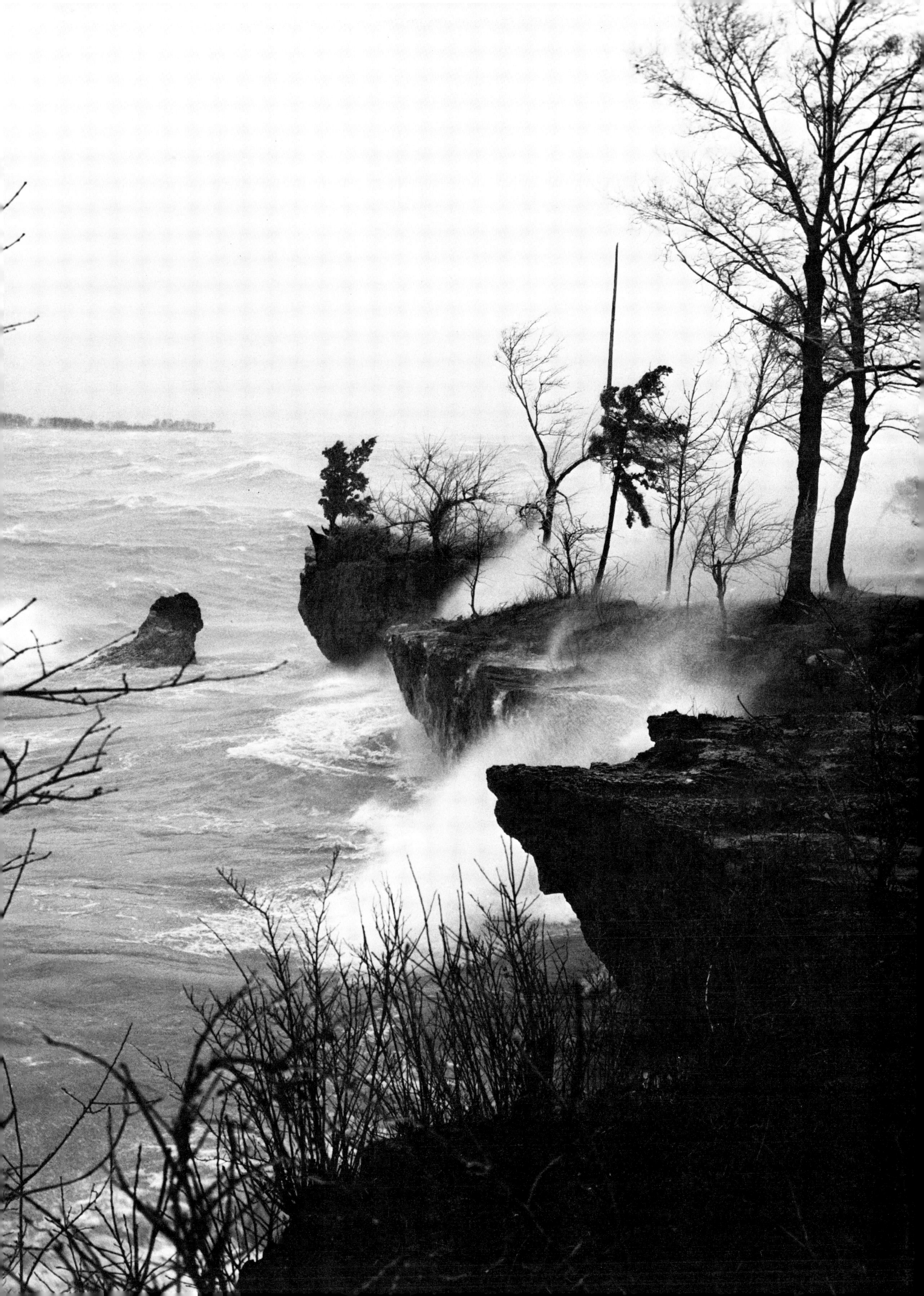

Chapter 13
Lake Erie
and the Islands

by Charles E. Herdendorf

Ronald L. Stuckey

LAKE Erie is one of Ohio's greatest resources. Each year more than 100 million tons of cargo pass through Erie ports. In Ohio alone, 2.7 billion of the lake's 100 billion gallons of water are used by cities and factories each day. And annually, American and Canadian commercial fishing efforts haul in a catch of 50 million pounds. The lake is just as important for recreation. Sport fishing takes good catches of yellow perch, walleye, and other game fish. During the summer 50,000 bathers use Erie beaches daily and additional thousands sail its blue-green waters. Twelve major islands are in the 3,500 square miles of lake controlled by Ohio. Many of these are rock-bound, and are popular recreation areas in summer. These islands are also important as rookeries for herons, gulls, egrets, and other birds, just as the marshes along shore are spawning grounds for northern pike and other important game fish.

Water quality is a continuing concern in Lake Erie, which is smallest in volume of the Great Lakes. The problem is one of polluted effluents from factories, cities, and run-off from farmlands into a low-volume lake which does not have the capacity to assimilate these wastes. Fortunately the water which enters the lake as rain and as inflow from tributaries remains in the basin for less time than in the other Great Lakes. This rapid turnover helps flush pollutants. Controls on what kind and how much waste can be dumped into the lake are being enforced, so the water quality is improving. Ohio owns 3,500 square miles of the lake, which makes it the largest American landowner (about one half of Lake Erie is in Canada).

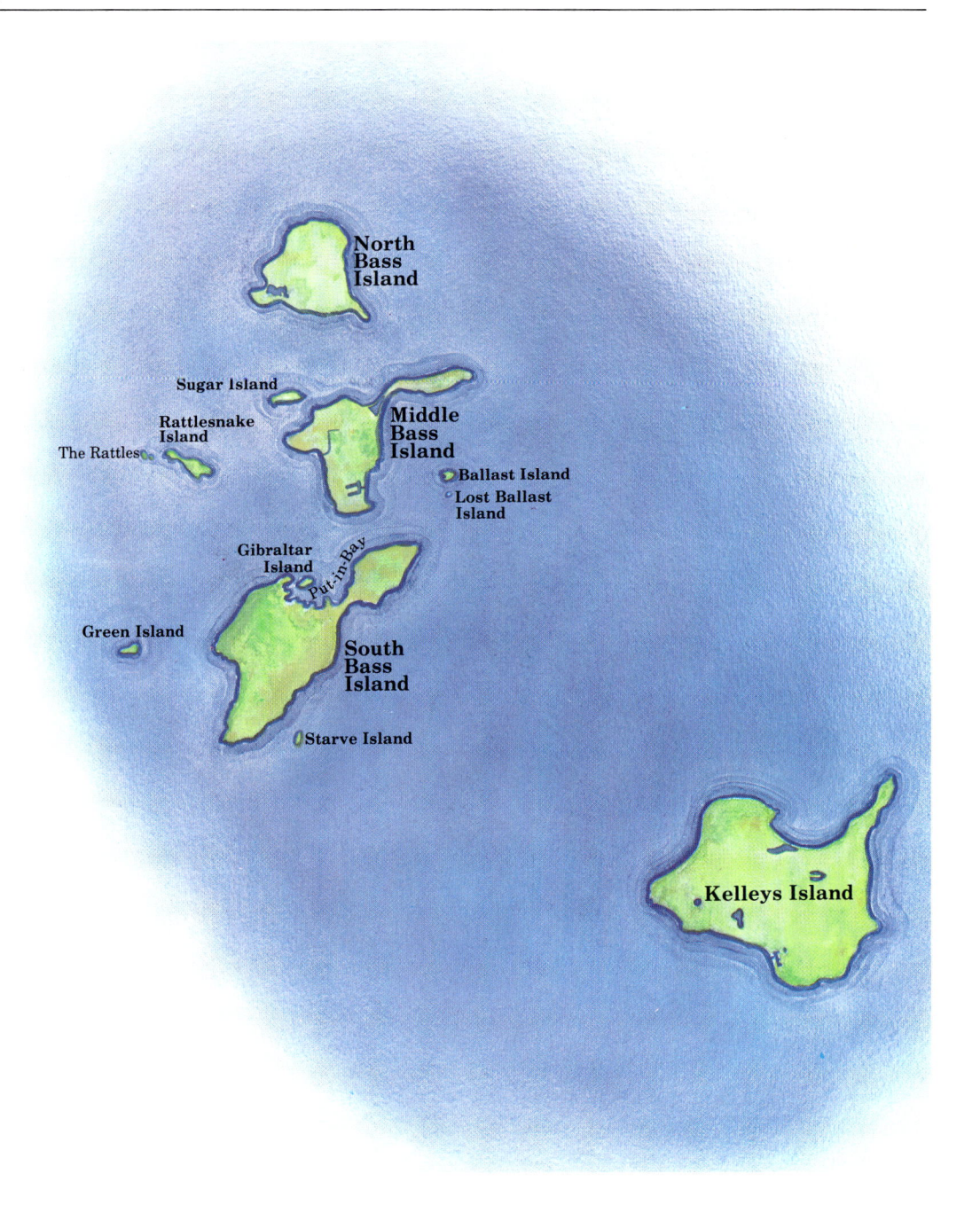

Shape of the Lake

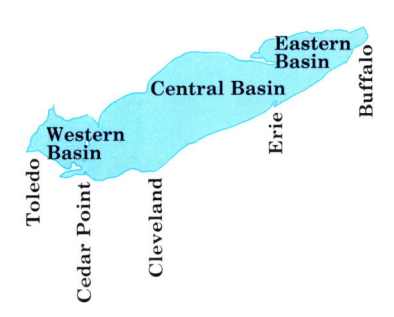

Lake Erie is long and narrow and is like a river connecting lakes Huron and Ontario. Erie is 240 miles long, but at its widest point only 57 miles separate Canadian and American shores, and in most places the lake is less than 40 miles wide. This narrowness, together with the fact that the lake's axis parallels the prevailing southwesterly winds, causes Lake Erie to function as a giant wind tunnel. Violent storms, powerful enough to sink large freighters, sometimes sweep the lake. An especially violent storm can generate 70 mile-per-hour winds which, in turn, can whip waves to heights of more than 12 feet and cause the lake level to rise or fall (termed a seiche) as much as 15 feet at the ends of the lake.

The Lake Basins

Lake Erie is divided into three basins. The western basin, which lies west of Cedar Point, Ohio, is the smallest and shallowest. Although the overall average depth of the lake is about 60 feet, the western basin averages only 25 to 35 feet deep. Its deepest portion, a small depression south of Starve Island, is only 62 feet deep.

The central basin is deeper. It stretches east from Cedar Point to Erie, Pennsylvania and averages 61 feet deep, while its deepest point is 84 feet. The eastern basin, which lies east of Erie, is deepest. Much of this basin lies below 120 feet, and the deepest point, about eight miles east-southeast of Long Point, Ontario, is 210 feet.

These basin depths are due to the differences in the hardness of the bedrock under the lake. When the glaciers scoured the Erie basins about 12,000 years ago, the ice cut deeper into the soft Devonian and Mississippian shales of the eastern basin. Farther west the shale widens, and the effects of the weight and cutting action of the ice were lessened, forming the broad but shallower central basin. Even farther west the shale diminishes and is replaced by more resistant Silurian and Devonian limestone and dolomite. Except for the impressive grooves in limestone found on Kelleys Island and at other places in the western basin, the ice has had moderate effect on this tough limestone, so the erosion is least here.

This limestone is sedimentary rock, deposited as limey mud in shallow, warm Silurian and Devonian seas 410 to 365 million years ago. Species of more than 70 marine fossils have been found in bedrock on some of the islands.

Groundwater has dissolved portions of this bedrock, forming a rather unusual cave and sinkhole topography. Limestone and dolomite are carbonates, which are dissolved easily by weak, naturally-occurring acids, such as carbonic and various organic acids. Over millions of years, these acids slowly dissolved portions of the rock, producing caves and sinkholes. The process may have started soon after the ancient sea drained from the lime muds over 300 million years ago. First, sinkholes were formed. These were filled with dolomite fragments that had broken from the sinkhole rims producing a rock called breccia. These ancient breccia-filled sinkholes are particularly common on the west shore of South Bass Island. The 37 small caves on the islands were all formed in the last several thousand years. Just as with sinkholes, acid dissolved the bedrock, creating a cavity. The best known cave in the islands is Crystal Cave on South Bass Island, a small cave 40 feet underground about the size of a living room. This cave is especially unusual because it appears to be the inside of a giant geode, a hollow rock lined with crystals. Most geodes are no larger than grapefruits, but the largest crystals in the cave exceed 15 inches. The crystals lining the geode are celestite, a beautiful, bluish, transparent form of strontium sulfate.

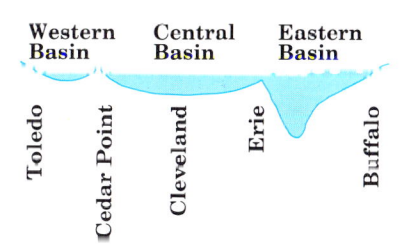

Relative sizes and depths of the three basins in Lake Erie

East-west section through South Bass and Kelleys islands showing form of the islands, the rock units, and the rock structure

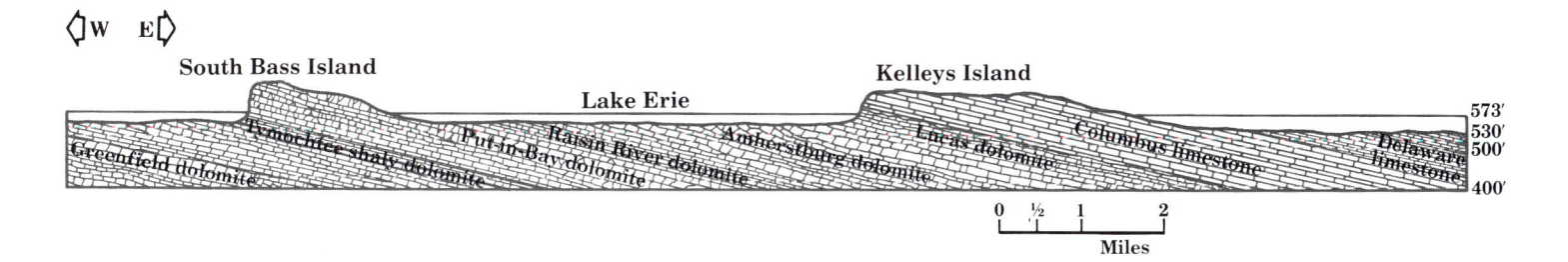

Most of the islands have rockbound shores surrounded by limestone and dolomite cliffs, especially on their western shorelines. These cliffs were formed after thousands of years of constant pounding by waves. Through the centuries, the waves slowly eroded rock at the bases of the cliffs, undermining it and eventually causing it to fall forming sheer, vertical faces.

In contrast to the islands, most of the Michigan and Ohio shoreline in western Lake Erie is low and marshy. There are no cliffs and the mouths of the tributary streams are all flooded with lake water, forming fresh water estuaries — a sign that they were submerged in recent geologic time.

A Succession of Lakes

Erie is the last of a number of lakes formed by the Wisconsinan ice as the glacier alternately advanced and retreated over 20,000 years of time. Each time the ice advance halted, ridges or moraines of glacial till were built at the glacial margin. These moraines dammed the natural drainage. Then water backed up, forming large glacial lakes in the scoured depressions. Lake Erie is the remnant of such a lake. Originally, this lake was 810 feet above sea level, and it extended as far southwest as present-day Fort Wayne, Indiana. At that time, Lake Erie drained to the southwest into the Mississippi River. Later the climate warmed and the glacier retreated, uncovering new and lower outlets. The water drained through these new outlets and the lake stabilized at successively lower levels.

When the glacier retreated from near present-day Buffalo, New York, it uncovered a new outlet through the Niagara River. A flood of water escaped, draining the shallow western end of the lake and most of the central basin. Twelve thousand years ago, this outlet was 100 feet lower than it is today because the great weight of the mile-thick ice depressed the land surface. Both the Niagara River and Lake Erie have rebounded from this glacial depression, resulting in the modern lake level.

As the water drained, erosion began to reshape the bottom. The bedrock closest to the surface emerged and also underwent erosion, and this exposed bedrock now forms the islands and reefs in the lake.

The Lake Bottom

Most of the bottom of Lake Erie is covered with mud, especially the broad, flat areas of the western and central basins and the deepest areas of the eastern basin. Scattered throughout the lake are occasional bars which are comprised mostly of sand and gravel or glacial till. The only places bedrock is exposed are in the shoals and islands in the western basin, along the south shore of the central basin, and along both shores of the eastern basin.

In general, Lake Erie beaches do not have abundant sand. The only places extensive dunes have formed are in the eastern basin, notably near Long Point, Point Albino, and Sturgeon Point. The best island beach in western Lake Erie is on one of the Canadian islands at Fish Point. This two-mile spit at the southern tip of Pelee Island contains the largest deposit of sand in the islands. The sand probably comes from glacial moraine deposits of sand and gravel lying east and west of Pelee. The largest sand deposit in the Ohio islands is along the North Bay of Kelleys Island.

Water Circulation and Water Quality

The largest single source of water for the lake is the Detroit River. The river drains Lake St. Clair and the upper lakes and supplies over 90 percent of the water flow into Lake Erie. Every second, 219,000 cubic feet of water flow from the river into the lake, and it is this immense volume which controls water circulation in the western lake. The midchannel flow of the river penetrates deeply into the western basin with a branch that flows east toward the Pelee Passage north of Pelee Island.

Satellite view of western Lake Erie showing currents

Ice frequently coats the shores of Lake Erie islands

Eddies occurring on the sides of the Detroit River result in a sluggish movement that causes the water to cling to the shoreline. Near the Michigan shore and to a lesser extent, Ontario, these eddies tend to retain water, causing a build-up of pollutants. In contrast, the Maumee River, the second-largest stream flowing into the lake at 4,700 cubic feet per second, carries 37 percent of the sediment loading the lake. The Maumee contributes so much silt and soil because it flows through northwestern Ohio farmland before reaching the lake.

Farther east, the prevailing southwest winds have a great effect on water movement. However every time the wind changes direction, the surface flow also changes. Strong winds from any direction can drive the surface currents over most of the basin toward the windward shore.

Lake Erie water temperatures range from a winter low of about 32° to a summer high of about 75°F. During really cold winters, up to 100 percent of the lake is covered with ice two feet thick. These thick slabs can pile up to 60 feet high in ice wind rows. Commercial navigation normally ends in mid-December and begins again in mid-March. After the lake freezes, ice boating and ice fishing are popular, and auto traffic on the ice from the islands to the mainland is common. Islanders strip down old automobiles to make them as light as possible, and then drive them to the mainland.

In March or early April the ice breaks up. The water warms faster along the shore because of warm run-off water. South-shore water warms very fast, because prevailing winds push the warmer surface water towards the south shore.

During most seasons water in the shallow western basin is usually the same temperature top to bottom. This shallowness allows the water to respond more quickly to temperature changes in the air. Sometimes water in the western basin forms layers according to temperature for short periods in the summer. When this happens, oxygen is kept from circulating to the bottom and the available oxygen is consumed by bacteria, making it difficult for other bottom organisms to survive.

Dissolved oxygen in the surface water varies considerably depending on the time of day and the season of the year. Oxygen is absorbed directly from the atmosphere and is transferred to the lower layers by mixing until water is saturated for a particular temperature (the colder the water, the more oxygen the water can hold). Supersaturation can occur after a sharp increase in temperature or as a result of oxygen produced by photosynthesis in aquatic plants.

One of the most serious problems in the lake is pollution — the result of too many nutrients or too many toxins from pesticides, heavy metals, and organic compounds. Nutritional overenrichment speeds the natural aging of lakes.

Overenrichment stimulates algae growth, and when these algae decay life-giving oxygen is consumed (called eutrophication) rendering the water unfit for fish life. Some blue-green algae produce noxious odors, clog intake pipes, and appear as unsightly scums. Fertilizer carried into the lake by run-off, along with municipal and industrial water discharges, have in a few decades aged Lake Erie by several thousand years. Dissolved solids have increased 35 percent in the last 50 years, with the increase being the greatest for chloride and sulfate compounds — both of which are indicators of domestic and industrial wastes. Phosphorus concentrations in the western basin are so abundant that they never limit algal growth.

Run-off is the major agricultural pollution problem. Millions of tons of silt are washed into the lake each year along with fertilizer, pesticides, and heavy metals attached to the soil particles.

Severe oxygen depletion was observed as early as 1958 in the bottom waters of central Lake Erie during periods of thermal stratification. Concentrations of less than one part per million (ppm) have been found over extensive areas. Dissolved oxygen levels are a continuing problem in the central basin where thermal stratification occurs. In the shallow western basin, bottom-dwelling fauna have changed from clean water forms such as mayflies to pollution-tolerant sludge worms. Game fishes such as whitefish and walleye are more scarce, while less valuable fish such as carp and freshwater drum are more common.

All of these changes have occurred even though nearly 40 percent of the lake volume flows over Niagara Falls annually, giving Lake Erie a flushing time of about 2½ years. The primary reason for the inability of Lake Erie to cleanse itself is that nearly 90 percent of the water flowing into the lake is via the Detroit River which is heavily polluted in the short distance between Lake Huron and Lake Erie. For example, in the early 1970s, 80 percent of the total dissolved solids, 70 percent of the chlorides, 65 percent of the nitrogen, and 60 percent of the phosphorus entering Lake Erie came from the Detroit River. The Maumee and Cuyahoga Rivers are also polluted by effluents from Toledo and Cleveland. All of the major metropolitan areas in the Lake Erie basin are constructing advanced water treatment facilities which should result in better water quality in the future.

Shore Erosion and Storms

Erosion is continual, but it became especially serious in the early 1970s when the water was at record high levels. The high water submerged the beaches in front of the rocky cliffs, and the waves crashed directly onto the cliffs. Large blocks of dolomite loosened and fell into the lake. The shoreline had eroded so much at the south point of South Bass Island that the U.S. Coast Guard light tower was in danger of falling into the lake and had to be moved 60 feet inland.

Wave action follows wind action very closely on Lake Erie because of the lake's shallowness. The strongest Lake Erie winds blow most often from the west and, frequently, from the northeast. The average monthly wind speed ranges from about 8 to 18 miles per hour but the highest winds usually occur during winter in the eastern half of the lake.

The predominant southwest and west winds over Lake Erie are explained in terms of "streamlines" of air movements in the Great Lakes region. The southwest wind is produced when masses of air moving from the west are abruptly shifted toward the northeast. This phenomenon causes the highest winds to occur in the eastern half of the lake during winter.

The depth of the water and the direction, velocity, duration, and open-water fetch (distance) of the wind determine the characteristics of waves at a given location. The maximum wave for the lake is formed in about 20 hours, given a 30 mph wind blowing over about 150 miles of lake. A 12-foot wave is formed and waves over six feet often persist well into the next day after a storm. Waves this high break offshore, but reformed waves up to 3½ feet high can reach the shoreline of the islands.

As waves approach the shoreline, the water level rises and the excess water escapes, forming currents along shore which transport sand, while wave impact transports rocks as large as cobbles and boulders. The waves and currents are slowly eroding the shore of the islands, especially in the spring and fall during storms. Ground water seeping into cracks and joints in the rocks freezes, expands, and tends to split rock from the cliffs, a process known as frost wedging. As a result large blocks of dolomite have fallen from the shoreline cliffs of the islands.

Low shores also flood during high water, and many homes and cottages have been destroyed or severely damaged by waves during northeasters. These waves possess immense energy, and because of the shallowness of the lake, they are steep-sided and destructive as they break at the shoreline. Constant pounding of the shoreline has washed much land into the lake. Expensive homes that 20 years ago were several hundred feet away from the lake edge are now close enough for their owners to feel the spray when waves break against the high bluffs during storms. Some homeowners have built rock-retaining walls and other defenses to reduce the force of the wave attack, but these efforts have not always been successful.

Wind from an approaching thunderstorm also can build up waves from a few inches to three or four feet within 30 minutes. This combination of wind and wave plays havoc with boats. Many small boats have been lost along with all hands after capsizing in Lake Erie thunderstorms, and the lake is the grave for over 100 larger vessels unable to weather severe gales.

Shore road washout near Vermilion.

Climate of the Islands

The climate of the Erie Islands is completely unlike the mainland. The range of the annual mean temperature is greater in the islands, the daily range between the maximum and the minimum temperatures is smaller, the precipitation is less, wind velocities are greater, and the frost-free seasons are longer.

In comparison with the mainland, the islands are colder in winter, warmer in summer, and drier year-round. The average monthly fluctuation between maximum and minimum temperatures is 13.7°F for

Wave beaten home

Put-in-Bay compared with 21.5°F for Bucyrus, a city only 50 miles from the lake. The lake temperatures change very slowly and the water acts as a damper between sudden heating and cooling. Put-in-Bay has the lowest average temperature in January in Ohio because of the frozen lake and the highest average temperature for July, because more sunlight shines on Put-in-Bay as compared to other stations at the same latitude.

However, it rains and snows less on the islands. In summer, thunderstorms are deflected around the lake. The storms that do cross the water do not form as much rain because higher air temperatures over land can maintain the energy needed to develop thunderstorms, whereas cooler temperatures over the lake do not provide enough energy. Because of low rainfall, high solar radiation, and continued movement of the air, evaporation actually exceeds precipitation in June, July, and August.

South Bass and the other islands, although nearly the most northern part of the state, have the longest frost-free period of any area in Ohio because of the stabilizing effect of the lake. South Bass has an average frost-free period of 205 days, while Bucyrus has an average of only 154 days. The long frost-free period, however, does not necessarily provide for a longer growing season. Although the last killing-frost for the islands is around April 15, contrasted with May 20 for the interior of Ashtabula County nearly at the same latitude, and with April 30 as far south as Columbus, the overall spring temperatures are lower because of the influence of the lake. Therefore, the threshold temperature, or temperature denoting the beginning of the blooming period of the flora in the spring, occurs much later on the islands than on the mainland. Conversely, later in the season, the lake retains heat and prolongs summer temperatures far into autumn. The average date for the first killing-frost in the fall is around October 30 for the islands, contrasted with September 30 for Ashtabula County, October 15 for Columbus, and October 20 for Cincinnati.

Put-in-Bay and Perry's Victory Monument

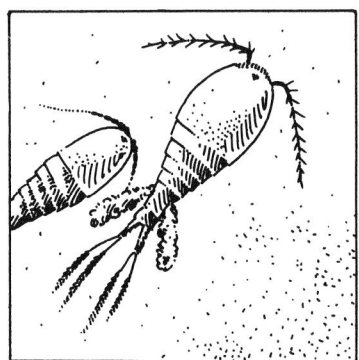

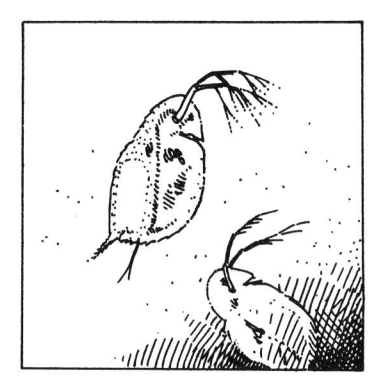

Life of the Lake and Islands

Lake Erie has an abundance of life. Walleye, smallmouth and white bass, perch, carp, and other fish swim in the lake. Plankton is plentiful. Thousands of animals such as aquatic earthworms and clams live on and in the lake bottom. Marshes close to shore support cattail, bulrushes, and water lilies. Among these plants dart small forage fish — their fate eventually to be devoured by larger fish.

The larger fish in turn are preyed on by herons and other birds. These birds use the islands as places to make their rookeries. The islands are also home to invertebrates, amphibians, reptiles, and mammals, as well as one of the most diverse plant communities in the United States.

When the Erie Islands were settled in the early 1800s, there were probably only a small number of large animals present. The most likely included grouse, porcupines, deer, bears, foxes, squirrels, rabbits, quail, raccoons, and muskrats. The deer, bears, and grouse were probably killed by hunters before the islands were permanently settled.

In addition to those that migrated from the mainland, ring-neck pheasants were brought to the Bass Islands and Kelleys Island in the early 1920s, and today many of these birds are harvested on the Lake Erie Islands. Cottontail rabbits, also abundant, are hunted. Muskrats are trapped in wetlands and marshes scattered throughout the islands.

The islands serve as "stepping stones" for whistling swans, Canada geese, and many species of ducks in the migration hop over Lake Erie each spring and fall. Some of these birds merely pause as they pass north or south, while others nest on the islands. The birds feed on fish, but a great many also feed on insects.

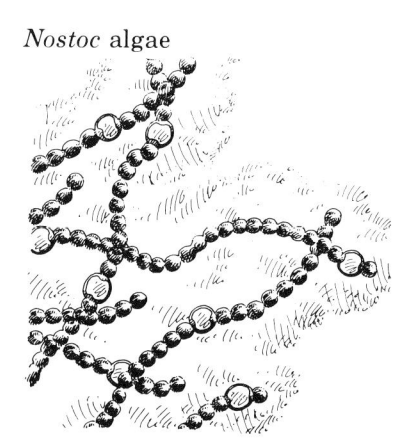

Plankton

Cup a handful of water from the lake and the plankton — the tiny plants and animals — can easily be observed. Their presence translates into millions of tons throughout the lake. These organisms are an important food base for all higher aquatic life. The phytoplankton around the islands consists mainly of diatoms and green and blue-green algae. Diatoms are the most plentiful. These one-celled plants are most common in spring and fall, while green algae are most abundant when the lake water warms in midsummer, and blue-green algae are most abundant during late summer. These seasonal population surges, known as pulses or blooms, account for well over 50 percent of the year's plankton production.

The algae are increasing in abundance. Growth has been stimulated by nitrogen, phosphorus, and other nutrients from waste dumped into the lake. As a result, the amount of algae in the water at the Cleveland water supply intake has doubled in the past 50 years, and there have been changes in the species composition of the phytoplankton.

In Lake Erie, animal plankton are mainly microscopic crustaceans (copepods and cladocerans), rotifers, and protozoans. Just as phytoplankton have increased, zooplankton populations have doubled since 1930. Zooplankton populations are low during the winter months. Adult crustaceans are rare in the spring and fall, but nauplius (immature copepods) are most abundant in late spring and form an important part of the diet of larval fish. The adult crustaceans are most abundant during the summer when they are a significant link in the

Sunset from Gibraltar Island

food web of Lake Erie fish. All fish probably eat zooplankton, at least as fish larvae right after hatching, but few eat phytoplankton (except carp and gizzard shad).

Invertebrates

The bottom fauna (benthos) of the western basin are mostly aquatic earthworms or sludge worms, midge larvae, fingernail clams, and snails. Most of these forms are very tolerant of pollution and are most abundant near the mouths of the Detroit, Maumee, and Raisin rivers. Organic material flowing from these rivers provides food for the benthos. Aquatic worms and midge larvae can tolerate low amounts of oxygen and are most abundant (up to 500 per square foot) and most widely distributed.

Pollution-sensitive organisms such as amphipods, mayfly nymphs, larger clams, and caddisfly larvae are scarce near the river mouths and more common near the islands. Freshwater mussels (clams) occur in small numbers around most of the islands. The larger populations are in the most sheltered habitats such as Fishery Bay on the north side of South Bass Island. At least 25 species occur there. The species around the islands are found mostly on gravel bars in shallow water. Some freshwater mussels are also found on silt bottoms in deeper water. They are generally smaller and slower growing than those living on gravel bars, because in the deeper water less food is available to the organisms. The bottom animals of the central basin are generally similar to those found in the western basin, although there are fewer species and more individuals from east to west. The phenomenon is a response to more food flowing in from the western basin.

The major biological changes in Lake Erie have occurred in the bottom fauna of the western basin. Prior to the early 1950s the population of mayfly larvae in the islands region averaged about 40 per square foot of lake bottom. In the summer of 1953 a long period of very calm weather resulted in thermal stratification of the lake and the severe oxygen depletion in the bottom water. The mayfly population dropped to about one tenth its original size, while there were large increases in worm and midge larvae populations. This change also occurred in the central basin where midge larvae replaced the mayfly nymph as the dominant bottom organism. However, fauna of the eastern lake has changed less.

Early each summer there is an extensive emergence of mayfly and midge larvae. The mayflies of genus *Hexagenia*, known locally as Canadian Soldiers, emerged in such great numbers before 1953 that they were a great nuisance along the shoreline. Their slippery bodies and first- and second-cast skins washed on to the beaches to rot or accumulated under light posts, making driving hazardous. Although the numbers of mayflys have decreased dramatically, the midges are still a minor nuisance to island dwellers.

The dominant groups of insects present on the Erie Islands are caddisflies, flies, bees and wasps, beetles, and dragonflies. Species of dragonflies are distributed according to their use of wetlands in different stages of succession. In addition to the insects, more than 200 species of spiders live on the islands.

Fish

Lake Erie in its 200-year history of commercial fishing has produced greater numbers and varieties of commercial species of fish than any other Great Lake. The annual Erie fish catch nearly equals the combined catches of all other Great Lakes. Annual production since 1930 has averaged about 50 million pounds, and at least 17 species have been important in the landings at one time or another. The reason for the high production is the chemical make-up of the lake. Compared to the other Great Lakes, Lake Erie has a higher nutrient level and warmer temperatures.

The estuaries and marshes along the western basin are valuable fish-spawning and nursery grounds — thus sport fishing is a big attraction in the basin. Ninety-five species of fish have been caught in waters surrounding the islands. When the area was first settled, lake sturgeon, cisco, whitefish, blue pike, and walleye were the most important. Dominant species today are perch, smallmouth and white bass, channel catfish, alewife, smelt, gizzard shad, carp, goldfish, freshwater drum, and emerald shiner.

Early catch records suggest a fairly stable fishery until shortly after the turn of the century when overfishing and environmental changes began affecting populations. The sturgeon almost disappeared from the catch about 1900. Cisco, once the dominant commercial species, experienced a drastic decline in 1926 and is now rarely caught.

Cisco

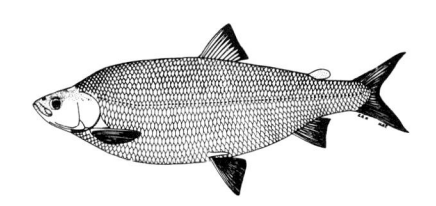

Whitefish catches declined rapidly in 1955 and are now insignificant, and the blue pike, which constituted a considerable portion of the fishery up to 1958, may be extinct in Lake Erie. Walleye production peaked in 1956, declined drastically in 1959, but is now showing signs of recovering.

The yellow perch has been an important commercial fish from the earliest days of the industry. In recent years the smelt has become commercially exploitable and it, along with yellow perch and, to a lesser extent, freshwater drum, white bass, catfish, and carp, is sustaining the fish industry.

The deterioration of the fishery was the result of several factors: (1) changes in the watershed, such as erosion and siltation of stream beds

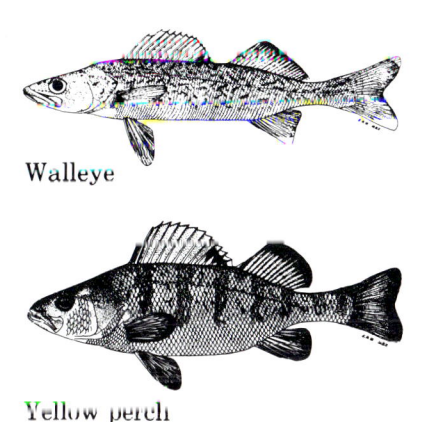

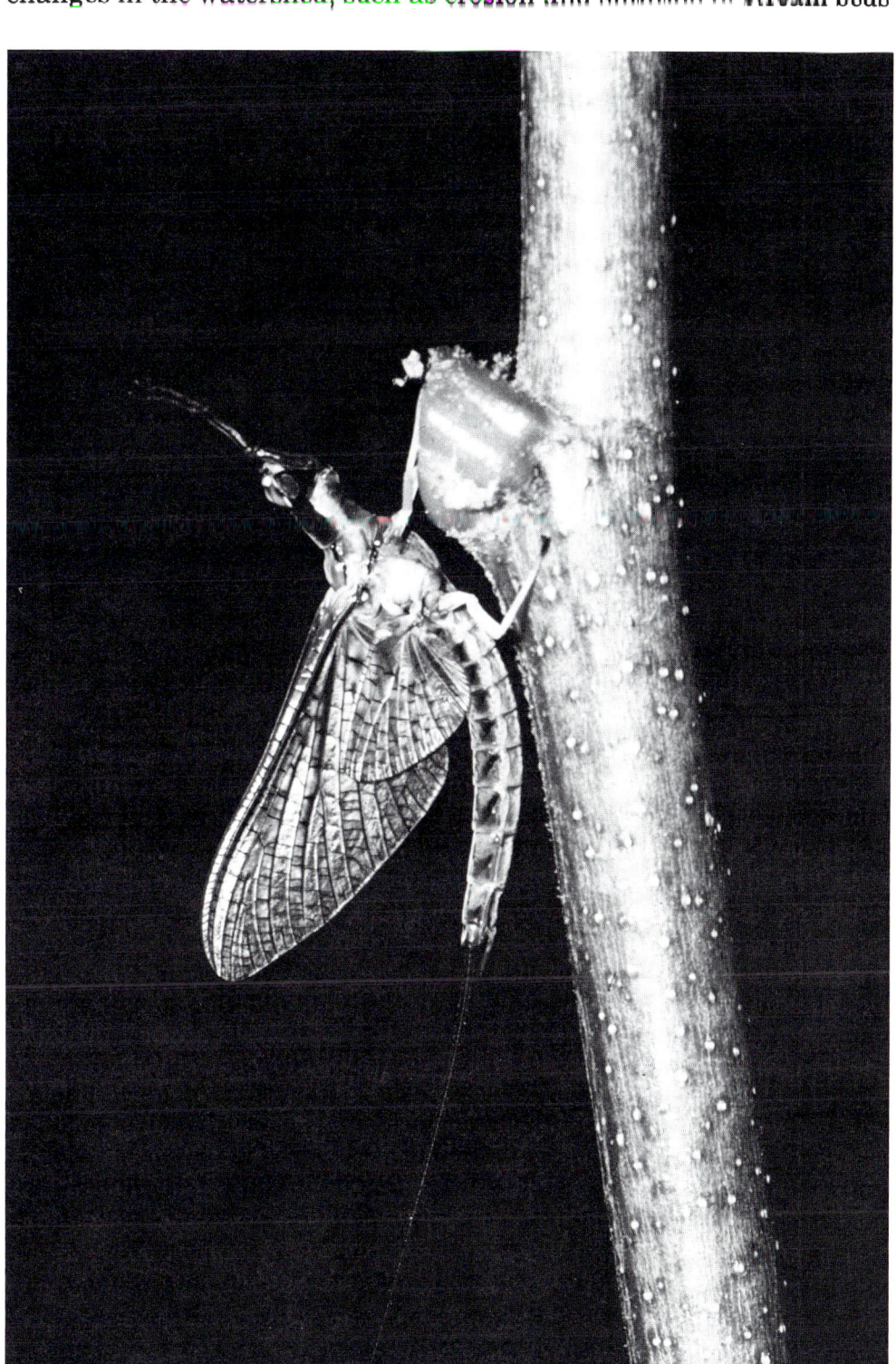

Walleye

Yellow perch

Mayfly

Great blue herons and nest

and inshore lake areas and construction of dams in tributaries and dikes in wetlands; (2) pollution, causing a reduction in dissolved oxygen; (3) competitive and predatory activities of invading species; and (4) better methods of fishing which land desirable fish faster than they can be naturally replaced.

Amphibians and Reptiles

The amphibians and reptiles of the Erie Island fauna are found in ponds, marshes, caves, along the shore, and on dry land. The mudpuppy is fairly common in the open water. Several species of salamanders, frogs, toads, and newts are found in a variety of habitats.

Many snakes once lived on the islands. Early explorers and settlers told of such great numbers of rattlesnakes that it seemed almost impossible to walk anywhere without stepping on one. After years of being slaughtered on sight and hunted by herds of hogs shipped to the Islands, the snakes are probably all dead. A timber rattlesnake has not been sighted since 1951. Settlers also feared a "hissing snake" which was said to blow a "nauseous wind," killing victims unlucky enough to inhale it. The hissing snake was probably the Lake Erie water snake, a nonpoisonous subspecies of the northern water snake. Typical of the species, it bites viciously when attacked and secretes a foul smelling substance from its musk glands. The Lake Erie water snake is fairly common around the islands, particularly the uninhabited ones. It can be seen swimming along the shore with its head above water, sunning on the flat rocks, or entwined around a shrubby branch near the water. The most common snakes on South Bass Island are this water snake, DeKay's, ringneck, fox, eastern garter snake, and the blue racer.

Populations of rare triploid salamanders of the genus *Ambystoma* live on Kelleys, Middle Bass, and North Bass islands. More common reptiles include snapping turtles, map turtles, and painted turtles.

Waterfowl and Other Birds

The islands in western Lake Erie are home to a wide variety of birds and waterfowl. A rookery of black-crowned night herons, great egrets, great blue herons, and green herons is on West Sister Island, a national wildlife refuge. Since thousands of birds nest on the islands, they are forced to go great distances to feed in the mainland marshes and around the other islands. An occasional nest can be found on the other islands, particularly the uninhabited ones, but nowhere in the area are colonies as extensive as on West Sister.

Large numbers of common terns nested on rocky, largely barren Starve Island until they were crowded out by herring gulls. In 1939, 1,052 tern nests were counted on this island, but by 1964, herring gulls had taken over completely. Other nesting sites include the Rattles of Rattlesnake Island, Lost Ballast, and several rock outcroppings occurring around the islands. The nearby Canadian islands also are popular nesting areas for herons, gulls, egrets, and cormorants. An occasional tern can be seen amidst the flocks of gulls following the ferry boats, but the numbers of these smaller more delicate birds have been drastically reduced since the arrival of the herring gulls. One theory is that DDT in the environment may have caused terns to lay eggs with thinner, more breakable shells, thus leading to their decline.

Common tern

In 1921 the ring-necked pheasant was stocked on South Bass Island. With few natural enemies, the pheasants multiplied and became a nuisance to orchardists and grape growers throughout the islands. Rattlesnake Island was stocked with golden pheasants and wild turkeys about 1950, but neither remains today, although the ring-necked pheasant is still common.

Single nests of the northern bald eagle once were located on South Bass, Green, Kelleys, Rattlesnake, and West Sister islands. Eagles still nest in mainland marshes along the Erie shore. Rare bird species include the least bittern, king rail, common tern, and orchard oriole.

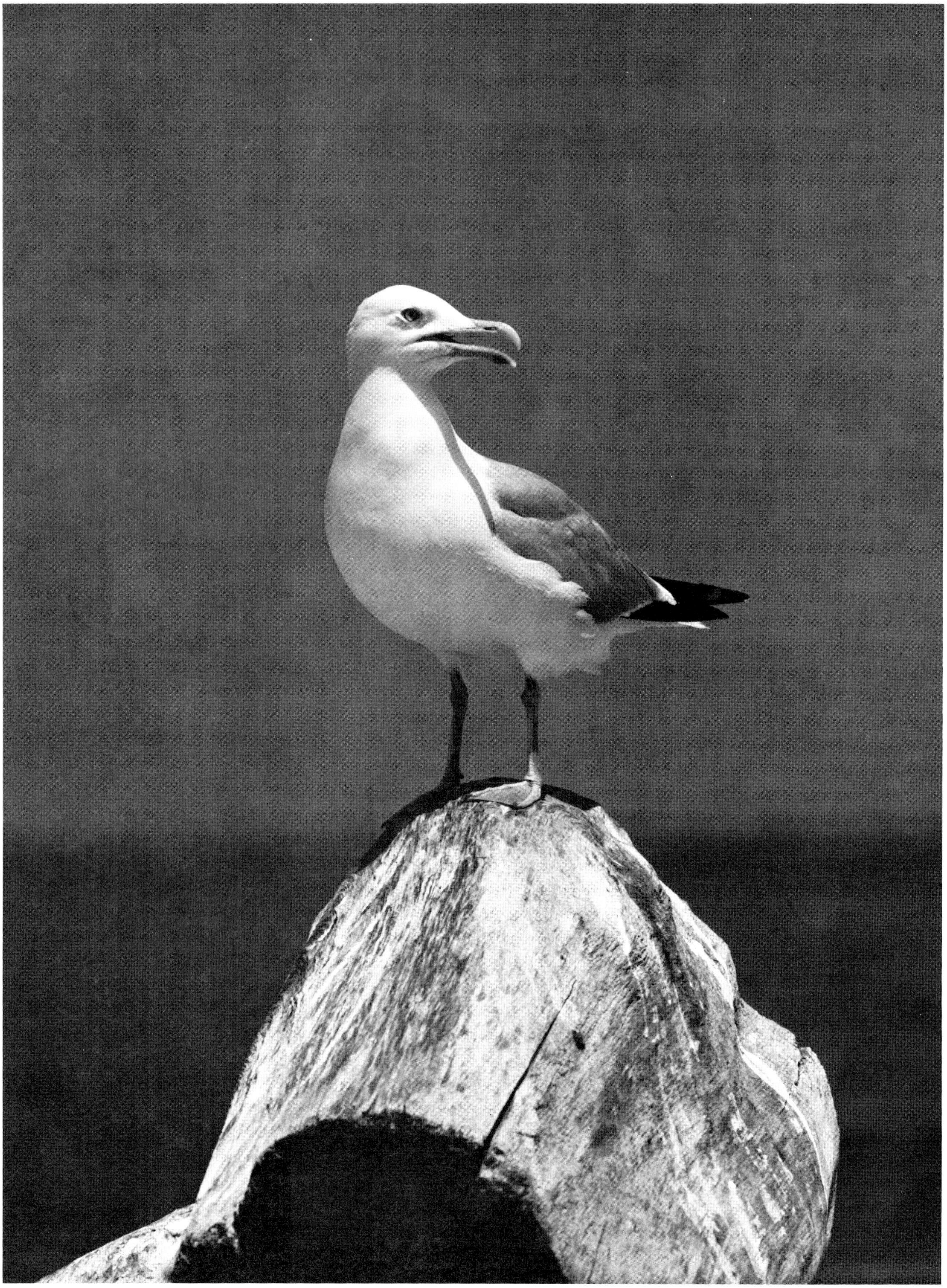

Other species which have decreased in numbers include the pied-billed grebe, American bittern, common gallinule, black tern, purple martin, crow, warbling vireo, northern oriole, and rough winged swallow

Mammals

As compared to the mainland, few mammals live on the islands. Only 13 small species have been recorded. Several species of mice exist, usually near humans. The Norway rat is particularly dependent upon humans since it lives mainly in dumps. Unfortunately, a campaign to poison the rats on South Bass Island in 1959 backfired. Instead of killing all the rats, many eastern gray squirrels ate the poison and died. Islanders imported several black squirrels from Belle Isle Park in Detroit in an attempt to bolster the squirrel population. The two varieties interbred and the resulting population is mixed with both gray and black squirrels. Cottontail rabbits are very common. But raccoons, red foxes, and muskrats are not common because they lack suitable habitat. The little brown bat is a permanent resident of the islands, but it is rarely seen because of its secretive nature. It remains dormant throughout the winter in empty cottages, boat houses, sheds, barns, and caves, and withstands extremely cold temperatures.

One of the interesting island animals is non-native — the African mountain sheep. A herd of these animals roams wild on Rattlesnake Island where they were introduced in the 1960s, but during the severe winter of 1976-1977, the herd was reduced from nine to three. A small number of deer live in the remaining wild areas of Catawba Island on the adjacent Marblehead Peninsula. During cold winters when the lake freezes over they occasionally cross the ice to some of the islands.

Plants

The flora of the islands and shoreline in western Lake Erie is one of the most diverse in Ohio. More than 847 species of vascular plants live there. Add to that the plants growing on the mainland shore and the total is nearly 1,300 species.

These plants have spread to the islands and main shoreline since the retreat of the Wisconsinan glacier 12,000 years ago. Common native species, those occurring throughout North America, grow just about everywhere on the islands and comprise about 70 percent of the native flora. Other less common plants grow in more specialized habitats such as in marshes, along cliff tops, and on rocky beaches. These habitats were most common when the glacier retreated, and these species live there today much as they did 12,000 years ago.

Within the past 100 years, some of these distinctive species have invaded human-created habitats. The best examples of those habitats are in the abandoned limestone quarries on Kelleys Island and on the Marblehead Peninsula, where wet depressions and falling rock provide continually disturbed habitats. Here, for example, grow the white-flowered houstonia, golden ragwort, small skullcap, and heath aster. Two orchids, yellow twayblade and nodding ladies' tresses, grow only in disturbed habitats with a high lime content.

Plants from Europe and from other parts of North America have invaded the islands since the late 1800s. These species now grow in abandoned orchards and vineyards, along roadsides, near docks, and in

Herring gull (opposite page)

Yellow water lily

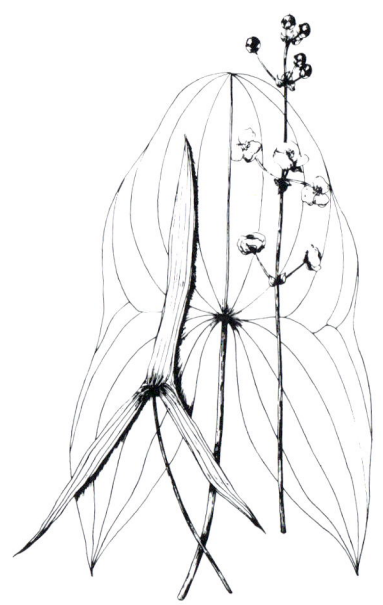

Arrowhead

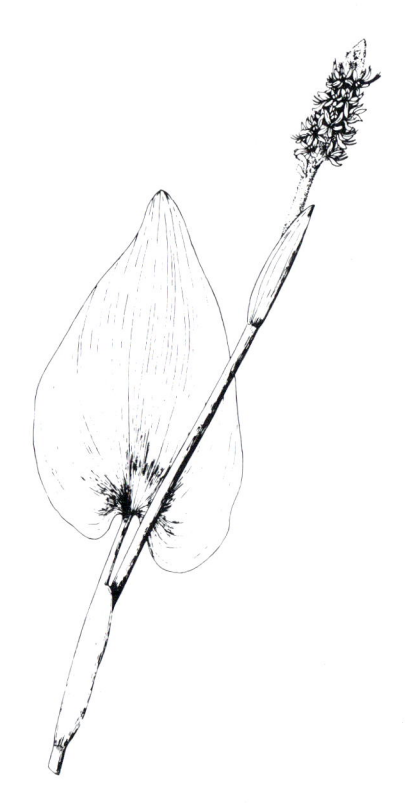

Pickerelweed

dumps and gardens. The plants survived because the human-disturbed habitats and climatic conditions are similar to those of Europe. These plant immigrants, often called weeds, have spread rapidly and have eliminated many of the native plants.

Bays and ponds . In the open water of the lake and larger bays, submersed aquatic plants are few, limited mostly to wild celery, coontail, water milfoil, and curly pondweed. The ponds contain many more species, among them the small floating duckweeds, which form dense floating mats in quiet, stagnant water. The duckweeds may be eaten by ducks and other waterfowl. White and yellow water lilies are uncommon, but where they do grow, extensive colonies are formed. The edges of the ponds are lined with cattails, bur reed, flowering-rush, arrowhead, swamp mallow, water smartweed, and pickerelweed.

Island aquatic plants have suffered from construction and other human activity. The building of retaining walls and docks, dredging, boating, and soil run-off from the vineyards all have made the water more turbid. In Put-in-Bay harbor alone, half the native species have disappeared since 1900. Dredging and construction have destroyed several ponds; the remaining ponds are the refuges for most of the submersed aquatic plants.

High lake levels periodically reduce populations of shore plants such as cattail and arrowhead, which emerge above the waterline, while submersed or floating-leaved plants such as white water lily and water milfoil increase.

Marshes and swamps . Marshes and swamps, once extensive along the main shoreline of western Lake Erie, still support a great diversity of plants. Near the edges of the marshes grow stands of tall grasses such as bluejoint grass and cord grass. Rushes and sedges also grow in the marshes as well as submersed species such as coontail, water milfoil, sago pondweed, and curly pondweed. However, the most noticeable plants are those with large showy flowers such as white water lily, spatterdock, swamp mallow, pickerelweed and arrowhead, the latter, also known as duck potato because ducks have been thought to eat the tuberous stems. These plants add brilliant color to the marshes.

Perhaps the most spectacular is the yellow water lotus, also known as the American lotus. This species is the largest and one of the most beautiful of all water plants in Ohio. The yellow flowers of this lotus are about six inches in diameter and are supported on slender, erect, leafless stalks. The circular leaves can grow to nearly 20 inches in diameter. These leaves stand like umbrellas in the water, or the blades float on the surface.

Of the foreign species, the flowering-rush is one of the conspicuous plants on the mudflats in the marshes. The plants grow in clumps with tall stalks, each one containing a loose cluster of pink flowers. Western Lake Erie has been home to this foreign species since the 1930s. It has been a successful colonizer because of its viable tiny seeds, rootstalks, and bulblets which float in the water and wash ashore. Muskrats are also believed to aid in the dispersal of the flowering-rush.

Today the marshes are not as extensive as they were before the coming of the European settlers. After the forests, which held the soil in place, were cut, the once clear water of the marshes began to become muddy. Extensive dredging and diking of the marshlands has continued to keep the water muddy. With the introduction of carp in the late 1800s, these fish continually uproot plants and keep the bottom silt stirred. Species of aquatic plants that normally live in clear, well-oxygenated waters have disappeared because of these altered conditions. Gone are the northern pondweeds, flexed naiad, and water marigold. Only the more tolerant pondweeds, coontail, waterweed, and water star-grass have survived in these newly muddied waters. European species, such as spicate water milfoil, curly pondweed, minor naiad, and flowering-rush, are quite tolerant of muddy waters and are now becoming thoroughly established. Because of these physical changes in the marshes, coupled with the ever-changing water-levels of Lake Erie, certain species are becoming scarce. Even the once plentiful wild rice may now be gone.

The swamps, dominated by woody plants, occur in small units in the low wet areas along the lake shore. Willows, cottonwood, sycamore, silver maple, and ashes are the dominant trees. American elm, once common, has been killed by Dutch elm disease. Swamp shrubs are mostly dogwood, elderberry, willow, buttonbush, and wild rose. Only a few species of herbs grow here — mostly shade-tolerant plants such as nettle, false-nettle, and spotted touch-me-not.

Pondweed

Sand beaches . Sand beaches are scattered and not very extensive along the main shoreline. Because the beaches are low and dunes have not formed, the beaches are particularly vulnerable to fluctuating water levels and wave action. Today, most of the sand beaches are used for swimming and camping. Because of these natural and artificial disturbances, most of the species unique to this type of habitat have disappeared. Distinctive herbs now rare include sea rocket, seaside spurge, beach pea, Canadian milk vetch, and beach grass, while shrubs that are today also rare or extirpated are sand-dune willow, sand cherry, and ground juniper. Common trees include cottonwood, willow, dogwood, and ash, and thick growths of vines such as wild grape, Virginia creeper, poison ivy, bittersweet, and trumpet creeper grow among the branches. European weeds have invaded in the open areas, and along with Russian thistle, winged pigweed, umbrella-wort, and sandbur grass, now form a new distinctive beach flora.

Gravel beaches . Low gravel beaches and bars are common on the islands, but little permanent vegetation grows on them because of the continuous wave wash and scouring of winter ice. Mats of the alga *Cladophora* often wash ashore, die, and decay. Farther up on the beach, where waves reach only during storms and periods of high water, willows, cottonwood, dogwood, and ash are dominant. Beaches are often tangled with wild grape, poison ivy, and Virginia creeper. Except for germander and smartweed, few herbs grow there.

Shoreline cliffs . The high, rugged cliffs on the north and west shores of the islands are among the most dramatic of shoreline habitats. *Cladophora* and *Bangia* algae inhabit the base of these cliffs along with vascular plants such as Dudley's rush, Kalm's lobelia, St. John's wort, mountain mint, heath aster, and beard tongue. Higher up grow herbs such as ivory sedge, nodding onion, barrens chickweed, purple and hairy rockcress, alumroot, harebell, and smooth cliff brake fern. Mosses and lichens are often on the rocks, and shrubs and small trees line most of the tops of the cliffs. Common woody plants include ninebark, chokeberry, hoptree, bladdernut, staghorn sumac, mulberry, dogwood, hop-hornbeam, and red cedar. Serviceberry and American yew are very rare. Dense growths of vines, such as poison ivy, Virginia creeper, and wild grapes, grow over large portions of the cliffs.

Cladophora algae

Woodlands. Originally the islands were covered with trees. Oak, hickory, maple, and red cedar were once common on the driest sites. These virgin forests were cut to supply firewood for woodburning lake vessels of the nineteenth century or to clear the land for agriculture. Today, second-growth forests occur throughout the islands. The most common of these is a sugar maple-hackberry-basswood community. Blue ash with its squarish twigs; Kentucky coffee tree with its large seed pods and exaggerated, double-compound leaves; and hop-hornbeam with its extremely hard wood are common associated species. Common shrubs include hoptree, chokecherry, and bladdernut. Wild hyacinth, Dutchman's breeches, wild leek, leafcup, and herb-Robert geranium are distinctive members of the herbaceous understory flora. In spring, portions of the forest floor appear solid white with flowers of Dutchman's breeches — a plant with blooms shaped like a pair of trousers. The appendaged waterleaf is a particularly distinctive understory plant. It has dark green foliage, a hairy stem, and clusters of light blue flowers. Wild licorice, easily identified by the licorice odor when its leaves are crushed and by its tiny white flowers, occurs in wetter areas of the woods. Unfortunately, garlic mustard is a pest plant replacing many of these understory species. The lack of leaf litter in the woodlands has been attributed to the large populations of snails.

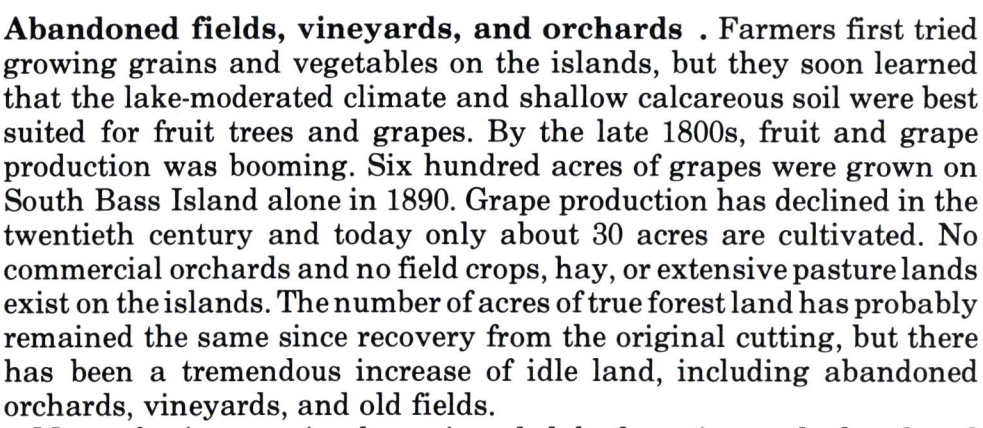

Abandoned fields, vineyards, and orchards. Farmers first tried growing grains and vegetables on the islands, but they soon learned that the lake-moderated climate and shallow calcareous soil were best suited for fruit trees and grapes. By the late 1800s, fruit and grape production was booming. Six hundred acres of grapes were grown on South Bass Island alone in 1890. Grape production has declined in the twentieth century and today only about 30 acres are cultivated. No commercial orchards and no field crops, hay, or extensive pasture lands exist on the islands. The number of acres of true forest land has probably remained the same since recovery from the original cutting, but there has been a tremendous increase of idle land, including abandoned orchards, vineyards, and old fields.

Many foreign species have invaded both active and abandoned vineyards. Some of these species include wild carrot, pigweed, lamb's quarters, sweet clovers, and many different grasses. These foreign species have had a large impact on the flora of the islands, particularly in the early successional stages. However, as the native woody species replace both the native and foreign pioneer herbaceous species, a slow return to a more stable forest community, similar in species composition to the original forests, is occurring.

Catawba grapes

Resource Value

Lake Erie is perhaps Ohio's most valuable water resource. The abundant natural resources of the coastal zone have attracted activities such as fishing, farming, commerce, and industry. The lake, its bay, and its estuaries are the source of a wide variety of fish for both commercial and recreational fishing.

More than thirty endangered wildlife species known to inhabit these waters and nearby coastal areas are being protected. The prolonged growing season and an average of nearly six months of frost-free weather, make the Lake Erie islands and bordering mainland an ideal

Sailboat at sunset

area for grapes and other fruits. The lake has been described as the busiest, most traveled, and most important lake in the world. While this description emphasizes the commercial importance of the lake, its importance to the people of Ohio extends far beyond these narrow boundaries. Gas, oil, limestone, sandstone, salt, gravel, clay, gypsum, and peat are all found in commercial quantities in the region. Over 100 million tons of goods are shipped through Ohio's lake ports each year. The lake also serves as a source of water for homes, industry, and power generation. The 262 miles of shoreline (41 miles of island shoreline) within the state, provide many fine beaches, scenic vistas, and opportunity for recreational pursuits. Three million of Ohio's eleven million people have found the lake region an ideal area in which to live.

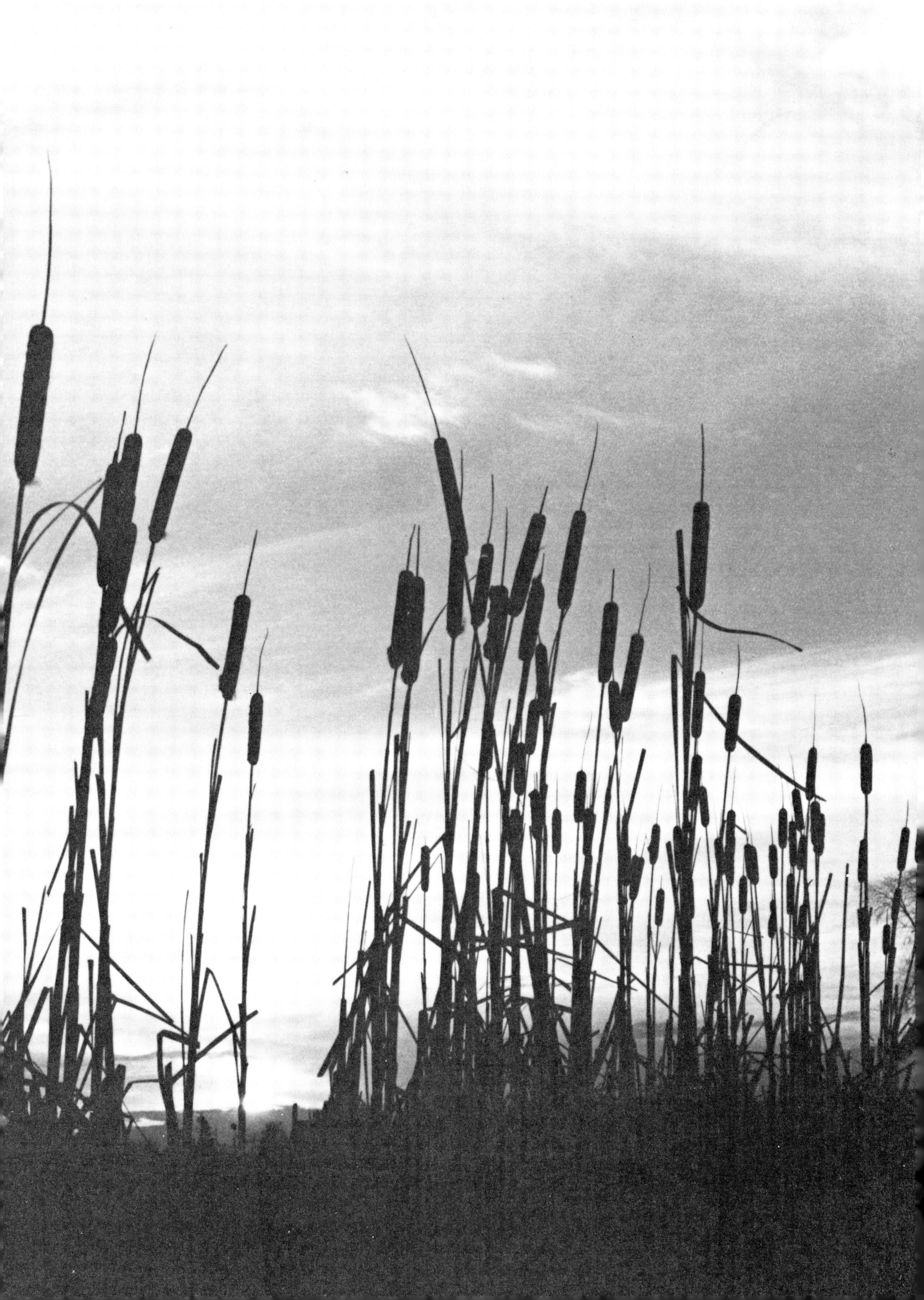

Chapter 14
Lake Plain

by Louis W. Campbell

THIRTEEN thousand years ago much of northwestern Ohio was covered by a vast sea from western New York State west to Fort Wayne, Indiana. Today, geologists call this Lake Maumee, a body of water created by the melting Wisconsinan glacier. As the ice retreated, unplugging outlets, the waters drained off and a series of lakes was formed eventually ending with present Lake Erie. Wave action and currents smoothed the fine clay sediments on the lake beds, leaving behind an extremely flat plain, interrupted only by remnants of glacial moraines and ancient beach ridges.

The succession of glacial lakes was instrumental in forming three unusual areas: the Great Black Swamp, the Oak Openings, and the Lake Erie and Sandusky Bay marshes. These areas were as much symbols of primitive America as the clouds of passenger pigeons east of the Mississippi River and the hordes of bison on the western plains. However, in their pristine wildness they were pieces that did not fit into the jigsaw puzzle which ultimately became the United States. Except where they are now preserved, these wildlands were sacrificed.

The Great Black Swamp

The swamp began forming after the lake waters drained away and left a great flat plain 120 miles long and 30 to 40 miles wide. It covered an

Phragmites or reed grass

area of about 1,500 square miles, beginning near Fort Wayne, Indiana and paralleling the Maumee River and bay to Lake Erie. The subsoil clay prevented water from sinking into the earth and the level terrain prevented water from running off readily. As a result, the land was flooded and muddy much of the year.

As temperatures moderated, vegetation invaded. First came tundra, then spruce, fir, pine, hemlock, birch, beech, and finally, dense swamp forest. Major tree species in the swamp forest were ash; elm; basswood; shellbark hickory; red, white, black, pin, bur, and swamp white oaks; and red and silver maples. Only scattered outcrops of limestone and sand ridges interrupted the surface. In places where the water was too deep for trees to survive, relatively small prairies persisted. They were covered with cattails, phragmites (a cane-like plant) and other herbaceous plants and were fringed with various shrubs. The only river of importance crossing the swamp was the Auglaize which flowed north joining the Maumee River near present-day Defiance.

This area was officially named the Great Black Swamp in 1812. The word black may have referred to the color of the soil or to the heavy shadow beneath the trees. Or perhaps it was meant to describe the forbidding character of the terrain. When explorers first encountered the Great Black Swamp, they found a vast expanse of trees which stood in water during spring and in oozy mud until ice formed in December. In early summer there were myriads of mosquitoes, and malaria was common. The Indians also avoided the dense growth and settled in the well-drained strips beside the Maumee River and its tributaries.

For years the Great Black Swamp was a barrier to the western movement of settlers. To avoid it, most travelers moved by boat on Lake Erie from Cleveland to Detroit. As a result, southern Michigan was much more densely populated than northwestern Ohio from 1830 to 1850. Travel through the swamp was difficult and major roads usually went around the border. As late as 1871 an overland trip of 35 miles from the Sandusky River to the Maumee River (probably Fremont to Perrysburg) took 2½ days of hard work.

It is significant that the principal cities of the area circled the swamp. Listed counterclockwise, they are Toledo, Maumee, Napoleon, Defiance, Fort Wayne (Indiana), Van Wert, Delphos, Findlay, Fostoria, Fremont, and Port Clinton. Only Bowling Green lay within it.

The problem of draining the land was solved by an 1859 law which provided for a system of public ditches. Still, the Great Black Swamp was only half cleared by 1870. A period of intense lumbering, during which "great gangs of men" were brought down from Canada, lasted from 1860 to 1865. And a large segment of the swamp was levelled in the 1860s when Eber Brock Ward purchased and cleared nearly 8,500 acres near Bono. In order to ship the timber, he dug Ward's Canal. Other lumbermen followed and by 1869, seven sawmills were being operated in and near the village.

By 1900 the swamp was drained and the fertile land produced good crops of corn. Martin R. Kaatz summed it up: "Within a few decades the Black Swamp was transformed from a useless, obstructive morass into the most productive region in Ohio." Looking back, we can see that transportation of people and materials, first by canal boat and then by railroad, was the important factor. One of the finest remaining examples of the Black Swamp forest is preserved in Goll Woods State Nature Preserve in Fulton County about three miles northwest of Archbold.

Modern studies indicate that climax forests such as the Great Black Swamp had (and have) very limited flora and fauna. The larger birds no doubt included the great-horned and barred owls, ravens, and wild turkeys. Passenger pigeons used the forests of the swamp as roosts if not breeding grounds. Ruffed grouse were probably rare. Songbirds must have included red-eyed vireo, scarlet tanager, flycatchers, and several warblers such as cerulean and redstart. Creepers and woodpeckers, especially the pileated woodpecker, were probably numerous. The

Fledgling screech owls

A young red fox

centers of bird and plant abundance would, of course, have been the prairies, sand ridges, and rock outcrops.

Mammals retreated to the swamp for safety after settlers invaded. During autumn, hunters from across Ohio came for organized shoots, and eventually game became scarce. Passenger pigeons, wild turkey, ruffed grouse, river otter, bison, wolverine, mountain lion, lynx, gray wolf, bobcat, black bear, porcupine, and deer were all extirpated by the mid-to-late 1800s.

Wildlife living in the region today has adapted to clearing and draining. Prairie and "backyard" birds took over and mammals such as the red fox, woodchuck, and fox squirrel became common. Brown rats and house mice occupied barns or fields. Almost nothing is known of the reptiles or amphibians which may have lived in the swamp forest, but undoubtedly they were very limited except in the prairie openings.

Clearing and draining also affected fish and other aquatic life. A foot of good topsoil has been washed into the streams from the treeless land. The great floods of 1913 were caused primarily by the rapid run-off of water, brought about by the heavy rains and frozen soils.

The levelling of these forests has provided almost a million acres of food-producing land and living space for Ohio's increasing population.

The Oak Openings

West of Toledo a broad ridge of fine yellow quartz sand extends from Liberty Center, near the Maumee River, northeast to Detroit. In Ohio, this region is known as the Oak Openings. The Oak Openings covers parts of Henry, Fulton, and Lucas counties; and it is bounded roughly by

Liberty Center, Colton, Whitehouse, Holland, and the western edges of Toledo, Sylvania, Raab's Corners, Swanton, and Brailey. The sand does not replace the clayey soil present in much of northwestern Ohio but lies upon it.

The question immediately arises: Where did all this sand come from? It came from Michigan over a period of thousands of years. Three of the lakes which preceded Lake Erie formed the Oak Openings. Geologists have named them Lake Warren, Lake Wayne, and Lake Lundy. They were much higher than Lake Erie. Lake Warren, for example, was 93 feet above Lake Erie. The sand along the edges of these glacial lakes was carried by longshore currents from Michigan to the southern ends of the various lakes.

When these sand beaches were first formed they were bare and fairly level. Then as the water dropped, the wind corrugated them, forming dunes that were constantly shifting. Vegetation began growing and the leaves and roots broke the wind and held the dunes in place. By the time French explorers traveled through northwest Ohio it is doubtful any expanses of bare sand were left.

The sand belt is not level but contains many dunes, some of them 35 feet or more above the clay base. The portion in Ohio is about 25 miles long and varies in width from 3½ to seven miles. Its depth ranges from 15 to 50 feet. Swan Creek and the Ottawa River cross the Oak Openings in Lucas County, but they circle around the portion where the sand is deepest. Drainage is very poor in the sand area, and the water table lies within three feet of the surface in many places.

Originally the Oak Openings was surrounded by dense swamp forest. On the dunes, however, trees were farther apart and drainage was better, providing easier travel and better living conditions. Artifacts discovered on the dunes indicate that people lived there as early as 12,000 years ago. Early explorers used the sand ridge as an important highway between Detroit and the fords in the Maumee River rapids.

Between 1830 and 1840, Toledo's population expanded rapidly and many families settled in the Oak Openings southeast of Whitehouse where the land was cheap, sand was thinner, and the soil was drained by several small streams. The opening of the Miami and Erie Canal in 1842, and later the coming of steam railroads and electric interurbans, also made the region more accessible. Intensive lumbering between 1910 and 1920 brought radical changes to the Oak Openings. Oak trees were cut for railroad ties. Larger trees from the swamp forest were leveled for timber. As the trees fell, plants needing more light invaded.

Away from the larger streams there was almost no drainage in the hollows between the dunes, so much of the land was flooded during the winter and spring. As late as 1910, people were crossing the big prairie between Old State Line Road and Bancroft Street in Lucas County in canoes or on ice skates. But the influx of immigrants brought a demand for drainage. Prairie Ditch, Wiregrass Ditch, and many others were dug to carry surplus water into Swan Creek and the Ottawa River. In 1930 the huge Drennan Ditch was built. This ditch connected with Wolf Creek near Holland and emptied into Swan Creek.

The coming of the automobile resulted in even more changes than the railroads had produced. In the mid-1930s most roads were surfaced by the WPA (Work Progress Administration). After World War II, a great expansion of house building took place and for the first time expensive homes were built in groves of oak. Today development continues and the cost of the land has skyrocketed.

Six well-defined habitats may be found within the Oak Openings. One of the great attractions is the closeness of these habitats to each other, making it easy to see a great variety of flora and fauna in a short time.

1) On the dunes and sandy plateaus, a scattering of black, white, and a few red oaks grow. This contrast with the dense swamp forests accounts for the name Oak Openings, which appeared as early as 1873. Bracken fern, huckleberry, chokeberry, wintergreen, wild indigo, lupine, wild sweet pea, butterfly weed, and various goldenrods and asters also grow here.

2) In hollows between the dunes are swamp forests of pin oak, red maple, wild black cherry, blackgum, poplar, and aspen. Before the peak of the Dutch elm disease in the late 1950s, American elm was common. Beneath the trees are buttonbush, blackberry, spicebush, wild spirea, spikenard, wild lily-of-the-valley, bedstraw, and several kinds of ferns.

3) The bogs are situated at the base of the dunes where they receive maximum moisture. Black soil is deepest there. Speckled alder, elderberry, willows, wild spirea, buttonbush, and ninebark flourish. Understory plants include wild raspberry, wild rose, skunk cabbage, marsh marigold, spotted jewelweed, yarrow, wild sunflowers, goldenrod, aster, and marsh ferns.

4) Wet prairies are few in number and, with the exception of those at Irwin Prairie State Nature Preserve and Schwamberger Preserve, acreage is small. The larger primitive prairies contain bluejoint grass, slough grass, sedges, and clumps of willow, buttonbush, ninebark, and aspen.

5) On the bare dunes and in the overworked, abandoned upland farm areas grow prairie plants such as big and little bluestem grass, Indian grass, low-running blackberry, lupine, sunflowers, and wild coreopsis. Many of these apparently moved in when Ohio's climate was drier 3,500 years ago.

6) The sixth habitat is technically not Oak Openings but the valleys of Swan Creek, the Ottawa River, and their tributaries which cut through the sand belt. In Wildwood Preserve and especially in Oak Openings Metro Park, there are steep cuts where the sand can be seen resting upon clay. Vegetation in the valleys is similar to that in all stream valleys near Toledo. Trees are mostly lowland species such as green ash, silver

Oak Openings sand dune area

Yellow warbler

maple, walnut, poplar, basswood, sycamore, and box elder. Beneath are giant ragweed, wood nettle, smartweed, coneflowers, spotted jewelweed and, in wetter spots, lizard's-tail, and water-willow.

The sandy soil of the Oak Openings is acid on the crests and slightly alkaline in the low spots. This condition, combined with the great variety of habitats, allows many plant species to grow that are rare in the remainder of Ohio. Even some northern plants still persist, because wet sand is not warmed by the sun as much as other soils.

Edwin L. Moseley was one of the first to study the vegetation of the sand country. He included 715 plant species in his *Flora of the Oak Openings* in 1929. Of these, 61 species were known in only two other Ohio counties. He estimated that 168 were more common in the Oak Openings than in the remainder of Ohio. Yet the Oak Openings is only about one-third as large as the average county. The presence of 17 species of asters and 20 goldenrods is a good indication of the abundance of flowers. Since Moseley's report, at least 100 additional species have been discovered, including a number of beautiful orchids.

No evergreens were native to the Oak Openings. Following the glacier, they had already moved north of the area before the sand belt formed. In the early 1940s however, thousands of pines, spruces, and a few other species were planted with WPA funds in Oak Openings Metro Park. A few other trees such as river birch were also introduced, laudable at the time but now confusing to students trying to learn the original vegetation.

Marsh hawk

Fungi are unusually common — over 70 species have been identified. The well-known forms, consisting of a stem with an umbrella-shaped cap, come in white, yellow, orange, brown, red, green, and purple. They range from tiny fragile specimens, which very often fall apart when touched, to husky ones eight or more inches in diameter. Shelf types attached to trees are numerous. Some forms which do not resemble the others include the sponge-like morels, puffballs, and coral mushrooms. Of course, great care must be taken when gathering mushrooms for food. Some of the most appetizing-looking are the most poisonous.

The Oak Openings also is the home of a great variety of wildlife, especially birds of which 110 species have been found breeding. Rarest breeding varieties are the Wilson's snipe; least flycatcher; Bewick's wren; summer tanager; Louisiana waterthrush; and Canada, mourning, magnolia, and Kentucky warblers. Bachman's sparrow and white-eyed vireo have been seen about every other year, but no nests have been discovered. Other species that bred once or twice, mostly on the Irwin Prairie, are the pied-billed grebe, least bittern, king and sora rails, gallinule, and long-billed marsh wren. Marsh and Cooper's hawks, which nested regularly through the 1940s, are no longer present, but the broad-winged hawk now breeds. The golden-winged and blue-winged warblers and their hybrids, the Brewster's and Lawrence's, were once seen regularly, but now only the blue-winged is left. Two other residents, Henslow's sparrow and the short-billed marsh wren, visit the sand belt from time to time.

Unusual but regular breeders include the red-shouldered hawk, barred and great-horned owls, the whip-poor-will which is declining rapidly, Acadian and willow flycatchers, and veery, blue-gray gnat-catcher, orchard oriole, scarlet tanager, rose-breasted grosbeak, and grasshopper and swamp sparrows. A few yellow-throated vireos, yellowbreasted chats, redstarts, and blue-winged, cerulean, chestnut-sided, and hooded warblers also nest. Most unusual are the few pairs of lark sparrows, considered the handsomest of their family.

Several of the more prominent birds of the sand country were noticed by early sportsmen. Twelve or 15 pairs of sandhill cranes nested on the big prairie until 1875. Prairie chickens were gone from the openings by 1880, wild turkeys by 1892, and the last ruffed grouse was seen in 1905.

Despite the wild character of the sand belt, comparatively few mammals are found there, no doubt because the soil is not rich enough to provide an abundance of food. The badger maybe the only one confined to it. Other species, fairly typical of the entire state, include raccoon, woodchuck, opossum, skunk, cottontail, fox, flying and red squirrels, chipmunk, eastern mole, white-footed mouse, meadow jumping mouse, vole, and short-tailed and least shrews.

Most often seen in the stream valleys are the muskrat, mink, and long-tailed weasel. The least weasel has been captured near Monclova. All the white-tailed deer were gone by 1889, but by 1930 had returned and have thrived since. Similarly, the red fox, gone by 1900, reappeared in 1935 and is now common. The gray fox returned in 1940, peaked in 1956, and has now dropped back to a few individuals.

No reptile is common in the Oak Openings. The most publicized is the massasauga, a small rattlesnake. It once lived in the wet prairies but now is very rare. The small, secretive ring-necked snake is also scarce. Other snakes found in the Openings include garter, ribbon, water, DeKay's, blue racer, hognose, and milk, a snake that the pioneers once thought milked their cows because it was often found in barns (searching for mice).

The spotted and the box are the most unusual turtles. Others are snapping, Blanding's, map, painted, and, in the streams, an occasional spiny softshell.

Amphibians include the cricket frog, spring peeper, gray treefrog, chorus frog, leopard frog, northern wood frog, green frog, bullfrog, and red-spotted newt, the Jefferson, spotted and red-backed salamanders, and Fowler's toads.

Much of the Oak Openings has been acquired by various state and local agencies and is open to the public. Oak Openings Metropark, with 3,400 acres, is the largest preserve. The 500-acre Secor Metropark protects about 250 acres of climax forest, and 460-acre Wildwood Preserve Metropark protects a stream valley and upland area. The largest forest area is the 3,068-acre Maumee State Forest. The state also maintains Irwin Prairie State Nature Preserve (172 acres). Other natural features can be seen on DeVilbiss Boy Scout Reservation and numerous railroad rights-of-way.

Lake Erie Marshes

Along the southwestern shore of Lake Erie between the mouth of the Detroit River and Port Clinton, and at several places bordering Sandusky Bay are huge cattail marshes. They average one to two miles wide and are interrupted by points of higher land, by human-made fills and by drainage for farming or subdivision. These marshes are caused by the changing levels of Lake Erie as it advances and retreats over the flat terrain.

Lake Plain marsh

Redwing blackbird nest in cattails

The upper Great Lakes furnish 90 percent of Erie's water, so the lake level is governed directly by lakes Huron, Michigan, and Superior. Precipitation and succeeding evaporation are the most important factors controlling the water levels, which vary from decade to decade. From 1965 to 1972, precipitation over the Great Lakes ranged from four percent to nine percent above normal, depending on the particular basin. This increase resulted in an all-time peak in the Lake Erie level in 1973. The run-off from precipitation has increased and will continue to increase in the coming years as forests, which retain water, are cut down and more drainage for highways and buildings is installed.

More predictable is a seasonal difference of 1½ feet each year — lowest in February and highest in June — due to the spring run-off. The slope, or gradient, of the land bordering the lake is only two or three feet per mile. Consequently, a half-mile strip would be alternately flooded and drained each year if there were no shoreline protection.

Northeast gales cause the greatest short-time change in Lake Erie levels. Sometimes these gales pile up the water to a height of six feet. When this mass of water moves back and forth, it is called a seiche. (Southwest winds lower water levels to the same degree). An elevation of four feet — a common occurrence — would flood the land two miles inland if there were no barriers.

Normally longshore drift builds up a sandbar at the lake edge of a marsh. This acts as a low dam, keeping the water impounded at a reasonable level except when northeast winds blow. But these are far from efficient because of the ever-changing lake level. For instance, on December 27, 1938, the lake reached its all-time recorded low of 562.9 feet above sea level. On April 19, 1973 a northeaster drove the reading up to 578, a difference of 15.1 feet. In other words, a person standing on the beach late in December of 1938 would be in 15 feet of water with six-foot waves above that if he could have stood on that same spot on April 19, 1973. It is no wonder that homes considered perfectly safe were flooded in 1973. Succeeding storms continue to destroy shoreline dikes.

Early settlers avoided the marshes because of the unpredictable changes in water level and the dense growth of reeds and cattails. As late as 1834, these areas were marked impassable on U.S. government maps and only a few French trappers had invaded them. Before roads were built, the strip of reeds and prairie grasses lying between the swamp forest and the cattails was sometimes used as a highway by travelers and troops moving from Toledo to Sandusky Bay, especially in autumn.

Earliest to utilize marshes were the duck hunters. They soon found that for best results earth barriers had to be built along Lake Erie's shores — to keep water out when lake levels were high and to keep water in when they were low. Farmers and real estate developers followed their example. By the turn of the century, scores of miles of dikes had been erected.

Later, during high water times, Lake Erie waves demolished some of the dikes. To protect them, huge chunks of rock were trucked from quarries and stacked along the beaches. These modern embankments are expected to hold Lake Erie in check even when further increases in levels occur — which they most certainly will.

Diking the marshes, although essential, was a mixed blessing for the sportsmen's clubs. It stabilized water levels, increasing waterfowl and all other forms of wildlife, especially those that prefer "edges." The earthen dikes provided dry upland breeding areas for waterfowl, mammals, and turtles. They increased the aquatic plants that ducks eat, but they also promoted greater numbers of raccoons, skunks, opossums, and snapping turtles, all of which destroy nests or ducklings. They caused the disappearance of wild rice, an important food item for waterfowl, and they prevented many species of fish from entering the marshes to spawn.

Bordering the marshes was the Great Black Swamp. When the rising water flooded the forest, the trees were killed. As the water receded, they were replaced by a zone of shrubs and saplings, reed, bluejoint grass and other grasses, cattails, and aquatic plants in the pools. However, not all of this vegetation was permanent. For instance, when the water level increased, cattails gave way to aquatic plants; when it dropped, cattails gave way to reeds and various grasses. The Lake Erie marshes are really composed of a variety of habitats including open ponds, cattails, reed, the tops of earthen dikes, shrub and sapling thickets, swamp forest remnants, and sand ridges.

Each of these habitats attracts its own species of plants, birds, mammals, reptiles, and amphibians. The result is more variety in plant and animal life then in any other area of equal size in the state. The overall conditions are very primitive. There are still sections visited by no more than two or three persons in a quarter century.

About 300 species of birds have been found in the Lake Erie and Sandusky marshes. Of these, 130 have been known to breed and 120 are found in winter. Recent flooding has greatly reduced the number of breeders such as bitterns, coots, gallinules, rails, black terns, and marsh wrens. Great numbers of migrating birds are present because branches of the Mississippi and Atlantic flyways pass over the west end of Lake Erie, and because conditions on the lake often prevent north-bound birds from crossing. When they are ready to proceed north, they take one of two routes — around the west end of the lake across the mouth of the Maumee River into Michigan, or by way of the Lake Erie islands to Point Pelee in Canada.

Sometimes in stormy weather great concentrations can be seen. In the last 15 years on various dates these totals have been reported on one-day counts: 35,000 mallards, 46,000 black ducks, 1,700 gadwalls, 20,000 wigeon, 7,575 redheads, 10,200 canvasbacks, 20,000 scaup ducks, 5,500 whistling swans, 30,000 Canada geese, 6,000 coots, 80,000 mergansers,

Hen mallard and ducklings

Whistling swans

Hooded merganser

Black terns

Herring gull

Goose family

Flying geese at sunset

1,000 great blue herons, 96,584 gulls (herring, ring-billed and Bonaparte's), 20,000 snow buntings, and blackbirds into the millions.

From 1972 through 1978, fields adjoining the marshes were flooded and thousands of shorebirds moved in together with common terns and Forster's terns.

A project of the Ohio Division of Wildlife that had an extraordinary effect on area waterfowl was the installation of a branch of the Canada Goose Management Investigations at the Crane Creek Wildlife Experimental Station in the Magee Marsh in 1967. Twenty pairs of giant Canada geese were wing-clipped and released. This group increased to 1,082 by 1972 and in that year raised 703 goslings.

Thousands of migrating geese have been attracted by this flock. The Crane Creek station and the adjoining Ottawa National Wildlife Refuge furnish food and sanctuary. Prior to this program, the maximum number of Canada geese recorded was 2,200 in 1946. But in 1972, 30,000 geese visited the area on December 3.

West Sister Island is 8½ miles from the mainland but is closely related to the marsh complex because of the huge heronry there. The birds make the trip to the wetlands daily for food. In 1976, 3,000 black-crowned night heron nests, 600 great blue heron nests, and 600 great egret nests were reported.

Another great blue heronry in the Winous Point Marsh on Sandusky Bay contained 1,600 nests in 1973. It began to fall apart due to the

Little green heron

rotting of the trees, and in 1977 only about 650 nests remained. But a branch has been established in a swamp near Sandusky Bay south of State Route 2 and west of State Route 6.

Bald eagles build the most spectacular nests in the marshes. A few of these can be found in the Ottawa National Wildlife Refuge, Winous Point Marsh, and Ottawa Marsh.

About 22 kinds of mammals, excluding bats, can be found in the marsh complex. Most important is the lowly muskrat. It furnishes more than 70 percent of Ohio furs with a cash value up to $1.5 million annually. In the last decade, the demand for the carcasses as food has greatly increased. Marsh water levels have stabilized and muskrat populations have soared. As in the remainder of northwestern Ohio, red and gray foxes and white-tailed deer reappeared in 1935 after an absence of 25 years. The gray fox has since declined greatly but red fox and deer are flourishing.

Reptiles and amphibians are more common in the Lake Erie and Sandusky Bay marshes than anywhere else in northwestern Ohio. However, amateur and professional collectors have reduced them to a minimum in portions of the Magee Marsh.

Common are the fox snake (the largest was 59 inches), common water snake, northern brown snake, and garter snakes including melanistic garters which are all black except for white throats. Most unusual are milk snake, Kirtland's snake, queen snake, and ribbon snake. No

American bald eagles live in the Lake Erie marshes.

massasauga or timber rattle snake has ever been reported. The marsh habitat is not favorable to either of these species.

Turtles are common. The snapping turtle, which has been reported weighing up to 50 pounds, is the largest. Painted and Blanding's turtles are the most numerous. Rare forms include the musk, map, and spiny soft-shelled turtles.

Frogs are represented by the bullfrog, green frog, leopard frog, striped chorus frog, cricket frog, and spring peeper. Salamanders include the mudpuppy, Jefferson, spotted, and red-backed. Red-spotted newts have been found at Catawba Island and may live near the marshes.

An estimated 1,000 vascular plants can be found in the marsh complex, of which 30 are shrubs and 75 are trees. The construction of the dikes and the stabilization of shorelines have added to the original number. The sand beach flora, which included some of the rarer forms, have suffered greatly from high lake levels and many species may have been eliminated.

Marsh vegetation is amazingly resilient. Areas of bare mud in spring will be covered by a waist-high growth of cattails, grasses, and herbaceous plants by late summer. Trees beside the canals grow very rapidly. Willows planted in 1927 are now over 20 inches in diameter. Originally the beaches must have held a conspicuous growth of red cedars. How else can we account for Cedar Point in Sandusky County, Little Cedar Point, and Cedar Island (now Turtle Island)? A few of these trees can still be found.

Marshes are most colorful in summer. Outstanding flowers are the pink rose mallow; the lavender Joe Pye weed; the white arrowhead and water lily; the blue skullcap, wild iris, and pickerel weed; the pale yellow American lotus, and bur marigold.

Swamp rose-mallow

Muskrat

Fox snake

Ohioans are fortunate that so many of the Lake Erie marshes have been preserved. If it were not for the efforts of hunters and trappers, many would have been drained or filled. Today several of the best tracts are owned by the U.S. Department of the Interior or the Ohio Department of Natural Resources, Division of Wildlife. In all, more than 21,000 acres of marshland have been protected by federal and state agencies and by private shooting clubs.

High Lake Erie levels and the accompanying flooding disturb the marsh environment. But the marsh is flexible and, once water levels within have been stabilized, a rapid return to previous conditions may be expected.

Of the three unique geographical areas caused by post-glacial lakes in northwestern Ohio, the Great Black Swamp has been changed the most. It was a serious obstacle to development of the state, and furthermore the soil which supported the trees was more valuable for growing crops. The Oak Openings, on the other hand, was less suitable for farmland and therefore remained relatively undisturbed. Naturalists had become aware of its unusual character and took action to preserve portions in a fairly primitive state. About 8,000 acres are contained in Toledo area metroparks or are controlled by the Ohio Department of Natural Resources. More control of habitat is needed if the prairie remnants are to be preserved. Because of overall drainage needed for the installation of highways and housing developments, prairies are being invaded by shrubs and aspens.

Snow goose (left) and Blue goose

As for the Lake Erie and Sandusky Bay marshes, a large portion of them will be preserved if the present attitude remains. The public is beginning to recognize their value as primitive areas and if owners decide to sell, no doubt other agencies will buy.

While the destruction of the Great Black Swamp was inevitable, it is fortunate that significant portions of the other two rare areas in northwestern Ohio are being preserved.

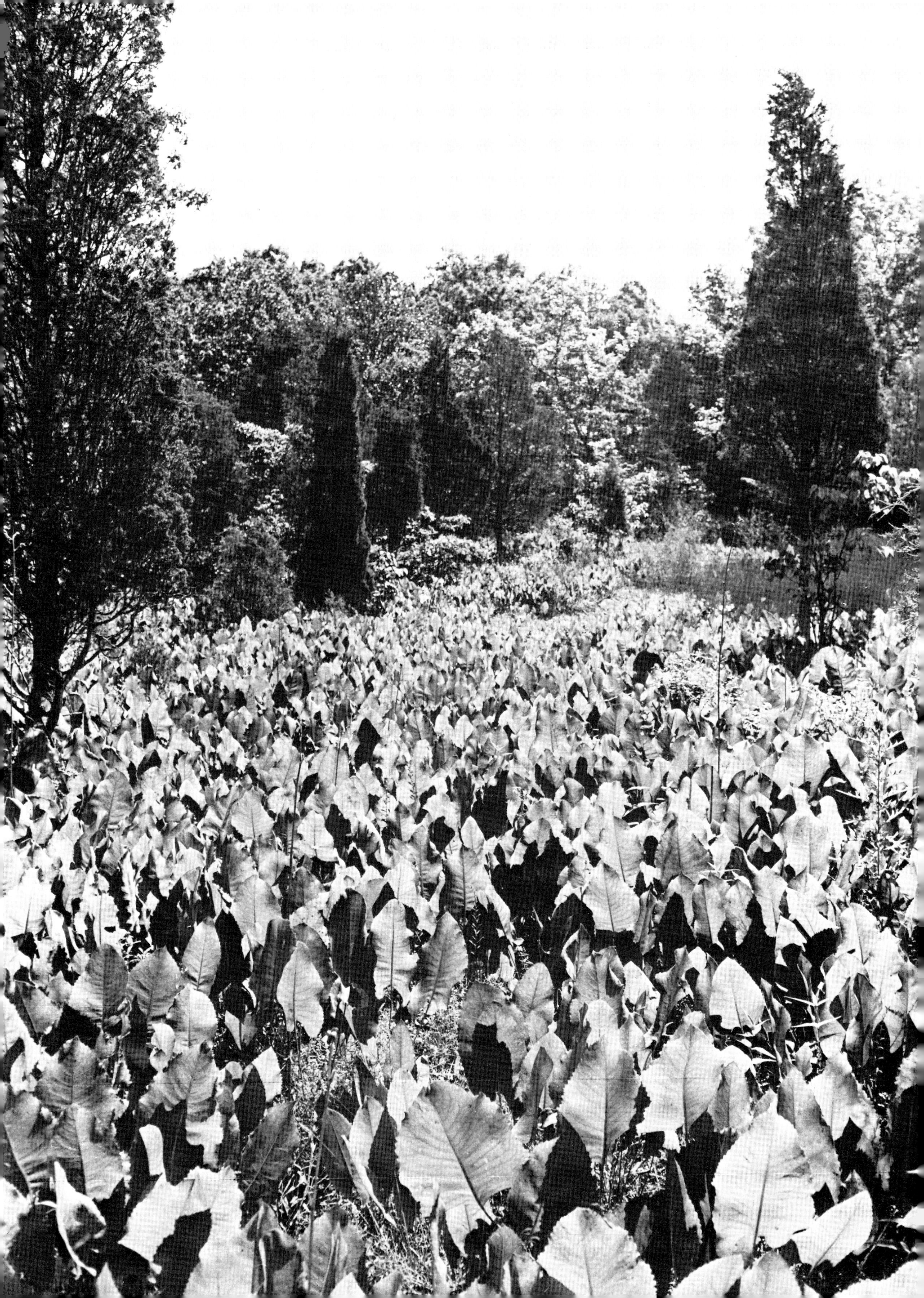

Chapter 15
The Bluegrass

JOHN Locke, an early Ohio naturalist, called it Split Rock; today it is known as Buzzardroost Rock. But no matter the name, the place still has the air of the wild woods about it. Vultures glide noiselessly on the air currents as they did 150 years ago. Ohio Brush Creek flows silently beneath a canopy of sycamores 400 feet below. The woods close in all around, and the only sound is that of the wind whistling through the trees and around the rocky outcrop. The roost, especially in winter, is a very lonely place.

The trail to the top is difficult, but just as rewarding as in 1835. A hiker earns a spectacular bird's-eye-view of one of the most interesting natural regions anywhere — the Bluegrass Region which stretches north, south, and west from Buzzardroost. A northern extension of the Bluegrass Region of Kentucky and the Interior Low Plateau Province, Ohio's Bluegrass Region is triangular-shaped with its northern tip in southern Highland County. The region covers most of Adams County plus the southeastern quarter of Brown County.

The region has a complicated geology. A blanket of Illinoian-age till marks the maximum movement of glaciers and smooths the region's northwestern boundary, while the Ohio River bounds the south. To the east, Mississippian sandstone caps the hills, locally called "knobs." Underlying the sandstone are Devonian shales and Silurian dolomite.

by Lynn Edward Elfner

Yellow-shafted flicker with Buzzardroost Rock in background

These hills were once joined to the high ground of the Appalachian Plateau to the east. But millions of years of erosion have cut down the terrain and the resistant dolomite points and cliffs are now separate. The result is some of Ohio's most spectacular relief. Greenbrier Ridge, south of Buzzardroost Rock, rises to 1,265 feet or 765 feet above Ohio Brush Creek.

Patterns of the Past

The Bluegrass has undergone much change, but past events have left many marks which help reveal its earlier appearance. Sediments of ancient Ordovician and Silurian seas formed the region's limestone, dolomite, and shale bedrock. Later uplifting of the Cincinnati Arch tilted the rock eastward.

Geologists believe that an ancient stream — a predecessor to Ohio Brush Creek — was once as high as Buzzardroost Rock. The top of the rock was part of a high-level stream divide which extended across what is now the valley of Ohio Brush Creek. Long before the creek was formed, rain falling on this ridge may have flowed either north or south and entered tributaries of the Teays River — Ohio's prehistoric master stream which flowed northwestward. A massive amount of meltwater from one of the early glaciers was trapped between this ridge and the ice front 15 to 20 miles north. Something had to give. Water from the glacial lake cut through the ridge and formed Ohio Brush Creek which drained to the south into the newly formed Ohio River. The peculiar undercut shape at the base of Buzzardroost Rock may be part of a stream bank which existed thousands of years ago and is now high and dry more than 300 feet above the present stream. This feature is strikingly similar to modern stream banks elsewhere in the region, especially at the Edwin H. Davis State Memorial near Peebles — a nature preserve administered by the Ohio Historical Society.

Ohio Brush Creek has many small tributaries which keep cutting back into the hills heading into the Appalachian Plateau. In several places, especially near the small hamlet of Lynx, eastward-flowing streams have been captured or "pirated" by westward-flowing tributaries of Ohio Brush Creek. Evidence for stream piracy is the "barbed" branches of these highland streams. Normal streams follow a "dendritic" or leaf-vein pattern. Pirated streams can be seen in the Wilderness Preserve at Lynx, owned by the Cincinnati Museum of Natural History. This area lies on a narrow transition between the Interior Low Plateau Province and the Appalachian Plateaus Province.

Purple cliffbrake fern

Holes in the Hills

Funnel-shaped depressions shunned by local landowners have developed near the edges of some of the dolomite hills. These are "sink holes" which formed when the underlying limestone and dolomite dissolved and the resulting caverns collapsed. Sink holes are natural obstacles to farming on these hills. Developed over thousands or even millions of years through the slow dissolving of the rock by rainwater, these cavities often mark the beginning of streams which eventually flow into Ohio Brush Creek or other streams.

E. Lucy Braun, who probably knew more about the Bluegrass than anyone, discovered that mist rises in these sink holes on hot summer days and the moist rock faces are green with mosses and liverworts. Ferns are abundant, and wild flowers such as anemonella, hepatica, and trillium, in Miss Braun's words, "convert the sink holes into a sunken garden in springtime."

But what may be just a hole in the ground to a farmer or a sunken garden to a naturalist, is much more important to a bat. Because of the number of sink holes, small caves, and rock crevices, Ohio's Bluegrass may be the bat capital of Ohio. At least nine of the eleven species of Ohio bats are found here. Species include the little brown bat, Keen's bat, silver-haired bat, eastern pipistrelle, evening bat, red bat, big brown bat, eastern big-eared bat, and the Indiana bat, an endangered species. Just how many bats are there? No one knows for sure but a few years ago one researcher, using an almost invisible "mist" net, captured, banded, and released 844 bats of five species over a thirteen-night period.

Very little is known about other animals which may live in the sink

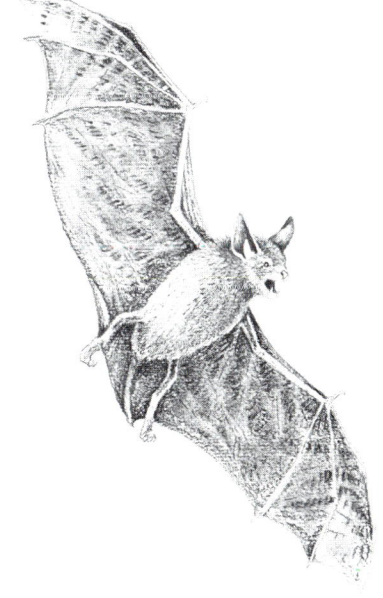

Indiana bat

Lynx

Looking southwest, an aerial view of the northern tip of the Bluegrass Region shows the unusual Serpent Mound meteor crater. The forested area to the left is the western edge of the Appalachian Plateau.

holes, small caves, and rock crevices, although a cave-dwelling form of an isopod similar to common pillbugs, rolly-pollies, or sowbugs found in dark, damp basements and under rocks, does live in them. No doubt foxes, raccoons, skunks, salamanders, and snakes sometimes live in the holes. And in pioneer days some of these caves may have hosted hibernating black bears or served as lairs for lynx, the name of a small Adams County town. Because the geology of this terrain is similar to that in other portions of the Interior Low Plateau Province — where farther south Kentucky's Mammoth Cave is so well known — it is possible that future researchers will uncover more cave-dwelling organisms, and more caves.

The Meteor Mounds

"I don't know whether it's a crater or not or just what it is, but something sure ain't right here...there's an awful lot of strange-looking rocks around." That's the opinion of a local landowner living on what may be a crater caused by a meteorite crashing to the earth millions of years ago. No one knows for sure how the unusual area was formed but two theories have been offered. In 1936 W.H. Bucher of the University of Cincinnati thought the area was formed by "cryptovolcanism." He thought such structures elsewhere in the world may have been caused by the sudden liberation of pent-up volcanic gases. A more modern theory holds that the area is an "astrobleme" or star wound caused by a meteorite.

Located at the common boundary of Adams, Highland, and Pike counties, the area is known as the Serpent Mound cryptoexplosion structure. On the southwest side of this five-mile circular area is the world famous Serpent Mound effigy constructed by Pre-Columbian Indians.

Most of the thousands of visitors to Serpent Mound are probably unaware of the unusual nature of the bedrocks. Like an impression made by a giant doughnut, the area contains three divisions. The center, which would have been squeezed up through the doughnut's hole, is comprised of highly faulted or broken rocks of Ordovician age displaced upwards over 950 feet above their normal level. Some layers are so jumbled they are completely upside down. Next, a ring of folded and faulted Silurian dolomite is displaced upward less than the center. The outer ring has the youngest rocks — Mississippian age — which have been displaced downward nearly 400 feet.

This area was first described in 1838 by John Locke who wrote:

> Although we travelled on that level which should have presented us with cliff limestone [Silurian], yet we were surprised with its total disappearance as we approached the spring [Sinking Spring in the southeast corner of Highland County], and in its place was found the sandstone [Mississippian] in large unturned and broken masses. In short, it became evident that a region of no small extent had sunk down several hundred feet, producing faults, dislocations and upturning of the layers of rocks.

Research continues; however, more questions are raised than answered. Did a star fall from heaven? Why did the Moundbuilders construct Serpent Mound here? Did they know something we don't know? Does the mound really resemble a falling star with a long serpent-like tail?

Soils Reflect Land Use

There is more to soil than meets the eye. Soil mirrors land use, both past and present. Viewed from the air, the light and brightly colored soils of the Bluegrass, now farm land, once supported extensive forests of white, red, shingle, chinquapin, swamp white, and bur oaks, and white and blue ash in association with less numerous species such as tuliptree, blackgum, red elm, sugar maple, pawpaw, and wild black cherry. These colors are due partially to mineral content, but they also reflect the lack of organic matter common to soils of the region, a feature of soils developed under forests. In contrast, small areas in this region have shallow, dark-colored soils because they developed under grassland. The extensive root systems of grass provide more organic matter and so the soils are darker.

Although pioneers cleared the forests for agriculture, much of the destruction probably occurred because of the tremendous amount of wood needed to make charcoal for iron furnaces at nearby Cedar Mills and Steam Furnace. Many of the oaks were cut to obtain tannic acid from their bark. Those natural areas spared from the ax and plow include both grasslands and inaccessible cliffs.

Cedar Barrens with Prairies

To someone from Iowa or Illinois who may expect acres and acres of waving grasses and other colorful plants, prairies in Ohio's Bluegrass Region are mere openings in the forest. Nonetheless, the presence of many prairie species makes them true prairies. Prairie dock, big bluestem, little bluestem, side-oats grama grass, and several species of liatris or blazing stars are found here. With its leaves resembling yucca, the false aloe or agave gives these areas an almost desert-like appearance. Indeed, close relatives of this species of agave (or century plant) are common in southwestern deserts.

The prairies of the Bluegrass are some of the best places to watch nature's annual progression. As Lucy Braun and her sister Annette observed of summer foliage:

> Through June and July the variety increases until by August the riot of flower color--of butterfly weed, coneflowers, coreopsis, physostegia, euphorbia, sabatia, liatris, and the smaller and delicate spikes of lobelia and fragrant agave--surpasses anything of the deciduous forest...One by one the summer flowers drop out; inch by inch the prairie grasses increase in height until the rich green and sienna of the grass stems and leaves and their silvery spikelets dominate the landscape. Just at the end of the season when the shrubs and surrounding trees are coloring the forests their richest, the asters and most of all the gentians again enhance the prairie with delicate blues and violets.

One of the best places to observe what the Brauns describe is Lynx Prairie, which has been dedicated as a memorial to E. Lucy Braun and the important work she accomplished during her career as a leading American ecologist.

To be accurate, the prairies of this region are more like strips, patches, or openings in areas of extensive "cedar barrens." Shallow, dark soils, developed in place on dolomite, reflect the persistence of prairies for many years. More recently, prairie type vegetation has developed on roadsides and old fields along with encroaching red cedar trees.

Purple coneflower

Red cedar or juniper

Zones of red cedar and hardwoods at Abner Hollow reflect the bedrock geology of the area.

Cedar Falls

Grama grass

An Important Point

But how did prairies develop in this region and from where did they come? Nearly a century passed before John Locke's observation of Buzzardroost Rock became significant. Many of the same plants he saw in the early 1830s were observed in the 1920s by E. Lucy Braun. Indeed, many of the same species are here today. Several, like big bluestem and side-oats grama grass, Texas rock sandwort, and blazing star, are prairie species. This prairie has existed for over 140 years; and there is further evidence that it is something out of the distant past.

The prairie on Buzzardroost Rock and similar prairies on nearby dry, rocky promontories probably developed during eastward migration of prairies in a period after the last glacial advance when the climate was warmer and drier; or, they may have developed during such periods between earlier glaciers. These relict prairies "seeded" old fields and roadsides.

Thanks to the special efforts of The Nature Conservancy, many of the prairies in the Bluegrass are being preserved and deeded to organizations like the Cincinnati Museum of Natural History for permanent care.

Northern Visitors Who Stayed

But the prairies are not the only connections to the past. A few northern plants that migrated into the area as the glaciers advanced have remained. Probably the most important of these is the white cedar, which grows extensively at Cedar Falls in Adams County. Cedar Falls contains one of the most impressive stands of white cedars this far south in North America. When hikers enter the gorge they are suddenly transported thousands of years back in time. The falls consists of a deep gorge flanked by wet, slippery blocks of dolomite. Even when the sun shines brightly, the narrow gorge is dark, damp, and cool, making conditions ideal for white cedar.

Northern Michigan and Canada can lay claim to extensive stands of white cedar where thousands of acres are covered by extensive swamps. In Ohio, white cedar is found in Cedar Bog near Urbana and in a few isolated spots on dolomite or limestone outcrops such as in Clifton Gorge in Greene County and from Adams County north to a handful of trees in Delaware County at Bellepoint, where Mill Creek flows into the Scioto River. However, the Cedar Falls population is the oldest in Ohio.

An extensive forest of northern species such as white cedar, spruce, and fir apparently migrated in advance of an early glacier. The ice front was 15 to 20 miles to the north. When the ice melted, the white cedars remained in isolated locations such as Cedar Falls where local conditions still favor their existence over other species.

The specific sites are rugged. Cliff edges are lined with broken blocks of dolomite. The drier slopes harbor almost pure stands of white cedar; other stands are mixed with red cedar, scarlet oak, white oak, sugar maple, basswood, and tuliptree. In Cedar Falls gorge, white cedar grows to over three feet in diameter, and this is the home of the largest white cedar known in Ohio. Tree ring counts reveal these cedars are at least 300 years old.

Other vegetation in the gorge is exceptionally luxuriant. Moist mats of mosses and liverworts cover the rocks. Walking fern, whose tapering tips touch the soil and give rise to new plants, can be found here. Maidenhair fern and bulblet ferns are common. The moist air and damp rock faces also support miterwort, hepatica, bloodroot, wild ginger, yellow touch-me-nots, and stonecrop. Here in Ohio's Bluegrass, northern visitors have found conditions hospitable and have stayed for thousands of years.

Isolated pockets of southern plants also exist on the plateau. One, Canby's mountain lover, is a small ground-hugging evergreen which is common on the Piedmont Plateau of North Carolina; this small plant probably migrated into Adams County by way of the Teays River. It is believed a live twig or branch from the plant fell into the river and was transported north to Ohio. The only other Ohio population of Canby's mountain lover is also on dolomite at Fort Hill in Highland County. Each patch is possibly a clone of great age.

The Bluegrass, a region which has been carved by glacial meltwater, now harbors isolated colonies of plants and animals of the West, North, and South. Although small in size, this natural region, including the meteorite structure, is one of the most fascinating in Ohio.

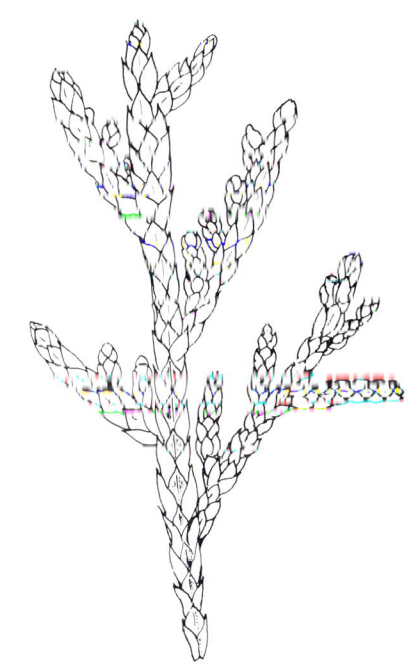

Northern white cedar or arbor vitae

Maidenhair fern

Canby's mountain lover

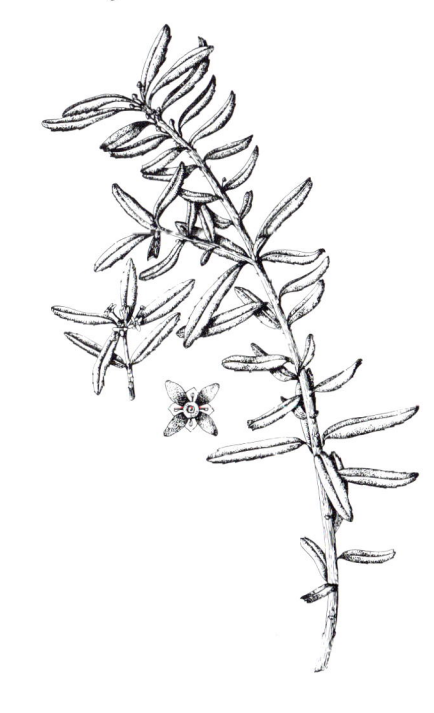

Part III
Impact of Man

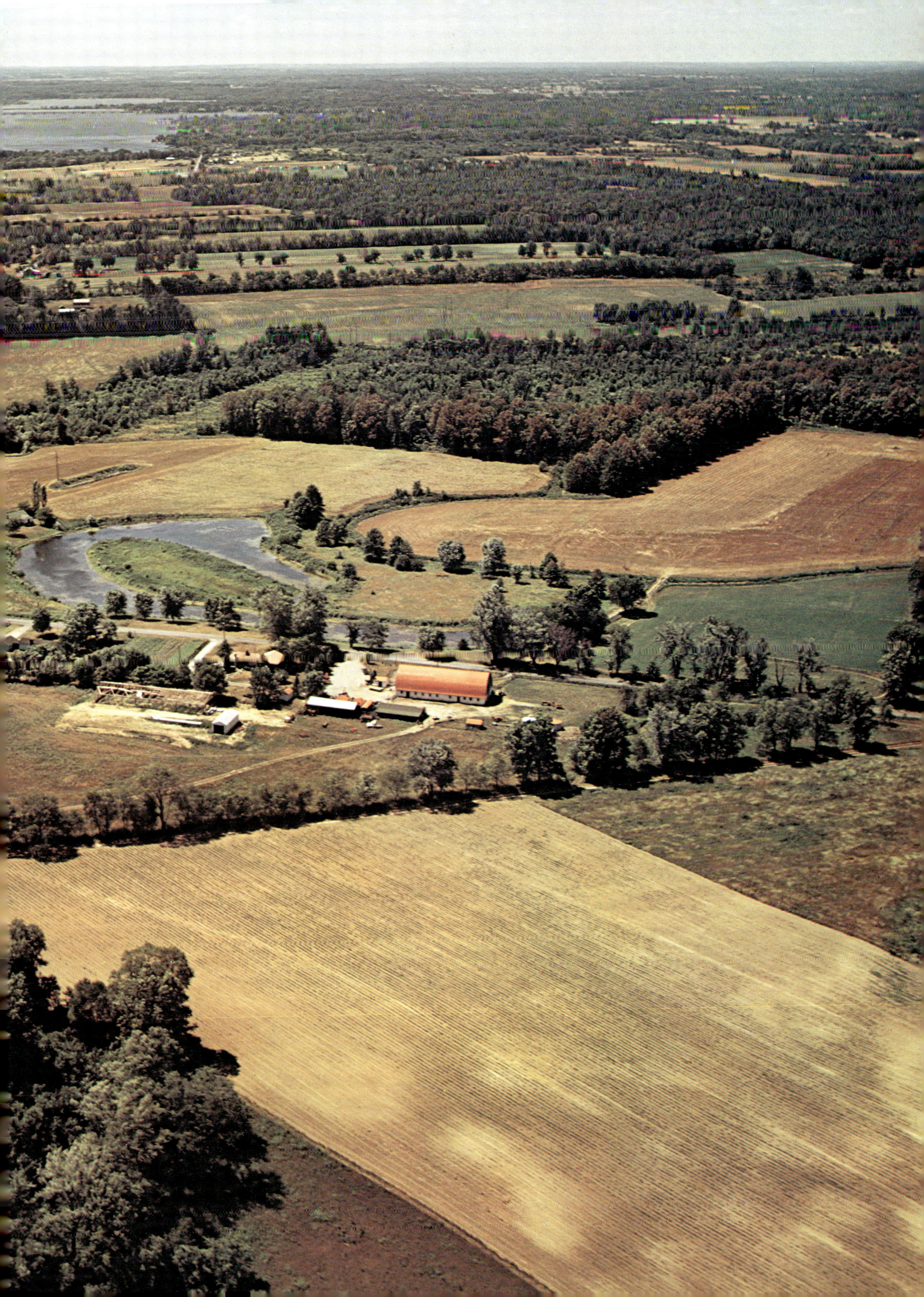

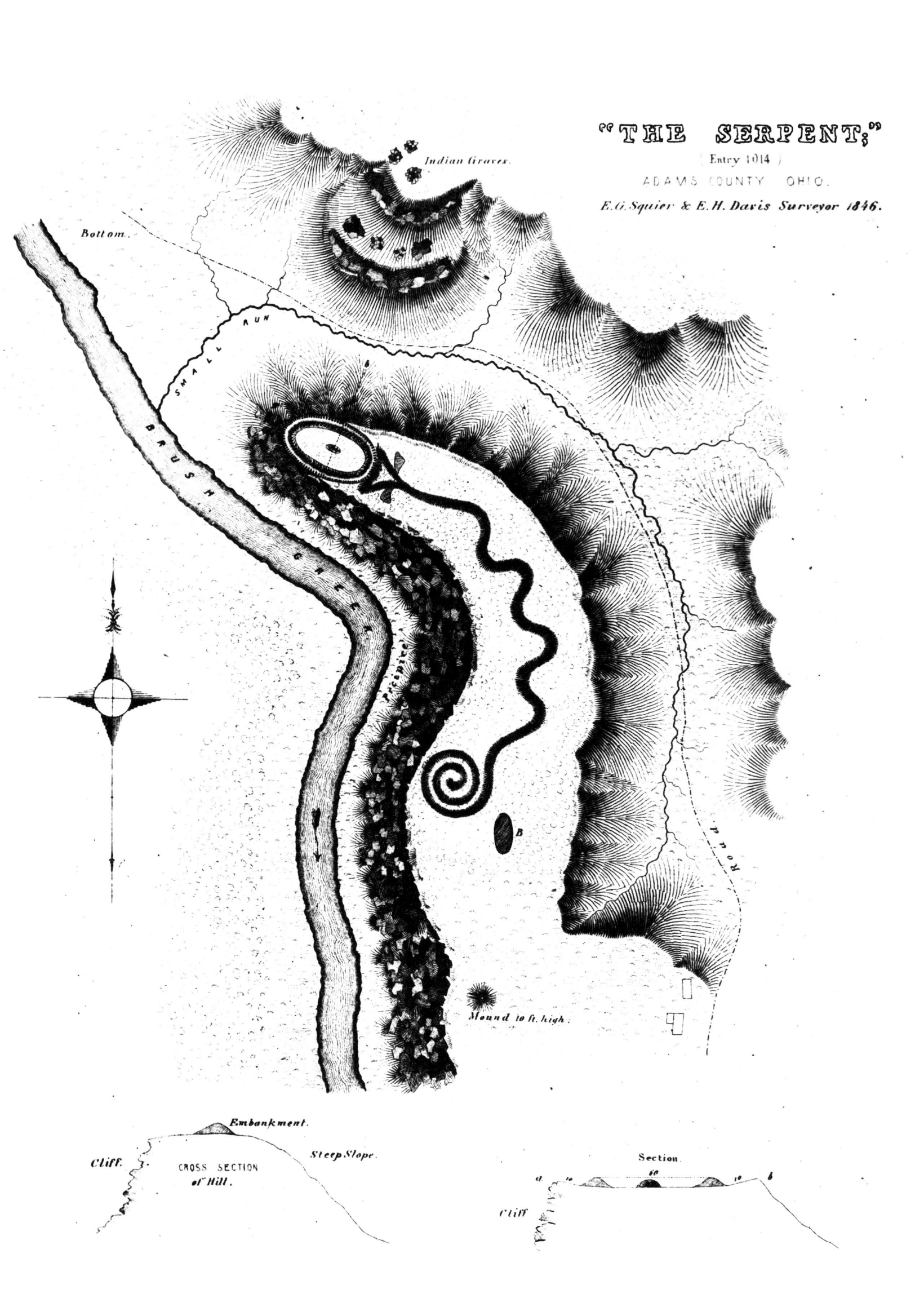

"THE SERPENT;"
(Entry 1014)
ADAMS COUNTY OHIO.
E. G. Squier & E. H. Davis Surveyor 1846.

Chapter 16
The First Ohioans

by Martha Potter Otto

THE first Ohioans were American Indians. Between 20,000 and 40,000 years ago their ancestors crossed from Asia to Alaska on the land bridge that formed when the glaciers covered much of the land. From Alaska these early people migrated south and east, constantly searching for game, and then finally entered Ohio about 13,000 B.C. Thus began the state's rich Indian heritage — perhaps the richest and most diverse in America — which ended when settlers crossed the Alleghenies into the Ohio Country 15,000 years later. As the centuries passed, the culture of each successive group was a little different from that of their predecessors. The earliest peoples were nomadic hunters. Then the Indians learned to supplement their diets with wild grains and fruits and finally to plant and raise their own crops. All shared a common characteristic — they lived in a delicate balance with nature. When hunting was bad, meat was scarce. When the hot sun parched the ground their crops withered. Disease took its toll. And simple luck — just being in the right place at the right time as we might call it — was an important part of their existence.

Palaeo—Indians

The earliest group of nomads to live in Ohio were Palaeo-Indians. Palaeo is Greek for "old" — an appropriate name for the first Ohioans.

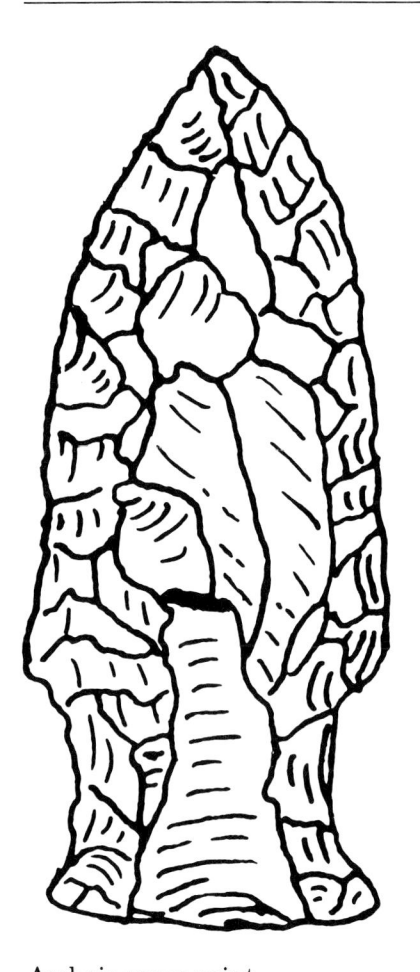

Archaic spear point

Archaic fluted point

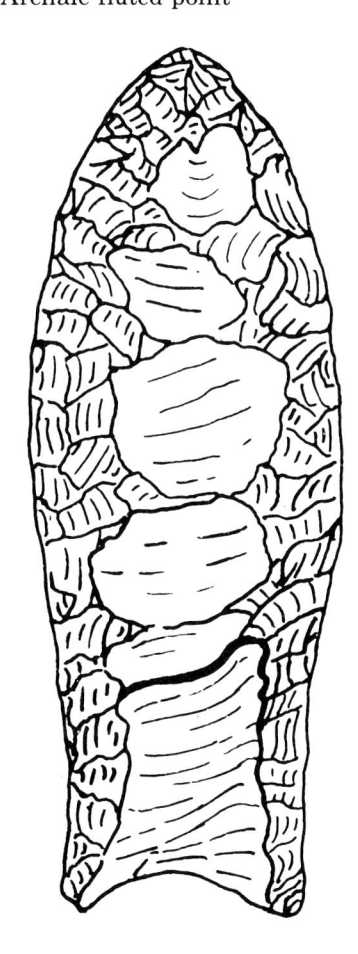

One group camped for a time in a rock shelter in southwestern Pennsylvania about 13,000 B.C. and it is likely other Palaeo-Indians lived in Ohio about the same time.

As the Wisconsinan glacier retreated, seeds from spruce, fir, pine, sedges, and grasses sprouted across the barren land. The plants attracted animals which ate or hid in the vegetation. There were elephant-like mastodon and mammoth, giant beaver perhaps six feet long, muskox, and caribou. The Palaeo-Indians were primarily hunters. They spread through Ohio's river valleys following the game. How far north they moved depended on the location of the lakes that existed before modern Lake Erie. At times, water covered much of northwestern Ohio. At other times the lake was much smaller than today. There is evidence from northwestern Ohio that Palaeo-Indians were living on the beaches of these lakes around 7,000 B.C. In the interior, the best areas for wildlife and humans were not in the dense spruce forests, but in the more open country. There, clumps of trees that provided protection were scattered through the grasslands on which the animals foraged.

The only direct evidence of the Palaeo-Indians consists of flint spearpoints, knives, and chopping and engraving tools left at a campsite or lost during a hunt. Since these nomads left no written records describing their lifestyle, archaeologists must study living societies such as the Eskimo in order to reconstruct the cultures of the Palaeo-Indians. Being hunters, the first Ohioans probably did not have permanent, year-round settlements. Instead they lived in small groups of 30 to 50 people, and moved from place to place in order to intercept the game. Water holes, salt licks, river fords, and other areas where animals congregated were probably ideal campsites. By running the animals into the mud of a waterhole or into a river, the hunter found the job easier.

Mastodons and other large animals may have been hunted by several Palaeo-Indian men working together. Smaller game could be killed by a lone hunter. Traps and snares of various kinds may have been just as effective hunting tools as the wooden spear tipped with a finely-made flint spearpoint. Hunting provided the Palaeo-Indians not only with their main food source, but also hide for their clothing, sinew for sewing their garments together, and bone for tools and ornaments. Hides could have been used to make tents or to cover lean-to shelters.

Unfortunately, archaeologists have not yet found any remains of Palaeo-Indian houses although they have discovered the locations of some of their camps. Several campsites have been discovered along the Walhonding River in Coshocton County. There, the Indians came to quarry flint for tools. They roughly formed some of the material to be made into finished tools later. Other pieces of flint were carefully chipped into complete spearpoints and knives. Most of the tools were probably used by the people who made them, but sometimes they were bartered to other individuals, probably constituting Ohio's earliest trade system.

While the Palaeo-Indians were living in Ohio, the climate was gradually warming. Animals like the muskox and caribou moved farther north, and some — mammoth, mastodon, giant beaver — became extinct. Some archaeologists think that the Palaeo-Indians were so successful in hunting these animals that they contributed to the extinctions. Maple, oak, chestnut, and other varieties typical of Ohio forests today gradually replaced the conifers. Much of northwestern Ohio that had been covered by earlier glacial lakes remained swampy. The Great Black Swamp, stretching south of the Maumee River between

Toledo and the Indiana border, was a barrier to settlement and communication between Ohio and southeastern Michigan until the late 1800s. Exactly how the Palaeo-Indians reacted to these changes is difficult to know but probably they slowly, perhaps unconsciously, adapted to them.

Archaic Indians

In southern Ohio, modern forest types became established as early as 8000 B.C., and by 6500 B.C., forests containing oak, elm, and maple covered much of northern Ohio. The Indians living in these forests, known as the Archaic people, were different from the Palaeo-Indians, although they almost certainly were descendants of these earlier groups. The Archaic Indians were hunters of deer, bear, wild turkey, and waterfowl—some species of which still live in Ohio forests. They also fished and gathered clams from the streams and rivers. For hunting, Archaic people used wooden spears with flint tips. While individuals probably went after game alone, the Archaic Indians also may have hunted in groups in which hunters drove game into concealed enclosures for easy slaughter. Fish may have been caught with bone hooks and lines made of plant fibers, but a larger quantity could be collected at one time by using nets, traps, or even by poisoning them with the juice of certain plants.

In addition to hunting, the Archaic Indians became adept at collecting plants. From early spring through summer and fall, tender shoots, tubers, roots, leaves, berries, seeds, wood, and nuts, were gathered for food, tools, beverages, medicines, and fibers. Indeed, the presence of certain plants and animals at particular times of the year meant that the Archaic Indians had to move from place to place during each 12-month cycle. In early spring, they might camp near sugar maple groves to collect sap and fish in nearby streams. Maple was also good for making bowls and canoe paddles. In summer the Indians probably gathered raspberries, blackberries, blueberries, strawberries, and black currants. In late summer and early fall, they collected goosefoot seeds, pawpaws, and a wide variety of nuts. Food not eaten right away was stored, perhaps intact, or ground into meal for winter use. Hunting continued all year, and in the fall, hunters killed migrating water birds such as ducks and Canada geese. Because of the severe winter weather, the Archaic Indians probably divided into family units, perhaps just single families, each of which established a small camp. Some of these groups may have lived in the rock shelters in southeastern Ohio, especially in the Hocking Hills where the rock overhangs are large enough to protect small groups of people. Some shelters were so suitable for habitation that they were used over several thousand years by Archaic peoples as well as by later cultures.

Of course the Archaic Indians also relied on other resources. Flint was basic to the lifestyle of all prehistoric cultures, and Archaic people used it for spearpoints, knives, and other sharp-edged tools. This type of stone occurs in many parts of Ohio, but some varieties are of higher quality and more workable than others. The Vanport Flint from Flint Ridge in Licking and Muskingum counties is particularly outstanding for its high purity and its variety of colors. Upper Mercer Flint from Tuscarawas and Coshocton counties was also a favorite material. Archaic Indians in southwestern Ohio collected spherical shaped

A scraper made from Ohio flint

nodules of flint from southeastern Indiana. In addition to these main sources, there were smaller deposits of flint in the gravels left by the glacier.

The Archaic Indians imported some materials, especially marine shells from the Atlantic or Gulf coasts and copper from Isle Royale and the Keweenaw Peninsula in western Lake Superior. From these materials, craftsmen made ornaments — pendants from the shells, and bracelets and beads from copper. Since these items are not strictly utilitarian and were made from hard-to-obtain materials, the shell and copper artifacts may have been status symbols for their owners. These objects were produced by one Archaic group in particular — the Glacial Kame Indians of western and northwestern Ohio. Archaeologists have given them that name because they buried their dead in glacial kames, small hills of gravel and sand deposited by the glaciers. Unfortunately, except for their burial practices, very little is known about these people and none of their campsites has been found.

One thing that is known is that the environment apparently played an important role in the religious beliefs of Glacial Kame people and probably all other Indian groups. Archaeologists have found masks made from skulls of wolves and bears in Glacial Kame sites that may have been worn on ceremonial occasions by shamans (medicine men). Some Indians believed that most elements in nature — animals, plants, bodies of water, the moon, rain, and wind — had spirits in the same way that humans do. Sometimes individuals felt a particularly close relationship to a certain spirit, perhaps a bird or animal, and believed that the spirit could help them cure illness, foretell the future, or bring good luck. By wearing a costume made of the animal's skin, the person could summon the spirit for help. It is likely that the carefully made wolf and bear masks found in Glacial Kame sites are the only remnants of such costumes.

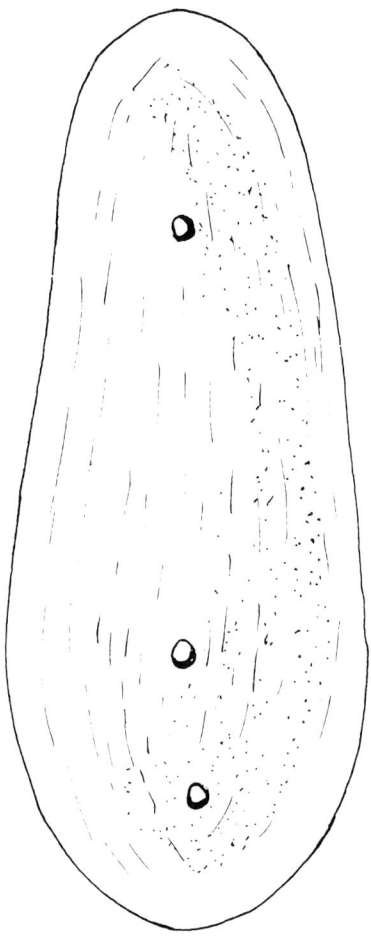

Glacial Kame Indian "sandal sole" neck ornament made from a shell

Adena Indians

In many areas of the United States, Indians continued the hunting and gathering lifestyle of the Archaic almost until the twentieth century. Certainly in areas where food and other resources were abundant, life may have been quite comfortable. However, sometime around 1000-800 B.C. changes occurred in the food gathering practices of the Ohio Indians that would have far-reaching effects. Women collected seeds from several types of wild plants. Perhaps by accident, the Indians, probably the women, noticed that if they put a seed into the ground in the spring the plant would grow and produce in the fall. Gradually they no doubt realized that they could cultivate their gardens near the settlements rather than traveling long distances for food. A cultivated plant also was a food source they could count on each year, unlike many wild plants such as nut trees that often bear heavy quantities of nuts only every two or three years. In other words, this group of Ohio Indians, whom we call the Adena, were at last able to control a certain portion of their food supply and their environment by raising crops.

The Adena, who lived primarily in central and southern Ohio, domesticated a number of native plants such as goosefoot, pigweed, smartweed, marsh elder (in Kentucky), and sunflowers. In addition, other types of plants such as squash and maybe corn, that had been domesticated first in Mexico, were gradually introduced into Ohio.

Adena pipe

Pieces of squash seeds were found in a Lorain County site that was inhabited in 520 B.C. by Early Woodland peoples, a group related to the Adena. An Adena mound in Athens that was built in approximately 280 B.C. also contained bits of corn. By combining their cultivated crops with game, fish, and wild plant foods, the Adena had enough supplies to settle in permanent communities.

Many ancient cultures are named for the locations where archaeologists first found evidence for their existence. In the case of the Adena, it was the Chillicothe estate of Ohio Governor Thomas Worthington, which the governor called Adena, the Hebrew word for delightful place.

Their communities probably included three or four circular wooden houses located on relatively high ground near a river. Of course, none of

Archaeologists excavate a site once occupied by early Ohio Indians

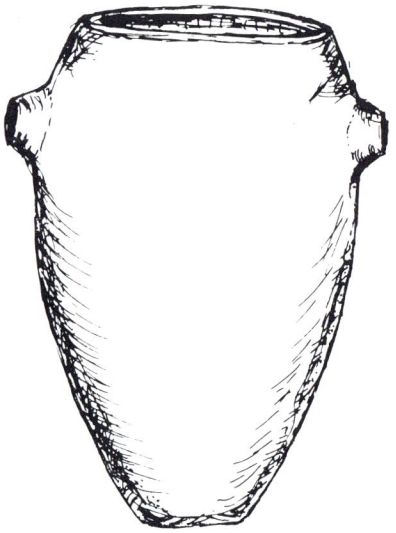

Adena pottery vessel

Adena incised stone tablet

Adena shoveler duck effigy pipe

their houses are standing today because they were made of wood and other materials that rot easily. However, archaeologists have found the filled-in-holes that originally held wall posts, and so they can determine the size and general shape of the dwellings. The houses of the Adena were 18 to 45 feet in diameter. Perhaps several related families lived in the larger ones. A fire in the center of the house floor provided heat and light; wooden racks and benches were probably used for storage and sleeping.

Because the Adena had some control over their food supply, they lived in fairly permanent villages. But they also had to devise ways to store their produce. Pottery was the answer. They learned to take clay, mix it with crushed stone (to keep the pots from cracking when they were fired), and form it into rope-like coils. By piling several coils on each other, the Adena made large jars that they then fired until hard. The first pots were crude. As they gradually became more skilled, the Adena made thinner, harder vessels.

Another result of the Adena's more stable life probably was an increase in their population and additional time available for other activities such as trading. Of course, the Archaic people and probably the Palaeo-Indians traded with other groups for supplies, but the Adena, and the Hopewell who followed them, seem to have been excellent businessmen. The primary materials that the Adena exchanged were knives and spearpoints made from Flint Ridge flint and tubular pipes carved from Ohio pipestone. The pipestone came from hills along the Scioto River just north of Portsmouth. It is soft when first dug from the ground and can be easily carved and polished. Later, the pipestone becomes quite hard. Archaeologists have found Adena Flint Ridge flint tools and pipestone pipes in sites around Chesapeake Bay and as far north as Vermont, hundreds of miles from Ohio. However, except for copper from the western end of Lake Superior, it is not known what the Adena received for their Ohio materials.

Some of the objects the Adena craftsmen made may have been status symbols for their owners. When these persons died, their possessions were frequently laid in their graves. Archaeologists feel that the Adena commemorated dead leaders and important community members by building mounds of earth over their graves. Frequently additional burials were added and the mounds enlarged to cover them, implying that entire families may have been honored in this fashion. Obviously the Adena were adapted well enough to their environment to have the spare time needed to construct the mounds.

Even though society became more complex, the Adena people still were greatly involved with their surroundings. From some of their pipes and engravings, it is clear that there were specific animals that were particularly important. About a dozen stone and clay tablets are decorated with stylized but recognizable engravings of hawks or vultures. Sometimes the bird images are combined with human hands or faces. It appears that the Adena people revered these birds for some reason, perhaps in the case of hawks because the birds are swift fliers and fierce hunters. Since vultures are attracted to dead animals, the Adena may have associated them with death and burial. Another bird seemingly important to the Adena was the shoveler duck. Several finely-crafted pipes have been found carved in the form of a duck's head with the bird's bill forming the mouthpiece. The details are so carefully engraved in the stone that the duck can clearly be identified as the shoveler.

Hopewell Indians

Around 100 B.C., evidently while the Adena were still living in Ohio, a new group of people (or at least their influence) called the Hopewell (for the Ross County farm where they were discovered) appeared in Ohio. They built their villages mainly in the wide river valleys of central and southern Ohio — the Miami, the Scioto, and the Muskingum. They were not as widespread as the Adena, whose mounds are scattered throughout the large valleys and the smaller ones too. Both the Adena and the Hopewell, or groups like them, lived in northern Ohio, but as a rule they did not build large earthworks as the Hopewell did in southern Ohio. Neither did they penetrate far into northwestern Ohio, probably because of the Great Black Swamp.

However in the broad valleys to the south, the Hopewell found conditions to their liking. For instance, near modern Chillicothe the Hopewell settled in an area where a variety of forest types merged — oak-hickory from the north, beech-maple and oak-hickory-chestnut from the south. There is evidence of large open grasslands where Paint Creek joins the Scioto River. This is ideal country for prehistoric village sites since the Indians could easily gather and hunt many different plants and animals. Unfortunately, archaeologists have not found many Hopewell villages, probably because most of them are located in the valleys where they have been buried beneath flood deposits accumulated during the past 2,000 years.

However, the Hopewell left magnificent earthworks in southern Ohio. Most of these earthworks were shaped as circles, squares, and sometimes octagons, and they covered anywhere from 20 to more than 100 acres. One of the most extensive complexes is at Newark, where earthworks and mounds originally were spread over an area of nearly four square miles. It seems that the Hopewell came to the enclosures at various times during the year for ceremonies and trading. Funerals were also conducted in the mound area and important leaders were buried there. Some archaeologists believe that particular earthworks were the centers of trading specific commodities: the Newark site may have been the main distribution point for Flint Ridge flint, and the Portsmouth works may have been important in the pipestone trade. Although a few people may have stayed at the earthworks year-round, most Hopewell probably lived in small villages up and down the river bottoms. There they hunted, fished, and gathered food in addition to cultivating crops such as corn — the staple for all Indian agricultural societies.

The Hopewell apparently had enough food that many of them could spend at least part of their time trading or practicing various crafts. Some were traders who exchanged Ohio flint and pipestone for copper, obsidian, and grizzly bear teeth from the Rocky Mountains, mica from North Carolina, marine shells from the Gulf and Atlantic coasts, and silver, possibly from Ontario. The materials were taken by artisans and formed into ornaments and other objects that may have been used in ceremonies or may have symbolized the high prestige of their owner. The artisans often copied forms in nature. Stylized hawks were cut from thin copper plates and decorated with very realistic feather patterns. A whole menagerie of animals is portrayed in a series of effigy pipes, including hawks, owls, cranes, wildcats, bears, turtles, toads, and even an effigy of an Indian's dog.

In addition to traders and artisans, another important group of specialists were the surveyors, who were skilled enough to lay out

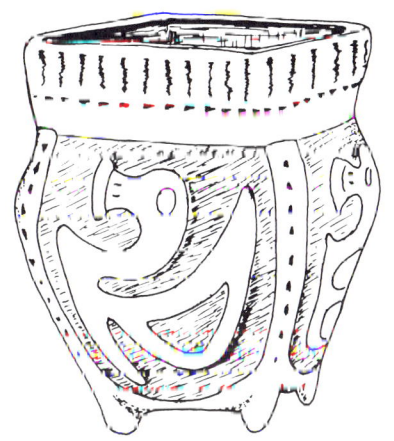

Hopewell pottery vessel

Hopewell knife made from obsidian, a stone of volcanic origin obtained from out of Ohio perhaps in trade for Ohio resources such as flint

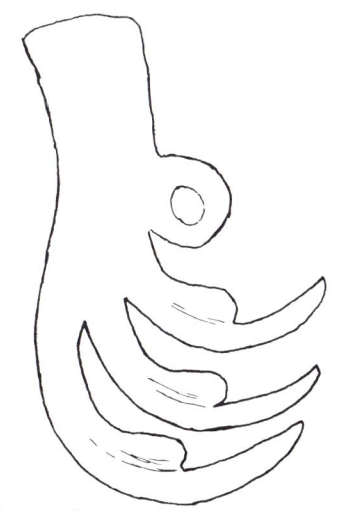

Hopewell mica bird claw ornament

Effigy pipe from the Hopewell Tremper Mound

perfectly circular earthworks enclosing many acres. Some archaeologists think that these large sites were oriented to various astronomical observations, perhaps like Stonehenge. Other Hopewells could organize work groups and direct them in the construction of the earthen walls, some measuring 50 feet wide at the base and 10 to 15 feet in height. It is probable that even the simplest enclosure required many years, perhaps several generations, to build.

The Hopewell culture ended around 500 to 600 A.D. The reasons for its decline and disappearance are not all clear. Early archaeologists blamed unknown conquerors. It is possible a terrible epidemic killed most of the people. More recently, some scientists have felt that somewhat cooler climatic conditions damaged the Hopewell's crops; a slight decrease in the number of frost-free days could have a disastrous effect on the corn. It is also possible that the Hopewell culture declined because of social disintegration.

Late Woodland Indians

The cultures that probably were the descendants of the Hopewell, which can be grouped together as Late Woodland, did not construct elaborate earthworks or large burial mounds. Neither is there evidence that they continued the extensive artistic activity of the earlier group. Whether they continued any farming is difficult to determine, although there is the possiblity that the weather conditions and the length of the growing season were still not favorable for agriculture. In northern Ohio, Late Woodland peoples apparently were more dependent upon the resources of the rivers and the lake. In many ways they were more like other cultures in southeastern Michigan and southern Ontario than the people in southern Ohio. Unfortunately, archaeologists just do not know much about the Late Woodland culture because they have not discovered enough village sites.

Fort Ancient/Whittlesey Indians

Around 800 to 1000 A.D. cultures called Mississippian, based in the central Mississippi River Valley, developed new strains of corn, beans, and squash. These crops enabled the Indians to form large towns containing hundreds, maybe thousands, of people. Some of the developments of the Mississippian people were influenced by ideas from Mexico. As these cultures expanded, they came into contact with other groups, such as Ohio's Late Woodland peoples. The new ideas were gradually accepted by the Ohioans, and what archaeologists identify as the Fort Ancient (for Fort Ancient in Warren County) culture gradually evolved in southern Ohio.

Many Fort Ancient villages were established in the broad river valleys where gardens could be planted in the rich river-bottom soil. The communities, composed of rectangular houses, were often enclosed with wooden stockades. Perhaps the increasing competition for good farm land required them to fortify their villages. These towns were permanent, that is they were occupied probably for 10 to 20 years until declining soil fertility and a dwindling firewood supply forced the people to move.

Although agriculture was an important activity, cultivation methods were crude. Sharpened sticks were the only ground-breaking tools they possessed, making it impossible to cultivate areas covered by heavy sod. Therefore, the Fort Ancient people probably cleared fields in the forests by girdling the trees, causing them to die. Any underbrush could be burned, thus conveniently providing ashes for fertilizer. As the crops matured, the Indian women cultivated them occasionally with hoes made from stone, clam shells, and the shoulder blades of deer and elk. Some corn was picked and roasted while still soft, much as we cut corn today. The remainder was dried and generally ground into meal, or boiled. Archaeologists excavating Fort Ancient villages in various parts of Ohio have frequently found large quantities of corn in storage pits.

While Fort Ancient communities existed in southern Ohio, Late Woodland peoples continued to inhabit the northern part of the state. Archaeologists working at several sites in the Cleveland area have discovered that one culture, Whittlesey, came into existence in that area around 1000 A.D. The Whittlesey Indians are named for Charles Whittlesey, a nineteenth-century Ohio geologist and archaeologist.

At first these people moved from place to place during certain seasons of the year. Later, after 1300 A.D., the Whittlesey people became more dependent on their crops and lived in their villages for longer periods, although they still fished and hunted waterfowl along the lake from the fall through early spring. Finally, between 1400 to 1600 A.D., the villages were inhabited year-round by people living in rectangular "long houses" somewhat like those used by the historic Iroquois Indians. There must have been a certain amount of conflict at this time since many of these late villages were located on high promontories protected by earthen walls and stockades.

Monongahela Indians

In Belmont, Jefferson, and Harrison counties of eastern Ohio, somewhat different things were happening. A group originating in northern West Virginia and southwestern Pennsylvania, called the Monongahela, expanded westward into neighboring areas of Ohio. This part of the state is quite rugged, but in some locations the Monongahela found enough space on ridge tops to establish villages. These people, again, lived by farming, hunting, and gathering. Unfortunately, none of these eastern Ohio villages has been completely excavated by a trained archaeologist and many have been destroyed by strip mining.

Exactly what happened to the prehistoric Indian cultures in Ohio in the late 1500s and early 1600s is quite difficult to determine. There is some evidence that groups began to move out of Ohio, the northern areas at least, perhaps because of additional pressures from other groups. In southern Ohio, specifically in village sites along the Ohio River, the Indian inhabitants possessed glass beads and objects made of brass manufactured by Europeans. This discovery does not mean these Indians had direct contact with Europeans, because many beads, iron axes, brass kettles, and similar artifacts were traded from one Indian group to another. These items reached the inland societies long before the English or French.

The prehistoric period of the American Indian cultures in Ohio ended in the mid-to-late seventeenth century when early Jesuit missionaries and explorers began recording their experiences in this area. In a very short time Indian wars and the mounting pressures of Euro-Americans for land in Ohio completely disrupted the culture and finally caused the Indians to be removed from the state completely.

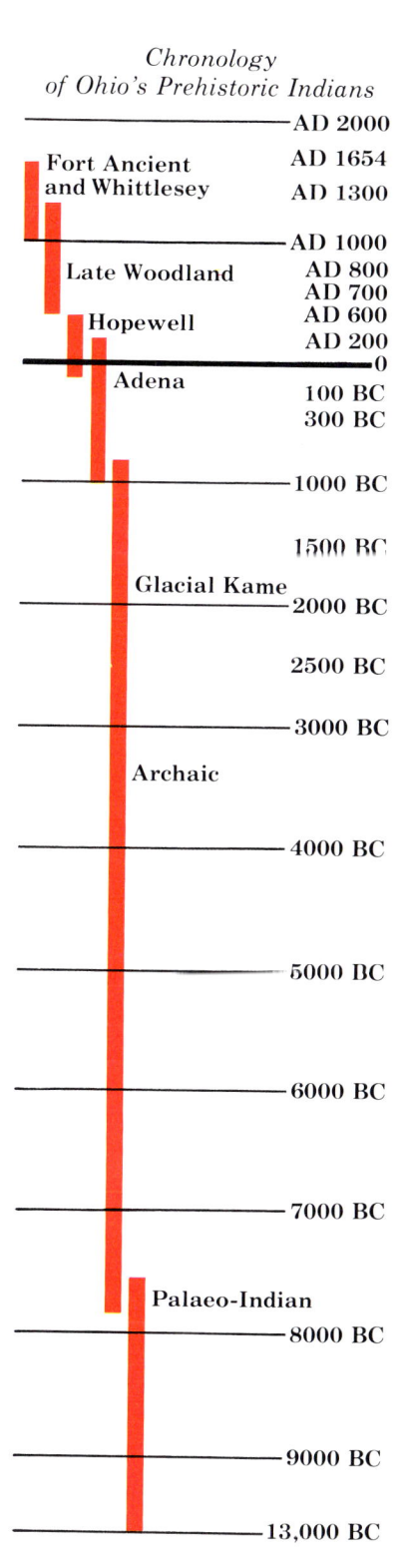

Chronology of Ohio's Prehistoric Indians

- AD 2000
- Fort Ancient and Whittlesey — AD 1654
- AD 1300
- AD 1000
- Late Woodland — AD 800
- AD 700
- Hopewell — AD 600
- AD 200
- Adena — 0
- 100 BC
- 300 BC
- 1000 BC
- 1500 BC
- Glacial Kame
- 2000 BC
- 2500 BC
- 3000 BC
- Archaic
- 4000 BC
- 5000 BC
- 6000 BC
- 7000 BC
- Palaeo-Indian
- 8000 BC
- 9000 BC
- 13,000 BC

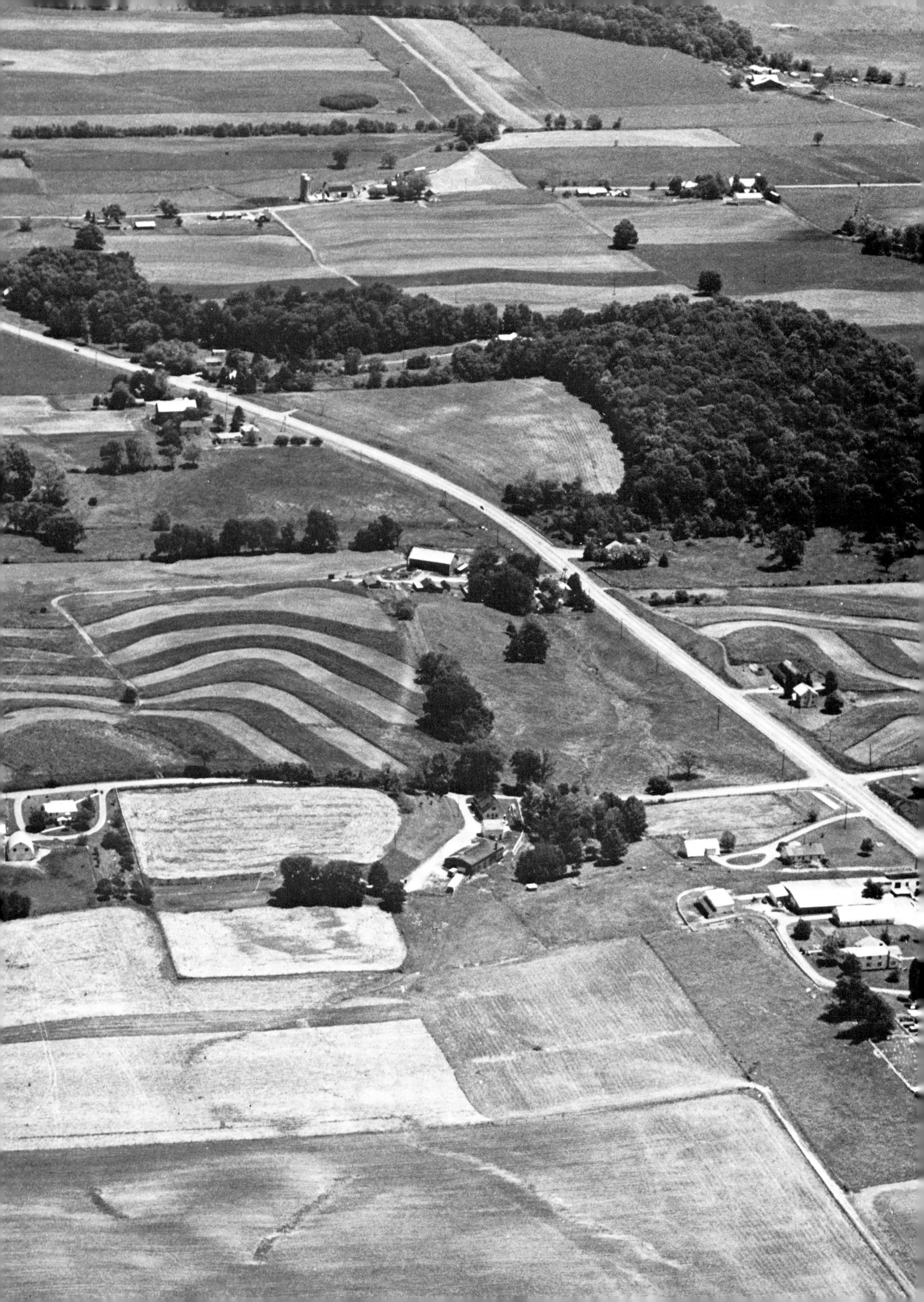

Chapter 17
Changing Land Use

IF a naturalist climbed into H.G. Wells's time machine and teleported 200 years into the past, he or she would not be able to get around much more easily than if they traded places with a pioneer trapper who suddenly appeared in front of the Terminal Tower in Cleveland. The landscape has been altered greatly in the nearly 200 years since pioneers began carving a place in the vast wilderness. Change has not been all bad for the state. Ohioans have a host of modern conveniences at their fingertips. But these conveniences have come at a heavy price to the natural world. Forests have been cut, water polluted, and wildlife destroyed.

Change cannot be avoided. Nature continually erodes the landface, and sooner or later an ice sheet will probably move south again pulverizing everything in its path. Lightning will spark a fire turning a forest to ashes, or a volcano will explode transforming a rich, verdant land into a "moonscape." But just as clouds are seeded to make rain, modern technology can be applied to temper the human impact on the environment. People are but one higher life form among countless organisms, and in applying technology, the human species owes it to future generations to ensure that the needs of all living species are taken into account.

by Kenneth Laub
Sherman L. Frost
Ruth W. Melvin

Forests, Farm Lands, and Wildlife

Kenneth W. Laub

Forests

The immensity of Ohio's primeval forests is difficult to comprehend today. After endless days of travel beneath the shading canopy, travelers often fell to their knees and thanked God when they reached a clearing and could feel the warmth of the sun or see the sky. Pioneers reported the upland forests contained an abundance of chestnut, black walnut trees over six feet in diameter, and towering oaks whose lowest limbs were 50 feet from the ground. Trees clung to the banks of streams and rivers, holding the soil in place and keeping the waters clean. Huge sycamores grew along almost every stream. Since these trees were usually hollow, settlers often used them as barns or temporary shelters, and on rare occasions actually lived in them. Other trees were almost as large. Daniel Boone carved a 60-foot dugout canoe from the log of a single tuliptree.

But this forest was far from park-like. Often undergrowth was dense and giant trees were toppled — victims of windstorm, disease, and old age. The Battle of Fallen Timbers, near modern Maumee in Lucas County, was fought on a battleground littered with trees uprooted and thrown over by violent winds. Nowhere in Ohio were travel and settlement so difficult as in the Great Black Swamp, a great boggy forest the size of two Rhode Islands which extended from Paulding and Van Wert counties to the Lake Erie marshes in Lucas and Ottawa counties. Tangles of wind-felled trees combined with waterlogged soils to slow travel.

But incredibly dense as Ohio's forests were, 150 years after our nation's birth almost every tree had been cut. Early explorers looked at the forests as producers of goods. They trapped beaver and other furbearers for the European fashion market. However, to the first settlers, the forest stood in the way of survival and civilization. The trees grew in soil needed for grain and livestock, and the forest harbored wild animals which threatened both crops and domestic animals. Christopher Gist, assessing Ohio's southeastern hill country for the Ohio Land Company about 1750, summed up the attitude of the land sellers and settlers: "...in short it wants Nothing but Cultivation to make it a most delightful Country."

Making Ohio a "most delightful Country" required an end to Indian raids, the mass immigration of settlers, and removal of the forests. The settlers fell to their task with zeal, cutting, sawing, burning, and girdling in such a frenzy of activity that the 24 million acres of woodland in 1800 were reduced to a mere four million acres by 1883. By 1940 the woodland was further reduced to about 3.7 million acres. Today the trend is reversed and forest land has nearly doubled in amount to about 6.5 million acres. The human energy required for a comparative handful of settlers to reduce millions of acres of forest in a few decades of the nineteenth century — without chain saws, bulldozers, and other powered equipment — was prodigious. Ax and fire were the primary tools. Many trees were cut, rolled into huge stacks, and burned later. Others were cut just halfway through, weakening them so they would tumble like stacked dominoes in the next violent windstorm.

Not all the timber was wasted. Some was sawed into lumber for homes, barns, and furniture, or split into fence rails, roof shakes, and firewood. As cultivation pushed back the frontier, wood became more important in commerce and industry. Many oaks, especially chestnut oak, were cut solely for their bark, which was used in the tanning industry. In the 1860s Ohio railroads burned a million cords of firewood a year and laid uncounted thousands of wooden ties to support the iron tracks. From 1818 to the turn of the century thousands of acres of woods were chopped down to fuel the charcoal iron industry. Some areas were cut three or four times. In the mid-1800s, Ohio was the nation's leading producer of iron for implements and weapons. At its peak 46 furnaces were firing in Ohio's six-county Hanging Rock Iron Region, and an estimated 250 to 350 acres of woodland were cut every year to supply each furnace. It is little wonder that many furnaces were closed for lack of wood long before the lode of iron ore gave out.

In the First Annual Report of the State Forestry Bureau, in 1886, the secretary opined that "...for climatic influence, for the supply of the demand upon forest products, and for shelter, 25 percent of a country should be kept in forest." At the time, only 14 percent of Ohio was wooded. Today the figure is almost exactly 25 percent. And with the exception of the Maumee and Miami valleys, there are more woods in every part of Ohio than in 1886. But since Ohio's population has increased dramatically, perhaps even more woodlands are needed.

However, the forest successions which followed the virgin stands differed in both size and character. Oak-hickory forests, in which white oak was dominant, were replaced by mixed oaks and hickories. Black walnut, today one of the most precious of hardwoods, must have been extremely common a century ago, judging from its use in homes and farm buildings erected in the nineteenth century. Except for white pine, Ohio's native pines — Virginia, pitch, and short-leaf — probably were confined to the driest, rockiest ridges, where hardwoods could not survive. As the hardwoods were removed by ax and fire, the pines rapidly colonized the hillside openings, and today they are much more widely distributed.

In glaciated Ohio and in the 26-county unglaciated hill country region, forest acreage declined at about the same rate through the nineteenth century. But the difference in the capacity of the two regions to support agriculture is revealed by today's figures. Beginning about 1920, woodland in the hill country expanded rapidly. Grain farming and pasturing had caused the thin, acid soils to erode. Crop yield declined and landowners, unable to pay their taxes, simply packed up and moved to greener pastures, leaving the worn-out land to revert to forest. Today the hill country contains one third of Ohio's land, but supports more than 70 percent of the woodland. Forest in glaciated Ohio persists mainly along stream banks and in farm land "back forties."

In northwest Ohio's Great Black Swamp, thousands of miles of ditches and drains were installed between 1859 and 1875 to drain water from the swamp. Doctors believed draining the swamp would "purify" the soil and eliminate mosquitoes. With water levels lowered, farmers were able to enter and cut down the trees. From 1853 to 1883, 2½ million acres of the Maumee Valley were cleared. By 1885 the region looked much as it does today — seemingly endless farm fields dotted here and there with small woodlots. The region also contains 159 municipalities and more than 3,000 miles of roads. Today the counties with the most forest cover in the Maumee Valley — Defiance, Lucas, and Williams —

Early lumbering site

In 1976 a black walnut tree near Pioneer in Williams County sold for $30,000 - one of the highest amounts ever paid for this species.

have barely 10 percent of their land in woods and the entire valley averages just six percent woodland. Forest acreage in Ohio's western counties is still declining. In northwest Ohio the downward trend is so precipitous that, if continued, the woodlots will be gone by the year 2030.

Ohioans who have visited the larger state forests or the Wayne National Forest may be surprised to learn that more than 90 percent of Ohio's woodlands are privately owned. The forest industry, which practices the most intensive management, owns only two percent of the state's woodlands. Farmers own 42 percent of the trees and 50 percent are held by private landowners for speculation or for recreation.

Farm Lands

People have been farming in Ohio since at least 1000 B.C. General Anthony Wayne was astounded by the extent of Indian cornfields at the confluence of the Maumee and Auglaize rivers in 1794. Indians were few, and although they practiced slash and burn agriculture which left the soil depleted, the land was extensive enough that their impact was minimal. But less than two centuries after the Battle of Fallen Timbers, agriculture had permanently altered much of Ohio.

After Wayne's victory, settlers from the East and Southeast swarmed into the Ohio Country. New Englanders brought their sheep and hogs to northeastern Ohio. Pennsylvania Dutch introduced their livestock and mixed-grain farming experience into Columbiana, Stark, Wayne, Holmes, and Coshocton counties. Virginians brought skills in livestock raising to southern Ohio. And later, Germans from Pennsylvania and Germany drained and cropped the swamp forest soils of northwestern Ohio with their careful farming practices.

Completion of the canals and later, the railroads, helped spur agricultural production. By 1850 Ohio led the nation in farming. In 1880, 93 percent of the land was considered to be in farms — including

A northeast Ohio rural scene

woodlots and "wasteland" acreage. Since then, farm acreage has declined steadily except for a brief, moderate upswing during World War II.

Pioneer farms were subsistence farms with production supplemented by hunting and gathering. Later, the small general farm provided the settlers' needs. The typical farmer raised grain, vegetables, hay, hogs, beef cattle, a dairy cow or two, and some poultry. Corn was the only important row crop, and farm fields were small enough to be managed with the human and animal power available. But the subsistence farming of the nineteenth century has become the agribusiness of the twentieth century. Modern cultivating, planting, and harvesting machines allow one person to do work once needing many field hands and animals. Reliance on fossil fuels released thousands of acres once used to produce food for horses and mules. Use of fertilizers, monoculture, and hybrid seeds, combined with a multitude of herbicides and insecticides, has resulted in vastly increased yields. The 36 bushels-per-acre corn yield in 1900 has climbed to over 100 bushels. Since 1900, the average wheat yield per acre has risen from 14 to more than 45 bushels.

Farming efficiency, measured by yield per acre and yield per person-hour, has increased steadily. But as agriculture has become more energy intensive — depending heavily on fossil fuels to power machinery and produce fertilizers and pesticides — it has become less efficient ecologically. Mechanized farming demands far more energy per unit of output than does farming which relies on human and animal power.

In the twentieth century, the number of farms has steadily declined, while average farm size has increased. In 1900 about 276,000 farms averaged 88 acres in size. But by 1970, the 111,000 remaining farms were over 150 acres each. In the process, land was dropped from production. In 1900 more than 24 million acres of Ohio were considered to be "in farms." Today less than 17 million acres are farmed. The decline in farm land acreage probably will continue as more land is withdrawn for urban areas, highways, and commercial, industrial, mining, and recreation sites. Urban and built-up areas increased from 400,000 acres in 1900 to more than three million acres today.

These numerical changes were accompanied by changes in management. With fewer horses and mules, the need for pasture has declined, as has the need for hay. And, until recently, small grain plantings have decreased, while row crops such as corn and soybeans have increased in acreage. Whereas corn acreage today is almost the same as in 1920, soybeans — which was not a significant agricultural crop in Ohio until the 1920s — have climbed rapidly, and now rival corn in total acreage.

Wildlife

The first settlers probably would not have understood the term "conservation" in a land of seemingly inexhaustible resources of woods, water, and wildlife. They shot the turkey, grouse, deer, and passenger pigeon, and caught numerous fishes for food. Furbearers had many uses — the famous Coonskin Library at Amesville was started in 1804 with books purchased from the sale of raccoon pelts by settlers in Athens County. Actually, the settlers began exterminating wildlife as soon as they arrived. The mountain lion, wolf, and bear were threats to livestock, and the sooner killed, farmers thought, the better. Gray squirrels were a constant threat to the corn crop. In 1807 and 1808 Ohio taxpayers were required to submit a quota of squirrel scalps with their tax payments. By 1874, Ottawa County commissioners were paying a half cent for the scalps of red-winged blackbirds which were endangering the new corn crop. The Great Hinckley Hunt in Medina County in 1818 was an organized effort to eradicate stock-killing predators from a remnant virgin woods.

The general history of Ohio's wildlife, as settlement progressed, was of eradication of predators and the most valuable furbearers, elimination or reduction of species requiring extensive mature forests, and increases in wildlife which thrived on vegetational variety and the open lands created by agriculture. The beaver, wolf, mountain lion, elk, turkey, and passenger pigeon were exterminated. Deer, gray fox, and gray squirrel populations declined, while the red fox, fox squirrel, crow, quail, and cottontail rabbit increased in numbers. This trend probably continued into the 1930s until Ohio's forest acreage stopped declining.

Two pairs of related wildlife species — the gray squirrel and the fox squirrel, and the gray fox and red fox — illustrate the effects of changes in the ratio of forest to farm land. Ohio was originally gray squirrel and gray fox country. As timber was cut, the fox squirrel expanded its range from the Midwest prairie edge into Ohio while the red fox moved in from the north. Today the fox squirrel is characteristic of the woodlot country of agricultural western Ohio; the gray is predominant in the forested hill country and in cities and parks with large hardwood trees. And the red fox is more common than the gray fox in much of western and northern Ohio.

In southeast Ohio the rejuvenation of forest succession on abandoned farm lands encouraged upswings in populations of deer, grouse, gray squirrels, and many other woodland species. In the late 1950s the Division of Wildlife of the Ohio Department of Natural Resources restored the wild turkey in Ohio's second-growth woodlands by importing wild stock from other states. But the passenger pigeon, in the latter part of the nineteenth century was deprived of the enormous acreages of mast-producing hardwood forests required by its huge colonies. It was hunted without respite until too late, and was exterminated.

While forest wildlife populations began their resurgence in southeast Ohio, farmers continued to cut forest and streamside trees in western Ohio. The small cropfields, wide and brushy fencerows, and virgin woodlots of the self-supporting general farm were replaced by larger fields designed for the planting and harvest machines coming into use in the early 1900s. Few "idle" areas were left for small game cover, and quail numbers dropped so drastically that in 1913 bobwhite quail hunting was stopped. In spite of this protection, quail continued their downhill slide as flatland farms were more intensively managed and hillside farms were abandoned to forest. Today the bobwhite is most abundant in southern Ohio where there is still a mixed pattern of cropfields, brushy fencerows, and woods. Cottontail rabbits, not so dependent on croplands, are still well distributed, but their population densities clearly reflect land use and soil fertility. Rabbits consistently produce larger litters on the fertile soils of western Ohio than in the hill country, but there are fewer in western Ohio because of the scarcity of permanent cover.

Meanwhile, a gamebird habitat new to North America was being created in the bountiful grain crops growing on vast acreages of fertile

ring-necked pheasant

soils. The ring-necked pheasant, an exotic species from Asia, was introduced. By the 1930s all of glaciated Ohio was home to the ringneck, with the greatest numbers in the old Great Black Swamp Country, which probably would not have supported a pheasant population at all 100 years earlier. Pheasant numbers continued to climb until the early 1940s when farming was intensified. Grain crops were emphasized, cropfields were enlarged, brushy fencerows and idle areas were cleared and put to work, and power mowers were commonly used. Night mowing, especially, spelled death for nesting hens. Before World War II small grain stubble provided widespread winter roosting cover; afterward, virtually all of this stubble was clipped. The increasing importance of alfalfa and its early mowing during the pheasant's nesting period lowered the ringneck's nesting success. Reduction of winter food and cover by fall plowing and woodlot removal also helped put the pheasant population on a downward trend from which it has never recovered.

Many other farming changes have affected wildlife populations. Crop rotations, which in the 1950s included one to three years of meadow, have been replaced by two-year rotations of corn and soybeans. Nitrogen-fixing legumes and other green manures have been replaced by fast-acting commercial fertilizers and the practice of returning most of the crop stubble to the soil. On the productive farm lands of northwest Ohio, it is not unusual to see a rotary mower and plow following directly after the corn picker-sheller — in one joint operation removing winter food and cover from the reach of wildlife.

Feedlots are more common in dairy herd management, eliminating the need for fencerows between cropfields and pastures. Grass waterways in cropfields are now plowed up, tiled, covered, and planted over. Soybeans provide some food in fall and winter, but offer little cover for wildlife. Soybean stems now are mulched in the combining operation, leaving no more tangles in which cottontails can hide.

On the positive side, free-stall cattle housing and slatted housing for pigs are reducing the need for straw, and changes in small grain stubble clipping practices could prove beneficial to wildlife. With cattle out of the pasture and the hay crop in, more wildlife can be produced if mowing schedules are adjusted to allow nesting success. In the hill country, contour strip cropping and other conservation practices are improving soil fertility and intermixing food and cover. Such intermixing is particularly valuable to small animals such as quail and rabbits, which may spend their lives on only a few acres.

The trend to more forest land in eastern Ohio has been a boon to some wildlife. Since their reintroduction, wild turkeys have thrived in the heavily forested areas of more than 20 counties and ruffed grouse populations have expanded considerably in areas of early forest succession. Ohio's deer herd is the largest of any time in the twentieth century. Management of woodlands on a sustained-yield basis, with moderate-sized clearcuts properly spaced in distance and time, can maintain diverse habitat types for many forest wildlife species.

Ohio is blessed with abundant furbearers, because of the state's rich mixture of habitats and the adaptability of many furbearers to human developments. With our increasing encroachment on their habitat, and in the absence of large predators, sound management is necessary to maintain furbearer populations within desirable limits.

Fish have been greatly affected by drainage, forest removal, farming practices, and pollution. Today water tables are much lower and many streams have become intermittent or dried up entirely. In the great spawning grounds of the Great Black Swamp's tributary streams, the lake sturgeon, Great Lakes muskellunge, and northern pike were already in decline in the early 1800s. Mill dams blocked their passage upstream from Lake Erie, and silt covered their eggs and buried stream bottom vegetation. Declining oxygen levels at the bottom of Lake Erie in the early 1900s also were beginning to eliminate the seemingly boundless supplies of mayflies (an important food for fish), mollusks, and other foods. Today both the lake sturgeon and the Great Lakes muskellunge are endangered species in Ohio.

Populations fell so rapidly that in 1880 the Ohio Fish Commission prophesied gloomily, "It affords substantial grounds for believing the total extinction of fish life in Ohio is drawing near." Although these fears were not borne out, declines in Ohio fish life have been substantial. Of the 179 kinds of fishes recorded for the state, fewer than 130 are here today in at least fair numbers.

But there were few permanent lakes in pioneer Ohio. Today the state has over 100,000 acres of lakes and reservoirs built for canal feeders, water supply, flood control, and recreation. In some areas, off-stream or upground reservoirs are being built for city water supplies. Nearly all these human-made bodies of water are habitats for largemouth bass,

Fall plowing produces fallow fields in winter which eliminates necessary cover for many species of wildlife.

bluegills, crappies, and various catfishes. Many contain walleye, muskellunge, smallmouth bass, yellow perch, and other sport species. In addition, most of Ohio's 40,000 small farm ponds are havens for largemouth bass and small sunfishes.

As beneficial as the lakes may be for fishing, they require huge amounts of land. Some reservoirs flood many acres of choice farm land, woodlands, and the habitat of many fish and wildlife species. So reservoirs are increasingly being opposed in favor of protecting beautiful valleys, scenic river systems, and historic and archaeological sites.

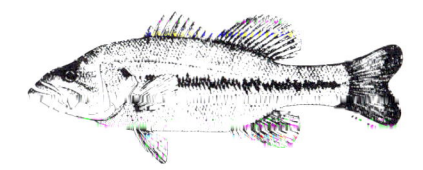

Largemouth bass

Water

Sherman L. Frost

The first reservoirs were built to provide water for the canal system. Buckeye Lake, a 3,000-acre lake east of Columbus, was the first large reservoir constructed in America and, for a long time, 13,500-acre Grand Lake-St. Marys was the largest reservoir in the world. Buckeye Lake was set aside as a public park in 1894 and it became Ohio's first state park. Eventually other canal lakes at Indian Lake (originally Lewiston), Portage, Grand Lake-St. Marys (originally Celina Grand), Guilford Lake, and Summit Lake were made parks and formed the basis of the state's park system.

Farm products were transported east on canal boats and manufactured goods were brought west until railroads and better forms of land transportation supplanted them. Even then, they exerted a great influence on transportation since highways or railroads were often constructed along the abandoned canals. Today some abandoned canal lands are state parks and nature preserves (Loramie in Shelby County and Black Hand Gorge in Licking County) and local parks (Canal Fulton in Stark County); a few provide local water supplies (Portage,

A mural in Coshocton depicts nineteenth century life along the Ohio-Erie Canal in Roscoe Village.

Streams and Water Power

Farming not only stimulated the need for canals, it also spurred construction of grist mills and saw mills along Ohio rivers. Water was an unlimited energy source in those days and pioneers turned to it for power to grind their grain and saw their timber. The state's first grist mill was built by Mayor Hatfield White in 1789 on Wolf Creek near Marietta. And by 1860, there were more than 1,200 grist mills and 2,000 saw mills on Ohio streams.

The dams soon caused problems for boaters and fish alike. In the early nineteenth century, land travel in Ohio was still very difficult. Much travel and transportation was done on the state's major rivers. Since the dams interfered with river travel, especially on major streams like the Muskingum, in 1813 the Ohio General Assembly banned building dams which would obstruct river traffic. The dams also interfered with fish migrations. Dam construction is blamed for the disappearance of the lake sturgeon from northern Ohio streams and of the paddlefish from the Scioto and other southern rivers. But it was not until 1843 that legislators approved a law requiring owners of dams on the Sandusky River to build a slope around their dam enabling sturgeon and other fish to swim upstream to spawn.

In the early twentieth century Ohio rivers underwent another spurt of dam-building. In 1913, flood waters ravaged much of the state and the rampaging Great Miami River practically destroyed Dayton. City streets were flooded to the tops of lamp posts, and many people escaped drowning only by climbing into attics, then chopping their way through roofs to crawl to safety. Determined the water-borne devastation would never again smash the city, a citizens' committee raised money to plan a giant flood-control project for the Great Miami and several major tributaries which converge at Dayton. Using the slogan "Remember the promises you made in the attic," the committee raised $2 million as seed money for the project. Committee members and their attorneys also wrote a bill, later approved by the Ohio General Assembly, creating the Miami Conservancy District. It was the district's job to oversee construction of the project and then to operate and maintain it. A network of five huge concrete and earth dams on the main streams, together with miles of channel modifications and levees, was completed in 1922 with tax money assessed on the value of the property protected.

The Miami dams created detention reservoirs. During periods of normal stream flow, water flows downstream unhindered. The dams act as giant drains and, just as only a maximum amount of water can flow out of a bath tub drain, during periods of high rainfall and stream flow, only a fixed maximum of water can flow through the dam. The remainder backs up in storage basins behind each dam. Water has accumulated countless times in the years since the dams were completed. Some of the land behind the dams is used by the Dayton-Montgomery County Park District for parks and nature areas.

In contrast, the Muskingum Watershed Conservancy District, Ohio's other large flood-control network, uses dams which form multiple-use reservoirs, primarily on tributaries of the Muskingum River. The lakes

The famous 1913 flood in Columbus.

Clifton Mill, a privately operated grist mill at the headwaters of the Little Miami River, is open to the public for visits. (opposite page)

Changing Land Use 283

Pleasant Hill Reservoir of the Muskingum Watershed Conservancy District near Loudonville in southern Ashland County.

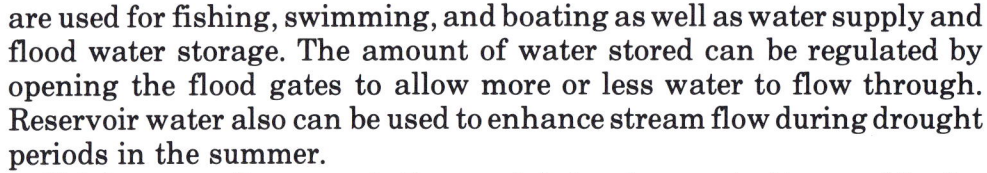

Freeways use enormous amounts of land.

are used for fishing, swimming, and boating as well as water supply and flood water storage. The amount of water stored can be regulated by opening the flood gates to allow more or less water to flow through. Reservoir water also can be used to enhance stream flow during drought periods in the summer.

Ohio's expanding population and intensive agriculture, with the associated pollution, also have caused major changes in the state's once-pristine streams. Urban land area has increased from one percent of the state's area to 11 percent and the cities are still expanding. As the sidewalks, streets, parking lots, and housing and factory complexes snake into the countryside, natural drainage patterns are being fundamentally changed. A human-made drainage pattern is slowly covering the natural one. The problem is that rivers and streams are adjusted to the natural and not an artificial pattern. Blacktop and storm sewers collect and channel water very quickly, rushing it into streams instead of allowing it to soak into the soil and drain into rivers more slowly.

In much of Ohio, this change began more than 100 years ago when the Northwest Territory was surveyed into townships six miles square and into sections one mile square. The survey lines did not follow natural drainage contours, and since roads and highways were often built on the survey lines, neither did the highways. Homes and farms, and later larger and larger communities, followed the roads. Every blacktop road in Ohio became a watershed as did every city street and paved shopping center.

The same thing happened in northwestern Ohio when farmers installed intricate and expensive tile drainage systems to drain excess water in the heavy soils of the old lake bed. Drainage made the region one of the most productive in the world, but the increased soil drainage meant the natural drainage could not drain the water fast enough. First the ditches, and later the creeks and larger streams, had to be enlarged. Trees and brush were cut and logs were cleared from streams so the water could flow freely.

As roads, more towns, shopping centers, and waste treatment plants added more sewage and storm water runoff, natural stream channels proved inadequate. To offset these changes, stream channels had to be widened to alleviate flooding and to permit the continued drainage of prime farm lands.

The greatest impact from urban land on streams is pollution. Expanding population creates vast amounts of municipal and industrial waste which pollutes many streams and lakes. But all pollution does not come out of the sewer pipes of cities and industries. Water running off urban areas also is polluted by fertilizers from lawns; grease and oil from parking areas, highways, and airports; dust and dirt on roofs and streets; fecal materials from birds, pets, and other animals; pesticides and herbicides applied on city gardens, flower beds, lawns, and street trees; and from salts used for snow removal.

In many cities sanitary sewers and street sewers are combined to run through wastewater-treatment plants. During severe storms, the volume of water often is too great for treatment and much sewage and runoff is bypassed to streams without treatment. This overflow can be disastrous.

Ground Water

Ground water is an important part of our water supply. As such it should be protected just like water in streams and lakes. Like stream flow, ground water can be replenished. During droughts, we frequently hear of "falling water tables," so ground-water levels are directly tied to the amount of rainfall. Artificial droughts can be created when humans tamper with the environment. For example, in the Mill Creek Valley near Cincinnati, hydrologists (water scientists) learned that falling water tables were a result of paving highways, parking lots, and other areas. The pavement, impervious to water, was keeping the rain water from soaking into the soil. Instead, the water was being shunted down sewers, direct to streams and rivers. To relieve the problem, they proposed to pump treated water into the ground through injection wells.

Like any other kind of water, ground water can become polluted by improperly constructed septic tanks, water wells, and drainage from dumps and waste disposal. For many years, ground water beneath more than one million acres in northern Ohio was contaminated by nearby waste from 1,600 disposal wells. Waste from septic tanks in highly permeable areas in Summit, Montgomery, and Franklin counties has caused ground water pollution, and nearly half the water wells in southeastern Ohio have been found contaminated by Ohio Department of Health experts.

In Montgomery County a study reported that only 12 of 50 landfills in the county were not polluted. Contamination from landfills has been reported in Pike, Hamilton, Ashtabula, Trumbull, Lucas, and Clark counties.

Ground water also can become polluted from salt brine pumped from oil wells, as happened once when the entire well field of the village of Cardington in Morrow County had to be abandoned after chloride content in the water rose 100 times. Ground water often sustains stream flow during droughts, and when polluted it can affect the quality of streams.

Of course the problem with polluted ground water is that once polluted, the water remains contaminated for a long time. Ground water moves very slowly — a few feet per year — compared to stream flow which is measured in feet per second. Thus underground pollution lingers longer and is more costly to eliminate.

Coastal Zone

A fragile necklace ties Lake Erie to its hinterland. It is 240 miles long and we call it Ohio's coastal zone. It has no sharp boundary, because it is more than a changing shoreline. At times part of the land side of the zone may be flooded from high lake levels. And sometimes, when the Great Lakes basin suffers from drought, areas commonly underwater may be exposed mud flats. The coastal zone also includes a variety of natural, commercial, recreational, industrial, and historic resources.

As a result of the federal Coastal Zone Management Act of 1972, public attention has been focused on the unique resources of Lake Erie's shore. We are becoming aware of the great erosive forces which chew up and change the coast, washing back the land and discoloring the lake with a long ribbon of silt. The silt from the eroded lake shoreline is almost twice that which comes from the watersheds.

We are becoming aware of the quiet remoteness and beauty of isolated stretches of the zone which still abound with native plants and animals. Just as important is the great economic relationship between shoreline cities and industries and their dependence on Lake Erie for vast quantities of water, often replaced much the worse for use. The coastal zone provides harbors for a vast waterborne commerce and recreation for a major segment of Ohio's population which lives in or near the coastal strip.

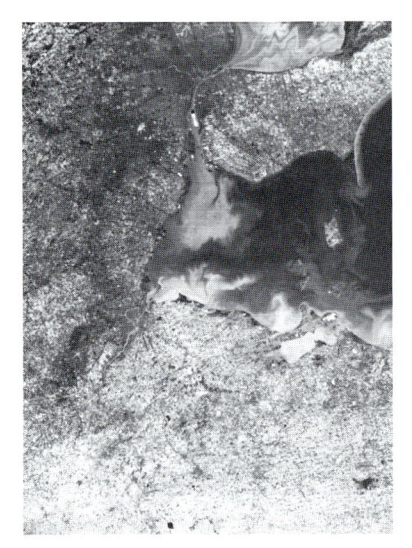

Erosion — A Barometer of Land Use

Erosion is a natural process which carves valleys and gives character to the landscape. A certain amount is normal as it results from the force of water flowing down hill. One look, however, at muddy Maumee Bay and at many of Ohio's streams will show how rapidly the land surface is currently being eroded. The annual silt load carried down the Maumee River to Maumee Bay would fill 40,000 freight cars, and most of this is due to current land use practices.

This satellite view of western Lake Erie and the Maumee River Valley shows human impact on water resources. The plumes of the Detroit River (top center) are visible as lighter areas in Lake Erie.

A silt-laden stream

An early salt works at a salt spring.

Topsoil in fields continuously planted to corn will erode on the average at a rate of about seven inches in 50 years. When corn, wheat, and clover are rotated, the rate slows to seven inches in 550 years. If the same land is kept in grass pasture, about 3,500 years would be required to erode seven inches. Over four million acres of Ohio crop land have an erosion hazard, and less than half has adequate protection.

Another great sediment threat to Ohio streams and lakes comes from highway construction and the bulldozing for new houses, shopping centers, and streets. Erosion from construction projects is usually about 10 times greater than from land in crops, acre for acre.

Severe soil loss from housing development

Hidden Wealth

Ruth W. Melvin

Bedrock and surface deposits make Ohio a leader in mineral production. This wealth comes not from precious gold, silver, and gems, but from a tremendous supply of mineral fuels such as coal, natural gas, and oil, and from industrial minerals such as salt, iron ore, limestone, dolomite, sandstone, sand and gravel, clay and shale, and gypsum.

Salt

Salt was the first mineral mined in Ohio. Bison, elk, bear, and smaller species, probably even the extinct mastodon and mammoth, had long visited wilderness springs or licks such as those along Salt Creek near Jackson to satisfy their salt needs.

The Indians and pioneers evaporated the brine water and collected the salt. Later, many salt-producing operations sprang up in eastern and southeastern Ohio, and the area around Pomeroy became the state's leading salt-producing region in the last half of the nineteenth century. By then, salt wells were being drilled into Upper Silurian beds far below the surface, and brines were pumped from the wells and evaporated. More recently, deep rock salt beds were discovered under the northeastern Ohio area. At several locations fresh water is pumped into these beds, returned to the surface as a brine, then evaporated to produce a purer and finer salt at less cost than pumping natural brines from drilled wells. Large mines are now located at Fairport Harbor in Lake County and at Cleveland.

Salt, chemically known as sodium chloride, has the greatest use in the soda ash and chlorine industries. Salt for cooking ranks well below its uses for industry, livestock, meat packing, and water-treatment plants. Smaller quantities are used in soap making, tanning, glass making, and more recently, in the manufacture of synthetic rubber and plastic. One of the largest current uses for rock salt is for snow and ice removal on highways, a mixed blessing since it pollutes the water runoff and speeds up rusting of vehicles.

Iron

Iron, since settlement, has always been in demand in Ohio. Farmers needed axes and plowshares; housewives needed pots and pans; and carpenters needed hammers and nails. Many settlers carried equipment with them as they traveled west, but the settler who broke or lost a tool or cooking pot faced a long period of doing without. Fortunately, Ohio's bedrock contained narrow bands of iron ore. This was mined and smelted in crude furnaces.

The first Ohio furnace was hidden away in the hills along Yellow Creek in Mahoning County. Prophetic of events to come, it was called "Hopewell" in 1804. It processed kidney ore from the neighboring hills. The furnace had an output of two tons per day, and the iron was cast immediately into stoves, kettles, irons, and similar articles for sale to the settlers.

From Hopewell, the industry expanded into the Hanging Rock region of southern Ohio. Nearly 50 charcoal furnaces were built before 1845, the year coal began replacing charcoal as a fuel, and after which furnaces with greater production capacity were constructed. Several hundred wood cutters, teamsters, ore-diggers, blacksmiths, bookkeepers, and managers were needed to operate a furnace. A blast of air from a water-powered blowing engine produced sufficient heat to melt the ore with its limestone flux. It took 150 to 200 bushels of charcoal, 5,000 pounds of ore, and about 300 pounds of limestone to make one ton of pig iron.

After the forests were depleted, the ironmakers substituted coal to fuel some of the furnaces. Eventually, as better transportation permitted finer grade ore from the Lake Superior region to be brought into Ohio and smelting techniques improved, small furnaces became impractical. By 1890 many of them were in ruins. One exception was the Vesuvius Furnace near Ironton, which was one of the first and last in the Hanging Rock Iron District embracing parts of Kentucky, West Virginia, and Ohio. Reserves of iron ore still exist in the rocks of Ohio but there is little likelihood that they will be utilized in the gigantic modern industry of iron and steelmaking.

The Jefferson charcoal furnace in Jackson County, established in 1854, had an output of over eight tons of pig iron per day. This furnace made its last blast in 1916.

Coal

Coal, Ohio's mineral king, reigns supreme. From the time of earliest settlement to the present, despite the many cultural and industrial changes, this natural deposit has played a vital role in the lives of Ohioans. It was first used as fuel for home heating, and for producing iron. Later, it was shipped down the Ohio and Mississippi rivers to the sugar refineries at New Orleans. And today more than half of all coal used in the U.S. is burned in the coal-fired boilers of power plants.

Many of the deposits of the 32 counties in eastern Ohio underlain by coal lie relatively near the surface. This encourages strip or surface mining, a method of extraction responsible for two-thirds of the annual production in the state. The 25 coal-producing counties, of which Belmont, Harrison, Muskingum, and Jefferson are still most important, account for nearly two thirds of the total tonnage mined in Ohio.

It has taken roughly two hundred million years for coal to be formed by geologic processes. This brings us to the stark reality that this resource will diminish gradually. Although not renewable, there is an encouraging coal reserve of 21 billion tons. However, this means strip mining will continue to be an environmental problem for years to come. The great gashed and denuded hillsides, the degradation of living conditions in the surrounding countryside, the contamination of watersheds, and the loss of land for forests and agriculture have moved society to enact strict state and federal reclamation laws. The federal law of 1977, closely following the Ohio law which is regarded as one of the most stringent in the nation, requires pre-planning, consideration of

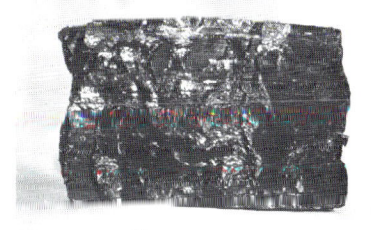

Coal is Ohio's mineral king

Coal strip mining in Meigs County

A reclaimed coal strip mine now used for cattle grazing

In the past, one miner used a dog team to pull coal cars from an underground mine.

how the surrounding land will be affected by mining, and stringent reclamation measures. Such planning also gives consideration to environmentally sensitive areas where mining should be prohibited altogether. In some cases where deep, abandoned mines continue to cause water-quality problems or where plugging has not worked, it is possible now to strip the area to remove the polluting rock material.

The beautiful blue waters of Lake Hope, one of the prettiest lakes in the state, contain so much acid from deep mines that few fish live there. The waters of Raccoon Creek in Gallia, Jackson, and Vinton counties contain so much acid that they are colored orange-red.

It is generally recognized that combustion of Ohio's coal creates a disturbing environmental impact. The culprits are a gas, sulfur dioxide, and fine particles which are dispersed in the air. These are presently expensive and difficult to control in high-sulfur coal. However, facilities are being constructed, such as coal-washing or coal gasification plants, which promise to make the use of Ohio coal more efficent.

It is clear that coal as a source of energy must remain available. It is equally evident that the environmental and social impact must be met with pre-planning and citizen support and with an understanding that coal used is coal gone, that the environment and the people in coal areas as well as entire drainage basins will be affected, and that an ecological balance cannot be restored overnight.

Oil and Gas

Waiting in line at the gas station and turning down thermostats in winter have created an awareness of the vital need for oil and natural gas. One of the first recorded oil wells in Ohio was drilled in Noble County in 1814 by two pioneers searching for salt. The product was of little interest at the time, but by the end of the century it formed the basis of an important industry.

In the early days of oil drilling, it was a catastrophe to the driller to find gas instead of oil. When the economic value of gas was finally recognized, wells began to appear on the landscape in large numbers. The glass industry in the Toledo area quickly adapted gas for its use; iron smelting, furniture making, lime burning, and brick making followed. Officials in Findlay, who thought the gas inexhaustible, promised free gas for new factories and allowed gas street lamps to burn 24 hours a day.

At the present time shortages of oil and gas have stimulated activity to increase Ohio's production. In 1976, drilling operations approached a new 10-year high. Estimated reserves of natural gas have increased, partly as a result of drilling wells into deeper rock strata. At the same time oil reserves have decreased.

Through the years, literally thousands of brine pits associated with the 200,000 oil wells drilled have created a reclamation dilemma. These pits, although not occupying great acreages, are necessary either for drilling overflow or for disposing of the salty sea water which comes up with the oil. Many leaks and many overflows contaminating streams or springs continue to be a problem even years after reclamation.

Wood County oil field in the 1890's

Limestone, Dolomite, and Sandstone

Limestone, and the related abundant Ohio rock called dolomite, are Ohio's most versatile industrial minerals. Both are processed into hundreds of products for use in agriculture, steelmaking, cement, ceramics, and construction. Ohio ranks high in the production of limestone and first in the processing of lime for chemical and agricultural uses.

Most limestone is in western Ohio beneath the glacial till. Early settlers found slabs of limestone rocks lying in the fields and streams and used them extensively in home building. When they discovered that these rocks broke down from fireplace heat into quick lime they used the material successfully for making mortar and plaster. Eventually limestone was quarried for buildings, bridge foundations, and making concrete, the first use of which was for highway pavement in Bellefontaine in 1891.

Limestone and dolomite resources are almost boundless. But future use, which promises to increase with population, is dependent upon accessible deposits. The hundreds of acres of deep quarry holes now filled with water present a reclamation challenge. Near Columbus a cliff-homes condominium complex has been built along ridges surrounding the quarry lakes.

Sandstone has been important in Ohio's industrial growth since the stone was first cut for grindstones, or for the construction of bridges, canal locks, and buildings. Ohio once was first among the states in sandstone production, but demand is less and it now ranks fifth along with limestone. About two million tons are mined each year.

Piles of sandstone blocks often are all that remain to mark the sites of the first iron furnaces. Sandstone abutments are all that remain of the first paper mill west of the Allegheny Mountains along Little Beaver Creek in Columbiana County. Many Ohio cities are graced by beautiful churches built from Black Hand and Berea sandstones, and they mark

Limestone quarry on Kelleys Island

the era of Ohio's prominence as a sandstone producer. Today, a larger percentage of sandstone is crushed for use in the glass and pottery industries, for manufacturing, and for lining in metallurgical furnaces.

In addition, Ohio's sandstone formations are reservoirs of oil and gas and are constantly being probed in a search for fuels. Even after they have given up their fuel supplies, many of the sandstones continue to serve as underground storage reservoirs for natural gas.

Sand and Gravel

The rivers carrying water from the melting glaciers deposited great volumes of sand and gravel in their valleys. This lowly material is of extraordinary value to the basic construction industry.

Industrial aggregates, a term used to describe the sand, gravel, limestone, and dolomitic rock extracted for paving, building, and fill, did not come into importance until the twentieth century. Sand became important when lime processing was developed. But the invention of Portland cement and steel-reinforced concrete really brought sand and gravel production into its present prominence.

Mining consumes the land at a rate of more than 2,000 acres annually. Land use problems have been created because urban areas have frequently spread out to surround quarries. The reclamation requirements may be met by filling in worked-out quarries with waste materials and then grading to restore the land for agriculture, recreation, or adjacent home and cottage sites.

One of the earliest reclamation projects, begun back in the 1920s, is known as Wayne Lakes near Greenville. The excavation process left 16 lakes totalling about 100 acres which provide an attractive residential community with backyard recreation. Eastwood Park in Dayton is a pre-planned joint venture on the part of the excavator and the city. The area was excavated to conform to a detailed park plan which included three miles of lakes for power boats, sailing, canoeing, and fishing. In addition, these lakes provide recharging basins for the city's adjacent water well fields.

Clay and Shale

Ohio has long been a leader in shale and clay production and in the manufacture of ceramic ware. One of the earliest recorded uses was in the building of Campus Martius in Marietta in 1788, where "the houses were all provided with good brick chimneys — the brick being made upon the grounds and burned by men experienced in that line of industry."

Ohio's pottery business appears to have begun in Cincinnati, and the "yellow ware" industry using native clays was introduced at East Liverpool in 1840 when an English potter judged the clays in the surrounding hills to be of excellent quality. The business developed from yellow ware to white and semivitreous china and porcelain electrical fixtures and supplies. Zanesville also became famous for its Bluebird Stoneware and floor, wall, and vitreous tile. The firebrick industry expanded throughout eastern Ohio where flint clays of excellent quality were discovered. Ohio originated the sewer pipe industry, developed fireproofing material from clay, and vitrified brick for paving.

Clay sewer tile

Some of the shales and clays of Ohio are found in association with coal formations where they are called fire clays. The supply, except for the flint fire clays, is abundant. The clays are not good for high-grade china and porcelain, but Ohio will continue to be a major producer.

Gypsum

Since the turn of the century, most of us unlucky enough to have a broken arm or leg are familiar with plaster of Paris casts. The molding material was largely the mineral gypsum which was heated at a low temperature, then mixed with water, and shaped. This process is called "calcining" and the resulting material also can be made into wall board and lath and gypsum plaster. Modern construction techniques make extensive use of wallboard, and most houses and apartments built fairly recently have interior walls of that material.

Ohio's gypsum industry began in 1821 when two boaters discovered the soft mineral in an outcrop along the north shore of Sandusky Bay. Quarrying was begun and has continued in the area to this day. Other deposits have been reported from a broad area in northeastern Ohio, but the Sandusky Bay deposits are presently the only ones of economic value.

Gypsum is composed of calcium sulfate and water. Research is being done on the mineral anhydrite, which is calcium sulfate without water. Most of Ohio's reserves are probably in this form, and favorable results of research could greatly increase the importance of the gypsum industry in the state.

Through the years the face of Ohio has changed. Vast forests gave way to productive farm land which provided food for more and more energetic settlers. Muddy roads, intermingled with railroads coming on the heels of canals, were replaced with a great network of highways and super-highways. Valuable minerals were discovered in the rocks and, when processed, provided tools, heat, and construction materials. Rivers and Lake Erie became waterways and furnished water for further extraction and industrialization. Villages became towns, towns became cities, and cities developed into great urban complexes.

With each multiple change the quality of life seemed to improve for large numbers of Ohioans, though people and minerals were extravagantly exploited and the land and waters abused. Laws, frequently too weak and too late, were enacted to curb the physical and social ills. Planning bodies at the federal, state, and sometimes local government levels were created. Ohio with its valuable farm land, mineral resources, and large metropolitan areas has not yet struck a balance to maintain its beauty and natural diversity.

There is a strong conviction among citizens to maintain, conserve, and protect our natural resources and guarantee a high quality of living. Land-use planning, to be effective, must begin with understanding and action at the local level. As local officials gain a knowledge of all viewpoints and act constructively to chip away at each problem as it arises, progress will be made. Regional and state planning councils, acting in an advisory capacity, must convince local officials of the importance of the programs they deem desirable. It is citizen concern and active involvement which will lift the richly endowed face of the Buckeye State and achieve a happier outlook for generations to come.

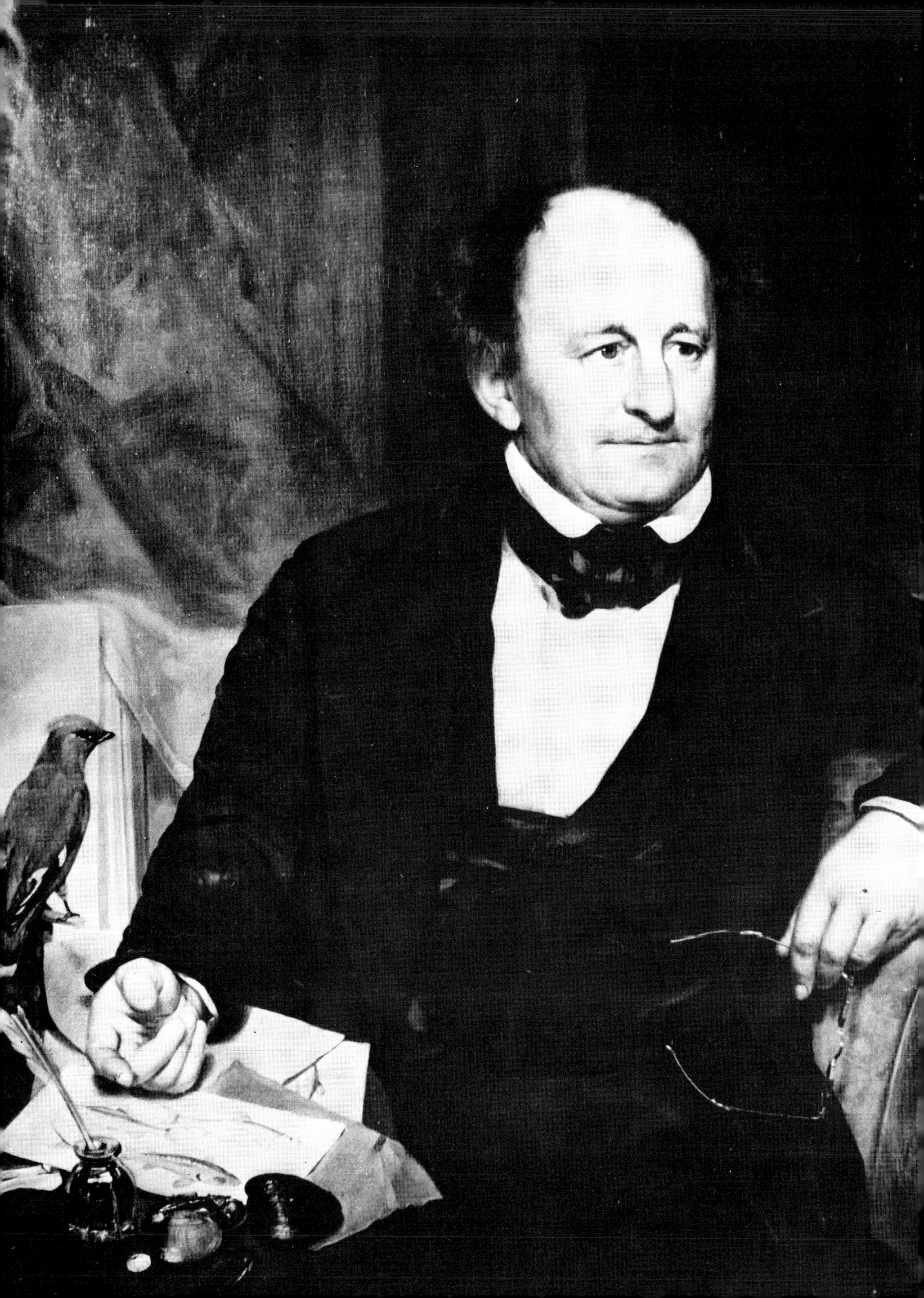

Chapter 18
The Naturalists

by Ralph W. Dexter

OHIO, first stop on the westward trek of settlement beyond the Alleghenies, attracted a variety of amateur rock hounds, zoologists, and botanists lumped under the convenient term "naturalists."

In the nineteenth century, the study of science — of rocks, animals, plants and the like — was called natural philosophy. Early naturalists were often physicians, and the person who bound a wound could just as easily offer an opinion on the distribution of pawpaw trees or speculate on the presence of granite boulders thousands of miles from their bedrock origin. When these physicians were not treating patients, they could often be found traveling the countryside observing, reporting, and taking notes on the natural features. Their reports constitute the earliest scientific observations of the state, forming the basis of work for a continuing stream of naturalists who have lived and worked in Ohio for about 175 years.

David Zeisberger

The Earliest Naturalists

The earliest reports of the Ohio Country came from trappers, soldiers, and very hardy pioneers. Among these were Christopher Gist (ca. 1706-1759), a surveyor who explored the Ohio Country in 1750-51, and David Zeisberger (1721-1808), leader of the Moravian mission community at Schoenbrunn in Tuscarawas County, who described the dark forests of the Tuscarawas River Valley.

Samuel P. Hildreth

Daniel Drake

Jared Potter Kirtland (page 294)

Perhaps the first scientist in Ohio was Dr. Samuel P. Hildreth (1783-1863), a physician who arrived in Marietta in 1806. He described the region around Marietta in detail and is credited with organizing the first local club for the study of natural history in the state. However, Hildreth is best known for his continuous records of weather and flood conditions along the Ohio River. His flood records date from 1772, and his published weather records extend for 35 years, from 1828-1863. An avid collector, Hildreth started a museum in his home and the collection was later given to Marietta College.

Medical doctors such as Hildreth were often interested in natural history because of the medicinal properties of plants. At the time Hildreth reached Marietta, another physician, Dr. Daniel Drake (1785-1852), returned to Cincinnati to practice medicine and study the natural history of southwestern Ohio. Drake traveled extensively, studying glacial drift and boulders before the concept of continental glaciation had been formulated. He founded the Western Museum Society in 1818 to fill the cultural gap in southwestern Ohio. Two years later the Western Museum, housed in the Cincinnati College building, opened its doors to the public. In the 1820s this museum was the fourth largest in the country, but the future of the parent society was to be short. Apparently there were financial problems from the start; the now famous bird artist, John James Audubon, who worked as a taxidermist for the Western Museum Society during 1819 and 1820, later claimed that he was never paid in full for his work. In any case the Society gradually withered and died. At an 1835 meeting of the so-called "Friends of Science", the dynamic Dr. Drake organized his second scientific society — the Western Academy of Natural Science. Its "life" was none too long either, and early in 1870 the Cincinnati Society of Natural History was organized, rising from the remains of the Academy and the Western Museum Society, all forerunners of the Cincinnati Museum of Natural History.

Drake's work attracted Dr. John Locke (1792-1856) and Dr. John L. Riddell (1807-1865) to the Cincinnati area in the 1830s. Locke, best known for his inventions of scientific instruments, was also a geologist who published a report for the Ohio Geological Survey concerning the geology of southwestern Ohio. Riddell, a botanist-physician, who developed the first binocular microscope, prepared his "Synopsis of the Flora of the Western States," his most important contribution to Ohio botany and the first flora west of the Alleghenies. He also was one of several naturalists to make repeated requests for a geological survey of the state's resources.

However, probably the best-known early naturalist was Caleb Atwater (1778-1867), a leading lawyer and politician from Circleville. Recognized as a historian, Atwater also had an intense interest in natural history. He first explained the existence of Ohio prairies on the basis of limited precipitation rather than periodic grassland and forest fires. Years ahead of his time, he was one of the first individuals to champion forest conservation — odd at a time when the forest was thought by many people to be limitless and a headache to be eliminated. Atwater was correct in his concern. After only about 20 years, the seemingly endless forest was proving very limited. It was rapidly giving way to the expanding nation. Roads and canals were built across the land, towns were built, crude factories and mills were turning out finished products, a wilderness was being replaced by industry and agriculture.

The Geological Surveys

There has always been as much interest concerning what is underground as what is above ground. In the early days of statehood, land speculation was fed by dreams of untold and unknown riches simply waiting to be dug. Often, the speculators were dishonest. They misrepresented or simply lied about the minerals beneath the land they owned. Geologists of the day also were misinformed. For example, Hildreth believed coal deposits could be found a few feet beneath the surface of western Ohio. The General Assembly approved a geological survey of the state to learn exactly what was under the ground. Finally, it was thought, people would have reliable information for planning mineral exploitation.

John L. Riddell

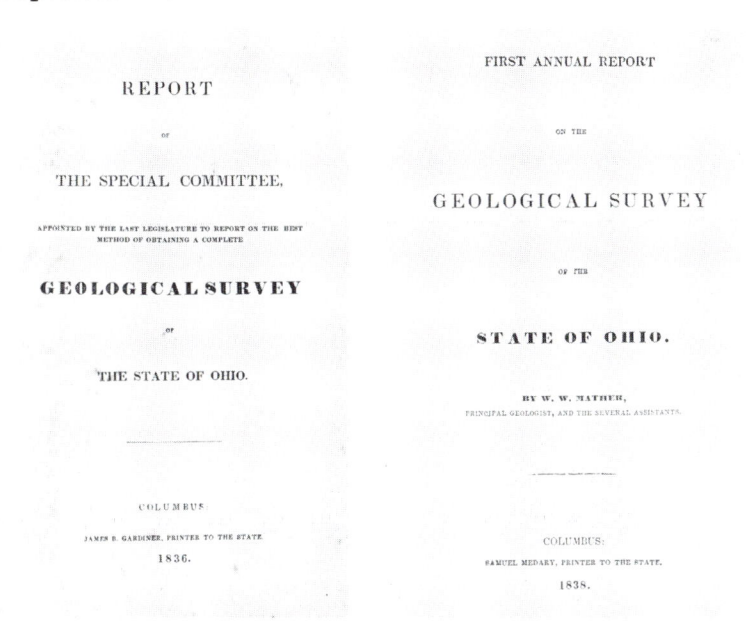

The Legislative Report which recommended the establishment of The Ohio Geological Survey (left)

The first Report of The Ohio Geological Survey

William W. Mather (1804-1859) was commissioned to head the survey, the first of three conducted during the nineteenth century. These surveys were important not only to determine the economic aspects of mineral exploitation, but also to serve as the first comprehensive, statewide examination of the flora and fauna. Mather was one of the first geologists to draw attention to Lake Erie shore erosion. The Mather survey lasted two years, 1837-1838, and it was really no more than a hurried overview of the state. Still, working without the aid of base maps, Mather and his co-workers charted the basic stratigraphy of Ohio geology and investigated salt, clay, and coal deposits before the survey was abandoned in the financial panic which swept the nation in the late 1830s.

William W. Mather

John Locke served as an assistant geologist on the survey and one of his most important contributions was the mapping of Adams County — the first county geologic map in Ohio and perhaps the first in the United States.

The first survey provided a geologic framework for the state, but it also included the first statewide investigation of the animals found in Ohio. This report was written by Dr. Jared Potter Kirtland (1793-1877), who was to become one of the best known American naturalists. A Connecticut native, Kirtland joined his father, who founded the town of Poland near Youngstown, in 1810. In his early years he collected shellfish in the Mahoning River. Like so many other early naturalists, Kirtland became a medical doctor, sandwiching trips to the woods and

John Locke

Charles Whittlesey

John S. Newberry

streams between an extensive medical practice and his duties at Western Reserve College.

In Kirtland's first statewide assignment with the geological survey, he described several new fish species. One of his most important contributions came in the establishment of the Cleveland Academy of Natural Sciences, later named the Kirtland Society of Natural History, which evolved into The Cleveland Museum of Natural History. Kirtland was also one of the founders of the American Society of Geologists and Naturalists, which, in time, became the nation's largest group of scientists — the American Association for the Advancement of Science.

Kirtland corresponded with naturalists throughout the country from his farm near Rockport (now Lakewood). He conducted many experiments in horticulture and arboriculture there, and the farm became a gathering place for others interested in natural history.

Two close associates who often visited Kirtland were Colonel Charles Whittlesey (1808-1886) and Dr. John S. Newberry (1822-1892). A graduate of the academy at West Point, Whittlesey is best known for his studies of archaeology and glacial geology. He helped the fledgling science of glacial geology make great strides in the state when he became the first person to study kettle hole lakes. In fact, glacial Lake Whittlesey in northwest Ohio is named in his honor. Newberry also became a renowned geologist, stimulated in his youth by the fossils he discovered in his father's coal mine near Tallmadge. Greatly interested in the outdoors, he prepared Ohio's first state list of plants before he entered college. However, Newberry became more interested in geology after he received his medical degree; and from that time on, he spent more time with rocks and fossils than with patients.

After an intensive investigation of the botany and geology of northeast Ohio, Newberry turned his attention to the remainder of the state when he accepted a position to direct the second geological survey. The Mather survey had been abandoned several years before its scheduled completion, and it was not until 1869 that the General Assembly authorized another survey. The second survey was to produce detailed information about Ohio's mineral wealth. Newberry, a strong believer in basic research, approached the problem fundamentally and began his survey by investigating the state's fossil deposits. Although his descriptions in the first few volumes of geological survey publications represented the first work on fossils in Ohio, the fossil work landed Newberry in trouble with legislators impatient for information about coal and other minerals. Actually, Whittlesey, bitter for being bypassed to head the survey in favor of Newberry, helped foment the dissatisfaction. Newberry survived a legislative investigation nevertheless and went on to provide the state with the most comprehensive mineral report to that time, concentrating on coal, clay, iron ore, gypsum, and salt. Once again a zoological study was included. Plant research also was accomplished, but the botanical manuscript was lost before publication, forcing the state to wait a few more years for a comprehensive study of plant life.

Newberry exerted tremendous influence on natural history study during the nineteenth century with his work for the survey, three trips as physician-naturalist on major U.S. government exploration parties, and his organization of the Department of Geology and Paleontology in the Columbia University School of Mines at New York City.

One of Newberry's assistants on the 1870-1872 geological survey was Newton H. Winchell (1839-1914), who in 1881 was to help organize the Geological Society of America and serve as its president in 1902. In addition, he was one of the founders of the *American Geologist* which he edited for 18 years.

The Newberry survey had barely ended when "oil mania" swept the nation. The General Assembly appropriated money for a third survey under the direction of Edward Orton, a prominent geologist and former president of The Ohio State University. In the late 1880s, the discovery of oil and gas deposits in northwestern Ohio sparked a tremendous oil boom near Findlay and Lima. Much natural gas was wasted. Hundreds of millions of cubic feet were flared into the atmosphere and the city of Findlay offered free gas for any factory built there. Gas torches lighted the streets night and day.

The Orton survey delineated the gas and oil deposits in the state, and in 1890 he prophetically warned that the petroleum boom could not last long:

> ...It is little less than vandalism to turn this superfine fuel, in amounts aggregating many millions of feet every day, to the commonest uses of fuel; as, for example, the burning of common brick or draining tile, or in calcining common limestone, or to be consumed in an iron mill. For such use no adequate justification exists. Neither cupidity nor stupidity should be allowed to work out these evil results. If the State were wise enough and were armed with proper power, it would surely forbid such an abuse of its priceless resources...

But few persons paid any attention, and by 1900, a mere 24 years after its birth, the great northwest Ohio oil boom collapsed. There has never been anything like it since.

The Orton survey mapped the gas and oil deposits within the state, but Orton also was successful in completing zoological, paleontological, and economic geology surveys. A state botanical survey was finally published which included the first serious mapping of Indian mounds within the state.

Ohio attracted several natural scientists from Europe. Edward Claypole (1835-1901), an internationally known geologist from England, helped found The Ohio Academy of Science, and he served as its first president in 1891. Later, Victor Sterki (1846-1933), a Swiss physician, practiced medicine in New Philadelphia and became the nationally recognized expert on fingernail clams and tiny land snails. In time, like so many other physician-naturalists, he gave up the practice of medicine and became associate curator of mollusks at the Carnegie Museum at Pittsburgh.

The Naturalists Specialize

As they learned more about the environment, naturalists began specializing in narrower fields of interest. Sterki of land snail fame was only one of several prominent specialists who lived and worked in the state. Their interests spanned from lowly, ground hugging mosses to the soaring American eagle. For example, William S. Sullivant (1803-1873), a central Ohio businessman and son of the founder of Columbus, became the nation's leading bryologist; and his extensive collection of mosses was eventually donated to the Farlow Herbarium at Harvard University. Leo Lesquereux (1806-1889), one of his close associates, carried on the work after Sullivant's death and eventually published the *Manual of Mosses of North America*. He was also one of the leading experts of coal fossils in the United States. Cincinnatian Charles Dury (1847-1931) was interested in beetles, and William A. Kellerman (1850-

Edward Orton, Sr.

Natural gas torches once lighted the streets of Findlay as shown in this old illustration from *Harper's* Magazine

William S. Sullivant

William A. Kellerman

Now preserved in the Herbarium of The Ohio State University, this dried specimen of a Pink moccasin-flower was collected in 1840 by William S. Sullivant of Columbus, Ohio.

The Ohio Naturalist

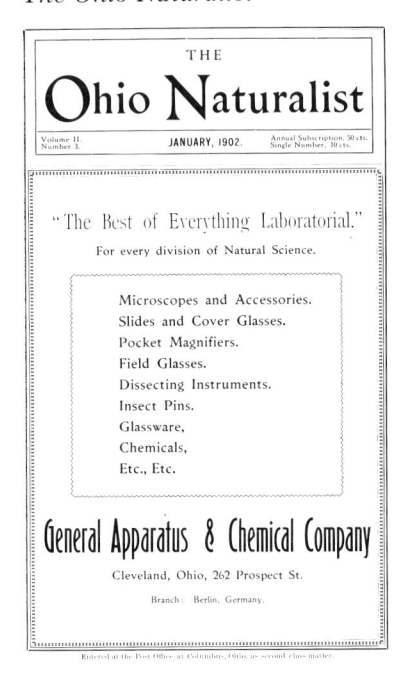

The Ohio Journal of Science

1908) of The Ohio State University became a nationally recognized authority on fungi, especially parasitic species. He was founder and editor of the *Journal of Mycology* and leading founder of *The Ohio Naturalist*, the official publication of The Ohio Academy of Science now known as *The Ohio Journal of Science*. One of the unique applications of natural history involved three Lloyd brothers from Cincinnati — John U. (1849-1936), Nelson A. (1851-1926), and Curtis G. (1859-1926), who extended an interest in pharmaceuticals into the study of fungi and medically useful plants. One of their greatest contributions was founding the journal *Lloydia*, concerned with natural drugs. They also founded the Lloyd Library and Museum in Cincinnati, one of America's foremost botanical libraries.

While C.G. Lloyd tracked fungi, Francis H. Herrick (1858-1940) was researching and writing about the American lobster for which he is best known. However, Herrick also investigated American eagles at Vermilion near Lake Erie and published one of the most comprehensive studies ever completed of this bird.

Dr. J.M. Wheaton (1840-1887) was a central Ohioan with a great interest in birds. Wheaton was a medical doctor, but he was especially interested in how the activities of birds related to agricultural production. He collected specimens from boyhood and eventually gathered a sizeable home museum. His collection of birds is now in the Museum of Zoology at The Ohio State University. Wheaton was honored when James S. Hine (1866-1930) formed the Wheaton Club in 1921 for serious central Ohio birders.

The state also had several outstanding educators of science and natural history. Edwin L. Moseley (1865-1948) taught science at Sandusky High School for 25 years before moving, in 1914, to Bowling Green Normal College (now Bowling Green State University), where he headed the science department for many years. While there, he organized a natural history museum and remained its curator after retirement from teaching in 1936.

Other high school science teachers were Auguste F. Foerste (1862-1937) at Steele High School in Dayton, and A.D. Selby (1859-1924) at Columbus High School. Foerste was especially interested in Ohio botany and geology, and he spent many summers working on geological surveys for both the United States and Canadian governments. Selby later was chief of the botany department at the Ohio Agricultural Experiment Station (1894-1924).

Biology education took a big step forward with the organization of the nation's first ornithology course at Oberlin College by Lynds Jones (1865-1951). Jones was the paramount birder in Ohio, and in 1903, he published a volume on the birds of Ohio. A founder of the Wilson Ornithological Club (1888), which has become a national society, he served as its president three times and as editor of its bulletin until 1924.

An important milestone in education and research was the formation of the Lake Laboratory in 1896 at Sandusky by David S. Kellicott (1842-1898). The laboratory served as a summer field station for both students

American eagle publication

Edwin Lincoln Moseley

Lake Laboratory advertisement (left)

Franz Theodore Stone Laboratory announcement

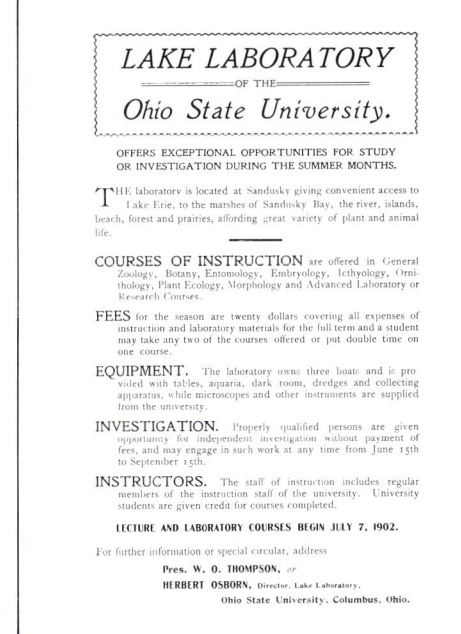

Herbert Osborn

Midwest naturalists (left to right): Milton B. Trautman, Paul B. Sears, Frank Preston, Edward S. Thomas, Robert B. Gordon, and Walter A. Tucker

Floyd Bartley

and researchers studying the biology of Lake Erie. In 1918, the laboratory's activities were moved to Put-in-Bay, and in 1925, when Gibraltar Island was acquired, it became known as the Franz Theodore Stone Laboratory, named for the father of its benefactor, Julius Stone. The Stone Laboratory of The Ohio State University has long been known for its tradition of students well trained in aquatic field biology.

Another major step was taken when Herbert Osborn (1856-1954) founded the Ohio Biological Survey in 1912. He served as director of the survey from 1912 nearly until his death and, from 1898 to 1918, as director of the Lake Laboratory. A former chairperson of The Ohio State University Department of Zoology and Entomology, Osborn was a prolific writer whose most important contributions are in the area of economic entomology.

A former Oberlin College faculty member who has had a great impact on education and research is Paul B. Sears (1891-). His publications on pollen analysis of Ohio's peat bogs, on the natural vegetation of Ohio's forests and prairies, and on the sequences of post-glacial vegetation and climate are classic. As a conservation educator he is nationally known for his popular writings: *Deserts on the March, The Living Landscape,* and *Lands Beyond the Forest.*

While Sears was working at Oberlin College and later at Yale University, botanists at The Ohio State University were making significant progress in education and research. Edgar N. Transeau (1875-1960) was chairperson of the Department of Botany from 1917 to 1946, during which time he developed a large teaching faculty that became known for its laboratory-demonstration-discussion procedures for teaching botany. Major research interests of the faculty ranged from experimental, physiological, and ecological approaches to descriptive floristic and vegetational studies on Ohio's plants. Many students were engaged in working out the natural vegetation of various counties and regions of the state. In the 1960s, one of these former students, Robert B. Gordon (1901-), with the help of others, collected this research into a large scale, single, multicolored map showing the original vegetation of Ohio at the time of the earliest land surveys. He soon followed with an accompanying publication, *The Natural Vegetation of Ohio in Pioneer Days,* published in 1969. Another of Transeau's students, John N. Wolfe (1910-1974), with his associates, published a now classic study on the microclimates of Neotoma, a small valley in Hocking County. Wolfe's research was one of the first detailed studies on the relationship of vegetation to microclimates in a very small area.

Most notable of recent workers on Ohio's birds and fishes is Milton B. Trautman (1899-), best known for his *The Birds of Buckeye Lake, Ohio,* published in 1940, and for his classic, *The Fishes of Ohio,* published in 1957.

Of course, this array of academics does not mean a naturalist has to be connected with a university to contribute to the understanding of Ohio's flora and fauna. Many lay citizens have made significant contributions. Two of the most famous are Floyd Bartley (1884-1974) and Homer Price (1895-). Bartley, a Pickaway County farmer, probably knew more about the plants of southeastern Ohio than anyone else. Bartley began collecting plants in 1928, and through the years, deposited thousands of specimens in The Ohio State University Herbarium. His personal collection of more than 5,000 specimens was donated to Ohio University and the herbarium is named in his honor. Homer Price, a farmer from Paulding County, made extensive collections of bird eggs, insects, and

Annette (left) and E. Lucy Braun in Lynx Prairie, Adams County, Ohio

One of Ohio's first history books was written by Caleb Atwater.

Several early books by Caleb Atwater are preserved in the Thompson Collection at the Cincinnati Historical Society library.

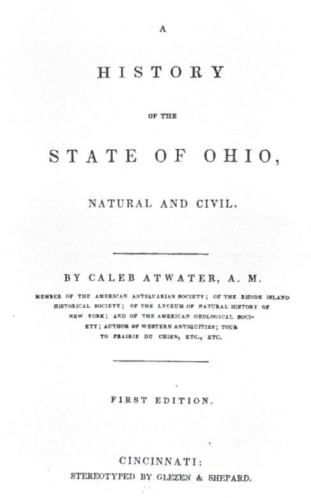

land snails in northwestern Ohio. From 1915 to 1962, Price collected the eggs of 119 birds—many from nests destroyed during hay mowing. His collection of 15,000 insect specimens is now in the Insect Collection at The Ohio State University.

Despite this formidable array of accomplishment and expertise, perhaps the best known twentieth century naturalist is E. Lucy Braun (1889-1971). An outstanding botanist and conservationist, Lucy Braun was one of the truly dedicated pioneer plant ecologists in the United States. She was associated with the University of Cincinnati her entire educational and professional life. Her publications, which total more than 180 articles, appeared in four books and 20 scientific and popular journals. She was an editor for the *Naturalist's Guide to the Americas,* and with Lynds Jones, contributed the chapter about Ohio. Her most recent and best-known works are the *Deciduous Forests of Eastern North America,* for which she was a recognized authority, *The Woody Plants of Ohio,* and *The Monocotyledoneae* [of Ohio].

The list of Ohio naturalists does not end with Lucy Braun. It could go on and on. A great many Ohioans have contributed their time and talent to increasing the understanding of the interrelationships of people, plants, animals, and soil. About two hundred years ago, the pioneer naturalists laid the foundation on which later naturalists sharpened their knowledge. This stream of investigation and learning has not ended — in fact probably never will end. No one has improved on Caleb Atwater's words in his 1838 book, *A History of the State of Ohio, Natural & Civil:*

> We have taken but a few steps into the path of Natural History leading the way and pointing ahead, for the young men of this state, to follow us, and when we stop short, and stand by the wayside, we pray them to march forward to the end of the path. Any one of them who feels within his own bosom, that he holds an appointment, to make a correct survey of Nature, not from any civil ruler but from Nature's God, let such an one move onward and fame and glory will follow his labors. No governor will appoint him, nor Legislature pay him. The Creator will reward him.

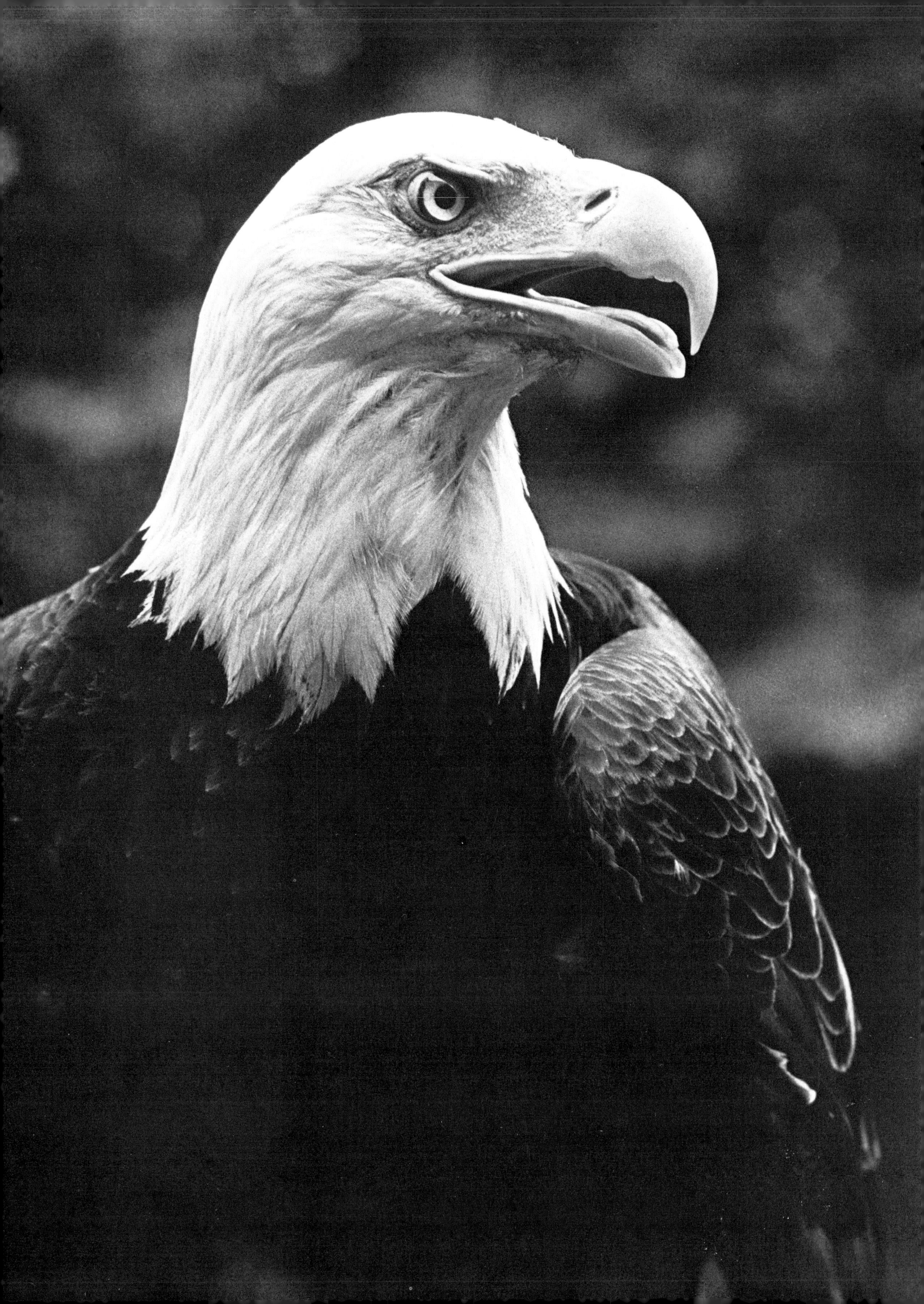

Chapter 19
Preserving the Heritage

BY the end of the nineteenth century, thanks to its bounteous natural resources, Ohio was well on its way to a position of leadership in agriculture and industry. The wilderness had been done in by the ax, plow, and cow. Few tracts of virgin forest remained. Plants of the tallgrass prairies persisted mostly in old cemeteries or along a few back roads and railroad rights-of-way. Nearly all the Lake Erie marshes had been drained or diked for management as private waterfowl shooting areas. Natural sand dunes had been replaced by resort beaches, and natural water courses had been straightened and cleared to carry away excess water from fields and human and industrial wastes from the cities. Dozens of species of animals were extirpated from Ohio and several had become extinct—gone from the earth forever.

by Richard E. Moseley, Jr.

Ralph E. Ramey

Early Concern for Ohio's Natural Areas

Fortunately, there were always a few Ohioans concerned about the increasing destruction of natural systems. Naturalists who walked the woods and fields protested the wholesale transformation of woods into crop fields and cities, and, before the turn of the century, members of The Ohio Academy of Science focused attention on the need to protect wild plants and animals.

In 1900, The Biological Club of The Ohio State University, initiated *The Ohio Naturalist* as a "journal devoted more especially to the natural history of Ohio." The Academy adopted the publication, and in 1915 changed the name to *The Ohio Journal of Science.* In 1912 upon the urging of the Academy, the Ohio Biological Survey was created as an inter-institutional organization with offices at The Ohio State University. Since then the Survey has published more lengthy and detailed technical research data on Ohio's flora and fauna than is appropriate for the *Journal.*

One of the most significant early preservation efforts in Ohio occurred in 1917 with the passage of Ohio's model Park District Law. This law allows establishment of special districts with the power to "acquire lands...for conversion into forest reserves and for the conservation of the natural resources of the state, including streams, lakes, submerged lands, and swamplands, and to those ends...create parks, parkways, forest reservations, and other reservations." The person largely responsible for the enactment of this unique piece of legislation was Cuyahoga County Engineer William Stinchcomb. It was A.B. Williams of The Cleveland Museum of Natural History whose farsighted interpretation of the law led to establishment of the many fine systems of metropolitan natural area parks in Ohio's highly populated counties.

In the late 1920s, garden clubs throughout the state began emphasizing preservation of natural habitats. The "Save Outdoor Ohio" movement under the leadership of the Ohio Association of Garden Clubs (OAGC) did much during the next several decades to educate voters about conservation and preservation legislation. Conservation programs sponsored by the OAGC, and articles on conservation issues which appeared in their publication, *The Garden Path*, played a significant role in the passage of hawk- and owl-protection legislation and in the establishment of state parks. The editor of *The Garden Path* during those early years was Walter A. Tucker of Columbus. His contributions toward the preservation of Ohio's natural areas span a half century. They include, in addition to his work with OAGC, a major leadership role in the establishment of the League of Ohio Nature Clubs in the 1930s, the Metropolitan Park District of Columbus and Franklin County in the 1940s, and the Ohio Chapter of The Nature Conservancy in the 1950s.

Although the official protection of natural areas by state government has only recently been mandated, significant areas came into public ownership when administrators of some state agencies recognized the plight of Ohio natural systems and boldly interpreted their authority to acquire land. The hemlock-lined Black Hand Sandstone gorges of Hocking County were acquired in the mid-1920s by the Division of Forestry. Hueston Woods, a 100-acre tract of virgin beech-maple woodland in Butler County, was purchased in the 1940s by the Division of Conservation in the Department of Agriculture. And in the early 1950s, the wet prairie area of Wyandot County, Killdeer Plains, became one of the first purchases of the newly created Ohio Department of Natural Resources (ODNR).

Cedar Bog in Champaign County was the first area purchased by the State specifically to assure protection of its unique natural features. In 1942, Edward S. Thomas, curator of natural history for the Ohio Archaeological and Historical Society (now the Ohio Historical

The cardinal flower brightens damp areas in August.

Ohio's State Bird, the cardinal

Society), learned of a plan to drain the area and use it as pasture. He convinced Governor John W. Bricker that the swamp had a more important use than feeding cows and, with the governor's help, won approval to acquire the area through the Department of Public Works. It was then assigned to the Society for management. Later, the Ohio Historical Society also acquired as nature preserves Glacial Grooves State Memorial on Kelleys Island, Wahkeena State Memorial in Fairfield County, and the Edwin S. Davis State Memorial in Adams County.

During this time, private efforts at natural area preservation were few. However, some were significant. Most notable was the preservation of the area along Yellow Springs Creek in Greene County known as Glen Helen. In 1929, Hugh Taylor Birch gave this beautiful area to Antioch College. The Glen, part of which is registered with the National Park Service as a Natural Landmark, now totals nearly 1,000 acres and includes an intrepetive center and resident outdoor education facility. In 1929 The Dawes Arboretum was established south of Newark in Licking County, while the Holden Arboretum in Lake County south of Mentor came into being in 1931.

During the 1930s, 1940s, and 1950s some natural areas were acquired by youth agencies and fishing, hunting, and conservation clubs. These were developed for summer camps or for fishing and hunting areas, and thereby received a measure of protection. In 1959, The Cleveland Museum of Natural History purchased Fern Lake in Geauga County in order to preserve its exceptional quaking bog and swamp forest.

In the 1950s and 1960s five privately-supported nature centers were developed over the state to save unique areas and promote interpretation of natural history. These are Aullwood Audubon Center north of Dayton, The Wilderness Center near Wilmot in Stark County, The Cincinnati Nature Center near Milford in Clermont County, Shaker Lakes Regional Nature Center in Shaker Heights in Cuyahoga County, and Brukner Nature Center near Troy in Miami County. Support for these projects comes from a variety of sources including local nature and Audubon clubs. The Garden Club of Ohio and its many affiliates assist greatly the preservation effort. The support given by the Canton Garden Center for The Wilderness Center was invaluable in all phases of its development.

The major private thrust statewide for natural area preservation began in 1958 when the Ohio Chapter of The Nature Conservancy was founded. Kenneth W. Hunt, then the Director of Glen Helen, had conducted a survey to determine the need for such a statewide organization to work for the preservation of Ohio's natural areas, and the Ohio Chapter of The Nature Conservancy was organized in response to Hunt's recommendations. The Nature Conservancy is a national non-profit organization whose single purpose is the preservation of natural areas. It traces its lineage to the old preservation committee of the Ecological Society of America. In 1946, some members felt the need for more aggressive action in natural area preservation and formed the Ecologist's Union. In 1951, at a meeting held in Columbus, the name was changed to The Nature Conservancy (TNC), and two years later the fledgling organization adopted a policy providing for state chapters.

Beginning in 1959, with the acquisition of Lynx Prairie in Adams County, the Ohio Chapter of The Nature Conservancy compiled a remarkable record for saving natural areas. Among the chapter's outstanding projects during the next 10 years were Clifton Gorge in Greene County —a project spearheaded by the Dayton Museum of Natural History, Dysart Woods in Belmont County, Mentor Marsh in Lake County, Redbird Hollow in Hamilton County, Brown's Lake Bog in Wayne County, Frame Bog in Portage County, and Buzzardroost Rock and Red Rock in Adams County.

An important move toward organizing the effort to preserve Ohio's vanishing natural areas occurred in 1958 when the Ohio Biological Survey, under the leadership of Charles A. Dambach, sponsored a statewide inventory of such areas. The following year, J. Arthur Herrick of Kent State University began the inventory, now referred to as the

Drops of dew on *Liatris* (or blazing star) and spider web greet the morning in an Adams County prairie. (opposite page)

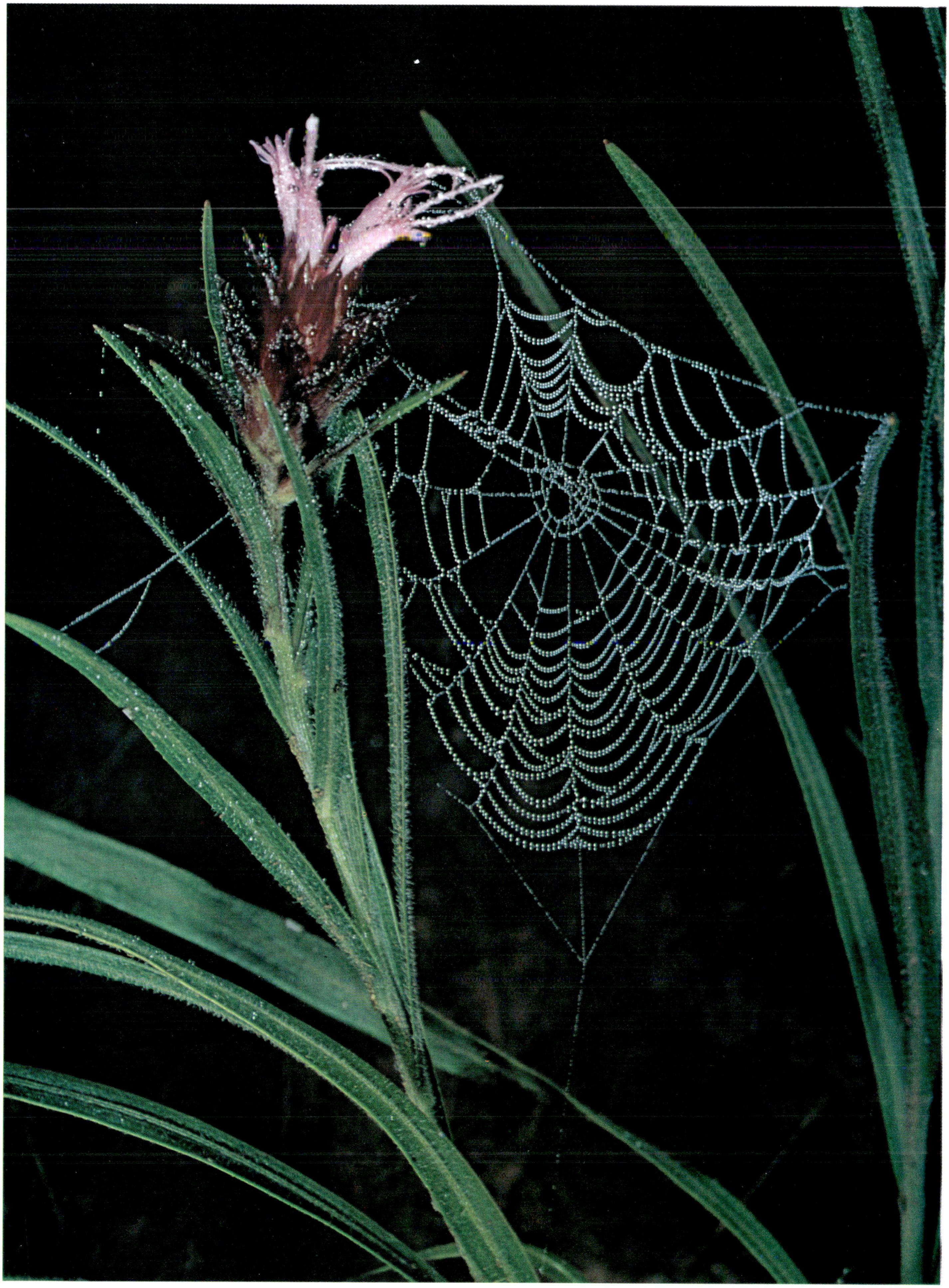

"Natural Areas Project." This list provided a firm foundation for the legislative effort that was to come.

The Ohio Nature Preserve System

By the mid-1960s, it was obvious that private efforts alone could not stop natural areas from being turned into shopping centers and subdivisions. Only the State, with its power of eminent domain, could protect some outstanding areas. At its annual meeting in 1966, the Ohio Chapter of TNC called for the creation of a state nature preserve system

Black Hand Sandstone Cliff at Black Hand Gorge State Nature Preserve near Toboso in Licking County. The legendary black hand pictograph which gave the name to the massive sandstone formation so prominent in the scenic Hocking Hills to the south was located here. During construction of the Ohio-Erie Canal in 1828 the pictograph was destroyed. A remnant of the canal remains at the bottom of the cliff.

Four-toed salamander

and a committee was formed to work toward that goal. The following January, at a chapter executive committee meeting, Walter A. Tucker reported that State Representative Robert A. Holmes of Columbus favored such a system. In August, the House adopted a Holmes-introduced resolution expressing concern over losses of wilderness and threats to the last remnants of Ohio's natural heritage. However, two years passed before the Ohio Legislative Service Commission approved a study of the "means of identifying, locating, and preserving areas of unusual natural significance for the beneficial use of generations to come." The result of this study was the introduction into the Senate of the Ohio Natural Areas Bill by State Senator Clara Weisenborn of Dayton. This bill, which later became a national model, was given final approval by the Ohio General Assembly and signed into law by Governor James A. Rhodes in 1970. It allowed the Ohio Department of Natural Resources to purchase and administer state nature preserves and to protect, through dedication, natural areas in private ownership. It also established the Natural Areas Council consisting of professionals from natural history disciplines who are appointed by the Governor.

Initially, the department acquired little land and thus management of these areas created no critical problems. However, as more areas came under protection, management problems increased for the department's small natural areas staff. In 1976, the General Assembly created the Division of Natural Areas and Preserves to provide the specialized management necessary for the acquisition and preservation of natural areas.

The goal of the program is to establish a statewide system of nature preserves which possess exceptional value or quality in illustrating or interpreting the natural history of the state.

The program's goals include:

• establishment of a comprehensive statewide inventory and registry of all ecologically significant areas in the state

• development of an effective public education program to promote an awareness, understanding, and appreciation for natural areas and preserves

• establishment of an effective protection program for all areas administered by the division

- development of a baseline data bank upon which sound preserve management decisions can be based
- establishment of a program through which all preserves can be developed for use without impairing their inherent natural values.

Today, the department, through the Division of Natural Areas and Preserves, has an active role in the planning, inventory, study, acquisition, and dedication of nature preserves. As a result of these efforts and the help of private citizens, the department has established a system of preserves that will help ensure the survival of Ohio's natural heritage for present and future generations. The existing system exhibits a great variety and wealth of natural diversity. Outstanding geological formations, bogs, fens, prairies, marshes, swamps, streams, forest, and areas of scenic grandeur are all represented.

The areas preserve the best that is left. They remain special places, relatively untouched by civilization or technology. Here, natural processes, remnant communities, and rare endangered species of plants and animals continue to live unimpeded by man. But preserves are not parks. They are not designed for masses of people or for mass-recreational activities such as swimming, boating, or camping. They are delicate ecosystems which need the respect of their visitors to continue to survive. Preserves are better-suited for more passive or non-consumptive recreational pursuits such as hiking, nature hobbies, art, photography, bird watching, and other similar activities not detrimental to their preservation. Protection of these priceless areas involves acquisition and sound management, and a good program must have both in order to assure adequately their continued preservation.

The preservation of Ohio's natural heritage has its critics. To some, preservation is merely a sentimental gesture, serving no useful purpose. Our ancestors took natural resources for granted and viewed the forests and wildlife as inexhaustible. We have built a mighty civilization during the last two centuries, but at a far greater cost than can be determined in dollars and cents.

Nature preserves, together with the natural communities of plants and animals, are of immense value for more than aesthetic or sentimental reasons. These priceless areas are needed as sites to conduct scientific research. As natural laboratories, they serve as environmental "barometers" or standards of reference in which to compare the health of the environment. As such, they can be useful in establishing environmental baselines or in analyzing and understanding conditions in a natural system. They are areas where present and future scientists can look for answers to questions and seek solutions to problems relating to the natural order of the system. As benchmarks, they provide standards against which environmental damage can be measured.

Uses of natural areas are broader than just for research. They are of value for teaching purposes, and serve as outdoor classrooms or "living textbooks" for those interested in the natural processes of an ecosystem or community of living things. They serve as habitats for rare and vanishing species and as places of historic and natural interest of scenic beauty. They also serve as living museums of the native Ohio landscapes where one may experience primeval conditions of a wilderness environment.

Lastly and more importantly, each natural area serves as a reservoir of genetic diversity, a gene pool, that is becoming increasingly more

A child's sense of wonder is enhanced in Ohio's natural areas.

Little Beaver Creek in Columbiana County

important to modern science. Because any species or organism may be important someday we cannot afford to reduce or destroy this genetic material. Many of the modern medicines and remedies for diseases that have afflicted the human race for centuries are derived from native plants and animals. Without these, who knows what the present condition and health of our civilization might be. We must indeed be selfish when looking at this genetic diversity, for we don't know what our needs will be in the future. Every one of our cultivated plants and domestic animals was originally a wild species.

But how do we save our priceless natural heritage from destruction? It begins with people caring. People, whether they be legislators, planners, engineers, homemakers, industrialists, factory workers, or students, need to be aware of the environmental implications of their actions, or the actions of others, and the problems they create.

There is still much to be done in Ohio. More areas must be identified and preserved before they are devastated, for they may be the last refuges of certain elements of our natural heritage. Your help is needed! Support those organizations which assist in efforts to acquire and set aside natural areas as preserves. Also, support the efforts of the local, state, and federal government in preserving these unique natural areas.

Landowners can either donate or dedicate land as a nature sanctuary. In so doing, they can enjoy the peace of mind that comes from knowing that the natural values of their land will be forever protected from destructive change. But the most satisfying and lasting reward will be the gratitude of the many future generations of Ohioans who will study, enjoy, and cherish this legacy.

As caretakers and stewards of this natural heritage, we all have an obligation and responsibility to use wisely these resources, to care for them, and to preserve them so they may be passed on to others unimpaired. Our very existence and the quality of life we enjoy depends upon the continued existence of the many elements of the natural world in which we live. Only when we understand and appreciate our natural heritage can we act intelligently to improve our enviroment and quality of life.

Wood duck

Additional Readings

A considerable quantity of basic information about the natural history of Ohio is available from publications of the following organizations:

The Ohio Academy of Science
445 King Avenue, Columbus, Ohio 43201

Ohio Department of Natural Resources
Publications Center
Fountain Square, Columbus, Ohio 43224

Ohio Biological Survey
484 West 12th Avenue, Columbus, Ohio 43210

Cincinnati Museum of Natural History
1720 Gilbert Avenue, Cincinnati, Ohio 45202

The Cleveland Museum of Natural History
Wade Oval, University Circle, Cleveland, Ohio 44106

The Dayton Museum of Natural History
2629 Ridge Avenue, Dayton, Ohio 45414

Ohio Historical Society
Interstate 71 and 17th Avenue, Columbus, Ohio 43211

The following publications are standard statewide references for specific subjects. Although some are out-of-print, they are usually available at most public and collegiate libraries or through inter-library loan.

Braun, E. Lucy. 1950. *Deciduous Forests of Eastern North America*. Blakiston Press. Reprinted in 1964 by Hafner Publ. Co., New York. 596 p.

_____. 1961. *The Woody Plants of Ohio*. Ohio State Univ. Press, Columbus. Reprinted in 1969 by Hafner Publ. Co., New York. 362 p.

_____ (with Clara G. Weishaupt). 1967. *The Monocotyledoneae: Cattails to Orchids*. Ohio State Univ. Press, Columbus. 464 p.

Conant, Roger. 1951. *The Reptiles of Ohio, 2nd Edition*. University of Notre Dame Press, South Bend, Indiana. 284 p.

Elfner, Lynn E., Ronald L. Stuckey, and Ruth W. Melvin. 1973. A guide to the literature of Ohio's natural areas. Ohio Biol. Surv. Info. Circ. No. 3. 56 p.

Frank, Glenn W., Editor. 1969. Ohio intercollegiate field trip [geology] guides 1950-51 to 1969-70. Kent State Univ. Printing Service, Kent. 268 p.

Gordon, Robert B. 1969. The natural vegetation of Ohio in pioneer days. Ohio Biol. Surv. New Series Bull. 3(2):1-109 plus map (1966).

Knepper, George W. 1976. *An Ohio Portrait*. Ohio Historical Society. 282 p.

Melvin, Ruth W. 1975. A guide to Ohio outdoor education areas. Second edition. Ohio Dept. Nat. Resources. 231 p.

Noble, Allen G. and Albert J. Korsok. 1975. Ohio — an American heartland. Div. Geol. Surv., Ohio Dept. Nat. Resources Bull. 65. 230 p.

Stout, Wilbur, Karl Ver Steeg, and G. F. Lamb. 1943. Geology of water in Ohio. Div. Geol. Surv., Ohio Dept. Nat. Resources Bull. 44. Reprinted in 1968. 694 p.

Trautman, Milton B. 1957. *The Fishes of Ohio*. Ohio State Univ. Press, Columbus. 683 p.

Trautman, Milton B., and Mary A. Trautman. 1968. Annotated list of the birds of Ohio. Ohio J. Sci. 68:257-332.

Walker, Charles F. 1946. The amphibians of Ohio. Part I, The frogs and toads. Ohio State Archaeol. & Hist. Soc., Columbus. 109 p.

Chapter 1. *The Ohio Country*.

Eckert, Allan W. 1967. *The Frontiersmen*. Bantam Books, New York. 751 p.

Howe, Henry L. 1900. *Historical Collections of Ohio*. C.J. Krebiel and Co., Cincinnati. Vol. 1, 992 p.; Vol. 2, 911 p.

Trautman, Milton B. 1977. The Ohio country from 1750 to 1977 — a naturalist's view. Ohio Biol. Surv. Biol. Notes No. 10. 25 p.

Chapter 2. *Written in the Rocks*

LaRocque, Aurele, and Mildred F. Marple. 1955. Ohio fossils. Div. Geol. Surv., Ohio Dept. Nat. Resources. Bull. 54. 152 p.

Smyth, Pauline. 1963, 1969, 1972. Bibliography of Ohio geology, 1951-1970. Div. Geol. Surv., Ohio Dept. Nat. Resources. Info. Circ. Nos. 32, 36, and 37. 63 p., 46 p., and 52 p.

Watkins, D.G. 1953. Bibliography of Ohio geology 1819-1950. Div. Geol. Surv., Ohio Dept. Nat. Resources. Bull. 52. 103 p.

Chapter 3. *Ice Over Ohio*

Goldthwait, Richard P. 1959. Scenes in Ohio during the last ice age. Ohio J. Sci. 59:193-216.

_____, Editor. 1972. *Till, A Symposium*. Ohio State Univ. Press, Columbus. 402 p.

Hough, Jack L. 1958. *Geology of the Great Lakes*. Univ. Illinois Press, Urbana, Illinois. 331 p.

Thomas, Edward S. 1952. The Orleton Farms mastodon. Ohio J. Sci. 52:1-5.

Chapter 4. *Today's Landscape*

Carman, J. Ernest. 1946. The geologic interpretation of scenic features in Ohio. Ohio J. Sci. 46:241-283. Reprinted in 1972 by Div. Geol. Surv., Ohio Dept. Nat. Resources.

Fenneman, Nevin M. 1938. *Physiography of Eastern United States*. McGraw Hill, New York. 714 p.

Ver Steeg, Karl. 1946. The Teays River. Ohio J. Sci. 46:297-307.

Chapter 5. *Climate and Weather*

Alexander, William H. 1923. A climatological history of Ohio. Ohio State Univ. Eng. Exp. Station Bull. 26. Columbus. 745 p.

Miller, Marvin E., and C.R. Weaver. 1971. Snow in Ohio. Ohio Agric. Res. and Devel. Center Research Bull. 1044. Wooster. 23 p.

National Weather Service. Monthly and annual summaries of local climatological data. Environmental Data Service, National Oceanic and Atmos. Admin., U.S. Dept. Commerce, Asheville, North Carolina.

Sanderson, Earl E. 1950. The climatic factors of Ohio's water resources. Div. of Water, Ohio Dept. Nat. Resources Bull. 15. 427 p.

Chapter 6. *Cradle of Life*

Division of Lands and Soil. 1973. Know Ohio's soil regions. Ohio Dept. Nat. Resources. Map and text. Columbus.

_____. Various dates. General soil maps and soil area maps and texts of individual Ohio counties by various authors. Ohio Dept. Nat. Resources.

Morse, H.H., and Samuel Bone. 1962. Understanding Ohio soils. Ohio Agric. Ext. Service, Ohio State Univ. Bull. 368. Columbus. 19 p.

United States Department of Agriculture. 1957. *Soil, The Yearbook of Agriculture*. U.S. Government Printing Office, Washington, D.C. 784 p.

Chapter 7. *Ohio Forests*

McCormick, Jack. 1966. *The Life of the Forest*. McGraw-Hill, New York. 232 p.

Chapter 8. *Ohio Waters*

Hynes, H.B.N. 1972. *The Ecology of Running Waters*. Univ. of Toronto Press, Toronto, Ontario. 555 p.

Oglesby, Ray T., C.A. Carlson, and J.A. McCann, Editors. 1972. *River Ecology and Man*. Academic Press, New York. 465 p.

Reid, George K. 1961. *Ecology of Inland Waters and Estuaries*. Reinhold Publishing Corp., New York. 375 p.

Usinger, Robert L. 1967. *The Life of Rivers and Streams*. McGraw Hill, New York. 232 p.

Chapter 9. *Relicts of the Past*

Prairies

Allen, Durward L. 1967. *The Life of Prairies and Plains*. McGraw Hill, New York. 232 p.

Cusick, Allison W., and K. Roger Troutman. 1978. The prairie survey project, a summary of data to date. Ohio Biol. Surv. Info. Circ. No. 10. 60 p.

Nichols, Stan, and Lynn Entine. 1978. Prairie primer. Univ. of Wisconsin — Extension, Madison, Wisconsin. 44 p.

Transeau, Edgar N. 1935. The prairie peninsula. Ecology 16:423-437.

Bogs

Aldrich, John W. 1943. Biological survey of the bogs and swamps in northeastern Ohio. American Midland Naturalist 30:346-402.

Dachnowski, Alfred. 1912. Peat deposits of Ohio. Div. Geol. Surv., Ohio Dept. Nat. Resources Bull. 16. 424 p.

Jones, Clyde H. 1941. Studies in Ohio floristics. I. Vegetation of Ohio bogs. American Midland Naturalist 26: 674-689.

King, Charles C., and Clara M. Frederick, Editors. 1974. Cedar Bog symposium. Ohio Biol. Surv. Info. Circ. No. 4. 71 p.

Caves

Poulson, Thomas L., and William B. White. 1969. The cave environment. Science 165:171-181

Verber, James L., and David H. Stansbery. 1953. Caves in the Lake Erie islands. Ohio J. Sci. 53:358-362.

White, George W. 1926. The limestone caves and caverns of Ohio. Ohio J. Sci. 26:73-116.

Chapter 10. *Hill Country*

Beatley, Janice C. 1959. The primeval forests of a periglacial area in the Allegheny Plateau (Vinton and Jackson counties, Ohio). Ohio Biol. Surv. New Series Bull. 1(1):1-182.

Hansen, Michael C. 1975. Field guide to the geology of the Hocking Hills State Park region. Div. Geol. Surv., Ohio Dept. Nat. Resources. Guidebook 4. 23 p.

Stout, Wilbur, and G.F. Lamb. 1938. Physiographic features of southeastern Ohio. Ohio J. Sci. 38:49-83. Reprinted in 1968 by Div. Geol. Surv., Ohio Dept. Nat. Resources.

Wolfe, John N. 1942. Species isolation and a proglacial lake [Lake Tight] in southern Ohio. Ohio J. Sci. 42:2-12.

Wolfe, John N., Richard T. Wareham, Herbert T. Schofield. 1949. Microclimates and macroclimates of Neotoma, a small valley in central Ohio. Ohio Biol. Surv. Bull. 41. 267 p.

Chapter 11. *Glaciated Plateau*

Banks, Philip O., and Rodney M. Feldmann, Editors. 1970. Guide to the geology of northeastern Ohio. Northern Ohio Geological Society (contact Earth Sciences Dept., Case Western Reserve Univ., Cleveland, Ohio). 168 p.

Coogan, Alan H., Rodney M. Feldmann, and Richard A. Heimlick. 1977. *Southern Great Lakes, Geology Field Guide Series.* Kendall Hunt Publ. Co., Dubuque, Iowa. 241 p.

Sampson, Homer C. 1930a. Succession in the swamp forest formation in northern Ohio. Ohio J. Sci. 30:340-356.

_____. 1930b. The mixed mesophytic community of northeastern Ohio. Ohio J. Sci. 30:358-367.

Chapter 12. *Till Plains*

Caster, Kenneth E., E.A. Dalve, and J.K. Pope. 1961. Elementary guide to the fossils and strata of the Ordovician in the vicinity of Cincinnati, Ohio. Cincinnati Museum of Natural History, Cincinnati. 47 p.

Forsyth, Jane L. 1965. Contribution of soils to the mapping and interpretation of Wisconsin tills in western Ohio. Ohio J. Sci. 65:220-227.

_____. 1970. A geologist looks at the natural vegetation map of Ohio. Ohio J. Sci. 70:180-191.

Chapter 13. *Lake Erie and the Islands*

Duncan, Thomas, and Ronald L. Stuckey. 1970. Changes in the vascular flora of seven small islands in western Lake Erie. The Michigan Botanist 9:175-200.

Herdendorf, Charles E., Suzanne M. Hartley, and L. James Charlesworth. 1974. Lake Erie bibliography in environmental sciences. Ohio Biol. Surv. New Series Bull. 4(5):1-116.

Langlois, Thomas H. 1954. *The Western End of Lake Erie and Its Ecology.* Edwards Brothers, Inc., Ann Arbor, Michigan. 479 p.

Stuckey, Ronald L. 1978. The decline of lake plants. Natural History Magazine 87(7):66-69.

Taft, Clarence E., and Celeste W. Taft. The algae of western Lake Erie. Ohio Biol. Surv. New Series Bull. 4(1):1-185.

Chapter 14. *Lake Plain*

Campbell, Lou. 1968. *Birds of the Toledo Area.* The Blade, Toledo. 330 p.

Easterly, N. William. 1979. Rare and infrequent plant species in the Oak Openings of northwestern Ohio. Ohio J. Sci. 79(2):51-58.

Kaatz, M.R. 1955. The Black Swamp: a study in historical geography. Annals Assoc. American Geogr. 45:1-35.

Mayfield, Harold. 1962. Changes in the natural history of the Toledo region since the coming of the white man. The Jack-Pine Warbler 40(2):36-56.

Niering, William A. 1966. *The Life of the Marsh.* McGraw-Hill, New York. 232 p.

Chapter 15. *The Bluegrass*

Braun, E. Lucy. 1928. The vegetation of the Mineral Springs region of Adams County, Ohio. Ohio Biol. Surv. Bull. 15:383-517.

Durrell, Richard H. 1967. Buzzardroost Rock, a nature preserve in Adams County. Cincinnati Museum of Natural History, Cincinnati. 10 p.

_____. 1972. Lynx Prairie — the E. Lucy Braun Preserve, Adams County, Ohio. Cincinnati Museum of Natural History, Cincinnati. 16 p.

Durrell, Richard H., and Lucile M. Durrell. 1975. The Wilderness, the Charles A. Eulett Preserve. Cincinnati Museum of Natural History, Cincinnati. 69 p.

Reidel, Stephen P. 1975. Bedrock geology of the Serpent Mound cryptoexplosion, structure, Adams, Highland, and Pike counties, Ohio. Div. Geol. Surv., Ohio Dept. Nat. Resources. Report of Invest. No. 95. Color map with text.

Chapter 16. *The First Ohioans*

Jennings, Jesse D., and Edward Norbeck, Editors. 1964. Prehistoric Man in the New World. Rice University, Houston, Texas. 633 p.

Potter, Martha A. 1968. Ohio's prehistoric peoples. Ohio Historical Society, 75 p.

Prufer, Olaf H., and Douglas H. McKenzie, Editors. 1967. *Studies in Ohio Archaeology.* Press of Western Reserve Univ., Cleveland. Revised edition of 1975, Kent State Univ. Press, Kent. 368 p.

Chapter 17. *Changing Land Use*
Forests, Farm Lands, Wildlife

Laub, Kenneth W. 1975. Wildlife conservation in Ohio: The role of hunting and trapping. Div. of Wildlife, Ohio Dept. Nat. Resources. Publ. 273. 81 p.

Sitterley, John H. 1976. Land use in Ohio, 1900-1970: How and why it has changed. Ohio Agric. and Res. and Devel. Center, Research Bull. 1084. Wooster. 92 p.

Water

Jenkins, Hal. 1976. *A Valley Renewed, the History of the Muskingum Watershed Conservancy District.* Kent State Univ. Press, Kent. 206 p.

Morgan, Arthur E. 1951. *The Miami Conservancy District.* McGraw-Hill, New York. 504 p.

The Ohio Soil and Water Conservation Needs Committee. 1971. Ohio soil and water conservation needs inventory. Available from Office of Information, Coop Extension Service, The Ohio State University, Columbus. 131 p.

United States Department of Agriculture. 1955. *Water, The Yearbook of Agriculture.* U.S. Government Printing Office, Washington, D.C. 751 p.

Hidden Wealth

Brant, Russell A., and Raymond E. Lamborn. 1960. Coal resources of Ohio. Div. of Geol. Surv., Ohio Dept. Nat. Resources Bull. 58. 245 p.

Division of Geological Survey. 1959. A century and a half of Ohio minerals. Ohio Dept. Nat. Resources Info. Circ. No. 24. 61 p.

The proceedings of two symposia in 1964 and 1975 relating to stripmining and reclamation have been published by the Ohio Journal of Science: 64(2) and 75(6).

Chapter 18. *The Naturalists*

Alexander, William H. 1941. The Ohio Academy of Science (mostly historical). Ohio J. Sci. 41:288-311.

Dexter, Ralph W. 1962. Conservation and the Ohio Academy of Science — an historical review. Ohio J. Sci. 62:274-280.

_____. 1976. Contributions of some Cincinnati-area physicians to the development of Ohio archaeology in the 19th century. Ohio State Medical Journal 73:409-411.

Hansen, Michael C., and Horace R. Collins. 1979. A brief history of the Ohio Geological Survey. Ohio J. Sci. 79:3-14.

Meisel, Max. 1924. *A Bibliography of American Natural History. Vol. I* and *Vol. II.* The Premier Publishing Co., Brooklyn, N.Y. 244p and 741p.

Stuckey, Ronald L. 1978. Medical botany in the Ohio Valley (1800-1850). Transactions and Studies of the College of Physicians of Philadelphia 45:262-279.

Chapter 19. *Preserving the Heritage*

Cahn, Robert. 1978. *Footprints on the Planet, A Search for an Environmental Ethic.* Universe Books, New York. 277 p.

Herrick, J. Arthur. 1974. The natural areas project, a summary of data to date. Ohio Biol. Surv. Info. Circ. No. 1. 60 p.

Leopold, Aldo. 1949. *A Sand County Almanac.* Oxford Univ. Press, New York. 226 p.

Schofield, Edmund A. 1978. *Earthcare: Global Protection of Natural Areas.* Westview Press, Boulder, Colorado. 838 p.

The Nature Conservancy. 1975. *The Preservation of Natural Diversity: A Survey and Recommendations.* Prepared for the U.S. Dept. Interior. Contract No. CX0001-5-0110. 314 p.

_____. 1977 and 1978. *Preserving Our Heritage. Vol. I, Federal Activities; Vol. II, State Activities.* Both volumes available from the Superintendent of Documents, U.S. Government Printing Office, Washington, D.C. Vol. 1, Stock No. 024-005-00681-8. 323 p.; Vol. II, Stock No. 024-005-00716-4. 671 p.

About the Authors

Robert L. Bates, Ph.D., a native of Brookings, South Dakota but a longtime Columbus resident, is a specialist in nonmetallic mineral deposits. Retired from the Department of Geology and Mineralogy at The Ohio State University, Dr. Bates is the author of the college textbook *Geology of the Industrial Rocks and Minerals* and co-author of *Geology: An Introduction.* He is a founder of the Forum on Geology of Industrial Minerals, past President of the National Association of Geology Teachers, and past Editor of *The Professional Geologist.* Since 1955, he has served as a columnist for *Geotimes,* and he also continues to do technical writing and editing.

James K. Bissell, M.S., a native of Ashtabula and now living in Geneva, is Staff Botanist and Natural Areas Coordinator for The Cleveland Museum of Natural History where he has been employed since 1971. An expert in the natural distributions of vascular plants in northeast Ohio, his additional areas of interest include local geology, glacial history, and local soil variations.

Roger W. Brucker, B.A., of Yellow Springs, is a nationally recognized authority on North American caves — especially the Flint Mammoth Cave System in Kentucky. A native of Shelby, Mr. Brucker is a director and past President of the Cave Research Foundation, and Honorary Life Fellow of the National Speleological Society. He is co-author of *The Longest Cave,* a book about Mammoth Cave, and co-author of *The Caves Beyond.* Mr. Brucker is President of Odiorne Industrial Advertising, Inc., but his additional interests for 25 years have carried him to cave exploration, writing, and photography.

Louis W. Campbell, a Toledo native and resident, is a retired outdoor writer for the Toledo *Times.* Although he has a wealth of knowledge about natural history, he is particularly interested in birds. One of his two books is *Birds of the Toledo Area.* Lou Campbell has been in charge of the Toledo-area Audubon Christmas bird count since 1924, and the leader of the annual spring bird census on Catawba Island and the Marblehead Peninsula since 1930. He also was one of the early promoters of the successful effort to protect part of the Oak Openings as public park land. He is past President of the Toledo Naturalists' Association and is the recipient of both an Ohio Conservation Achievement Award from the Ohio Department of Natural Resources, and a Wildlife Conservation Award from the department's Division of Wildlife.

Guy L. Denny, B.A., is a foremost authority on the formation and life of Ohio bogs. A native of Toledo, Mr. Denny is Assistant Chief of the Division of Natural Areas and Preserves of the Ohio Department of Natural Resources. Much of his 15 years of professional experience concerns interpreting nature to the lay citizen. He organized the first Ohio Department of Natural Resources program to interpret the natural world to inner city youths and several programs designed to interpret the outdoors to teenagers. He is the author of several booklets on Ohio natural history, including *Ohio's Reptiles, Ohio's Trees,* and *Ohio's Amphibians,* and he also developed the first ODNR self-guiding nature trail. Mr. Denny's other interests include camping, hiking, nature photography, and canoeing.

Ralph W. Dexter, Ph.D., is a biologist and ornithologist, and a native of Gloucester, Massachusetts. His special interests include ecology and the history of biology. Dr. Dexter is especially well-known for bird-banding studies and his research on the chimney swift. A Kent resident and member of the biology faculty at Kent State University for over 40 years, Dr. Dexter has been honored as an Outstanding Faculty Member and is a recipient of the university's President's Medal. He has served as President, Vice-president for Zoology, Secretary, and Historian of The Ohio Academy of Science. Also he is a former President of the American Malacological Union, and Vice-president of the Inland Bird Banding Association.

Lucile M. Durrell, M.A., and **Richard H. Durrell, D.Sc.,** of Cincinnati are both graduates in geology from the University of Cincinnati where Richard is Professor of geology. Both are avid outdoors people and world travelers. Active in state and national conservation efforts for many years, the Durrells have donated much time and energy to The Nature Conservancy and to various state and regional conservation organizations. Their major interest is land preservation, and they have contributed significant amounts of land to the Cincinnati Museum of Natural History's preservation activities in Adams County.

Lynn Edward Elfner, M.S., is the Executive Officer of The Ohio Academy of Science and a specialist in plant ecology. A native of Jamestown, he now resides in Delaware. He began his professional career in 1967 as a science teacher in the Mt. Orab Local School District in Brown County. Mr. Elfner has conducted studies of the Bluegrass region, and his additional areas of interest encompass photography, geology, and the history of science.

Jane L. Forsyth, Ph.D., is an expert in Pleistocene geology — glacial deposits and the history of the ice ages. A native of Hanover, New Hampshire, Dr. Forsyth is Professor of Geology at Bowling Green State University, and is interested in environmental geology and the relation of geological formations and history to the distribution of plants and animals. In addition to her research, Dr. Forsyth is a popular interpreter of geology and the environment to lay audiences in meetings, workshops, and classrooms throughout the state. A former Editor of *The Ohio Journal of Science,* Dr. Forsyth is a member of the Ohio Natural Areas Council and the Editorial Committee of the Ohio Biological Survey.

Glenn W. Frank, M.S., is a respected geologist, teacher, and civic leader. A native of Mayfield Heights and now residing at Kent, Mr. Frank is Professor of Geology at Kent State University where for 25 years he has specialized in the general and regional geology of northeastern Ohio. Selected for a Kent State Alumni Distinguished Teaching Award, he was also chosen as one of 30 faculty in the United States to write a unit in the book, *Excellence in University Teaching.* In addition to geology, Mr. Frank is knowledgeable about collections of stamps, coins, and paper money.

Sherman L. Frost, M.S., a native of West Haven, Connecticut, but a longtime resident of Columbus, is widely recognized as an authority on water management. His areas of specialization for 45 years of professional service include forestry and water resources. Presently a member of the Ohio Environmental Board of Review, Mr. Frost has also taught in the School of Natural Resources at The Ohio State University and has been a member of the Ohio Water Commission. Every Director of the Ohio Department of Natural Resources has requested assistance from Mr. Frost regarding water management problems in Ohio.

Richard D. Goddard, B.F.A., is a former Air Force meteorologist who is now Chief Meteorologist for WJKW-TV in Cleveland. With 27 years of experience, Mr. Goddard has worked at the U.S. Air Force Severe Storm Center and with U.S. Navy Hurricane Hunters. In 1963, he flew into the eye of hurricane Flora. A resident of Lakewood, this popular northeast Ohio meteorologist intersperses many of his forecasts with weather folklore and anecdotes. Mr. Goddard's other interests include sports and he serves as football statistician for the Cleveland Browns professional football club.

Richard P. Goldthwait, Ph.D., is an internationally respected authority on glacial geology. Originally from Hanover, New Hampshire, and with more than 43 years of experience, Dr. Goldthwait has studied the characteristics and movements of glaciers in Alaska, Antarctica, Greenland, New Hampshire, and Ohio. The author of more than 70 scientific articles and the editor of three books, he established the Institute of Polar Studies at The Ohio State University. After 31 years in Ohio, he is presently retired from the OSU Department of Geology and Mineralogy, and now resides in Florida.

Ernest E. Good, Ph.D., is a wildlife manager and ecologist. A native of Van Wert, Dr. Good worked for the Soil Conservation Service of the U.S. Department of Agriculture before coming to Columbus and The Ohio State University in 1948. A respected teacher and researcher, Dr. Good has been concerned with natural resources and has been teaching courses in their management for more than 30 years. He has been much involved with the Barnebey Center, the university's biological reserve in the Hocking Hills near Lancaster.

About the Authors

Charles E. Herdendorf, Ph.D., a native of Sheffield Lake, is Director of the Center for Lake Erie Area Research at The Ohio State University where he is also Professor of Geology and Zoology. In addition to these duties he is Director of Franz Theodore Stone Laboratory, OSU's biological field station on Lake Erie at Put-in-Bay, and the newly formed Ohio Sea Grant Program. Dr. Herdendorf with over 17 years of professional experience has conducted research on the physical limnology and aquatic ecology of the Great Lakes with particular interest in shore processes, sedimentation, water quality eutrophication, wetlands development, and fishery resources.

Nicholas Holowaychuk, Ph.D., is an authority on soil classification, development, and conservation. A native of Alberta, Canada, he has spent most of his 50 years of professional service in Ohio working with Ohio soils. He has also conducted soil research in Alberta, 17 states in the Central and Great Plains, Zaire, and Alaska. Dr. Holowaychuk was instrumental in developing the detailed county soil surveys currently being conducted in Ohio. He has recently retired from the Agronomy Department of The Ohio State University and has returned to his native Edmonton where he is once more conducting soil studies for the Research Council of Alberta.

Edward F. Hutchins, B.Sc., is the Director-Secretary of the Columbus and Franklin County Metropolitan Park District, a system of active-use, natural area parks. There his expertise in the history of conservation in Ohio is applied to the restoration and preservation of pre-settler ecosystems and forest associations, in part through the use of controlled ecological succession. A native of Columbus and currently a resident of Dublin, he is a former environmental and outdoor writer for the Columbus *Dispatch*. Mr. Hutchins is an active hunter, fisherman, and photographer.

Charles C. King, Ph.D., is the Executive Director and Editor of the Ohio Biological Survey. He is a native of Kittanning, Pennsylvania, but moved to Ohio in 1950 for his higher education at Marietta College and The Ohio State University. His graduate research dealt with insects and was conducted at the Ohio Agricultural Research and Development Center in Wooster. While teaching biology for 11 years at Malone College in Canton, Dr. King became involved in helping develop The Wilderness Center near Wilmot. He is interested in natural history and the communication to lay citizens of basic ecological concepts.

Michael B. Lafferty, M.A., is a free lance writer and editor specializing in environmental and agricultural topics. A native of Dayton, Mr. Lafferty is a former Public Information Officer with the Ohio Department of Natural Resources, and the former Managing Editor of *Buckeye Farm News* magazine. His other interests include hiking, camping, and sailing.

Kenneth W. Laub, M.Sc., a native of Detroit, Michigan, brings 17 years professional experience to his position as Technical Editor with the Division of Wildlife of the Ohio Department of Natural Resources. He now resides at Westerville.

Ruth W. Melvin, B.A., of Carroll, a consultant and lecturer, has had a long and stimulating career in outdoor education. Her specialty is geology, but Mrs. Melvin is also the author of two books on environmental education: *A Guide to Outdoor Education Areas* and *Ohio Environmental Education Areas*. Each of these volumes provides biological, geological, historical, cultural, and economic information concerning several hundred outdoor and environmental education sites in the state. Mrs. Melvin has taught geology at National Audubon Society summer camps and has lectured in geology and geography at Capital University in Columbus. She and her husband were inducted into the Ohio Conservation Hall of Fame in 1975.

Richard E. Moseley, Jr., B.S., from Columbus, is a naturalist and nature photographer. Instrumental in the formation of Ohio's system of state nature preserves and scenic rivers, Mr. Moseley is now Chief of the Division of Natural Areas and Preserves of the Ohio Department of Natural Resources. A former Chief Naturalist for the department's Division of Parks and Recreation, he has been active in the Association of Interpretive Naturalists and now chairs the Ohio Historic Site Preservation Advisory Board.

Martha Potter Otto, M.A., is a specialist in the archaeology of the Ohio Valley. A native and resident of Columbus, Mrs. Otto is now Head of the Department of Archaeology at the Ohio Historical Society where she has been employed since 1960. She has been involved in excavating a number of Adena and Hopewell Indian sites and is the author of *Ohio's Prehistoric Peoples,* a book on prehistoric Indians of the region and directed toward the lay reader.

Ralph E. Ramey, M.S., is Director of Glen Helen, Antioch College's 1000-acre nature preserve near Yellow Springs in Greene County. The preservation of the natural world is of great concern to Mr. Ramey, a native of Columbus, who is a specialist in natural area management and environmental education and interpretation. He was very instrumental in the development and passage of the Ohio Natural Areas Act in 1970. He formerly chaired the Ohio Chapter of The Nature Conservancy, and currently serves on the Ohio Natural Areas Council. Mr. Ramey is the recipient of the Green Leaf Award from The Nature Conservancy, the Conservation Achievement Award from the Ohio Department of Natural Resources and the Outstanding Achievement Award from the Ohio Chapter of The Nature Conservancy.

David H. Stansbery, Ph.D., a native of Upper Sandusky, is Director of the Museum of Zoology of The Ohio State University. A nationally-known expert on fresh water mollusks, Dr. Stansbery specializes in the zoogeography, ecology, evolution, and systematics of these animals and the effects of impoundments, dredging, and channelization on the bottom-dwelling fauna of rivers. A long-time educator, he began his career as a mathematics and science teacher at Plymouth in 1950 before moving to Columbus and The Ohio State University where he has taught and conducted research since 1955.

Ronald L. Stuckey, Ph.D., is the recognized authority on the flora of the Lake Erie islands and shore. A native of Bucyrus, Dr. Stuckey is expert in all phases of Ohio flora and of the introduction of non-native aquatic and wetland species into the United States. The author of more than 50 scientific articles over 20 years, he is co-author of *Index to Plant Distribution Maps in North American Periodicals through 1972*. A Columbus resident and Professor of Botany at The Ohio State University, Dr. Stuckey is also a biographer of early botanists and naturalists.

K. Roger Troutman, B.S, is a native of Wayne County and now resides near Mansfield. He is an interpretive naturalist and one of Ohio's foremost authorities on prairies. Mr. Troutman chairs the Ohio Biological Survey's Prairie Survey Project, a committee of nearly a hundred persons interested in finding, inventorying, and preserving Ohio's prairies. His other special interests include nature photography, bird banding, computer applications in the natural sciences, propagation of native plants (especially milkweeds), and the biogeography of Ohio's plant and animal communities.

Illustration Credits

Key

RA	Ron Austing
DB	DeVere Burt
CMNH	Cleveland Museum of Natural History
LE	Lynn Edward Elfner
JG	James Glover
CK	Charles C. King
HO	Howard Oberlin
ODNR	The Ohio Department of Natural Resources
OHS	Ohio Historical Society
OSUP	The Ohio State University Press
AS	Alvin E. Staffan
RT	Robert Tanner

(Credits are separated from top to bottom by a colon and from left to right by a semicolon)

Chapter 1 *The Ohio Country:* 4. Donald Hutslar 6. Columbus Public Library 7. RT: ODNR (Herb Hott) 8. Oliver D. Diller: Geauga County Historical Society 9. ODNR 10. DB 11. JG: DB: Anon. 12. RT: ODNR (Herb Hott) 14. Currier and Ives: Anon. 15. OSUP.

Chapter 2 *Written in the Rocks:* 16. HO 19. ODNR 20. RT 21. Cincinnati Museum of Natural History 22. RT: Anna Bory: RT: William Butcher 23. ODNR (Michael Hansen): RT 24. ODNR (Michael Hansen) 25. CMNH: ODNR (Michael Hansen) 26. CMNH: LE 27. ODNR 28. RT 30. ODNR (Michael Hansen).

Chapter 3 *Ice Over Ohio:* 32. OHS 35. ODNR 36. Jane L. Forsyth: Richard P. Goldthwait 38. CMNH 39. DB 40. both ODNR 41. LE 42. ODNR (Michael Hansen) 43. ODNR (Michael Hansen) 44. ODNR (Herb Hott) 45. LE 46. LE.

Chapter 4 *Today's Landscape:* 48. U.S. Geological Survey 50. RT 51. RT: Louis W. Campbell 52. RT 53. RT 54. LE 55. RT 56. ODNR 57. ODNR.

Chapter 5 *Climate and Weather:* 58. Jay Carter, III 60. RT 61. Ohio National Guard: Jay Carter, III 62. RT 63. LE: RT 64. LE 66. RT 67: RT 68: OSU Marching Band 69. RT.

Chapter 6 *Cradle of Life:* 70. LE 72. ODNR 73. ODNR 74. ODNR 75. RT 76. RT 77. RT 78. Anon.: CK 79. Malcom Emmons.

Chapter 7 *Ohio Forests:* 80. Oliver D. Diller 81. E.E. Good 82. OSUP 83. OSUP 84. ODNR (AS): JG: AS 85. ODNR (AS) 86. RA 87. OSUP: HO 88. ODNR 90. ODNR 91. ODNR (AS) 92. ODNR (AS): HO 93. ODNR (AS): HO: E.E. GOOD 94. Alfred C. Robinson: E.E. Good 95. JG: ODNR (AS): ODNR (AS) 96. JG: E. Lucy Braun 97. ODNR (AS) 98. JG: ODNR (AS): JG: ODNR (AS) 99. DB: DB: RA 100. all ODNR 101. Karl Maslowski 102. ODNR (AS) 103. C. Wayne Ellett: CK: CK: ODNR (AS) 104. ODNR (AS): E.E. Good: ODNR (AS) 105. ODNR (AS) 106. ODNR (AS) 107. DB 108. HO 109. ODNR (AS).

Chapter 8 *Ohio Water:* 110. LE 113. LE: JG 114. JG 115. OSU Museum of Zoology 116. JG: JG: Clarence Taft 117. Ohio Biological Survey: JG: ODNR (AS); ODNR (AS) 118. LE 119. OSUP: ODNR (AS): JG: ODNR (AS) 120. ODNR (AS) 121. ODNR 122. RT 123. JG; JG: ODNR (Richard E. Moseley, Jr.): JG 124. JG: OSUP 125. ODNR 126. ODNR (AS): JG 127. JG 128. CK 130. ODNR (AS).

Chapter 9 *Relicts of the Past:* 132. CMNH 134. ODNR (AS): OSUP 135. LE: ODNR (AS) 136. E.E. Good: OSUP 137. E.E. Good 138. K. Roger Troutman: ODNR (AS) 139. K. Roger Troutman: ODNR (AS) 140. ODNR (AS) 141. RT 142. ODNR (AS) 143. ODNR (AS) 144. HO 145. CK; OSUP: OSUP 146. OSUP: E.E. Good 147. ODNR (AS) 149. ODNR (Guy L. Denny) 150. ODNR (AS) 151. RT 152. JG 153. Roger W. Brucker 154. Roger W. Brucker 155. Kim Wells 156. Roger W. Brucker.

Chapter 10 *Hill Country:* 160. ODNR (AS) 161. ODNR (AS) 162. RT 163. CK 164. Kenneth Gerber 165. ODNR (AS) 166. OSUP: ODNR (AS) 167. CK: ODNR (AS): JG 168. ODNR (AS); CK: Kenneth Gerber: CK 169. ODNR (AS): DB: ODNR (AS) 170. ODNR (AS): ODNR (AS): JG 171. ODNR (AS): RT 172. LE; ODNR (AS): Edward F. Hutchins: HO 173. HO: ODNR (AS): E.E. Good; ODNR (AS) 174. Roger Burnard: Anon. 175. OSUP: RA 176. OSUP 177. DB: ODNR (AS): OSUP 178. Milton B. Trautman: David H. Stansbery 179. RA 180. CK: OSUP: JG 181. Virginia Rice: JG.

Chapter 11 *Glaciated Plateau:* 182. ODNR (AS) 184. RT 187. Anon. 188. Charles Dambach: Anon. 189. ODNR (AS): C. Wayne Ellett 190. Anon: C. Wayne Ellett 191. HO: ODnr C. Wayne Ellett 190. Anon: C. Wayne Ellett 191. HO: ODNR (AS): E.E. Good 192. E.E. Good: HO 193. CK 194. ODNR (AS) 195. ODNR (AS) 196. ODNR (AS): RA 197. ODNR (AS): JG.

Chapter 12 *Till Plains:* 198. LE 200. RT 201. William T. Butcher 203. Richard P. Goldthwait: Alfred C. Robinson: RT 204. RT 206. ODNR (AS) 207. LE: K. Roger Troutman 208. ODNR (AS) 209. ODNR (AS): JG: RA 210. ODNR (AS): Milton B. Trautman: ODNR (AS): ODNR (AS): JG 211. JG: ODNR (AS): ODNR (AS); ODNR (AS) 212. RA 213. ODNR (AS): DB.

Chapter 13 *Lake Erie and the Islands:* 214. Thomas H. Langlois 216. RT 217. RT 219. U.S. Geological Survey 220. Thomas H. Langlois 222. Thomas H. Langlois 223. John A. Blakeman: ODNR 224. JG 225. LE 226. OSUP 227. OSUP: OSUP: N. Wilson Britt 228. ODNR (AS) 229. JG 230. ODNR (AS) 232. LE: OSUP: OSUP 233. JG 234. Malcom Emmons 235. LE.

Chapter 14 *Lake Plain:* 236. HO 238. RT: Ralph E. Ramey 239. RA 240. ODNR (AS) 242. N. William Easterly 243. ODNR (AS) 244. RA 246. ODNR (Richard E. Moseley, Jr.): ODNR (AS) 247. JG: ODNR (AS): JG 248. ODNR (AS): JG: ODNR (AS); ODNR (AS) 249. Karl Maslowski: CMNH 250. ODNR (AS) 251. ODNR (AS): JG.

Chapter 15 *Bluegrass:* 252. Ralph E. Ramey 254. RT: DB 255. LE: DB 256. DB: Richard H. Durrell 257. Marvin Roberts: OSUP: Ralph E. Ramey 258. LE: OSUP 259. OSUP: LE: OSUP.

Chapter 16 *First Ohioans:* 262. OHS 264. OHS 265. ODNR 266. OHS 267. OHS 268. OHS 269. OHS 271. RT.

Chapter 17 *Changing Land Use:* 272. ODNR 275. Oliver D. Diller: ODNR 276. Kenneth Gerber 279. ODNR (AS) 280. LE 281. OSUP: Roscoe Village Foundation 282. *Columbus Dispatch* 283. ODNR (AS) 284. LE: Anon. 286. ODNR: Malcom Emmons 287. ODNR (JG): LE 288. O.E. Diller 289. ODNR: ODNR (Art Woldorf) 290. Ohio Power Co.: ODNR 291. Marathon Oil Co.: ODNR 292. Anon.

Chapter 18 *The Naturalists:* 294. CMNH 295. OHS 296. OHS 297. Ronald L. Stuckey: LE; LE: Anna Bory 298. Anna Bory: Anna Bory: Ronald L. Stuckey 299. Anna Bory: OHS: Ronald L. Stuckey: Ronald L. Stuckey 300. LE: The Ohio Academy of Science: The Ohio Academy of Science 301. OHS: Ronald L. Stuckey: The Ohio Academy of Science; Ronald L. Stuckey 302. Ronald L. Stuckey: Ralph E. Ramey: Harold E. Burt 303. Elizabeth Brockslager; OHS: LE.

Chapter 19 *Preserving the Heritage:* 304. CMNH 306. William E. Styer 307. Steve Maslowski 309. K. Roger Troutman 310. ODNR (Richard E. Moseley, Jr.) 311. ODNR (AS) 312. K.W. Pratt 313. ODNR (Richard E. Moseley, Jr.): ODNR (AS).

Index

Aberdeen — 22
Abner Hollow — 257
Acadian flycatcher — 95, 244
Adams County — 23, 50, 52, 53, 136, 151, 157, 163, 164, 169, 174, 178, 210, 253, 256, 259, 297, 307, 308
Adena Indians — 266, 267, 268, 269
Adena State Memorial — 26
African mountain sheep — 231
agave — 257
Age of Fishes — 24
agrimony — 106
Akron — 37, 41, 164, 185, 186, 190, 191
Akron Metropolitan Park District — 28, 190
Alaska — 37, 40, 66, 263
Alberta — 67, 134
Alberta Clipper — 67
alder — 145, 149, 177, 179
alder buckthorn — 149
alewife — 226
Alexandria soils — 205
alfalfa — 279
algae — 112, 114, 117, 119, 122, 172, 180, 221
Allegheny Escarpment — 50, 55, 162
Allegheny mountain dusky — 197
Allegheny Mountains — 5, 263, 291, 295, 296
Allegheny Plateau — 164, 167, 169, 174, 183, 187, 189, 190, 193
Altonian Stage — 36
alumroot — 233
Amanita — 103
Ambystoma — 229
American Association for the Advancement of Science — 298
American bald eagle — 211, 229, 249, 299, 301, 304
American bittern — 231
American columbo — 209
American lobster — 301
American lotus — 232, 250
American redstart — 174
American Society of Geologists and Naturalists — 298
American yew — 233
Amesville — 277
Amherst — 27
Amish — 187
amphipods — 155, 225
Anabaena algae — 224
Anderson's Ferry — 202
anemonella — 255
anemones — 172, 192
Anna — 202
annelid worms — 113, 117
ant(s) — 138, 143
Antarctica — 34, 40, 47
Antioch College — 308
Appalachian Escarpment — 50, 52, 162
Appalachian foothills — 186
Appalachian Highlands — 162
Appalachian Mountains — 22, 81, 165, 187, 193, 301
Appalachian Plateau — 54, 55, 78, 161, 186, 254, 255, 256
Appalachian Plateaus Province — 49, 50, 52, 255
appendaged waterleaf — 234
apple (trees) — 161, 174
arbor vitae — 149, 259
Archaic Indians — 264, 265, 266, 268
Archbold — 239
Arctic — 33, 47, 100, 145
Arkona — 42
arrow-arum — 145
arrowhead — 122, 145, 232, 250
arrow-wood — 145
ash — 8, 9, 81, 82, 89, 146, 233, 238
Ash Cave — 28
Ashland County — 164, 168, 169, 284
Ashtabula County — 66, 177, 183, 184, 192, 196, 223, 285
Asia — 149, 263, 279
aspen — 102, 177, 196, 242, 251
asters — 89, 97, 106, 209, 242, 243, 257
Athens — 267
Athens County — 178, 277
Atlantic Coast — 22, 29, 176, 266, 269
Atlantic Coastal Plain — 165
Atlantic flyway — 247
Atlantic Ocean — 65, 163
Atwater, Caleb — 296, 303
Atwood Lake — 168
Audubon, John James — 296, 308

Auglaize County — 51
Auglaize River — 238, 276
Aullwood Audubon Center — 308
Austrian pine — 168
Avonburg soil — 76
backswimmer — 117
bacteria — 31, 71, 102, 114, 119
badger — 139, 245
Baffin Island — 36
Bainbridge — 157, 204, 205
Baker Fork — 55
Baltimore — 62
Bancroft Street — 241
baneberry — 172
Bangia — 233
Barberton — 23, 24, 185
barred owl — 174, 239, 244
barrens chickweed — 233
barn swallow — 211
Bartley, Floyd — 166, 302
Bass Island Dolomite — 154
Bass Islands — 154, 224
basswood — 73, 208, 234, 238, 243, 259
bats — 100, 152, 157, 169, 173, 194, 255
Battle of Fallen Timbers — 274, 276
Battle of Lake Erie — 153
beach grass — 233
beach pea — 233
beans — 270
bear(s), black — 10-13, 103, 161, 169, 193, 213, 224, 240, 256, 265, 266, 269, 277, 287
beard tongue — 233
beaver — 177, 188, 196, 197, 213, 274, 278
Bedford Shale — 26, 27
bedstraw — 106, 242
beech, American — 8, 9, 38, 77, 81, 82, 103, 106, 108, 171, 174, 176, 177, 187-193, 206-208, 238, 269, 306
beef cattle — 277
"beef heart" fossil — 22
bees — 226
beetles — 99, 138, 152, 226, 299
beggar's-lice — 106
beggar's ticks — 167
Bellbrook — 123
Belle Isle Park, Detroit — 251
Bellefontaine — 18, 23, 31, 66, 155, 203, 209, 291
Bellefontaine Outlier — 51, 201, 202, 203
Bellepoint — 259
Bellevue — 155
bellwort — 93
Belmont County — 8, 166, 177, 271, 289, 308
belted kingfisher — 177
benthos — 225
Berea — 27, 28
Berea Sandstone — 26, 27, 28, 185, 291
Bewick's wren — 244
big bluestem — 134, 135, 136, 149, 178, 207, 242, 257, 258
big brown bat — 194, 255
Big Darby Creek — 115, 210
Bigelow Cemetery State Nature Preserve — 135
bigleaf magnolia — 173
birch — 103, 196, 238
Birch, Hugh Taylor — 308
bison — 139, 161, 169, 178, 213, 237, 240, 287
bitterns — 247
bitternut — 171, 176
bittersweet — 233
bituminous coal — 31
black and white warbler — 95
black ash — 207
black bass — 15
black currants — 265
black ducks — 247
Black Hand Gorge — 28, 281
Black Hand Gorge State Nature Preserve — 168, 310
Black Hand Sandstone — 28, 163, 178, 291, 306, 310
black huckleberry — 145
black locust — 180
black maple — 207
black oak — 81, 102, 166, 167, 238, 242
black racer — 170
black rat snake — 170, 173
Black River — 44
black snake(s) — 196
black snakeroot — 106
black squirrels — 231

black tern — 231, 247, 248
black vultures — 169, 170
black walnut — 8, 171, 170, 207, 274, 275
black widow spider — 98
black widow — 175
blackberry — 89, 242, 265
blackbirds — 248
black-crowned night heron — 229, 248
blackgum — 82, 83, 100, 102, 145, 167, 274
bladdernut — 233, 234
Blanding's turtle — 245, 250
blazing star — 139, 178, 257, 258
blazing star, dense — 136
blazing star, spiked — 149
Blizzard of '78 — 69
bloodroot — 93, 172, 192, 208, 259
Bloody Run Swamp — 13
Blossom Music Center — 190
Blount soils — 76, 204, 205
blue ash — 82, 208, 234, 257
blue catfish — 15
blue goose — 251
Blue Hole — 57, 154
blue jay — 103
blue phlox — 172
blue pike — 127, 226, 227
blue racer — 210, 229, 245
blueberries — 167, 189, 265
bluebird, eastern — 195, 211
Bluebird Stoneware — 292
bluegills — 281
bluegrass — 136
Bluegrass Region — 50, 52, 78, 253, 254, 255, 256, 257, 258, 259
blue-gray gnatcatcher — 100, 152, 174, 244
blue-green algae — 221, 224
bluejoint grass — 135, 136, 207, 232, 242, 247
bluets — 167
blue-winged warbler — 244, 245
bobcat — 169, 213, 240
bobolinks — 141, 211
bobwhite quail — 14
bog buckbean — 142
bog laurel — 145
bog lemming — 150
bog rosemary — 145
Bonaparte's gulls — 248
Bono — 239
Boone, Daniel — 274
Bourne, Alexander — 6
Bowling Green — 238
Bowling Green Normal College — 301
Bowling Green State University — 301
box elder — 176, 243
box turtles — 103, 173, 245
brachiopods — 21, 24, 26, 28, 199, 201
bracken fern — 242
Brailey — 241
Brassfield Limestone — 205
Bratton soil — 78
Braun, Annette — 257, 303
Braun, E. Lucy — 171, 255, 257, 258, 303
breccia — 217
Brewster's warbler — 244
Bricker, Gov. John W. — 307
brick making, brick industry — 27, 31
British — 5
British soldier lichen — 100
broad-winged hawk — 86, 95, 244
brook trout — 209
broomsedge — 89, 168
brown creeper — 107
Brown County — 253
brown rats — 240
Brown, Samuel R. — 10
brown thrashers — 89, 91
Brown's Lake Bog — 55, 308
Brownstone — 10
bryozoans — 21, 26, 201
Bucher, W.H. — 256
Buchtel — 178
buckeye — 176
Buckeye Lake — 13, 42, 127, 281
Bucyrus — 37, 233
buffalo — 10, 178
Buffalo Beats — 178
Buffalo, N.Y. — 42, 218
buffalofish — 15
bulbet fern — 259
bullfrog — 100, 245, 250
bulrushes — 224
bumblebees — 138
bunchflower — 148

bur marigold — 250
bur oak — 82, 191, 198, 207, 238, 257
bur reed — 232
Burton — 187, 188
Butler County — 34, 36, 306
Butler's garter snake — 210
butterfly shell — 178
butterfly weed — 136, 242, 257
butternut — 82, 176
buttonbush — 179, 233, 242
Buzzardroost Rock — 253, 254, 255, 258, 308
Buzzardroost Rock Nature Preserve 136
cabbages — 75
caddisfly — 225, 226
Caesar Creek — 123
California — 60
calopogon orchid — 142, 143, 148
Cambrian — 20, 21
Cambridge — 64, 69
Campbell Hill — 203
Campus Martius — 292
Canada, Canadian — 5, 6, 33, 34, 36, 38, 40, 44, 47, 59, 66, 67, 141, 186, 205, 215, 216, 218, 229, 239, 247, 259, 301
Canada Goose Management Investigations — 248
Canada geese — 10, 211, 224, 247, 248, 265
Canada mayflower — 146, 149
Canada warbler — 244
Canada yew — 173
Canadian Klondike — 66
Canadian milk vetch — 233
Canadian Shield — 20, 36, 286
Canadian Soldiers — 226
Canadice soil — 77
Canal Fulton — 281
Canby's mountain lover — 259
Canfield soil — 77
Canton — 64, 186
Canton Garden Center — 308
Cantwell Cliffs — 28
canvasbacks — 247
cardinal flower — 306
cardinals — 88, 89, 95, 101
Cardington — 285
Carey — 155
caribou — 38, 100, 264
Carillon Park — 282
Carnegie Museum — 299
Carolina chickadee — 174
Carolina coast — 67
Carolina parakeet — 12, 14
Carolina spring beauty — 190
carp — 124, 221, 224-227, 232
Carroll County — 53, 179
Castle Piatt Mac-A-Cheek — 47
catamount — 10
Catawba grapes — 234
Catawba Island — 231, 250
catbirds — 150, 211
catenas — 206
catfish — 15, 123, 281
cattails — 117, 122, 126, 145, 179, 224, 232, 238, 245-247, 250
cattle — 161, 280, 290
cave fishes — 152
cave pearls — 155
Cave Run — 157
cave salamander — 210
cecropia moth — 100, 174
cedar — 136
Cedar Bog — 147, 149, 259, 306
Cedar Bog State Memorial — 206, 207
Cedar Falls — 258, 259
Cedar Island — 250
Cedar Mills — 257
Cedar Point — 217, 250
Cedarville Dolomite — 57, 157
celandine — 93
celery — 79
Celeryville Bog — 42
celestite crystals — 151, 153
Celina — 37, 41, 201
Celina Grand River — 281
cement — 25
Cenozoic Era — 20, 31
Centerville — 63, 166
centipedes — 174
Central Lowland Province — 49
central stoneroller minnow — 119
century plant — 257
cephalopods — 28, 199
cerulean warbler — 174, 239, 245

Chagrin Falls — 184
Chagrin Shale — 25, 184
chambered nautiloids — 21
Champaign County — 45, 47, 147, 152, 157, 207, 306
channel catfish — 124, 226, 227
chara — 148
charcoal — 161, 257, 275, 288
Chardon — 69
Charm — 165
chert — 18, 24
Chesapeake Bay — 268
chestnut — 10, 81, 166, 167, 264, 269
chestnut blight — 167
chestnut oak — 81, 82, 108, 167, 275
chestnut-sided warbler — 245
chickadees —96, 104, 107
chickens — 194
chicory — 209
Chili soil — 77
Chillicothe — 7, 34, 41, 51, 54, 55, 267, 269
chimney swift — 211
chinquapin oak — 82, 103, 208, 257
chipmunks — 87, 89, 99, 100, 104, 107, 172, 213, 245
chokeberry — 145, 233, 242
chokecherry — 234
chorus frog — 92, 245
Christmas fern — 189
chub — 122, 209
Chuckery — 135
cicadas — 98
Cincinnati — 18, 21, 36, 42, 51, 55, 61, 62, 65, 66, 122, 124, 171, 176, 202, 205, 223, 285, 292, 296, 299, 300
Cincinnati Arch —18, 21, 31, 201, 254
Cincinnati College — 296
Cincinnati Historical Society — 303
Cincinnati Nature Center — 308
Cincinnati Reds — 62
Cincinnati Society of Natural History — 296
Cincinnati soils — 204, 205
Cincinnati, University of — 303
Cincinnati Zoological Gardens — 13
Cincinnatian — 200, 201
cinnamon fern — 145, 146
Circleville — 115, 296
cisco — 127, 226
Civil War — 181
Cladocerans — 224
Cladophora algae — 116, 233
clams — 21, 24, 28, 29, 199, 224, 225, 265, 271
Claridon Prairie — 136
Clark County — 47, 122, 147, 207, 285
clay — 18, 20, 29-31, 42, 43, 72, 75-77, 180, 185, 186, 235, 268, 292, 293, 297, 298
Clay Township — 181
Claypole, Edward — 299
Clear Creek — 165
Clear Fork — 113
Clendening Reservoir —168
Clermont County — 123, 207, 308
Clermont soil — 76
Cleveland — 11, 23, 25, 34, 50, 60, 64-66, 69, 185, 187, 190, 221, 224, 238, 271, 273, 288
Cleveland Academy of Natural Sciences — 298
Cleveland Indians — 62
Cleveland Metropolitan Park District — 26, 27, 190
Cleveland Museum of Natural History — 38, 298, 306, 308
Cleveland Shale — 25
Clifton — 47, 51, 122, 123
Clifton Gorge — 46, 203, 259, 308
Clifton Mill — 282
Clinton County — 36, 63, 205, 208
Clinton Sand — 22
Clinton Sandstone — 185
clover — 287
clubmosses — 171, 189
coal — 17, 18, 29, 30, 31, 114, 115, 161, 162, 180, 183, 185, 287-290, 293, 297-299
Coal Measures — 29, 31
Coastal Zone Management Act—286
cob shell — 178
Cold Creek — 154
Colton — 241
coltsfoot — 181
Columbia University School of Mines, Department of Geology and Paleontology — 298
Columbiana County — 53, 162, 164, 168, 185, 196, 276, 291, 313
columbine — 188
Columbus — 13, 14, 17, 24, 26, 34, 37, 43, 55, 62, 65, 115, 116, 157, 173, 201, 202, 210, 223, 281, 282, 291, 300, 306, 308, 311
Columbus High School — 301
Columbus Limestone — 24, 25, 57, 155, 201
Columbus Zoo — 128
common bullhead — 178
common gallinule —231
common shiner — 119
common tern — 229, 248
compass plant — 178
concrete — 25, 46
concretions — 25, 26
conglomerate — 17, 18, 183, 185
coneflower — 243, 257
Congress — 7
Conkles Hollow — 163
Connecticut — 297
Continental climate — 59
coontail — 232, 233
Cooper's hawk — 95, 244
coots — 247
copepod — 224
copper — 266, 269
Copperas Cliffs — 54
copperhead — 170, 210
coral mushrooms — 244
corals — 21, 22, 23, 24, 26, 41, 199
cord grass — 232
coreopsis — 257
cormorants — 229
corn — 8, 11, 14, 50, 65, 75-79, 136, 161, 199, 206, 239, 266-271, 276-280, 287
Coshocton — 281, 282
Coshocton County — 264, 265, 276
cotton grass — 145, 148
cottontail rabbit —109, 139, 169, 183, 193, 194, 196, 211, 213, 224, 231, 245, 278, 280
cottonwood — 82, 176, 181, 207, 233
cougar — 10, 96
cowbird — 211
Cowdery Cemetery — 78
cows — 102, 141, 194, 305, 307
coyote — 139
crab spider — 84
crabs — 21
cranberries — 143
Crane Creek Wildlife Experimental Station — 248
cranes — 269
crappies — 281
crawfish — 51, 52, 99, 115, 117, 119, 122, 124, 138, 140
Crawford County — 207
creepers — 239
Cretaceous — 31
cricket frog — 245, 250
crickets — 138
crimped-leaf pondweed — 126
crinoids — 28, 199
crows — 103, 108, 231, 278
crown vetch — 181
crustaceans — 113, 224
crustose lichens — 100
Crystal Cave — 153, 217
Crystal King stalactite — 157
Cuba Moraine — 51, 208
cucumber magnolia — 82, 171, 189, 208
cucumbers — 75
Culberson State Nature Preserve — 206
cultured pearl — 178
cumulonimbus — 63
cumulus clouds — 63
curly pondweed — 232, 233
Cuyahoga County — 27, 28, 66, 185, 187, 192, 308
Cuyahoga Falls — 29, 185, 186, 191
Cuyahoga River — 29, 41, 54, 184-186, 221
Cuyahoga River Valley — 188, 190, 191
Cuyahoga-Tuscarawas Portage — 191
Cuyahoga Valley National Recreation Area — 29, 185, 190
Cynthiana FLats — 42

dairy farms, cows — 77, 183, 188, 277, 280
daisy fleabane — 209
Dambach, Charles A. — 308
Darby Plains — 135
darters - 119, 122, 210
Dawes Arboretum, The — 308
Dayton — 18, 41, 62, 204, 207, 282, 292, 301, 308, 311
Dayton-Montgomery County Park District — 282
Dayton Museum of Natural History
Deep Lock Quarry — 28

deer mouse — 211
deer, white-tailed — 10-12, 14, 83, 91, 96-98, 103-105, 139, 161, 169, 172, 173, 176, 183, 188, 194, 211, 213, 224, 231, 240, 245, 249, 265, 271, 277, 280
Defiance — 238
Defiance County — 275
DeKay's snake — 229, 245
Delaware — 24
Delaware County — 157, 259
Delaware Limestone — 151, 157
Delphos — 238
Department of Agriculture — 306
Department of Public Works — 307
Detroit, Mich. — 10, 231, 238, 240, 241
Detroit River — 219-221, 245, 286
DeVilbiss Boy Scout Reservation—245
Devonian — 17, 18, 23-27, 31, 151, 183, 184, 199-201, 217, 253
diatoms — 116, 117, 119, 122, 224
dickcissel — 211
Dillon Dam — 115
dinosaur — 31
dittany — 167
diving beetle — 127
Division of Conservation — 306
Division of Forestry — 306
Division of Natural Areas and Preserves (ODNR) — 131, 311, 312
Division of Wildlife (ODNR)— 251, 278
dog(s) — 12, 269, 290
dogwood — 86, 89, 104, 107, 167, 172, 177, 233
dolomite — 18, 21-24, 41, 43, 52, 55, 57, 78, 151, 154, 173, 199, 208, 217, 218, 253-257, 259, 287, 291
Doughty Creek — 164, 165
Dover River — 163, 164
downy woodpecker — 96, 107, 174
dragonflies — 119, 120, 226
Drake, Daniel — 296
Drennan Ditch — 241
Dublin — 157
Duck Pond — 154
duck potato — 232
ducks — 10, 211, 224, 247, 265
duckweed — 117, 232
Dudley's rush — 233
Dundee — 180
Dunkleosteus — 25
Dury, Charles — 299
dusky salamander — 197
Dutch elm disease — 176, 207, 233, 242
Dutchman's breeches — 172, 192, 208, 234
dwarf willow — 37
Dysart Woods — 8, 166, 308

Early Woodland — 267
earthstars — 103
earthworms — 140
earthworms, aquatic — 224, 225
East Coast Lows - 67, 68
East Liverpool — 292
eastern big-eared bat — 255
eastern garter snake — 210, 229
eastern meadowlark — 211
eastern mole — 245
eastern phoebe — 194
eastern pipistrelle — 255
eastern plains garter snake — 140, 210
eastern wood pewee — 174
eastern wood rat — 165, 169
Eastwood Park — 292
Ecological Society of America — 308
Ecologist's Union — 308
Eden soils — 78, 205
Edwin H. Davis State Memorial — 255, 307
egrets — 211, 215
elderberry — 233, 242
elk — 10, 11, 139, 169, 193, 213, 271, 278, 287
elm, American — 8, 9, 14, 81, 82, 108, 146, 176, 181, 191, 207, 233, 238, 242, 265
elm bark beetles — 87
Emerald Necklace — 187
emerald shiner — 226
enchanter's nightshade — 106
England, English — 271, 292, 299
Erie County — 63, 135
Erie Islands — 62, 222, 224, 226, 228
Erie Lobe — 202
Erie, Pa. — 217
ermine — 197
Eskimo — 264
Etna Township — 7
Euclid — 66
euphorbia — 257
Euphrates River — 129
Eurasian — 135
Euro-Americans — 271

Europe, European — 47, 149, 168, 181, 231-233, 271, 274, 299
European black alder — 181
evening bat — 255

Fairfield County — 34, 36, 42, 55, 163, 186, 307
Fairport Harbor — 23, 288
fairy shrimp — 114
false aloe — 257
false asphodel — 148
false foxglove — 193
false-nettle — 233
Farlow Herbarium — 299
fence lizard — 169, 210
Fenneman, Nevin M. — 49
Fern Lake — 132, 308
ferns — 26, 28, 108, 143-146, 171, 242, 255
field crickets — 98
field sparrows — 89
Findlay — 18, 50, 238, 291, 299
fingernail clams — 299
fir — 38, 134, 141, 208, 238, 259, 264
firepink — 93, 167
fireweed — 37
Fish Point — 218
Fishery Bay — 225
Fitchville soil — 77
flame azalea — 173
flathead catfish — 15
flatworms — 152
flexed naiad — 233
flies — 138, 226
flint — 29, 264-266, 269
Flint Mammoth Cave System — 151
Flint Ridge — 29, 265, 268, 279
flowering-rush — 232, 233
Flushing Escarpment — 53, 164, 168
fluxstone — 25
fly mushroom — 103
flycatchers — 239
flying squirrels — 87, 105, 168, 169, 245
foamflower — 93, 172
Foerste, Auguste F. — 301
foliose lichens — 100
Forster's terns — 248
Fort Ancient — 22, 270
Fort Ancient Indians — 270, 271
Fort Harmar — 7
Fort Hill — 55, 259
Fort Wayne, Ind. — 42, 50, 218, 237, 238
fossil fuels — 185, 277
fossils — 18, 20, 21, 24-26, 28, 31, 41, 141, 199-201, 217, 298, 299
Foster — 122
Fostoria — 238
four-toed salamander — 311
Fowler's toad — 245
Fox — 210
fox(es) — 12, 84, 87, 100, 103, 107, 108, 139, 224, 245, 256
fox snake — 229, 249, 251
fox squirrels — 105, 107, 168, 213, 240, 245
foxtail grass — 89
fragipans — 77
Frame Bog — 308
Franklin County — 12, 27, 28, 185, 285
Franz Theodore Stone Laboratory — 301, 302
Fremont — 238
French — 5, 241, 246, 271
French and Indian War — 6
freshwater drum — 15, 221, 226, 227
"Friends of Science" — 296
fringed gentian — 148
frogs — 99, 107, 119, 140, 209
fructose lichens — 100
Fulton County — 7, 75, 239, 240
fungi — 102, 103, 112, 114, 119, 172, 244, 300, 301

gadwalls — 247
Gahanna — 28, 185
Gallia Beauty apple — 181
Gallia County — 63, 181, 290
gallinule — 244, 247
garden spider — 209
garlic mustard — 234
garter snake (common) — 140, 150, 197, 245, 249
gastropods — 26
Geauga County — 8, 30, 61, 66, 69, 132, 185, 187, 188, 308
General Assembly — 297-299
gentians — 257
geode — 153, 217
Geological Society of America — 298
Georgia — 165
geranium, wild — 208
germander — 233
Germany, Germans — 7, 276
giant beaver — 38, 213, 264
giant ragweed — 243

Index 321

giant reed grass — 207
Gibraltar Island — 225, 300
Gillette, Alanson — 181
Gist, Christopher — 274, 295
gizzard shad — 225, 226
Glacial Grooves State Memorial — 307
Glacial Kame Indian — 266
Glaciated Appalachian Plateau — 50, 55, 76, 79, 115, 183
glass industry — 271, 291
Glen Helen — 57, 308
Gnadenhutten — 6
golden pheasants — 229
golden ragwort — 231
goldenrods — 89, 97, 106, 209, 242, 243
golden-winged warbler — 244
goldfinches — 89
goldfish — 226
goldthread — 146
Goll Woods State Nature Preserve — 7, 239
goosefoot — 265, 266
Gordon, Robert B. — 302
Gorge Metropolitan Park — 29
grain farms — 183
grama grass — 258
Grand Lake — 42, 211
Grand Lake St. Marys — 281
Grand River — 34, 54, 186, 282
Grand River, Mich. — 42
grapes — 62, 229, 234, 235
grasshopper sparrow — 244
grasshoppers — 138, 139
grass-of-Parnassus — 148
grass-pink orchid — 142
gravel — 55, 141, 186, 204, 235
gray fox — 85, 169, 194, 213, 245, 249, 278
gray squirrels, eastern — 11, 105, 107, 168, 173, 213, 231, 278
gray tree frog — 98, 245
gray wolf — 169, 240
gray-headed coneflower — 134
Great Black Swamp — 10, 50, 75, 237-239, 247, 251, 264, 269, 274, 275, 279, 280
great blue herons — 119, 228, 229, 248
Great Buffalo Swamp — 13
great crested flycatchers — 96
great egrets — 229, 248
Great Hinckley Hunt — 11, 12, 278
great horned owl — 95, 173, 239, 244
Great Lakes — 44, 55, 67, 69, 126, 134, 215, 222, 226, 246
Great Lakes basin — 286
Great Lakes muskellunge — 280
"Great Lakes' Worst" — 69
Great Miami River — 5, 15, 21, 51, 55, 282
Great Plains — 60, 67, 81
Great Seal of Ohio — 54
Great Thanksgiving Day Storm — 69
grebes — 211
green algae — 224
green ash — 82, 207, 242
green frogs — 150, 245, 250
green herons — 229
Green Island — 229
green salamander — 174
greenbrier — 108, 167
Greenbrier Ridge — 53, 254
Greene County — 22, 34, 41, 44, 57, 61, 122, 203, 259, 308
Greenland — 34, 36, 40, 47
Greenville — 292
grizzly bear — 269
ground juniper — 233
ground sloth, giant — 38, 213
groundhog — 139
grouse — 10, 103, 104, 108, 172, 224, 277, 278
Guernsey County — 64
Guilford Lake — 127, 281
Gulf Coast — 266, 269
Gulf Coast Lows — 67
Gulf of Alaska — 59
Gulf of Mexico — 59, 60, 67, 134, 163, 186
Gulf of St. Lawrence — 21, 186
gulls — 215
Gypsum — 23
gypsum — 17, 18, 22, 23, 153, 235, 287, 293, 298

hackberry — 82, 83, 190, 208, 234
hail — 64, 65
hairy rockcress — 233
hairy woodpecker — 194
hairy-tailed moles — 168
halite — 23
Hamilton — 34, 41
Hamilton County — 55, 205, 210, 285, 308

Hanging Rock Iron Region — 275, 288
Hanover soil — 77
harebell — 233
Harrisburg peneplain — 53
Harrison County — 181, 271, 289
Harrison, William Henry — 176
Hartwell moraine — 51
Harvard University — 299
hawks — 84, 85, 92, 194, 196, 268, 269, 306
hawthorns — 89, 104
Haynes — 54
hazelnuts — 103
heath aster — 231, 233
Heath Family, heaths — 167, 178
Heidi Quarry — 205
hellbender — 177
hemlock — 28, 108, 168, 171-174, 187, 190, 191, 238, 306
Henry County — 240
Henslow's sparrow — 244
hepaticas — 93, 172, 192, 255, 259
herb-Robert (geranium) — 208, 234
herons — 211, 215, 224
Herrick, Francis H. — 301
Herrick, J. Arthur — 308
herring gulls — 229, 230, 248
Hexagenia — 226
hibernate — 103, 107
hickory — 38, 81, 89, 102, 103, 134, 161, 166, 168, 176, 188, 208, 269, 275
high bush blueberry —145
Highbanks Metropolitan Park — 26
Highland County — 22, 36, 52, 55, 66, 157, 173, 205, 253, 256, 259
Hildreth, Samuel P. — 11, 178, 296, 297
Hillsboro — 157
Hinckley — 12
Hine, James S. — 301
hispid dewberry —146
hobblebush — 190
Hocking County — 44, 53, 54, 151, 302, 306
Hocking Hills — 17, 28, 163, 165, 167-169, 172, 173, 178, 265, 310
Hocking Hills State Park — 172
Hocking River — 36, 46, 55, 165
hog-nosed snake — 170, 245
hogs — 103, 229, 276, 277
Holden Arboretum — 308
Holland — 241
Holmes County — 164, 165, 265
Holmes, Robert A. — 311
honey locust — 207
hooded merganser — 247
hooded warbler — 95, 245
Hopewell Indians — 268, 269, 270
"Hopewell" iron furnace — 288
hop-hornbeam — 108, 233, 234
hoptree — 233, 234
hornbeam — 172
horned lark — 89, 141, 211
hornets — 138
horses — 10, 161, 277
horses, wild — 38
house mouse — 213, 240
House of Representatives (Ohio) — 311
house sparrow — 211
house wren — 211
Hoytville soils — 75, 204
huckleberries —167, 242
Hudson Bay — 34
Hueston Woods — 306
Hueston Woods State Park — 22
Hueston Woods State Nature Preserve — 206
hummingbird moth — 100
Hunt, Kenneth W. — 300
Huron basin — 37
Huron County — 42
Huron Shale — 25
Hurricane Agnes — 64
hydra — 124

Ice Age — 36, 37, 42, 47, 132, 133, 141, 163
Iceland — 34, 36, 37
Illinoian — 34, 36, 42, 47, 51, 54, 73, 76, 77, 202-208, 253
Illinois — 31, 42, 47, 53, 134, 257
Indian(s) — 5-11, 14, 15, 28, 29, 38, 40, 52, 81, 139, 151, 154, 173, 177, 191, 238, 263, 266-271, 274, 276, 287
Indian grass — 134-136, 149, 242
Indian Lake — 42, 127, 211
Indian Lake Portage — 281
Indian mounds — 299
Indian plantain, tuberous — 148
Indian Signal Tree — 191
Indian Trail Cave — 155
Indiana — 31, 42, 50, 60, 140, 173, 201, 218, 237, 238, 265, 266

Indian-pipe — 172, 173
indigo bunting — 95
Interior Low Plateau Province — 50, 52, 253-256
Iowa — 257
iron — 59, 275, 287, 288, 291, 298
iron furnaces — 161, 257
Ironton — 69, 165, 288
ironwood — 172
Iroquois Indians — 271
Irwin Prairie State Nature Preserve — 242, 244, 245
Isle Royale — 266
isopod — 256
ivory sedge — 233

Jack-in-the-pulpit — 172
Jackson — 287
Jackson County — 29, 42, 163, 166, 168, 172, 173, 180, 288, 290
Jacob's ladder — 93
Jamestown — 34
Japan — 65, 178
Jefferson charcoal furnace — 288
Jefferson County — 271, 289
Jefferson salamander — 245, 250
jellyfish — 21
Jesuit — 271
jet streams, winds — 59, 65, 69
jewelweed — 209
Joe Pye weed — 250
John Bryan State Park — 22, 122, 203
Johnstown — 38
Jones, Lynds — 301, 303
June grass — 135
juniper — 257
Jurassic — 31

Kaatz, Martin R. — 239
Kalm's lobelia — 148, 233
Kansan — 34, 36, 42, 51, 54, 202, 205
Kansas — 61
karst topography — 154, 155
katydids — 85, 98

keeled green snake — 170
Keen's bat — 255
Kellerman, William A. — 299
Kelleys Island — 24, 32, 41, 201, 217, 218
Kennard Outwash — 46, 203
Keno — 78
Kent — 186
Kent State University — 308
Kenton — 37
Kentucky — 7, 31, 36, 52, 60, 78, 151, 163, 164, 173, 253, 266, 288
Kentucky coffeetree — 208, 234
Kentucky warbler — 84, 95, 174, 244
kestrels — 96, 141, 209
Keweenaw Peninsula — 266
Kilbourne, James — 10
Killbuck Creek — 34, 46, 55
killdeer — 89
Killdeer plains — 207, 306
Killdeer Plains Wildlife Area — 136
king rail — 229, 244
kinglets — 107
Kings Creek — 209
Kirtland, Jared Potter — 10, 294, 297, 298
Kirtland Society of Natural History — 298
Kirtland's snake — 249
knobbed rock shell — 178
Knox County — 34
Knox Dolomite — 185
Kokosing River — 46, 55, 165

Labrador tea — 145
lacewing — 84
ladies-tresses orchids — 148
Lake County — 23, 25, 64, 66, 288, 308
lake effect — 66, 67
Lake Erie — 7, 10, 15, 17, 23, 34, 36, 41, 42, 50, 54, 55, 59-69, 111, 112, 126, 127, 151, 184, 186, 215-234, 237, 238, 241, 245-251, 264, 280, 286, 293, 297, 301, 302
Lake Erie basin — 37, 186, 202
Lake Erie islands — 153, 234
Lake Erie marshes — 237, 249, 251, 274, 305
Lake Erie water snake — 229
Lake Hope — 290
Lake Huron — 42, 216, 221, 246
Lake Katharine State Nature Preserve — 172
Lake Loramie — 127
Lake Lundy — 241
Lake Maumee — 42, 50, 237
Lake Michigan — 42, 246

Lake Ontario — 126, 216
Lake Plain — 50, 51, 75, 76, 184, 216
Lake St. Clair — 219
Lake St. Marys — 127
lake sturgeon — 226, 280, 282
Lake Superior — 246, 266, 268, 288
Lake Tight — 42, 52, 53
Lake Warren — 241
Lake Wayne — 241
Lake Whittlesey — 42, 298
Lakewood — 298
lamb's quarters — 234
Lancaster — 7, 186
land snails — 299, 303
Langlade, Charles — 6
larch — 146
largemouth bass — 122, 280, 281
lark sparrow — 245
Late Woodland Indians — 270, 271
Laurelville — 44
Lawrence County — 69, 169, 174, 178, 181
Lawrence's warbler — 244
Lawshe soil — 78
leaf miners — 173
leafcup — 234
League of Ohio Nature Clubs — 306
least bittern — 229, 244
least flycatcher — 244
least shrew — 211
least weasel — 211, 245
leatherleaf — 142, 145
Lebanon — 202
leech — 124
Leesville Lake — 168, 177
leopard frog — 245, 250
Lesquereux, Leo — 299
Lewiston — 281
Lexington peneplain — 53
Liatris — 139, 257
Liberty Center — 240, 241
Liberty Township — 166, 173
lichens — 100, 102, 112, 172, 178, 233
Licking County — 7, 29, 36, 38, 55, 115, 168, 185, 265, 281, 308, 310
Licking River — 44, 46, 55, 115, 164, 165
lignite — 31
limestone — 17-25, 29, 31, 41, 43, 52, 55, 57, 76-78, 83, 114, 115, 148, 151, 157, 162, 165, 176, 183, 185, 199-202, 205, 208, 210, 217, 218, 238, 254-259, 287-291, 299
Limestone, Kentucky — 7
Little Beaver Creek — 167, 168, 173, 291, 313
little bluestem — 135, 136, 242, 257
little brown bat — 194, 211, 231, 255
Little Cedar Point — 250
Little Cuyahoga River — 186
little green heron — 249
Little Miami River — 21, 47, 51, 122, 124, 202, 282
Little Miami River Gorge — 123
liverworts — 255, 259
lizards — 87, 107
lizard's-tail — 243
Lloyd, Curtis G. — 300, 301; Lloyd, John V. — 300; Lloyd Library and Museum — 300; Lloyd, Nelson A. — 300
lobelia — 257
Locke, John — 253, 256, 258, 296-298
locust borer beetle — 180
Logan County — 23, 44, 47, 51, 147, 155, 201, 204
Long Point, Ont. — 217, 218
long-billed marsh wren — 244
long-horned grasshoppers — 98
longnose gar — 210
long-spurred violet — 94
long-tailed salamander — 174
long-tailed weasel — 194, 197, 211, 245
Lorain — 185
Lorain County — 27, 28, 185, 267
Loramie — 281
Lost Ballast Island — 229
Loudonville — 284
Loudonville soil — 77
Louisiana — 29
Louisiana waterthrush — 174, 244
Louisville, Ky. — 124
Loveland — 123
low-running blackberry — 242
Lucas County — 75, 240, 241, 274, 275, 285
luna moth — 100
Lundy — 42
lupine — 242
Lynx — 255, 256
lynx — 213, 240
Lynx Prairie — 136, 257, 308

Mad River — 46, 55, 209

Mad River Valley — 46, 147
Madison County — 38, 135, 198, 207
Magee Marsh — 248, 249
magnolia warbler — 244
Mahomet Valley — 42
Mahoning County — 185, 196, 288
Mahoning River — 297
maidenhair fern — 172, 259
mallard — 247
mammoth(s) — 38, 40, 204, 213, 264, 287
Mammoth Cave — 256
Manchester — 52, 178
Mansfield — 188, 203
map turtles — 229, 245, 250
maple(s) — 8, 38, 77, 81-83, 89, 234, 264, 265, 269, 306
maple-leafed viburnum — 86, 87
Marble Cliff — 201
marbled salamander — 170
Marblehead — 24
Marblehead Peninsula — 41, 201, 231
Marietta — 7, 62, 176, 178, 181, 282, 292, 296
Marietta College — 296
Marion County - 136, 140, 207
marl — 148, 149, 157
marsh elder — 266
marsh ferns — 145, 149, 242
marsh grass — 194
marsh hawk — 244
marsh marigold — 192, 242
marsh violet — 148
marsh wrens — 247
"Martha" — 13, 14
massasauga, eastern — 150, 210, 245, 250
Massie Creek — 42
mastodons — 37, 38, 40, 204, 213, 264, 287
Mather, William W. — 297
Maumee — 238, 274
Maumee Bay — 286
Maumee River — 220, 221, 238-241, 247, 264, 276, 286
Maumee State Forest — 245
Maumee Valley — 275
mayapple — 172, 192, 209
mayflies — 112, 113, 122, 221, 225-227, 280
Maysville, Kentucky — 7, 22
meadow jumping mouse — 245
meadow vole — 140, 211, 245
meadowlarks — 141, 211
Mechanicsburg — 45
Medina County — 187, 278
Megalomus — 22
Meigs County — 78, 168, 289
Mentor — 308
Mentor Marsh — 308
Mercer County — 51
Mesopotamia — 129
Mesozoic Era — 20, 31
Metropolitan Park District of Columbus and Franklin County — 306
Mexico — 266, 270
Miami and Erie Canal — 241
Miami Conservancy District — 282
Miami County — 157, 308
Miami Lobe — 41, 46, 202, 203
Miami River — 34, 46, 269
Miami River Valley — 202
Miami Valley — 34, 275
Miamian soils — 76, 204, 205
mica — 269
Michaux, Francois Andre — 176
Michigan — 10, 42, 134, 218, 220, 238, 241
Michigan Basin — 31
Michigan, University of — 68
Middle Bass Island — 229
midge — 143, 225, 226
midland painted turtle — 197
Milford — 123, 308
milk fever — 102
milk snake — 245, 249
milkweed — 209
Mill Creek — 25, 259
Mill Creek Valley — 36, 285
Milligan — 69
millipedes — 29, 99, 174
Minford Silt — 42, 53, 176
mink — 119, 139, 150, 177, 196, 245
Minnesota — 38
minor naiad — 233
Mississippi Basin — 190
Mississippi delta — 29
Mississippi flyway — 247
Mississippi River — 51, 218, 237, 289
Mississippi River Valley — 270
Mississippi system — 42
Mississippian Period — 18, 26-28, 52, 183-185, 217, 253, 256, 270
Missouri — 29
Missouri River — 134

miterwort — 259
mites — 174
moccasin-flower — 93, 189, 190
mockernut hickory — 81, 108, 166
Mohican Hills — 168
Mohican River — 46, 55, 165-168, 173
Mohican State Park — 113
mole (eastern) — 140, 211
mollusks — 10, 28, 113, 115, 117, 165, 178, 280, 299
monarch butterfly — 209
Monclova — 245
Monnett — 207
Monongahela Indians — 271
Monroe County — 53, 162, 164, 168
Montgomery County — 285
Montreal — 21
Moravian(s) — 6, 295
morel mushrooms — 206, 244
Morrow County — 185, 285
Moseley, Edwin Lincoln — 243, 301
mosquitoes — 82, 119, 152, 238, 275
mosses — 86, 142, 172, 233, 255, 259, 299
Moundbuilders — 256
Mount Logan — 54
Mount Pleasant — 186
mountain holly — 145
mountain laurel — 86, 108, 167, 168
mountain lion — 10, 193, 213, 240, 277, 278
mountain maple — 173, 190
mountain mint — 233
mountain teaberry — 190
mountain tiger — 10
mourning dove — 13, 92
mourning warbler — 244
mudpuppy — 228, 250
mudstone — 27
mulberry — 233
mules — 277
musclewood — 86, 172, 177
mushrooms — 103
musk turtle — 250
muskellunge — 15, 281
Muskingum basin — 165
Muskingum County — 42, 115, 265, 289
Muskingum River — 47, 53, 115, 164, 175-178, 269
Muskingum Watershed Conservancy District — 168, 282, 284
muskoxen — 38, 40, 264
muskrats — 177, 194, 196, 211, 224, 231, 232
mussels — 115, 177, 225
mycorrhizae — 103, 172

naiad mollusks — 115, 177, 178
nannyberry — 149
Napoleon — 238
"The Narrows" — 123
National Park Service — 308
National Road — 7
Native American — 129
Natural Areas Council — 311
Natural Areas Project — 310
natural gas — 18, 22, 26, 185, 235, 287, 290-292, 299
Natural Landmark — 308
Nature Conservancy, The (TNC) — 206, 258
The Nature Conservancy (TNC) Ohio Chapter — 306, 308, 310
nauplius — 224
Nebraska — 47
Nebraskan — 34, 205
Nelson-Kennedy Ledges State Park — 29, 185
Neotoma — 165
Neotoma Valley — 165, 166, 302
nettle — 233
Nettle Creek — 46
Nettle Lake — 124
New England — 6, 38, 43, 68, 165, 276
New England aster — 208
New Orleans — 289
New Philadelphia — 178, 299
New River — 201
New York — 23, 187, 189
New York City — 167, 298
New Zealand — 47
Newark — 28, 269, 308
Newberry, John S. — 293, 299
Newfoundland — 68
Newtown — 203
Niagara Falls — 34, 221
Niagara River — 218
Nimishillen Creek — 46
ninebark — 149, 233, 242
Noble County — 290
nodding ladies tresses — 231
nodding onion — 233
nodding thistle — 208

nodding trillium — 190, 192
nodding wild onion — 149
nodding wild rye — 135
North Bass Island —229
North Bay — 219
North Carolina — 53, 259, 269
North Pole — 66
"northeaster" — 68
northern brown snake — 249
northern copperbelly — 210
northern dusky salamander — 174
northern finches — 108
northern fly honeysuckle — 190
northern leaf shell — 115
northern oriole — 231
northern pike — 15, 215, 280
northern pondweeds — 233
northern red salamander — 174
northern smallmouth bass — 119, 122
northern water snake — 177, 197, 229
northern white cedar — 259
northern wood frog — 245
Northwest Territory — 284
Norway — 47
Norwood —202
Nostoc algae — 224
nuthatches — 96, 107

oak(s) —9, 38, 73, 81, 85, 89, 103, 106, 108, 134, 136, 146, 161, 168, 169, 171, 174, 176-178, 188, 190-193, 206-208, 234, 241, 264, 265, 269, 274, 275
Oak Openings — 75, 194, 237, 240-245, 251
Oak Openings Metropolitan Park — 50
Oberlin College — 301, 302
obsidian — 269
Ohio Academy of Science, The — 229, 300, 306
Ohio Agri. Exp. Station — 301
Ohio Agricultural Research and Development Center — 77, 181
Ohio Archaeological and Historical Society — 306
Ohio Association of Garden Clubs (OAGC) — 306
Ohio Biological Survey — 302, 306, 308
Ohio Black Shale —54
Ohio Brush Creek — 53, 253-255
Ohio buckeye — 176, 190
Ohio Canal — 28
Ohio Caverns — 47, 152, 155, 157, 201
Ohio Company — 5, 11
Ohio Department of Health — 285
Ohio Department of Natural Resources (ODNR) — 131, 206, 251, 278, 306, 311
Ohio Division of Wildlife — 15, 177, 197, 248
Ohio-Erie Canal — 281, 310
Ohio Fish Commission — 280
Ohio flint — 265, 269
Ohio General Assembly — 11, 176, 311
Ohio Geological Survey — 10, 296, 297
Ohio goldenrod — 148
Ohio Historical Society — 41, 206, 255, 306, 307
Ohio Land Company — 274
Ohio Legislative Service Commission — 311
Ohio muskellunge — 177
Ohio Natural Areas Bill — 311
Ohio River — 21, 23, 36, 42, 50-55, 76, 122-124, 127, 134, 151, 162-165, 168, 174, 176, 181, 201, 202, 205-208, 253, 255, 271, 296
Ohio River Valley — 52, 65, 76, 204, 208, 210
Ohio Shale — 25, 26, 29
Ohio State University, The — 10, 134, 165, 299-302
OSU, The Biological Club — 306
OSU Department of Botany — 302
OSU Department of Zoology and Entomology — 302
OSU Herbarium — 300, 302
OSU Insect Collection — 303
OSU Marching Band — 68
OSU Museum of Zoology — 301
Ohio University — 302
Ohio Valley — 115
oil — 18, 21, 22, 185, 235, 287, 290-292, 299
Oklahoma Panhandle — 67
Old Man's Cave — 163
Old State Line Road — 241
Olentangy Caverns — 155, 157
Olentangy River — 26
Ontario — 23, 40, 43, 217, 220, 269, 270
Ontario basin — 37
Opequon — 78

opossum — 87, 103, 108, 167, 169, 170, 193, 194, 211, 245, 247
orchard oriole — 229, 244
orchids — 108, 167, 243
Ordovician — 20-22, 52, 199-202, 205, 208, 254, 256
Orient, the — 167
Orleton — 40
Orleton Farms — 38
orographic lifting — 66
Orthoptera — 98
Orton, Sr., Edward — 299
Osborn, Herbert — 302
Oscillatoria — 116
O'Shaughnessy Dam — 128
Ottawa County — 10, 23, 24, 274, 278
Ottawa Indians — 6
Ottawa Marsh — 249
Ottawa National Wildlife Refuge — 248, 249
Ottawa River — 241, 242
otter — 213
ovenbird — 95, 174
owls — 84, 108, 194, 196, 269, 306
oxeye — 138
Oxford — 22, 206
oyster — 178

Pacific Ocean — 60, 65
paddlefish — 210, 282
Painesville — 23
Paint Creek — 44, 54, 165, 173, 205, 269
painted trillium — 191
painted turtles — 127, 150, 177, 210, 229, 245, 250
Palaeo-Indians — 263, 264, 265, 268
Paleozoic (Era) — 20, 31, 162, 199, 201, 205
Panama Canal — 180
Panhandle Hook — 67
panther — 10
Park District Law — 306
partridge-berry — 108, 146, 172, 192
passenger pigeon — 10-14, 213, 237-240, 277, 278
Paulding County — 274, 302
pawpaw — 86, 172, 257, 265, 295
peat — 30, 31, 71, 141, 145-149, 235, 302
Peattie — 129
Peck Road — 191
Peebles — 255
pelecypods — 26
Pelee Island — 41, 218
Pelee Passage — 219
Peninsula — 28
Pennsylvania — 23, 29, 31, 78, 187-190, 217, 264, 271, 276
Pennsylvania Dutch — 276
Pennsylvanian — 28, 29, 31, 180, 183-185
perch — 15, 224, 226
Permian — 20, 28-31, 33, 168
Perry, Commodore Oliver Hazard — 153
Perry County — 69, 185
Perry's Cave — 153, 154
Perry's Victory Monument — 153, 223
Perrysburg — 238
Persian Gulf — 185
persimmons — 89, 103, 161, 167
Pewamo soil — 76
Philadelphia — 62
phloem necrosis — 207
phoebe — 177
phragmites — 238
physostegia — 257
phytoplankton — 224, 225
Pickaway County — 207, 210, 302
Pickawillany — 5
pickerel weed — 232, 250
pied-billed grebe — 231, 244
Piedmont — 165
Piedmont Lake — 177
Piedmont Plateau — 259
Pierce, Capt. Milton B.   12
pig — 11, 12
pigeon — 211
pigmy shrew — 169
pignut — 166
pignut hickory — 81
pigweed — 234, 266
Pike County — 13, 28, 42, 157, 175, 205, 256, 285
205, 256, 285
pileated woodpeckers — 92, 96, 174, 239
pin oak — 82, 103, 176, 191, 207, 238, 242
pine(s) — 38, 89, 103, 108, 167, 168, 178, 208, 238, 243, 275
pine siskin — 194
pink ladyslipper — 189, 190
pink moccasin-flower — 167, 300

Index 323

Pioneer — 275
pipestone — 268, 269
pipsissewa — 193
Piqua — 37
pitch pine — 82, 168, 181, 275
pitcher plant — 143, 144, 148, 150
Pittsburgh — 299
pixie cups — 100
planarian — 127
plankton — 224
Platea soil — 77
Pleasant Hill Reservoir — 284
Pleistocene — 20, 40
Plum Run — 23
Point Albino — 218
Point Pelee — 247
poison ivy — 107, 233
poison sumac — 145, 149
Poland — 297
polyphemus — 100
Pomeroy — 288
pond snail — 117
pondweed — 117, 233
Pontius, Leslie — 166
poplar — 242, 243
porcupine — 213, 224, 240
porcupine grass — 135
pore fungi — 103
Port Clinton — 17, 23, 238, 245
Portage County — 29, 44, 55, 146, 185, 188, 308
Portage Lakes — 124, 186
Portage River — 10, 281
Portland cement — 292
Portsmouth — 23, 52, 69, 165, 201, 268, 269
Portsmouth River — 52
post oak(s) — 166, 178
Potamogeton — 117
poultry — 277
poverty grass — 89, 168
Powell — 157
Powell-Union City moraines — 37
power plants — 161
prairie chicken (greater) — 14, 140, 245
prairie cord grass — 149
Prairie Ditch — 241
prairie dock — 136, 149, 207, 257
Prairie Peninsula — 134, 140, 208
prairie vole — 140, 211
Precambrian — 202
Pre-Columbian Indians — 256
Preston, Frank — 302
Price, Homer — 302, 303
Proctorville — 181
promethea silk moth — 167
protozoans — 71, 174, 224
puff adder — 170
puffballs — 103, 244
puma — 10
pumpkinseed sunfish — 117
purple cliffbrake fern — 255
purple coneflower — 207, 257
purple cresses — 192
purple gerardia — 148
purple martin — 211, 231
purple rockcress — 233
purple trillium — 191
pussytoes — 167
Put-in-Bay — 151, 153, 154, 223, 232, 302

quail — 10, 224, 278, 280
Quebec — 21
queen snake — 119, 177, 210, 249
queen-of-the-prairie — 149, 207

Raab's Corners — 241
raccoon(s) — 12, 99, 100, 103, 107, 150, 152, 157, 169, 173, 193, 194, 211, 224, 231, 245, 247, 256, 277
Raccoon Creek — 290
radioactive elements — 18
radiocarbon — 36, 202, 204
ragweed — 89
ragwort — 93
railroads — 247, 275, 293, 305
rainbow darters — 210
raspberries — 100, 265
Rathbone Elm — 176
rattlesnake(s) — 229
Rattlesnake Island — 229, 231
rattlesnake master — 178
rattlesnake plantain — 167
ravens — 239
ravine salamander — 174
red algae — 154
red bat — 194, 255
red cedar — 78, 82, 83, 89, 208, 233, 234, 250, 257, 259
Red Delicious apple — 181

red elm — 257
red fox — 169, 193, 194, 211, 213, 231, 240, 245, 249, 278
red maple — 82, 92, 102, 145, 171, 176, 177, 181, 188, 189, 191, 207, 238, 242
red oak(s) — 7, 82, 103, 166, 171, 176, 206, 207, 208, 238, 242, 257
red pine — 168
Red Rock — 308
red squirrel — 211, 213, 245
red-backed salamander — 177, 210, 245, 250
red-backed vole — 197
red-bellied snake — 197
red-berried elder — 173
Redbird Hollow — 308
redbud — 83, 172, 208
red-eyed vireos — 95, 99, 174, 211, 239
redheads — 247
red-headed woodpecker — 211
red-shouldered hawk — 244
redside dace — 130
red-spotted newt — 245, 250
redstart — 239, 245
red-tailed hawk — 95, 174, 210
red-winged blackbird (redwing) — 126, 150, 246, 278
reed(s) — 246, 247
reed grass — 238
Reesville-Farmersville moraines — 37
reindeer — 38
reindeer lichen — 100, 178
reindeer moss — 100
Resthaven Wildlife Area — 135
Revolutionary War — 6
Rhode Island — 274
Rhodes, Gov. James A. — 311
rhododendron, great — 173
ribbon snake(s) — 150, 245, 249
Richter Scale — 202
Riddell, John L. — 296, 297
Riddell's goldenrod — 148
ring-billed gulls — 248
ring-necked pheasant — 194, 211, 213, 224, 229, 279
ring-necked snake — 87, 229, 245
Ripley — 32
Rittman — 23, 185
Rittman soil — 77
river birch — 176, 243
river otters — 177, 240
robin — 193, 194, 211
Rock House — 172
Rock Run — 172
rock salt — 23, 185
rockbass — 122
Rockport — 298
Rocky Fork — 22, 28, 43, 55, 157, 173, 185
Rocky Mountains (Rockies) — 31, 59, 67, 133, 134, 269
Rocky River — 26, 27
Rogers, Major John — 11
Rome Beauty apple — 181
Rome Township — 181
Roscoe Village — 281, 282
rose mallow — 250
rose pogonia — 143
rose-breasted grosbeak — 244
roseshell azalea — 188
Ross County — 36, 42, 54, 157, 183, 204, 205, 269
Rossmoyne soil — 76
rosyside dace — 177
rotifers — 174, 224
rough winged swallow — 231
round-headed bush clover — 136
round-leaf sundew — 148
round-leafed violet — 188
royal fern — 145
royal walnut moth — 100
Ruby apple — 181
ruby-throated hummingbirds — 95, 100
rue anemone — 93, 208
ruffed grouse — 14, 87, 94, 95, 173, 194, 213, 239, 240, 245, 280
Rush Creek — 42
rushes — 143, 145, 148, 149, 179
Russell soils — 204
Russian thistle — 233

sabatia — 257
saber-tooth tiger — 38
sago pondweed — 232
St. John's wort — 233
St. Lawrence River — 125, 126
St. Lawrence Valley — 34
St. Marys River — 51
salamanders — 107, 152, 174, 209, 229, 256
salmon — 15

salt — 18, 22, 23, 169, 235, 285-291, 297, 298
Salt Creek — 42, 54, 55, 165, 287
Salt Creek Valley — 44, 54
sand — 43, 55, 75, 141, 186
sand cherry — 233
sandbur grass — 233
sand-dune willow — 233
sandhill crane — 245
sandstone — 17-22, 26-29, 43, 52, 53, 55, 57, 77, 78, 114, 151, 162, 163, 167, 173, 183-185, 205, 235, 253, 256, 287, 291, 292
Sandusky — 34, 63, 64, 301
Sandusky Bay — 10, 245-249, 293
Sandusky Bay marshes — 237, 247-251
Sandusky County — 75, 250
Sandusky High School — 301
Sandusky River — 238, 282
Sandy Creek — 46
Sargent — 13
sassafras — 89, 167, 181
savannah sparrow — 211
"Save Outdoor Ohio" — 306
saw-whet owl — 196
Sayler Park — 61
scarlet oak — 81, 102, 259
scarlet tanager — 95, 174, 239, 244
scaup ducks — 247
Scenic River Program — 131
Schaff, Morris — 7
Schoenbrunn — 295
Schwamberger Preserve — 242
Scioto County — 69, 164, 169
Scioto Lobe — 41, 46, 202, 203
Scioto madtom — 210
Scioto River — 34, 46, 47, 53, 55, 115, 116, 128, 165, 168, 177, 259, 268, 269, 282
Scioto River Valley — 34, 202
Scotch pine — 168
screech owls — 96, 174, 239
scrub pine — 168
scud — 113
sea rocket — 233
Sears, Paul B. — 302
seaside spurge — 233
Secor Metropark — 245
sedges — 136, 143-149, 178, 179, 208, 242, 264
seiche — 246
Selby, A.D. — 301
Seneca Caverns — 154
Seneca County — 75, 154, 207
Serpent Mound — 52, 256, 262
Serpent Mound Cryptoexplosion Structure — 52, 256
serviceberry — 167, 233
sessile trillium — 190, 192
Seven Caves — 55
shagbark hickory — 81, 108, 166, 171, 176, 206, 207
Shaker Heights — 308
Shaker Lakes Regional Nature Center — 308
shale — 17, 18, 23-29, 43, 52, 57, 75-78, 114, 162, 168, 180, 183-186, 199-202, 205, 253, 254, 287, 292
Sharon Conglomerate — 29, 30, 163, 172, 173, 185
Sharon, Pa. — 29
Sharon Sandstone — 185
Sharonville — 203
sharp-shinned hawks — 174, 175
Shawnee Hills — 164, 167, 170
sheep — 11, 12, 69, 161, 276
Shelby County — 36, 157, 202, 281
shelf fungi — 244
shellbark hickory — 8, 206-208, 238
shingle oak — 103, 257
shinleaf — 188
short-billed marsh wren — 244
short-eared owl — 211, 212
short-leaf pine — 82, 275
short-tailed shrew — 99, 169, 174, 211, 245
short-tailed weasel — 197
shoveler duck — 268
showy lady slipper orchid — 146
showy orchis — 172
shrews — 96, 107, 108
shrubby cinquefoil — 149
Shumard's oak — 82
Siberia — 40
side-oats grama grass — 135, 257, 258
Sidney — 34, 36, 204
siltstone — 18, 26, 28, 29, 77
Silurian — 17, 18, 22, 23, 31, 52, 55, 151, 157, 185, 201, 202, 205, 217, 253-256
silver maple — 82, 176, 177, 191, 207, 233, 238, 243
silver-haired bat — 255

Sinking Spring — 256
skink, (large-headed) — 87, 169
skipper — 100
skullcap — 250
skunk — 87, 169, 173, 193, 194, 211, 245, 247, 256
skunk cabbage — 92, 93, 242
slough grass — 135, 136, 242
sludge worms — 221, 225
small skullcap — 231
smallmouth bass — 119, 224, 226, 281
small-mouth salamander — 210
smartweed — 89, 243, 266
smelt — 226, 227
Smith's longspurs — 211
smoky shrew — 174
smooth cliff brake fern — 233
snails — 21, 24, 28, 29, 199, 234
snakes — 107, 209, 256
snapping turtle — 123, 177, 210, 229, 245, 247, 250
sneezeweed — 135, 149
"Snow Bowl" game — 68
snow buntings — 211, 248
snow goose — 251
snow trillium — 93, 208
soft-shell turtle — 177
soil profile — 72, 73
Solomon's seal — 172
song sparrow — 211
sora rail — 244
sorrell tree — 82
sourwood — 82, 83, 167, 173
South Amherst — 27, 28, 185
South Bass Island — 41, 153, 217, 221, 223, 225, 29, 231, 234
soybeans — 50, 75, 76, 136, 199, 206, 277, 279, 280
sparrow(s) — 141
sparrow hawks — 209
sparta — 13
spatter-dock — 117, 145, 232
Specht — 175
speckled alder — 242
speleothems — 151, 154, 155
Spencer, Col. William — 11
Spencer, John — 11
sphagnum — 9, 141, 142, 146-149
spicate water milfoil — 233
spicebush — 86, 242
spiders — 21, 29, 83, 100, 174, 226
spikenard — 242
spiny back spider — 100
spiny softshell(ed) turtle — 245, 250
Spirogyra — 114, 116
Split Rock — 253
sponges — 21
spotted bass — 122
spotted jewelweed (touch-me-not) — 233, 242, 243
spotted salamander — 245, 250
spotted turtle — 150, 180, 210, 245
spring beauties — 93, 172, 192, 208
spring peeper — 92, 93, 98, 210, 245, 250
Springfield — 47, 51, 203, 204, 207
spruce — 37, 38, 103, 134, 141, 204, 208, 238, 243, 259, 264
squash — 266, 267, 270
Squirrel Scalp Law — 12
squirrels — 12, 89, 92, 96, 98, 100, 102, 103, 104, 105, 107, 108, 224
staghorn sumac — 233
stalactites — 151, 153, 155, 157
stalagmites — 151, 154
star-flower — 146, 149, 190
Stark County — 34, 44, 55, 165, 185, 188, 276, 281, 308
starling — 211
star-nosed mole — 197
Starve Island — 217, 229
State Forestry Bureau — 275
Steam Furnace — 267
steel — 59, 183
Steele High School — 301
Sterki, Victor — 178, 299
Steubenville — 65, 69
stiff goldenrod — 178
Stillfork Creek — 179
Stinking Benjamin — 191
Stone, Julius — 302
stonecrop — 259
stoneflies — 122, 123
Stonehenge — 270
strawberries — 265
"streamlines" — 222
striped chorus frog — 210, 250
stripmining — 116, 180, 271, 289, 290
sturgeon — 15
Sturgeon Point — 218
sub-bituminous coal — 31
sugar birds - 92
Sugar Grove area — 169

sugar maple — 81, 82, 85, 102, 166, 171, 176, 187-193, 206-208, 234, 257, 259, 265
Suillus — 103
sulfur bacteria — 180
Sullivant, Lucas — 173
Sullivant, William Starling — 14, 173, 299, 300
Sullivantia — 173
Sullivant's milkweed — 136
sumac, fragrant — 208
summer tanager — 244
Summit County — 23, 28, 44, 55, 124, 146, 187, 188, 285
Summit Lake — 281, 282
sundew — 143
sunfish — 281
sunflowers — 178, 242, 266
swallowtails — 99
swamp birch — 149
swamp loosestrife — 142
swamp mallow — 232
swamp rattlesnake — 150, 210
swamp rose-mallow — 250
swamp sparrow — 244
swamp white oak — 82, 191, 207, 238, 257
Swan Creek — 241, 242
swans — 211
Swanton — 241
sweet buckeye — 176
sweet cicely, wooly — 106
sweet clover — 234
sweet gum — 176, 181, 208
swift — 169
Swiss — 299
switch grass — 135
"Switzerland of Ohio, The" — 164
sycamore — 8, 175, 207, 233, 243, 253, 274
Sylvania — 241
Symmes Creek — 180

Tallmadge — 298
tamaracks — 37, 145, 146, 149, 150
Tappan Reservoir — 168
tawny cotton-grass — 145
Teay's River — 163-166, 173, 176, 186, 201, 202, 205, 255, 259
Teays (Valley) — 41, 42, 51-55, 202
temperature inversion — 65
Terminal Tower — 273
Terrace Park — 51
Texas — 134
Texas rock sandwort — 258
thimbleweed — 209
thirteen-lined ground squirrel — 139, 211
Thomas, Edward S. — 302, 306
Thompson Collection — 303
Thompson's Ledges — 30
thrushes — 100, 150, 194
Thurman — 63
tick trefoils — 106
ticks — 174
tiger salamander — 210
tiger swallowtail — 99
Tigris River — 129
Till Plains — 50, 51, 55, 76, 79, 199, 201-213
timber rattlesnake — 170, 171, 229, 250
Tinkers Creek — 185
Tinkers Creek Gorge — 27, 28
titmice — 104
toads — 98, 107, 269
tobacco — 65
Toboso — 310
Toledo — 18, 42, 50, 194, 221, 238-241, 247, 251, 265, 291
tomatoes — 75
tonguetied minnow — 209
toothwort — 93
towhees — 89
Townshend, Norton S. — 10
trailing arbutus — 93, 167, 168, 188
Transeau, Edgar N. — 134, 302
Trautman, Milton B. — 210, 302
Trautman's Riffle — 210
tree crickets — 98
tree frogs — 98
tree swallow — 194
Tremper Mound — 269
Triassic — 31
trillium, (large-flowered or white) — 93, 94, 172, 192, 208, 255
trilobites — 21, 199, 201
troglobites — 152, 155
trogloxenes — 152
trout — 57
Troy — 308
Troyer's Hollow — 164, 165
Trumbull County — 285

trumpet creeper — 233
Tucker, Walter A. — 302, 306, 311
tufted titmouse — 92, 96, 174
tuliptrees — 73, 81-85, 102, 108, 161, 166, 171, 176, 177, 181, 188, 208, 257, 259, 274
tundra — 238
turkey vultures — 169
Turtle Island — 250
turtles — 10, 107, 209, 247, 269
Tuscarawas County — 6, 180, 265, 295
Tuscarawas River — 46, 55, 164, 186
Tuscarawas River Valley — 295
two-lined salamander — 174

U.S. Coast Guard — 221
U.S. Department of the Interior — 251
Ulothrix — 116
umbrella magnolia — 173
umbrella-wort — 233
underwing moth — 100
Unglaciated Allegheny Plateau — 50, 53, 77, 161, 188
University of Cincinnati, The — 49, 171, 256
Upper Mercer Flint — 265
upland plover — 211
Upper Silurian — 288
uranium — 26
Urbana — 147, 206, 207, 209, 259

Van Wert — 238
Van Wert County — 51, 274
Vanport Flint — 29, 265
Vanport Limestone — 29
veery — 194, 244
Venango soil — 77
Vermilion — 222, 301
Vermont — 268
vesper sparrow — 89, 211
Vesuvius Furnace — 169, 288
viburnum — 107
Vigo — 54
Villars Chapel Wood — 206
Vinton County — 61, 168, 169, 290
violets — 93, 135, 172
Virginia, Virginians — 7, 53, 276
Virginia creeper — 172, 233
Virginia Kendall Park — 29, 185
Virginia pine — 82, 167, 177, 181, 275
Virginia polypody ferns — 172
vultures — 161, 253, 268

WPA (Work Progress Administration) — 241, 243
Wabash Moraine — 37
Wahkeena State Memorial — 307
Wakatomika Creek — 42
Walhonding River — 164, 242
Walker, C.M. — 10
walking fern — 259
walleye — 15, 127, 215, 221, 224-227, 281
walnuts — 81, 82, 243
War of 1812 — 12
warblers — 89, 106, 174, 194, 239
warbling vireo — 231
Ward, Eber Brock — 239
Ward's Canal — 239
Warren — 42, 186
Warren County — 122, 123, 205, 208, 270
Washington County — 168, 175
Washington (D.C.) — 62
Washington (State) — 59
wasps — 226
water lilies — 117, 126, 224, 250
water marigold — 233
water milfoil — 232
water pennies — 122
water plantain — 122
water smartweed — 232, 233
water snakes, common — 119, 150, 210, 245, 249
water star-grass — 233
water strider — 123
waterflea — 224
waterweed — 233
water-willow — 122, 243
Waverly — 28, 175
waxwings — 100
Wayne — 42
Wayne County — 23, 55, 64, 77, 276, 308
Wayne, Gen. Anthony — 276
Wayne Lakes — 292
Wayne National Forest — 276
Waynesburg — 165
Waynesville — 123
weasels — 84, 139, 169, 173, 196, 211
Weisenborn, Sen. Clara — 311

Wells, H.G. — 273
West Liberty — 155
West Point — 298
West Sister Island — 229, 248
West Virginia — 31, 53, 67, 78, 164, 271, 288
Westerly Lows — 67
Western Academy of Natural Science — 296
Western Museum Society — 296
western pack rat — 169
Western Reserve College — 298
Wet Cave — 157
wheat — 65, 77, 161, 199, 206, 277, 287
Wheaton Club — 301
Wheaton, Dr. J.M. — 13, 301
Wheelersburg — 53
Wheeling — 7
whip-poor-will — 94, 161, 244
Whiskey Island — 23
whistling swans — 224, 247
white ash — 171, 181, 188-191, 206, 208, 257
white baneberry — 172
white bass — 224, 226, 227
white basswood — 171
white cedar — 149, 207
white crappie — 126
White, Mayor Hatfield — 282
White Oak Hills — 188, 190
white oaks — 7, 81, 166, 171, 178, 187, 188, 190, 206, 208, 238, 242, 257, 259, 275
white perch — 15
white pines — 103, 168, 181, 190, 275
White River — 47
white snakeroot — 102
white water lilies — 232
white willow — 175
white-breasted nuthatch — 106
white-eyed vireo — 244
whitefish — 15, 127, 221, 226, 227
white-flowered houstonia — 231
white-footed mouse — 84, 87, 96, 100, 108, 168, 196, 211, 245
Whitehouse — 241
Whittlesey, Charles — 271, 298
Whittlesey Indians — 270, 271
wigeon — 247
wild black cherries — 82, 100, 108, 171, 177, 181, 188, 189, 207, 242, 257
wild carrot — 234
wild celery — 232
wild cherry — 167
wild coreopsis — 242
wild crabs — 89, 104
wild geranium — 93, 172
wild ginger — 172, 208, 259
wild grapes — 172, 233
wild hyacinth — 234
wild indigo — 242
wild iris — 250
wild leek — 234
wild lettuce — 209
wild licorice — 234
wild lily-of-the-valley — 242
wild phlox — 193
wild plum — 100
wild rice — 233, 247
wild rose — 89, 233, 242
wild spirea — 242
wild sunflowers — 242
wild sweet pea — 242
wild turkey — 10, 12, 14, 87, 94, 103, 172, 173, 229, 239, 240, 245, 265, 277-280
wildcats — 269
Wilderness Center, The — 308
Wilderness Preserve — 255
Wildwood Preserve Metropark — 242, 245
Williams County — 50, 124, 275
willow(s) — 149, 196, 207, 233, 242, 250
willow flycatcher — 244
Wilmington — 63, 206
Wilmot — 308
Wilson, Alexander — 13
Wilson Ornithological Club — 301
Wilson's snipe — 244
Winchell, Newton H. — 298
wine industry — 62
winged pigweed — 233
Winous Point Marsh — 248, 249
winterberry — 145
wintergreen — 108, 167, 190, 192, 242
Wiregrass Ditch — 241
Wisconsin — 43
Wisconsinan — 33-36, 42-54, 75, 76, 134, 141, 157, 186, 202-206, 218, 231, 237, 264
witch-hazel — 86, 87, 106
Wolf Creek — 241, 282
wolf(wolves), timber — 10-12, 96, 161, 193, 213, 266, 277, 278

Wolfe, John N. — 165, 302
wolverine — 240
wood aster — 192
Wood County — 291
wood ducks — 103, 106, 150, 177, 313
wood frog — 98
wood nettle — 243
wood peewee — 99
wood sorrel — 93
wood thrush — 95, 174, 179, 194
wood warblers — 93
wood-boring insects — 87
woodchucks — 71, 102, 107, 169, 194, 196, 211, 240, 245
woodcock — 194, 211
woodland asters — 192
woodland goldenrods — 192
woodland jumping mouse — 197
woodpeckers — 87, 96, 100, 103, 107, 239
woodrush — 167
Wooster — 64, 181, 185
Wooster soil — 77
World War I — 180
World War II — 180, 241, 277, 279
worm-eating warbler — 95
Worthington, Gov. Thomas — 267
Wyandot County — 136, 140, 155, 207, 306
Wycomyia mosquitoes — 143

Xenia — 34, 61, 123
Xerothermic Period — 134, 149, 208
Yale University — 302
yarrow — 89, 242
yellow birch — 145, 146, 191
yellow buckeye — 171, 176
Yellow Creek — 288
yellow perch — 215, 227, 281
yellow pine — 168
Yellow Springs (Creek) — 57, 308
yellow touch-me-nots — 259
yellow twayblade — 231
yellow warbler — 243
yellow water lily — 232
yellow water lotus — 232
yellow-bellied sap-sucker — 194
yellow-shafted flicker — 254
yellow-throated vireos — 244
Youngstown — 297
yucca — 257

Zaleski State Forest — 169
Zane Caverns — 155, 201
Zane Ebenezer — 7
Zane's Trace — 7
Zanesville — 7, 62, 69, 292
zebra swallowtail — 172
Zeisberger, David — 295
zigzag goldenrod — 192
zooplankton — 224, 225